Catching the Light

A Journey across Myanmar

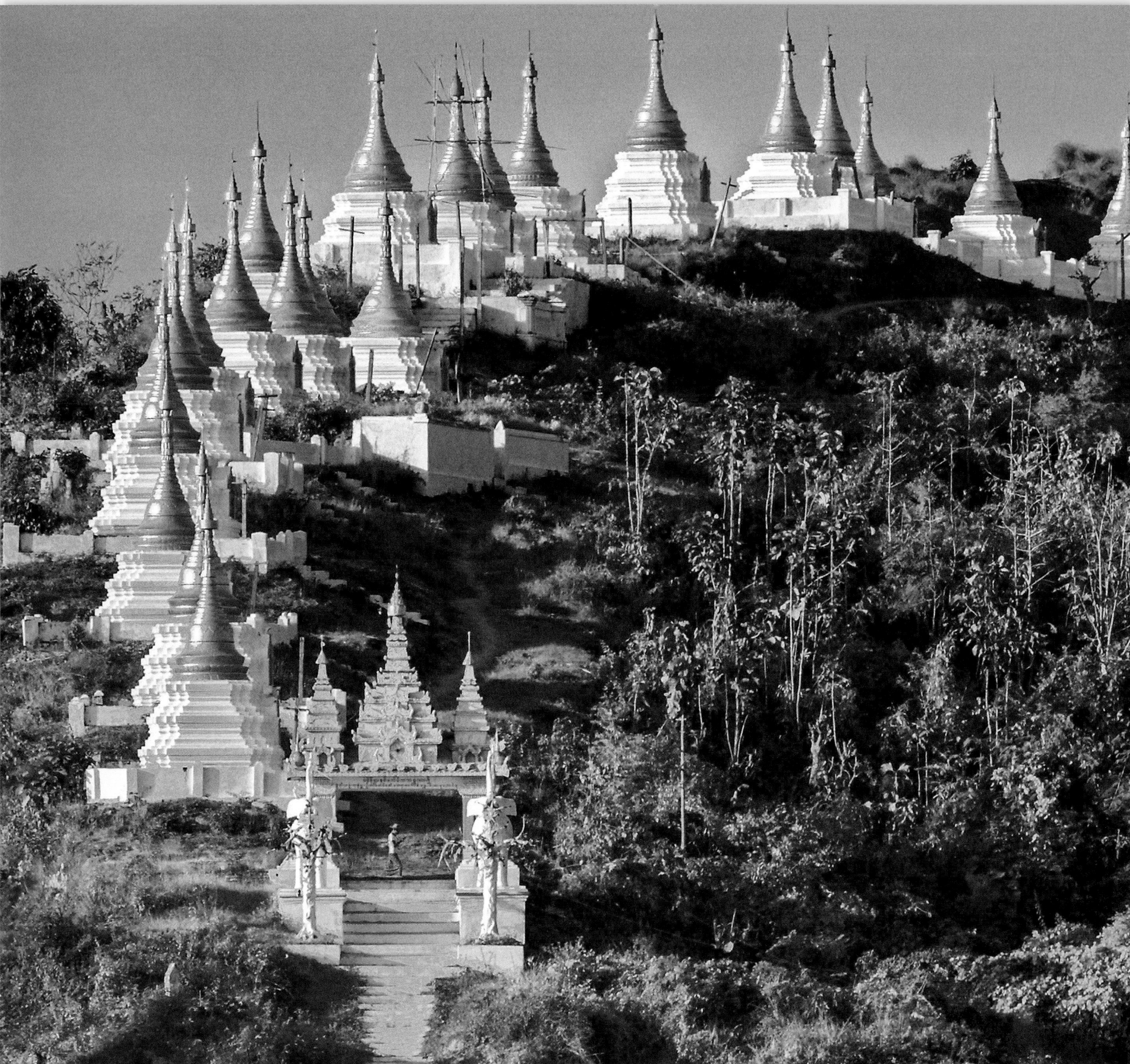

Catching the Light

A Journey across Myanmar

Birgit Neiser

RIVER
BOOKS

First published in Thailand in 2017 by
River Books Co., Ltd
396 Maharaj Road, Tatien, Bangkok 10200
Tel: 00 66 2 225 4963 | 00 66 2 224 6686
E-mail: order@riverbooksbk.com
www.riverbooksbk.com

Editor: Narisa Chakrabongse
Production: Paisarn Piemmettawat
Design: Ruetairat Nanta

ISBN 978 616 7339 83 2

Front cover: *Fishermen on Inle Lake renowned for a one-legged rowing technique that leaves their arms free to cast fishing nets, Inle Lake, Shan State, 2010.*

Back cover: *Pagoda ruins in Samka Village, Inle Lake, Shan State, 2010.*

Page 2: *Riverside pagoda complex, located between Thaungdut and Kalewa on the Chindwin River, Sagaing Region, 2010.*

Printed and bound in Thailand
by Sirivatana Interprint Public Co., Ltd.

Foreword

The photographs on the following pages document scenes that will soon be transformed or even vanish entirely. As Myanmar undergoes political reformation, ways of life preserved in the aspic of a dictatorship that had ruled for nearly half a century now face the possibility of dramatic change.

It was not long after Cyclone Nargis struck in 2008 that it became apparent the political climate in Myanmar was preparing to shift. The cyclone was a disaster of epic proportions, killing an estimated 138,000 people and destroying entire villages in the low-lying delta region. Immediately after the cyclone, the paranoid and self-protective military regime delayed the arrival of international emergency services and blocked aid from reaching the worst-hit areas thereby compounding an already catastrophic event. Yet, behind the scenes, the tectonic plates of change had been shifting with inexorable slowness for some time and, in the aftermath of that tragedy, their course was accelerated as the military rolled out a series of reforms. In 2010, a general election was held even though the hugely popular leader Aung San Suu Kyi, known simply as "the Lady", remained under house arrest; her party, the National League for Democracy (NLD), boycotted the process. She was later released and the NLD participated in a by-election held in 2012, an event depicted in two exhilarating images in this book and through which Aung San Suu Kyi won a seat in parliament. Three years later, in 2015, another general election was held and the NLD won by a vast majority. Today, the military still holds immense power in Myanmar but the dictatorship has been replaced by a parliamentary system and the country is on a course towards becoming a more democratic and open nation.

The photographs in this book were taken during these heady years of change. Birgit Neiser first went to Myanmar in 1981 but started making annual visits in 2010 and, since then, has been spending up to a couple months there each year. Keenly aware that the political changes will in turn instigate social, cultural, and economic change, she travelled across the country documenting life at this key moment in time – a moment when a country still entangled in its past is looking forward to the certainty of change and the hope of a better future. The imprint left by nearly half a century of military rule, however, will not be easily or quickly erased making every image fraught with this tension between the past and the future. Look carefully and you will see that even the most beguiling postcard-perfect vistas in this book are imbued with layers of history:

The timeless scene of oxcarts being used to transport water from a lake to a village is timeless because the country has been closed off from the outside world for so many years by isolationist military rule.

The lively image of a Ferris wheel spun by manpower reveals how development has been slow or nonexistent in many parts of Myanmar and how constant electricity is still a luxury not everyone has access to.

The bookstall owner selling books on a Yangon pavement is recycling well-thumbed volumes passed around through countless readers during a time when the written word was censored and imported literature was difficult to find.

Even the tribal dances and annual religious festivals are a by-product of Myanmar's decades of isolation. Large areas in the country's ethnic states have been off-limits due to numerous insurgencies, some of which remain ongoing. Untainted by globalization and interaction with other cultures through tourism or business, old-world traditions and rituals have survived intact.

Yet, if there is a constant hymn that animates these images, it is the inevitability of change and the Buddhist mantra of impermanence. After all, as Birgit's haunting photographs of ruined pagodas in long abandoned ancient citadels show, this is not the first transfer of power Myanmar has experienced. The photographs are not laid out in accordance with chronology or geography. Rather, this collection captures a diverse cross-section of life in Myanmar and, as such, provides an invaluable portrayal of a critical juncture in the country's modern history.

Emma Larkin
Bangkok, 2017

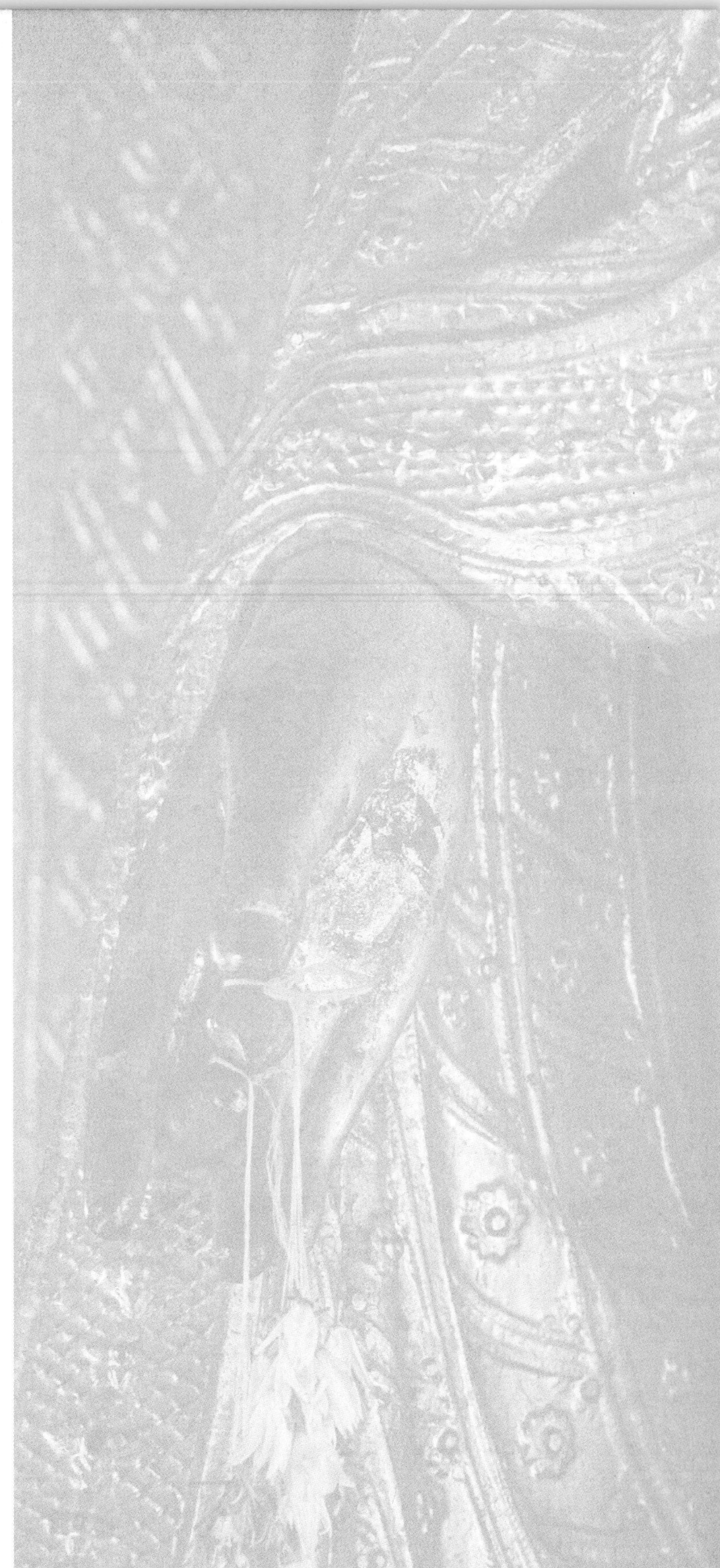

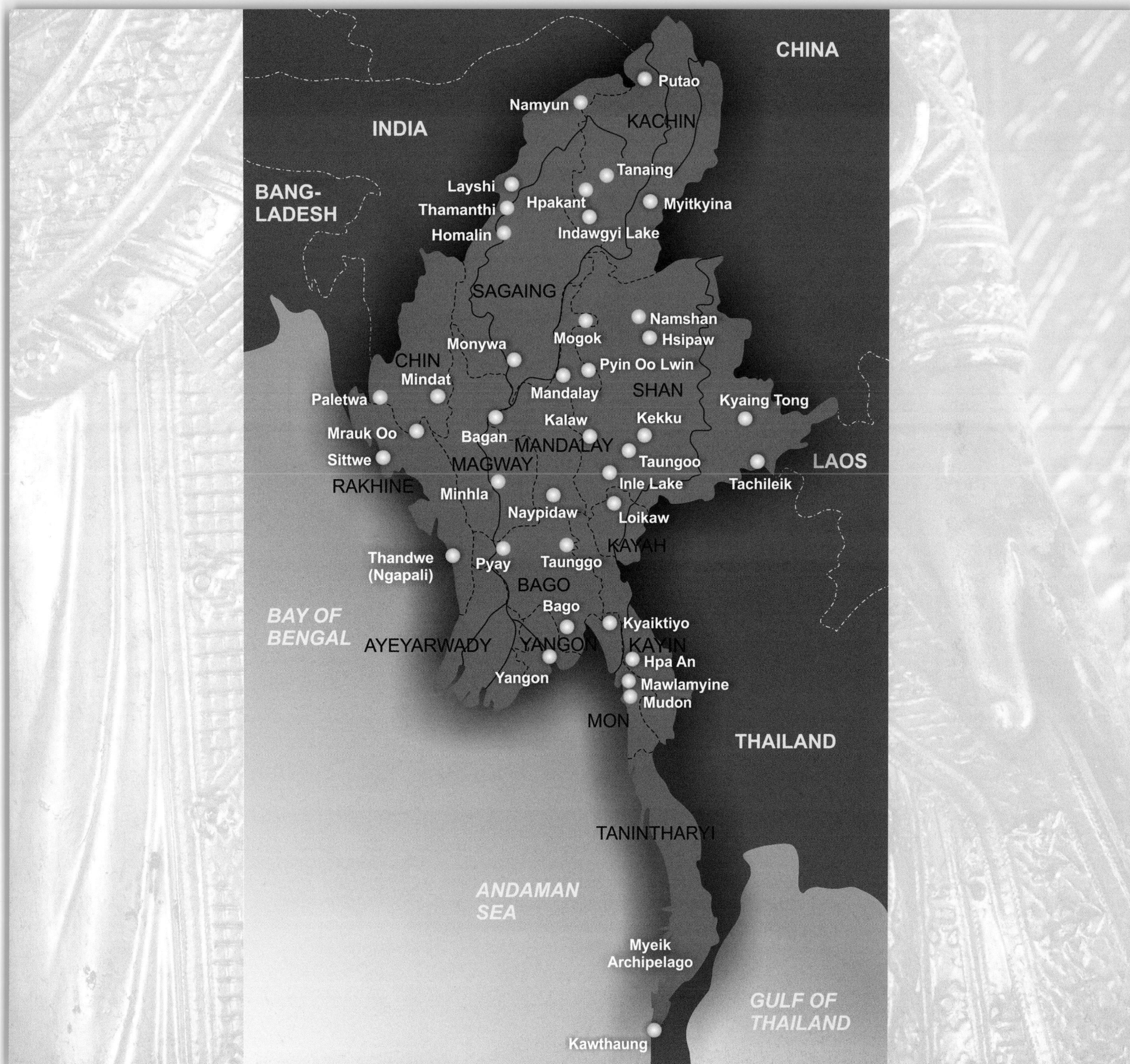

CHINA
Putao
Namyun
KACHIN
INDIA
Tanaing
Layshi
Hpakant
Myitkyina
BANG-
LADESH
Thamanthi
Homalin
Indawgyi Lake
SAGAING
Namshan
Mogok
Hsipaw
Monywa
CHIN
Pyin Oo Lwin
Mindat
SHAN
Mandalay
Paletwa
Kyaing Tong
Kalaw
Kekku
Mrauk Oo
Bagan
MANDALAY
Sittwe
Taungoo
MAGWAY
LAOS
Inle Lake
Tachileik
RAKHINE
Minhla
Naypidaw
Loikaw
KAYAH
Thandwe
(Ngapali)
Pyay
Taunggo
BAGO
Bago
BAY OF
BENGAL
Kyaiktiyo
AYEYARWADY
YANGON
KAYIN
Hpa An
Yangon
Mawlamyine
Mudon
MON
THAILAND
TANINTHARYI
ANDAMAN
SEA
Myeik
Archipelago
GULF OF
THAILAND
Kawthaung

MARBLE BUDDHA IN THE TAI LOW KO WOODEN MONASTERY, CHAUK, MAGWAY REGION, 2012

Monasteries in Myanmar are much more than places of worship. They provide accommodation for monks and serve as boarding schools and libraries. Entirely dependent on donations, they offer numerous services to the surrounding community. This constant use of monastery facilities leaves visible traces.

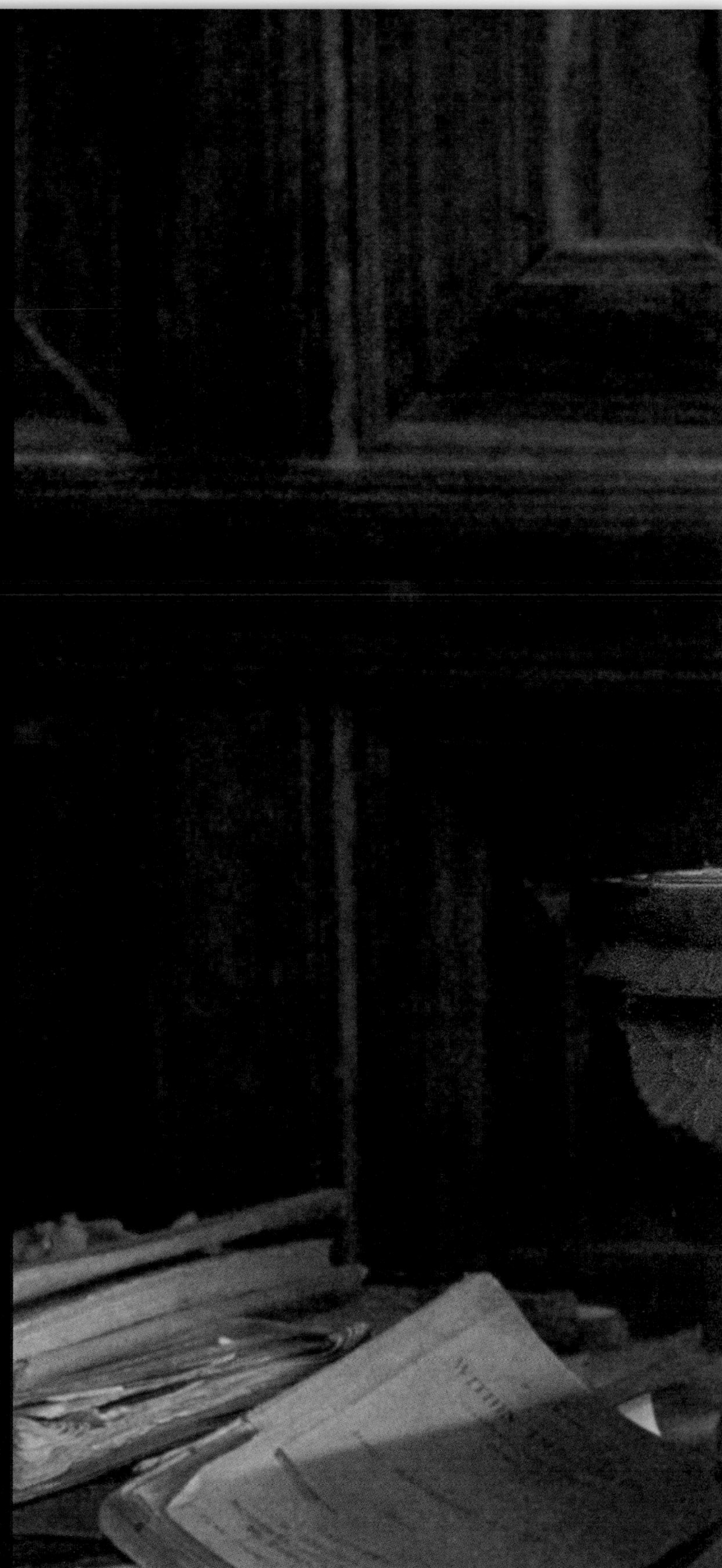

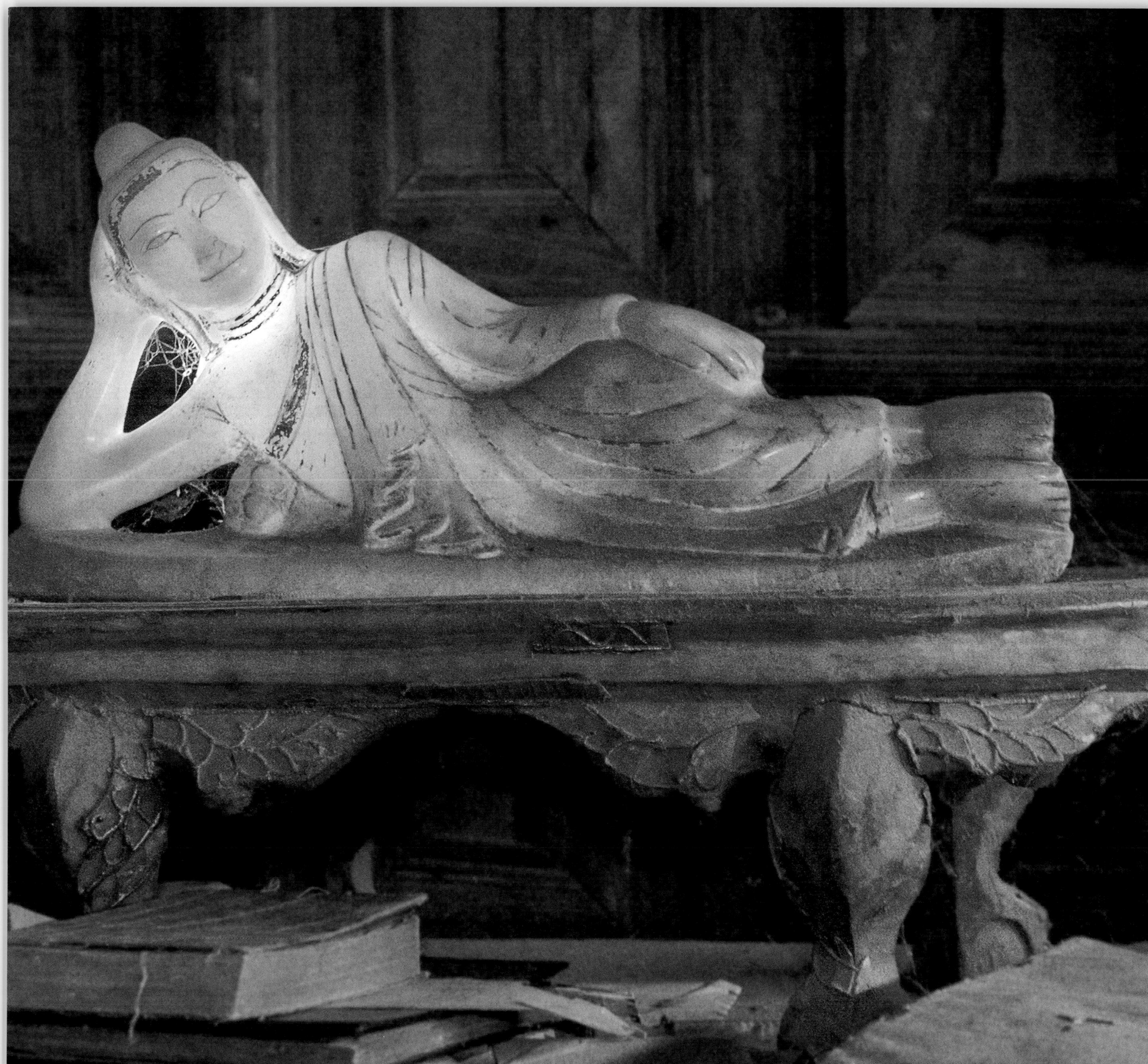

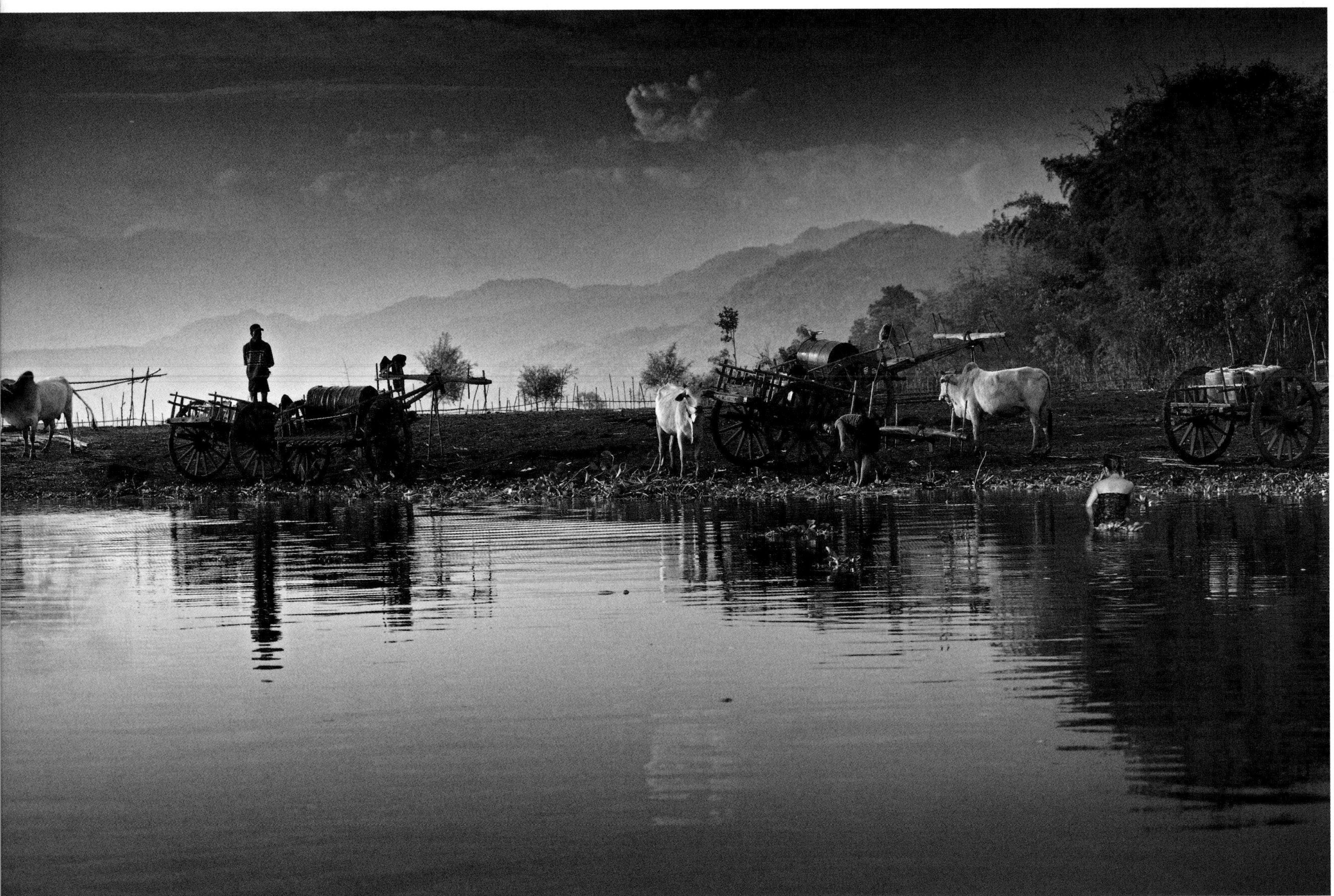

Inle Lake, Shan State, 2010

This early morning scene would have looked no different a hundred years ago. A nearby river or lake provides villagers with a source of clean water for bathing and laundry. Water for use in their homes is transported back to the village by ox cart. Gazing upon this view, I felt as if I had been transported back in time.

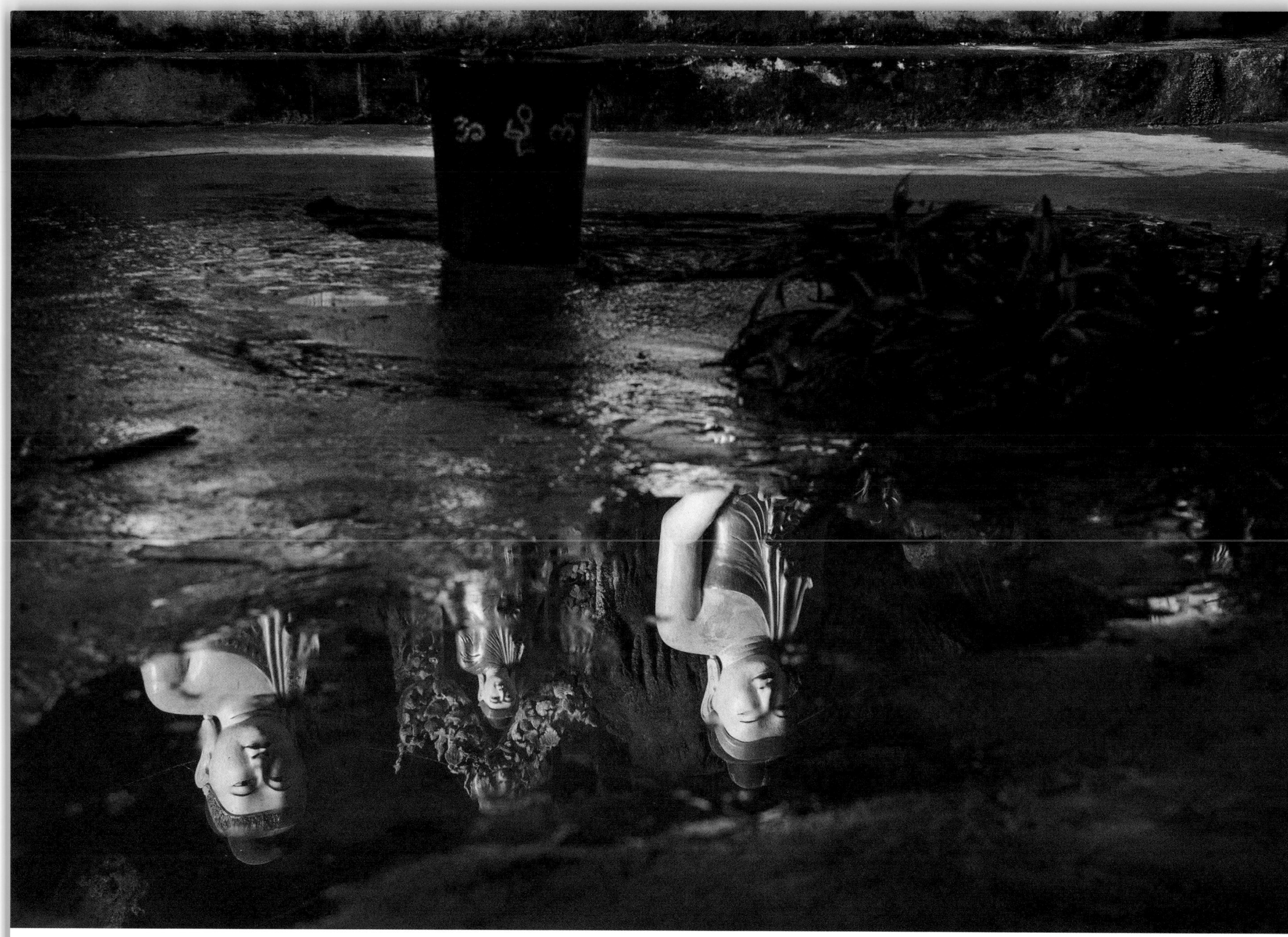

Kaw Goon Cave, Hpa An, Kayin State, 2011

Myanmar has many sacred caves that contain donated Buddha statues. These damp, poorly lit places of worship draw countless pilgrims. At Kaw Goon Cave, water seeps in everywhere. While some of it is collected in buckets meant for dumping rubbish, there is still enough left over for reflections.

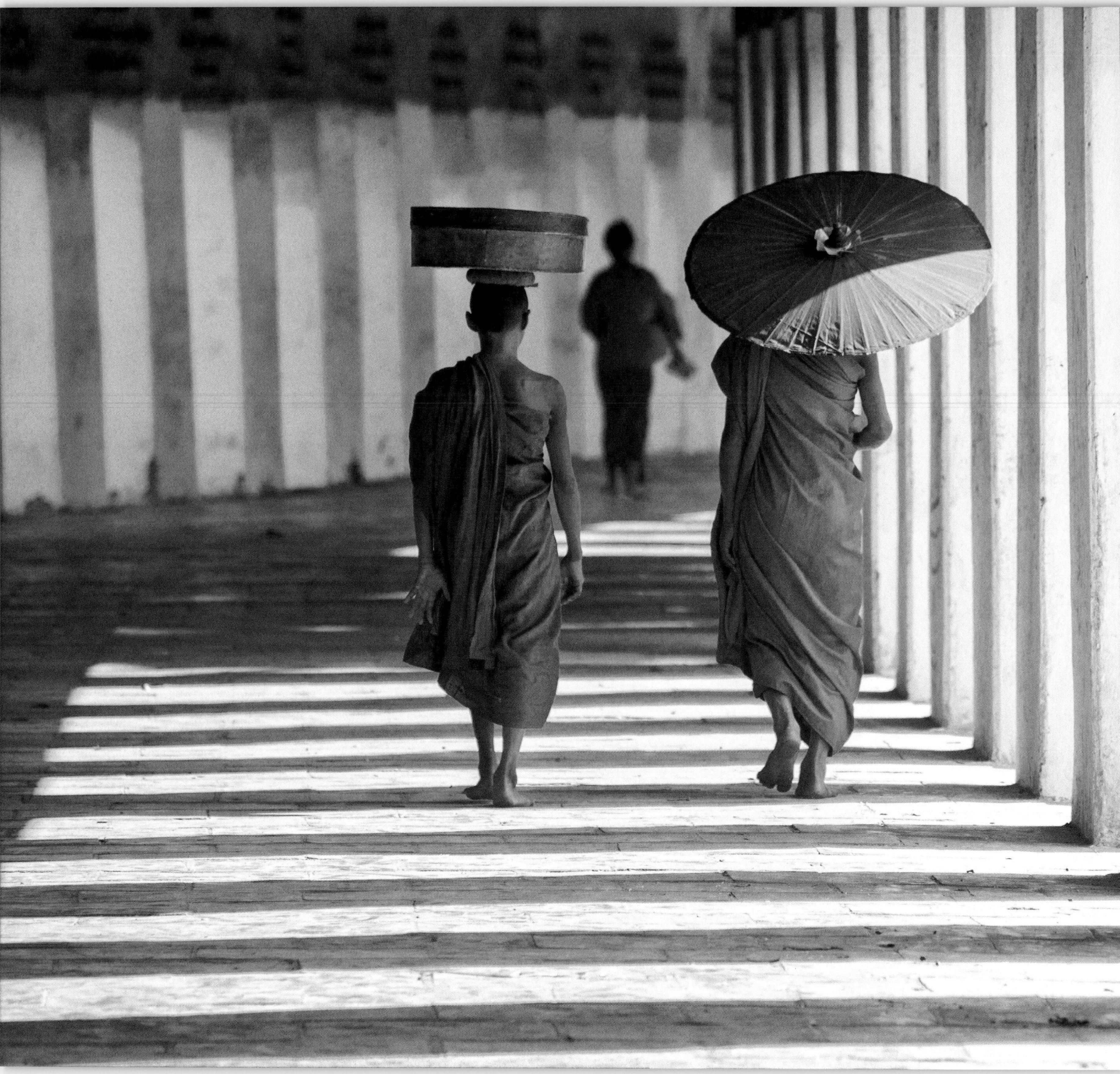

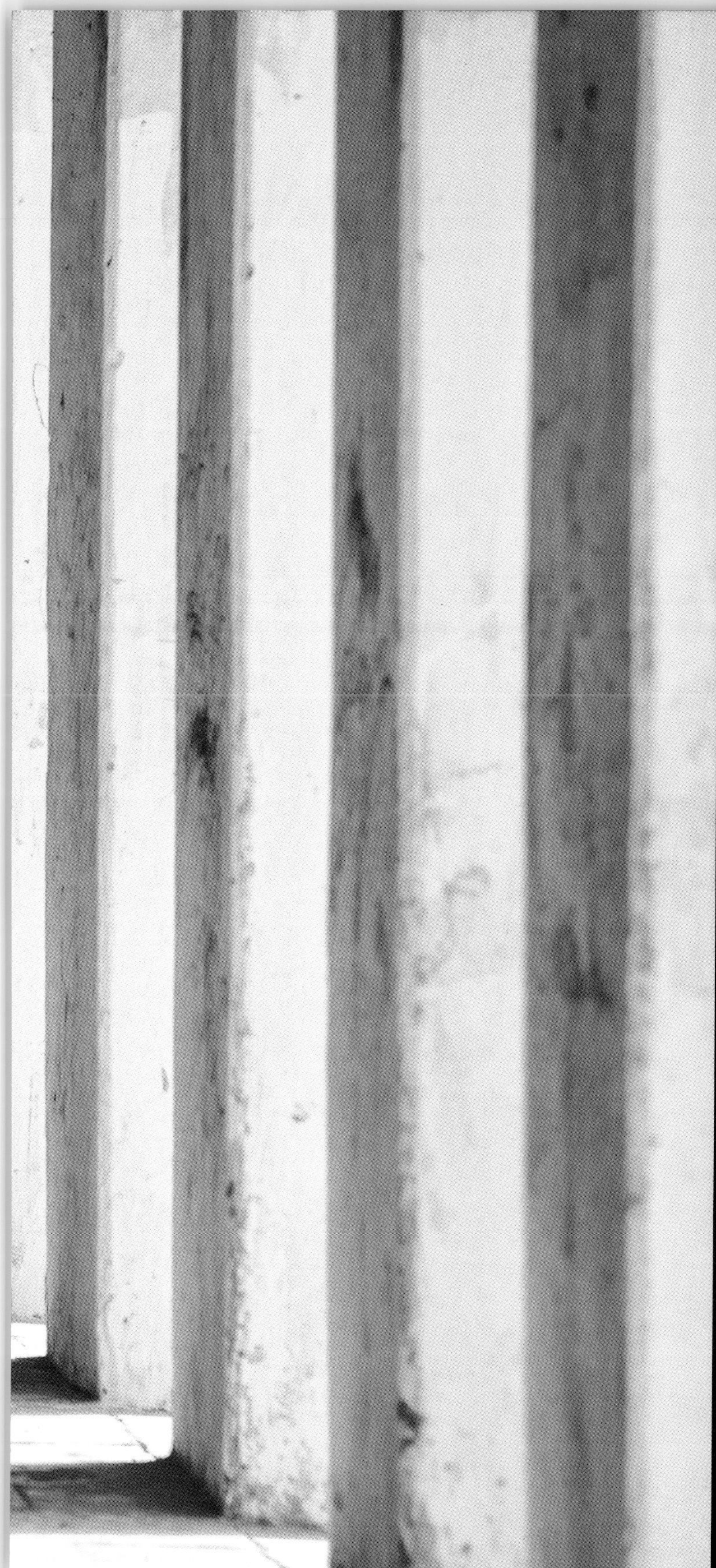

Shwezigon Pagoda, Bagan, Mandalay Region, 2010

A long corridor flanked by light and shadow leads to the famous Shwezigon Pagoda, which is visited by monks from the nearby monastery and visitors from around the country. Although Myanmar is a country full of colour, I chose black-and-white images for this book because they offer more insight into the country's soul than colourful travel images of the main tourist attractions.

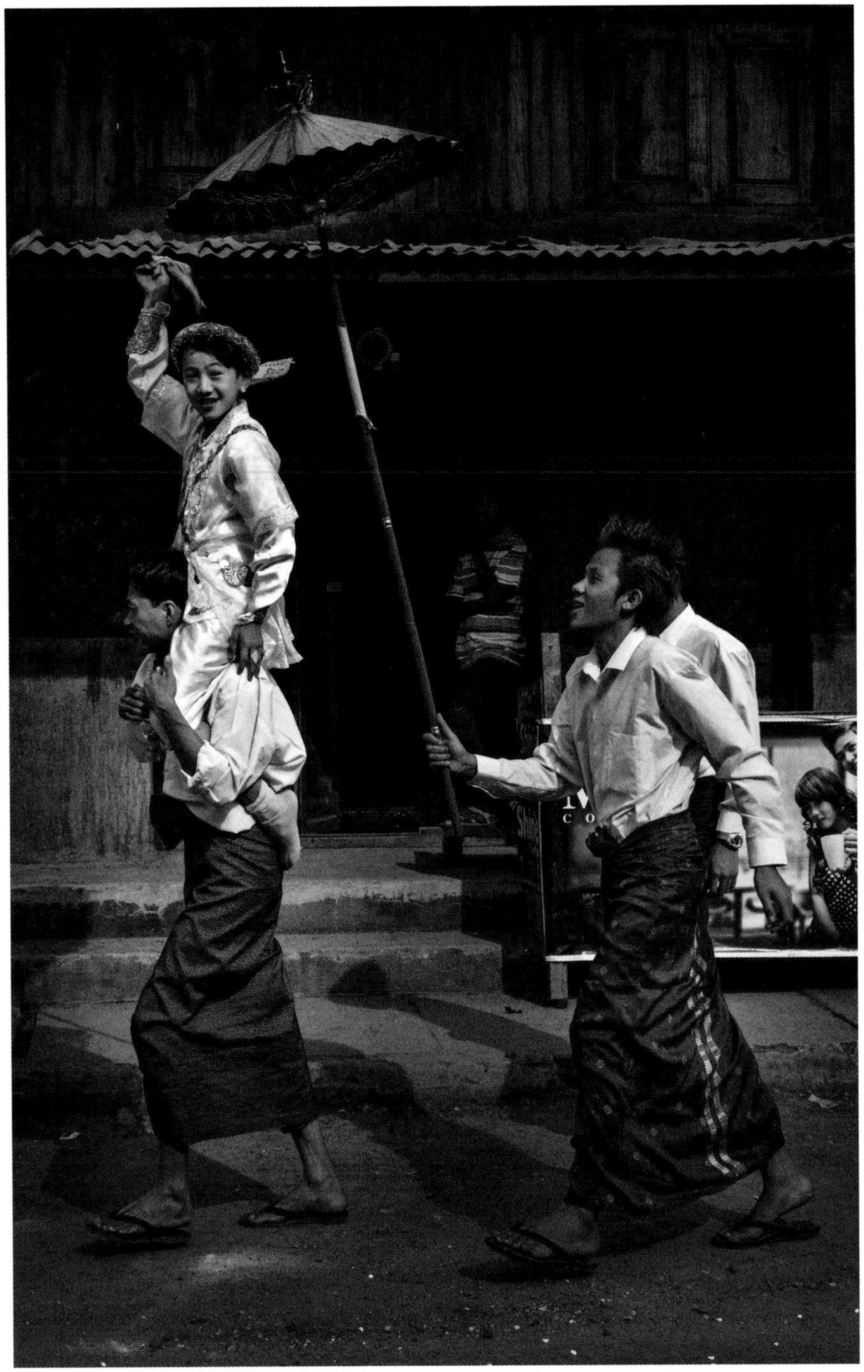

Left: Novitiation ceremony, Mogok, Mandalay Region, 2013

Opposite: Novitiation ceremony, Yangon, 2012

Every male Buddhist in Myanmar is expected to spend a certain amount of time in a monastery. His stay begins with a novitiation ceremony, which can be simple or sumptuous according to the financial means of his parents and his, or their, personal preferences. Either way, the boy puts on a princely costume and is taken to the monastery in a procession on the back of a pickup truck, a pony, or – as in this instance – carried by his father. After the ceremony, his head is shaved by monks and he is presented with a monk's robes and accessories.

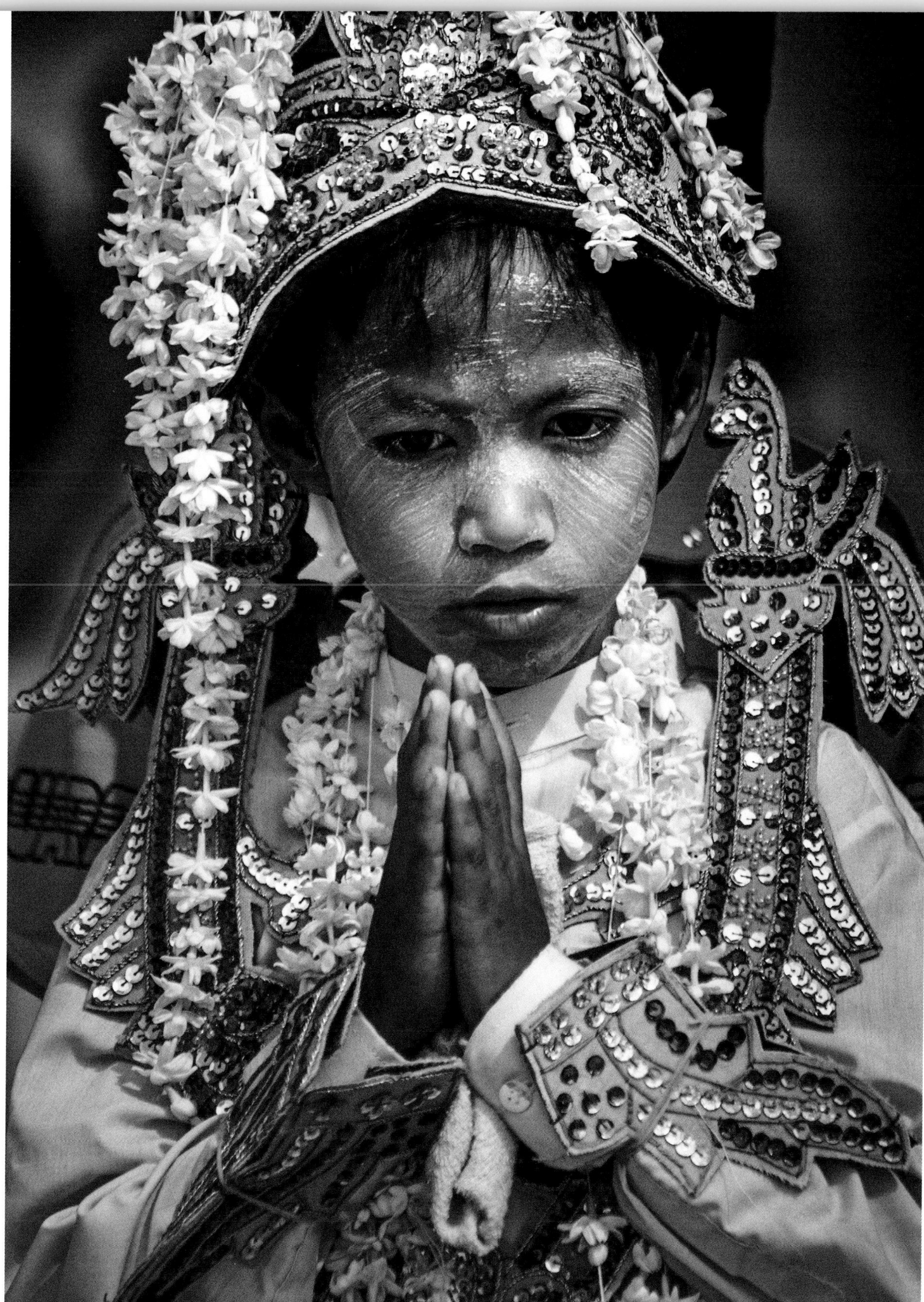

Monks after finishing their annual exams, Loikaw, Kayah State, 2012

A monk who commits to the monastic life must undergo an annual exam to achieve a higher ordination. The exam is taken in the ancient Pali language and has both written and oral components to test a monk's knowledge of Buddhist scripture and his ability to perform Buddhist chants with the correct intonation. The monks pictured here came from all over Kayah State to sit their exams. Once the exams were over, they rushed into the street to celebrate.

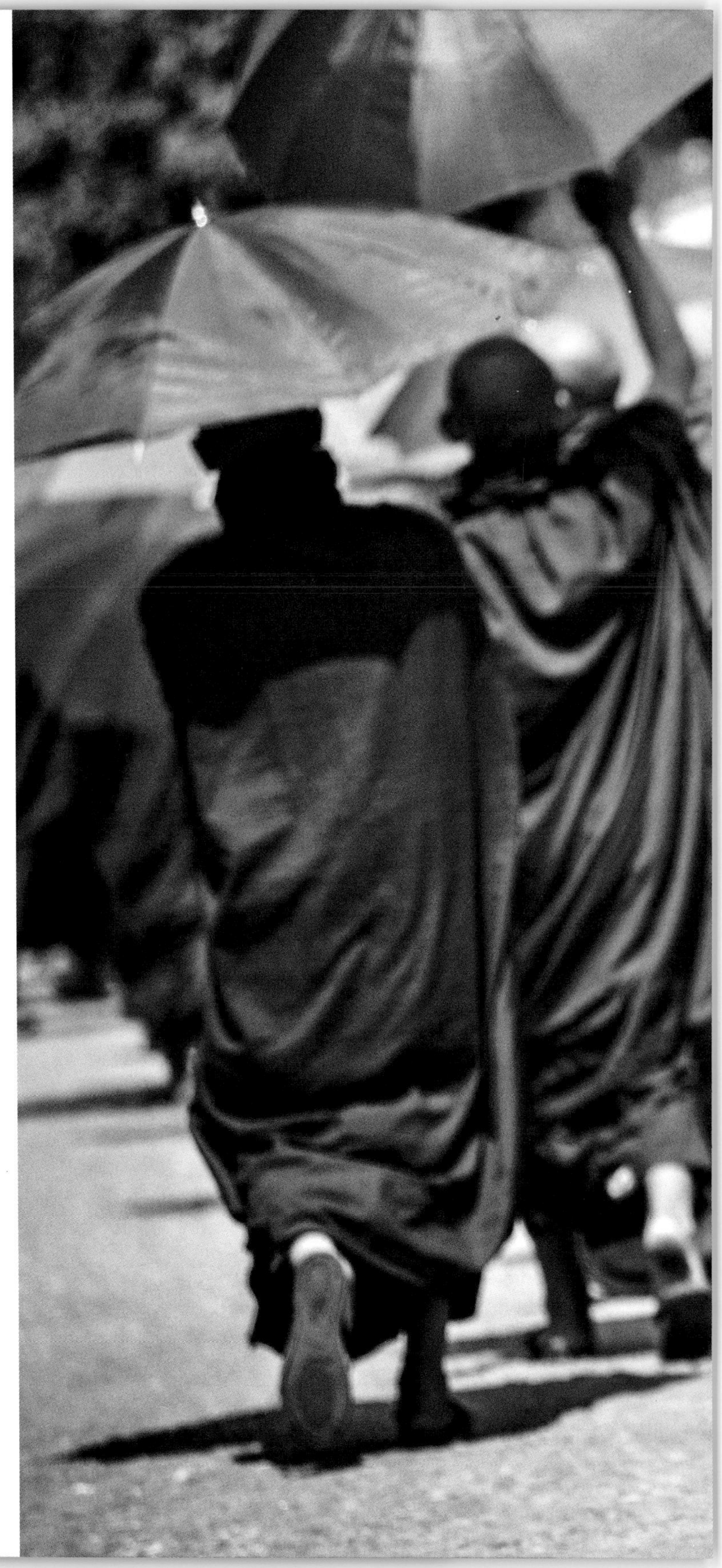

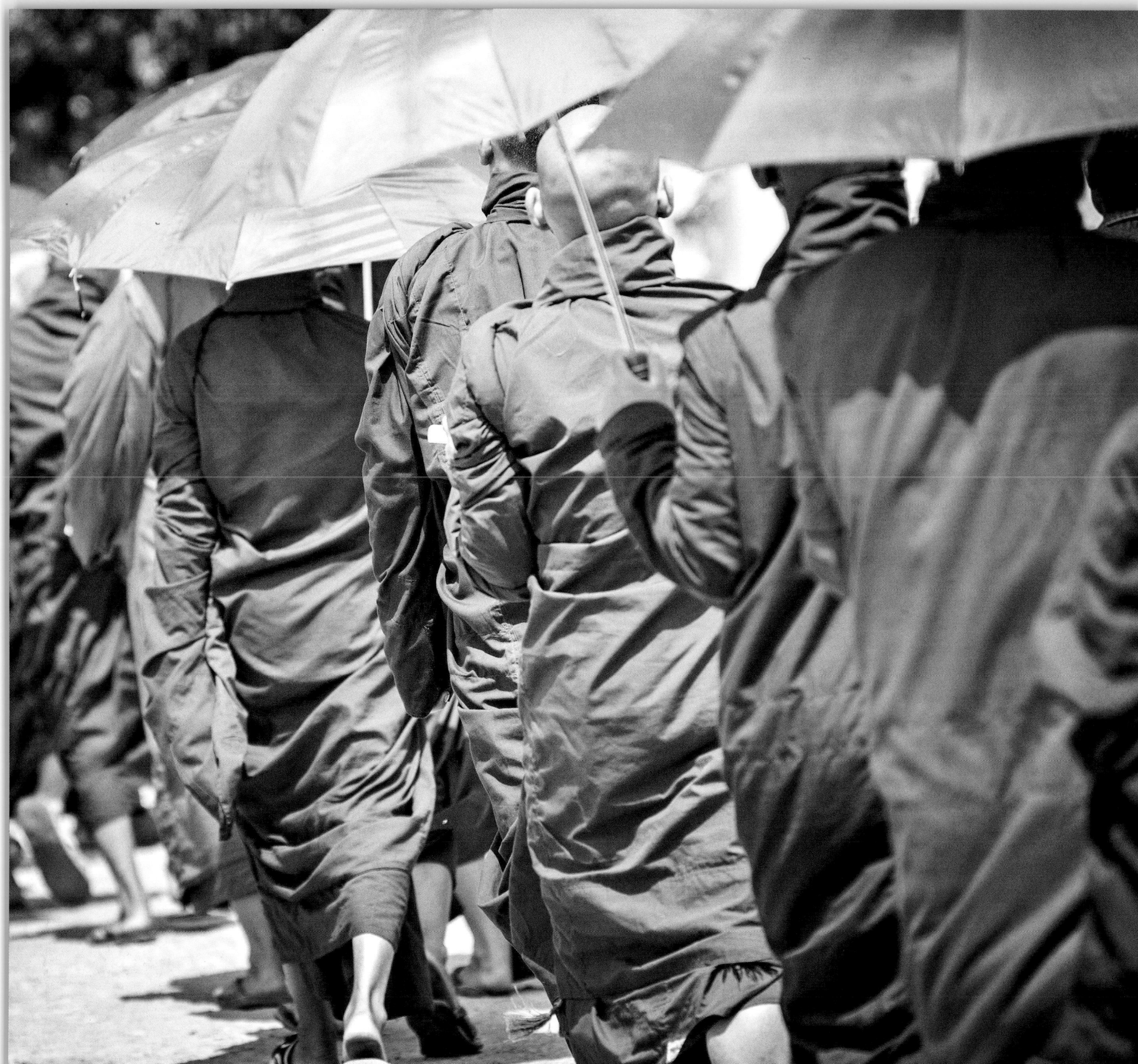

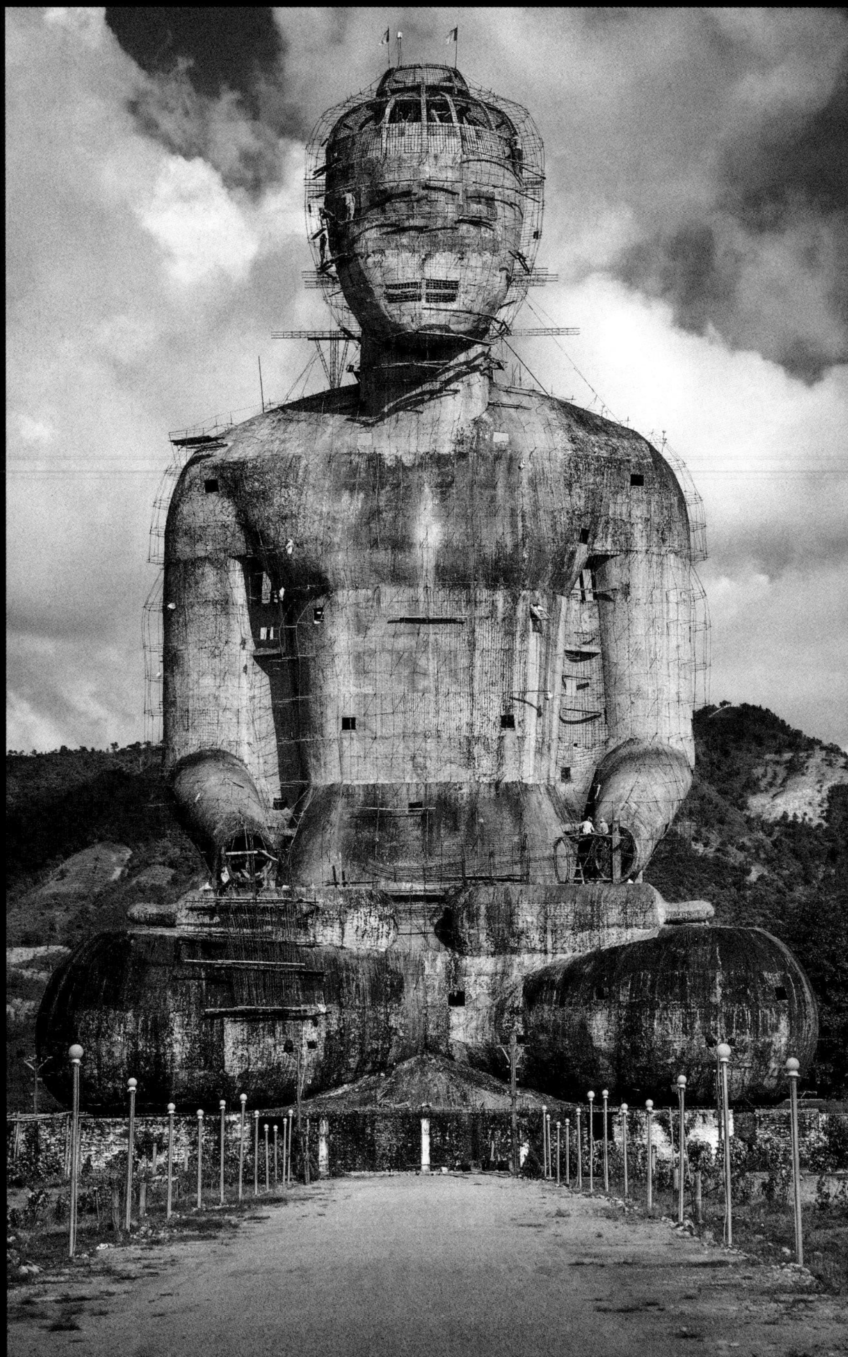

Left: Seated Buddha under construction, Mudon, Mon State, 2011

Right: On the scaffolding of the seated Buddha, Mudon, Mon State, 2011

To commission a new Buddha statue or the construction of a pagoda improves one's karma; the bigger, the better. In the case of a Buddha statue, the donor chooses a sitting, lying, or standing posture and adds detail according to his or her taste. Donors who can afford it will build the statue as high as possible. This seated Buddha is 80 metres tall. During construction, an open elevator was installed along the Buddha's spine and operated with a diesel engine. The one-eyed architect was very friendly and invited me to ride the elevator up into the head of the Buddha statue – a once-in-a-lifetime opportunity as the interior would be sealed off for good once construction was complete. After an adventurous ride up, I decided to descend using the internal staircase, which also gave me the chance to peek out from time to time and even walk out onto the scaffolding.

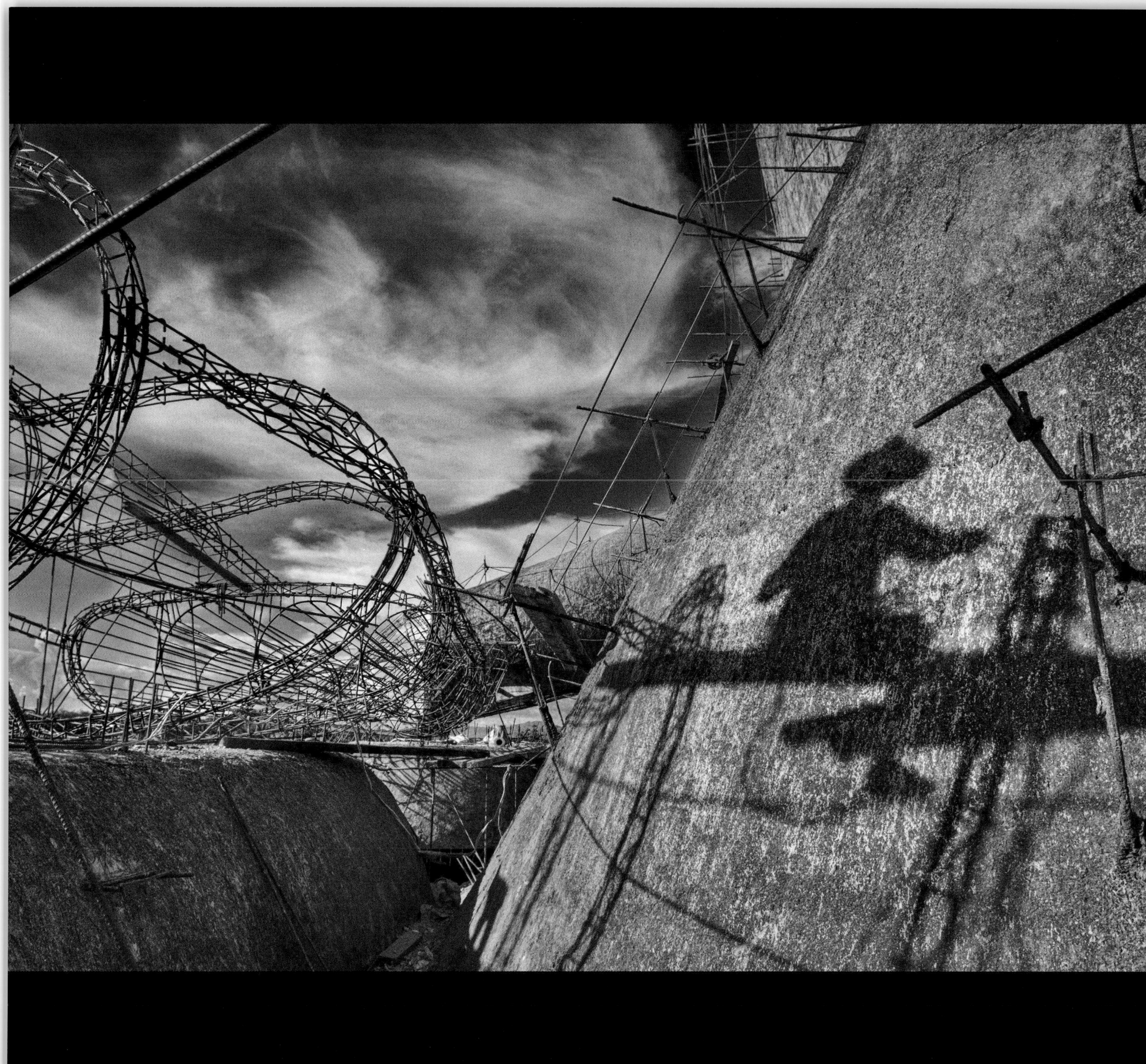

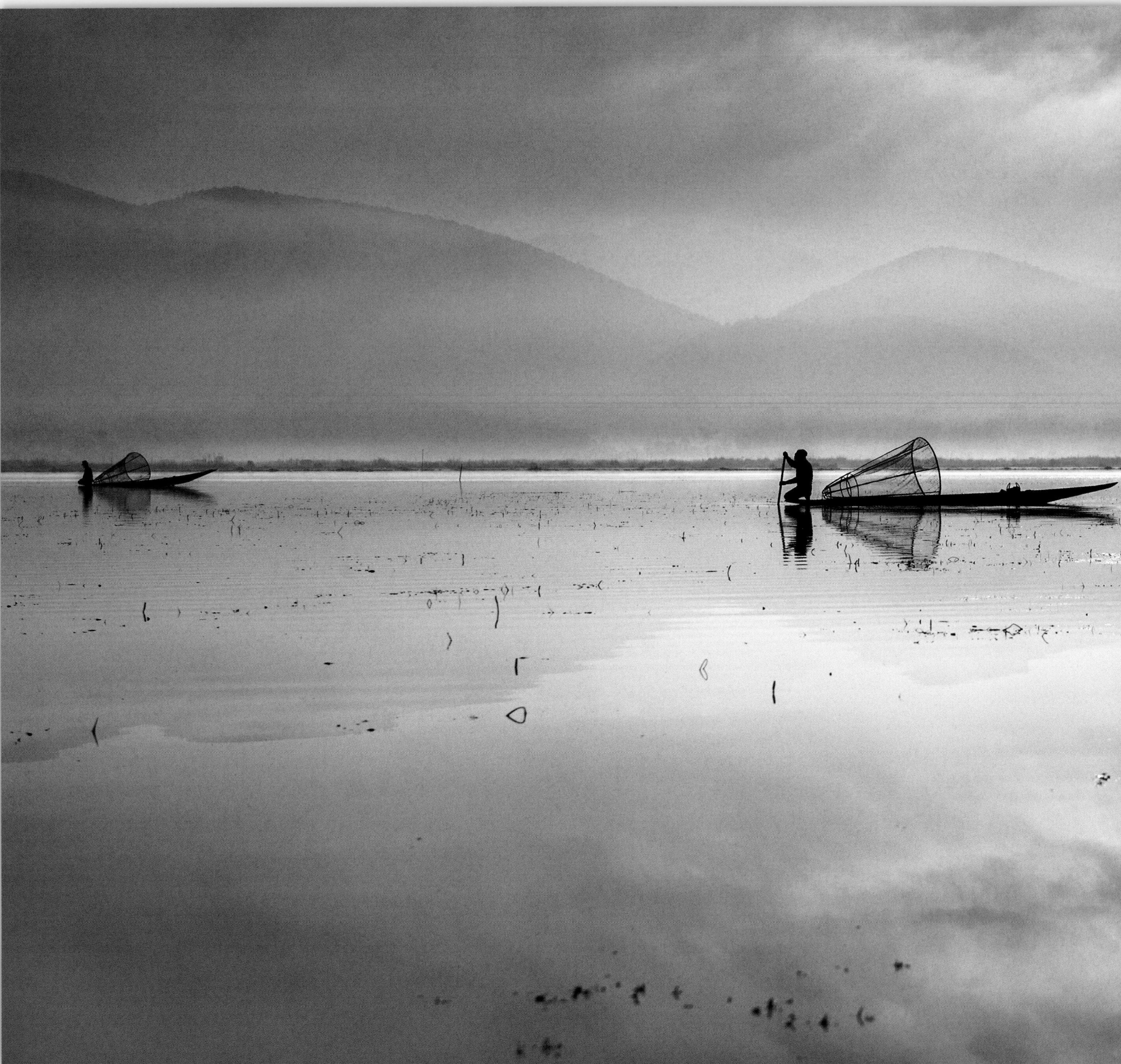

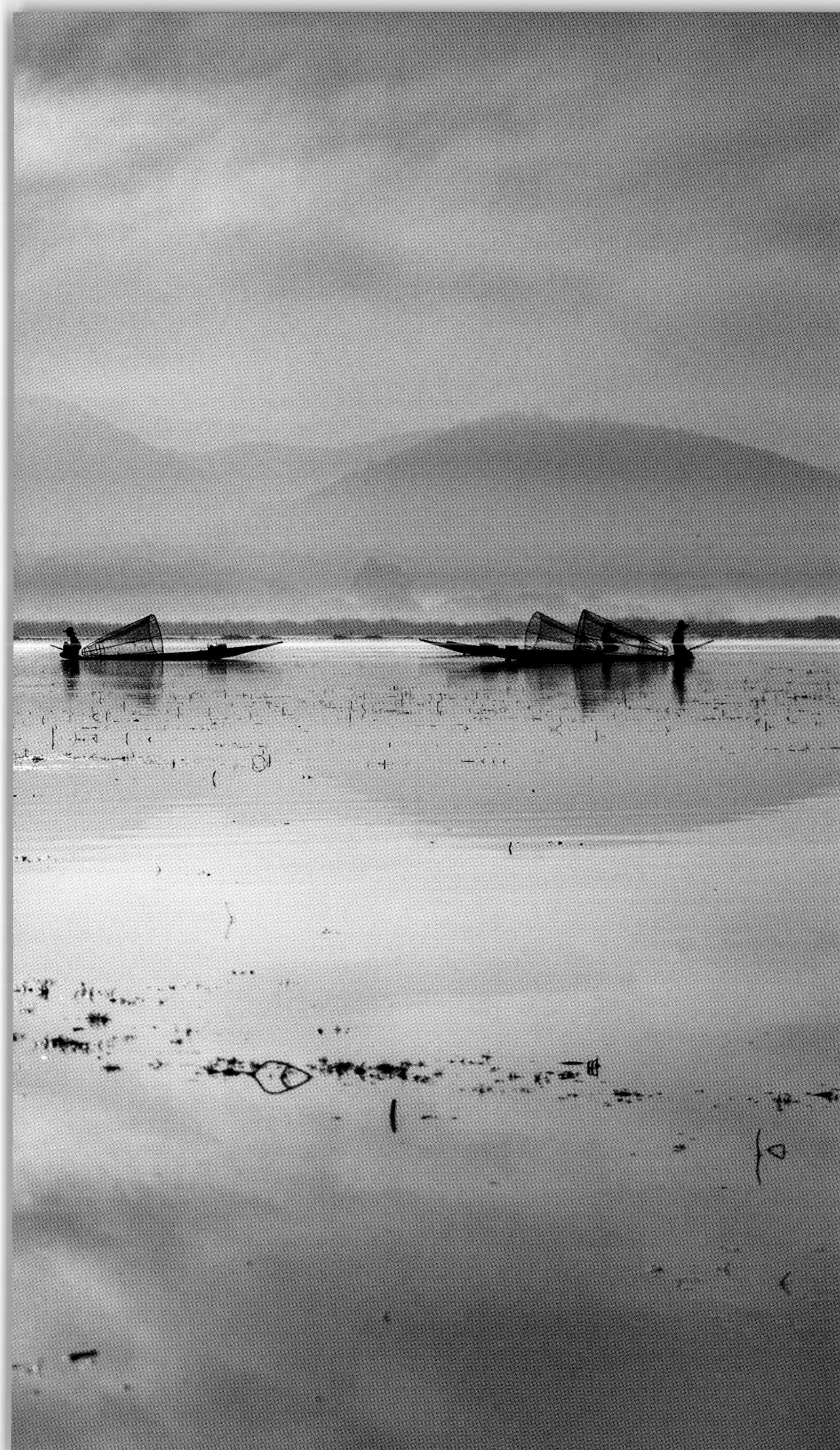

Inle Lake, Shan State, 2010

Early morning is my favourite time of day on Inle Lake, though I have never been able to beat the fishermen to the lake. They are at their chosen spots even before the first ray of sunlight climbs over the mountain and pierces the layers of fog. At this time of day, the scenery is engulfed in an otherworldly atmosphere.

In many regions of Myanmar, there are still people who have never seen a camera. As they have never been photographed, their reaction to a photographer varies from apprehension to fearless curiosity. This young boy never overcame his shyness but the enthusiastic group pictured on the opposite page couldn't get close enough to the camera.

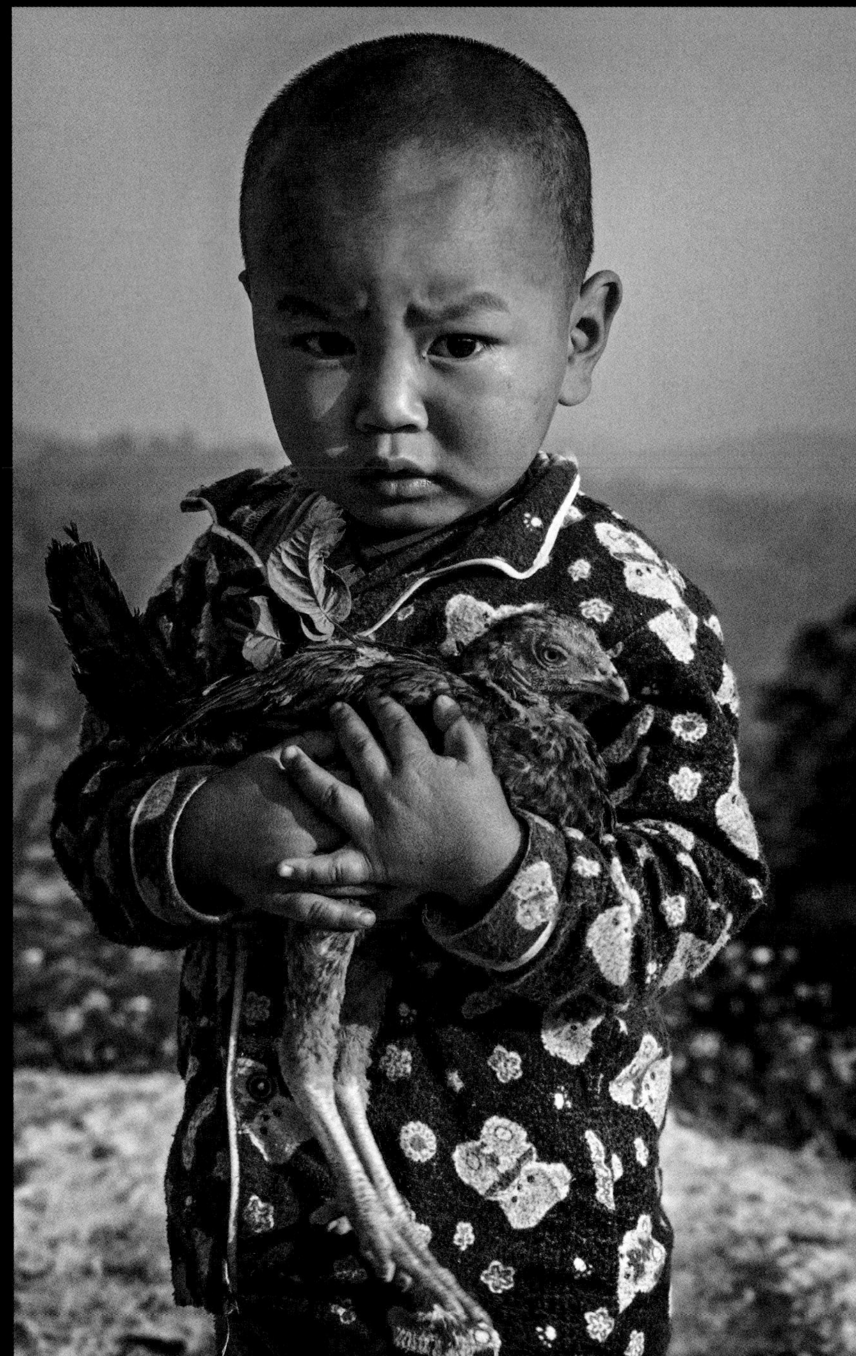

Boy holding a chicken, South Kunhawt, Shan State, 2013

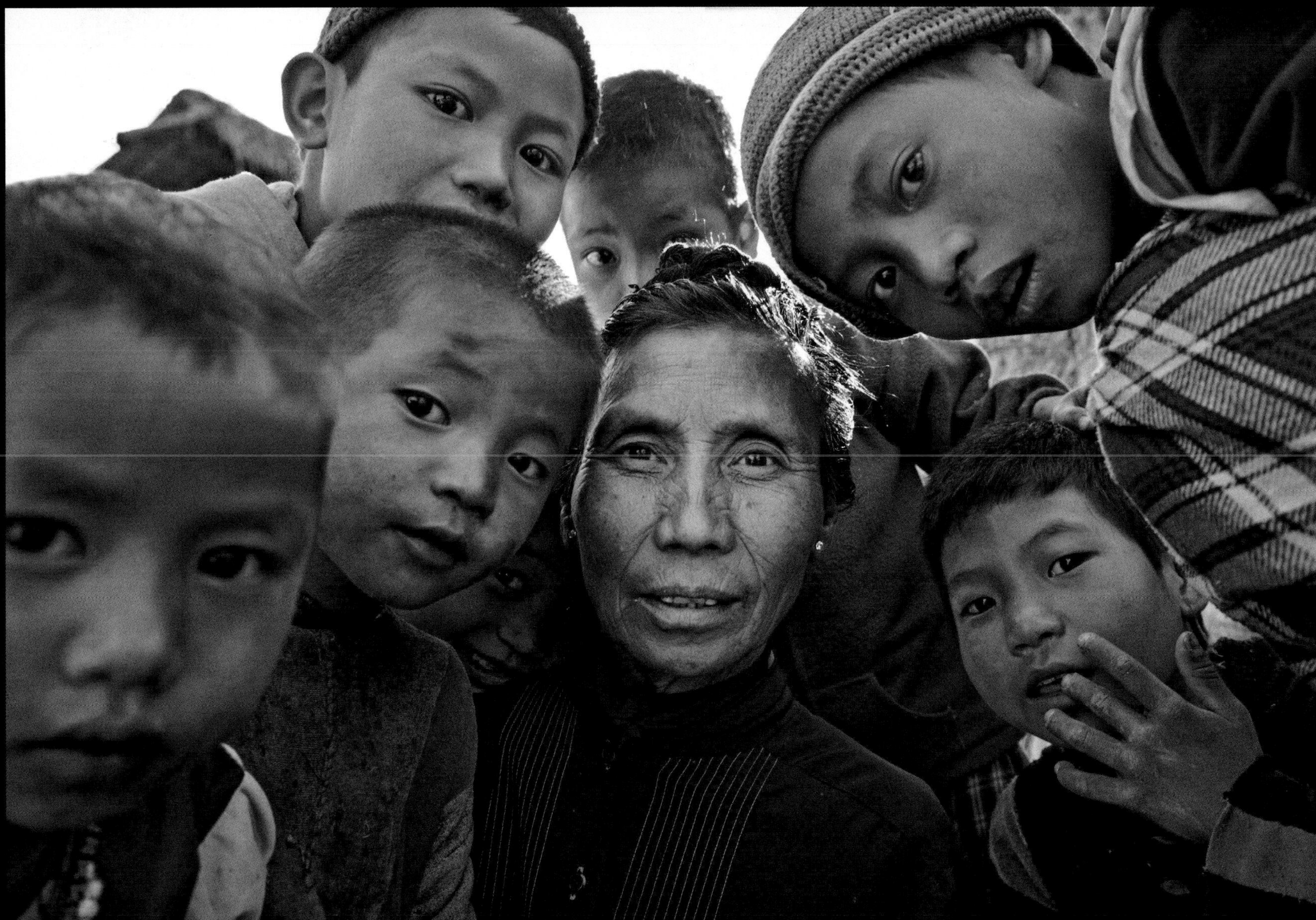

Grandmother with village children, Layshi, Sagaing Region, 2010

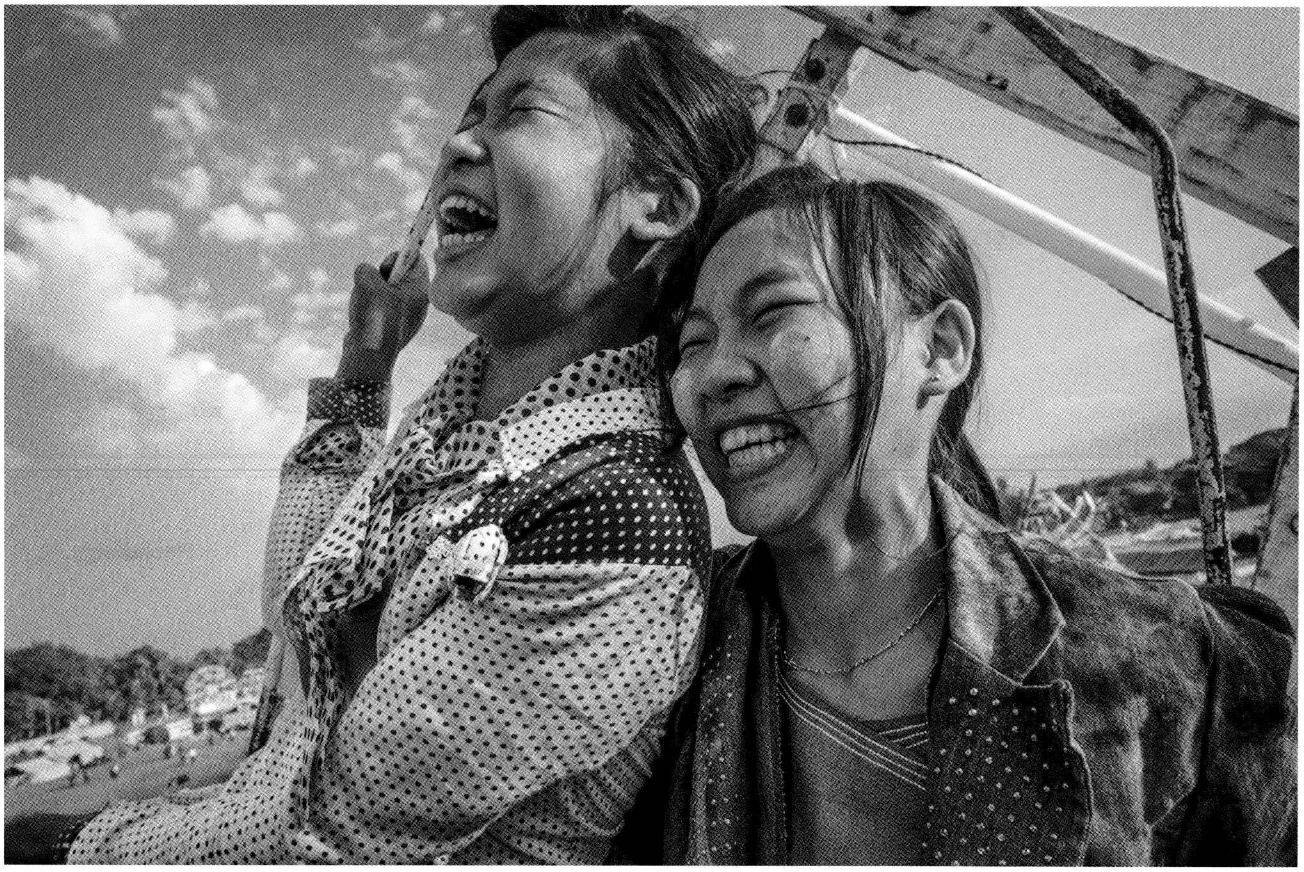

Girls on a Ferris wheel, Myitkyina, Kachin State, 2015

No festival is complete without a man-powered Ferris wheel. In the absence of electricity, young men climb up inside the structure and keep to one side, using their weight and the law of gravity to spin the wheel. They are incredibly skilled and impossibly elegant; they never seem to lose their flip-flops or the wallets and phones tucked into their *longyí* (sarong), or even the *longyí* themselves. Once the wheel is spinning fast enough, they hang onto one of the seats and wait for the right moment to jump off.

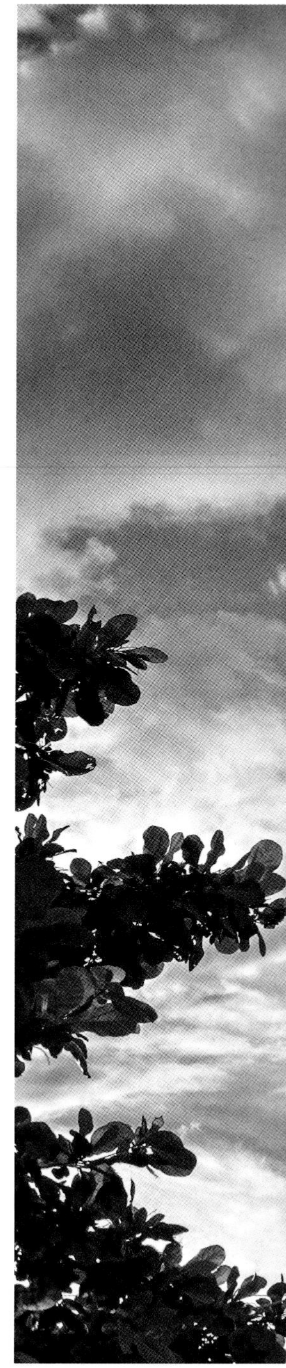

Opposite: Ferris wheel at a pottery fair, Mandalay, 2015

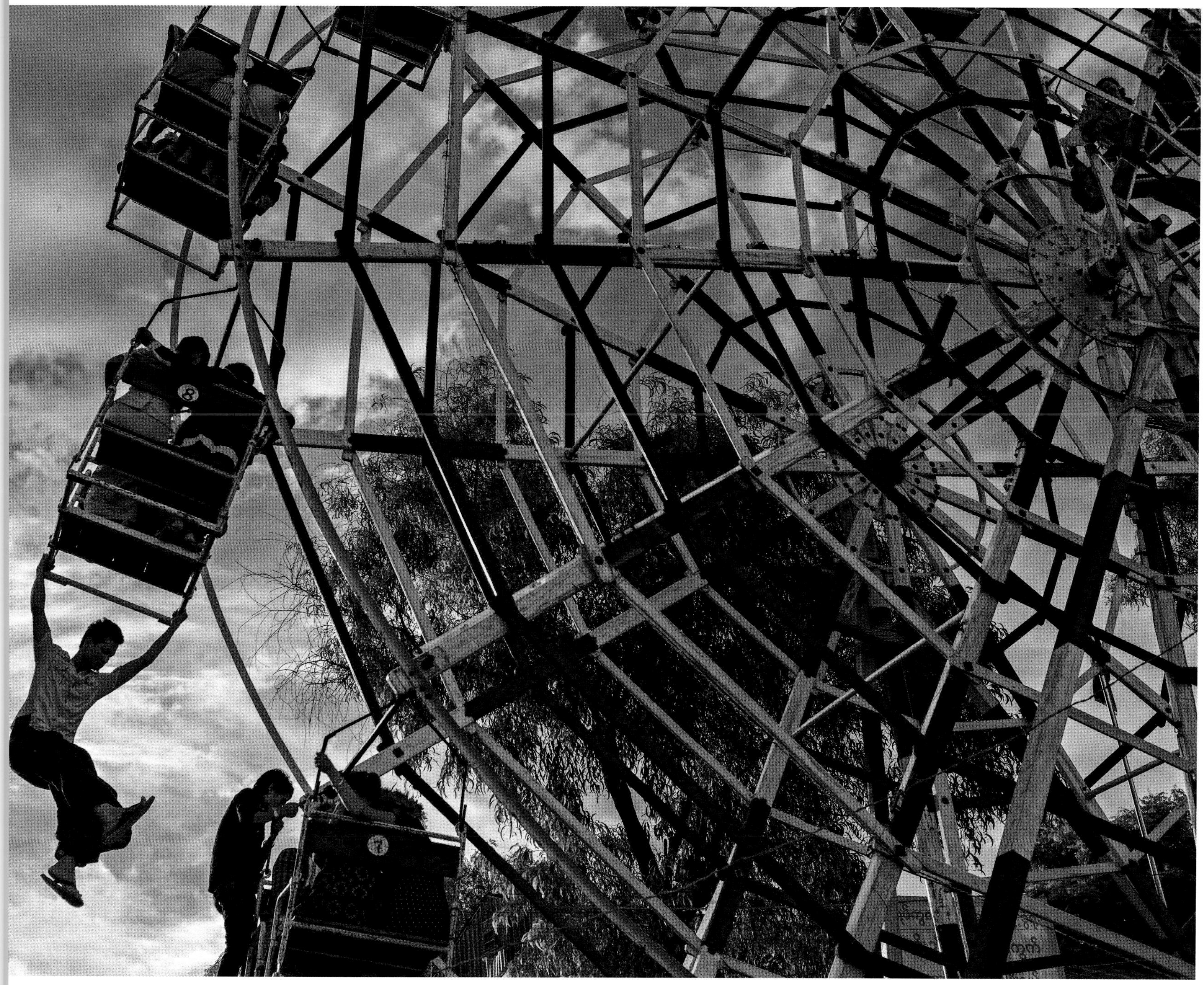
8
7

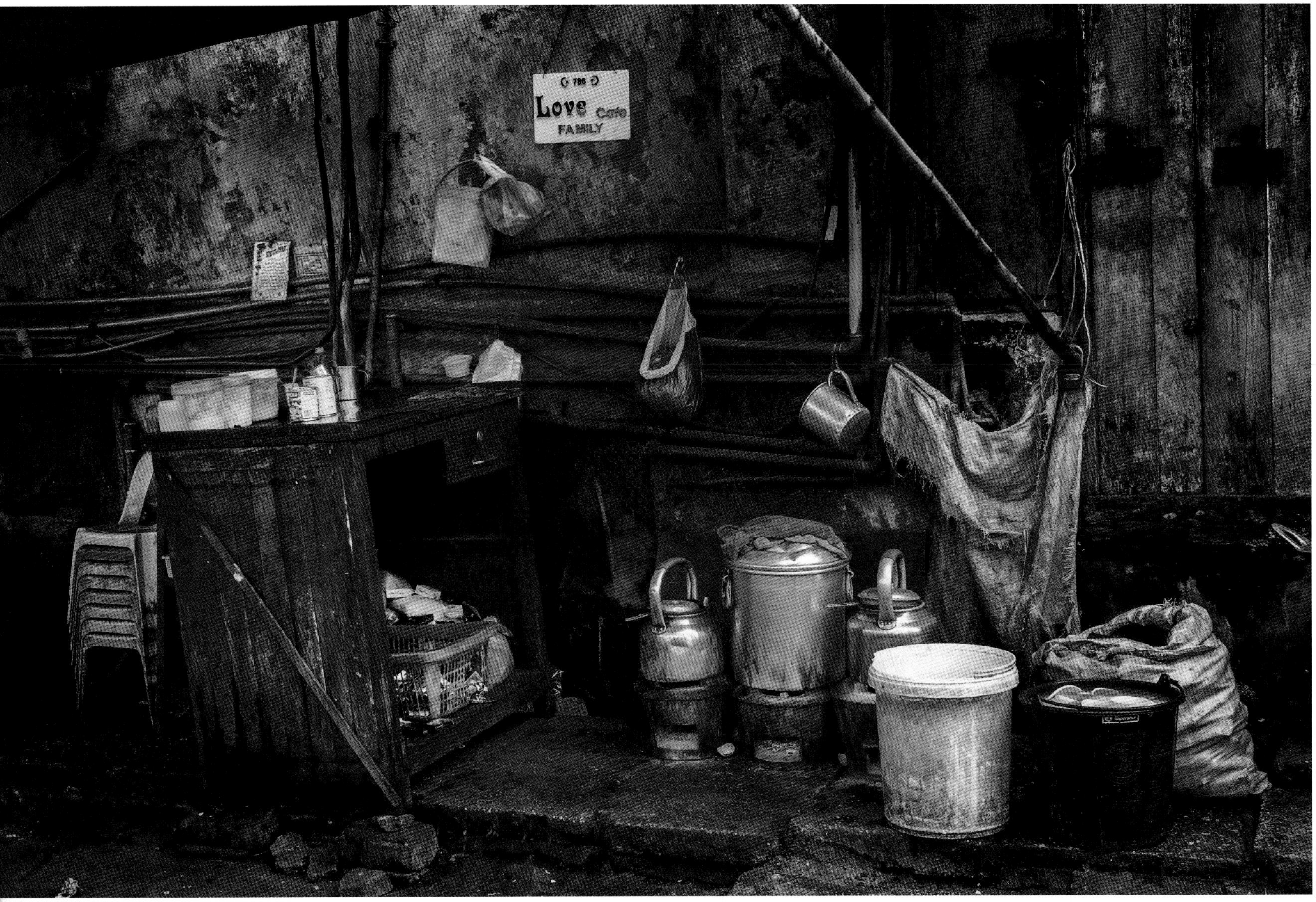

STREET-SIDE TEA SHOP, YANGON, 2011

Tea shops are abundant in Myanmar. A wide, or even narrow, expanse of sidewalk can invite an entrepreneur to open a tea shop. The patrons sit on kindergarten-size plastic chairs or wooden stools. With free pitchers of green tea placed on each table to compliment the milky brews, many hours can be whiled away in a tea shop.

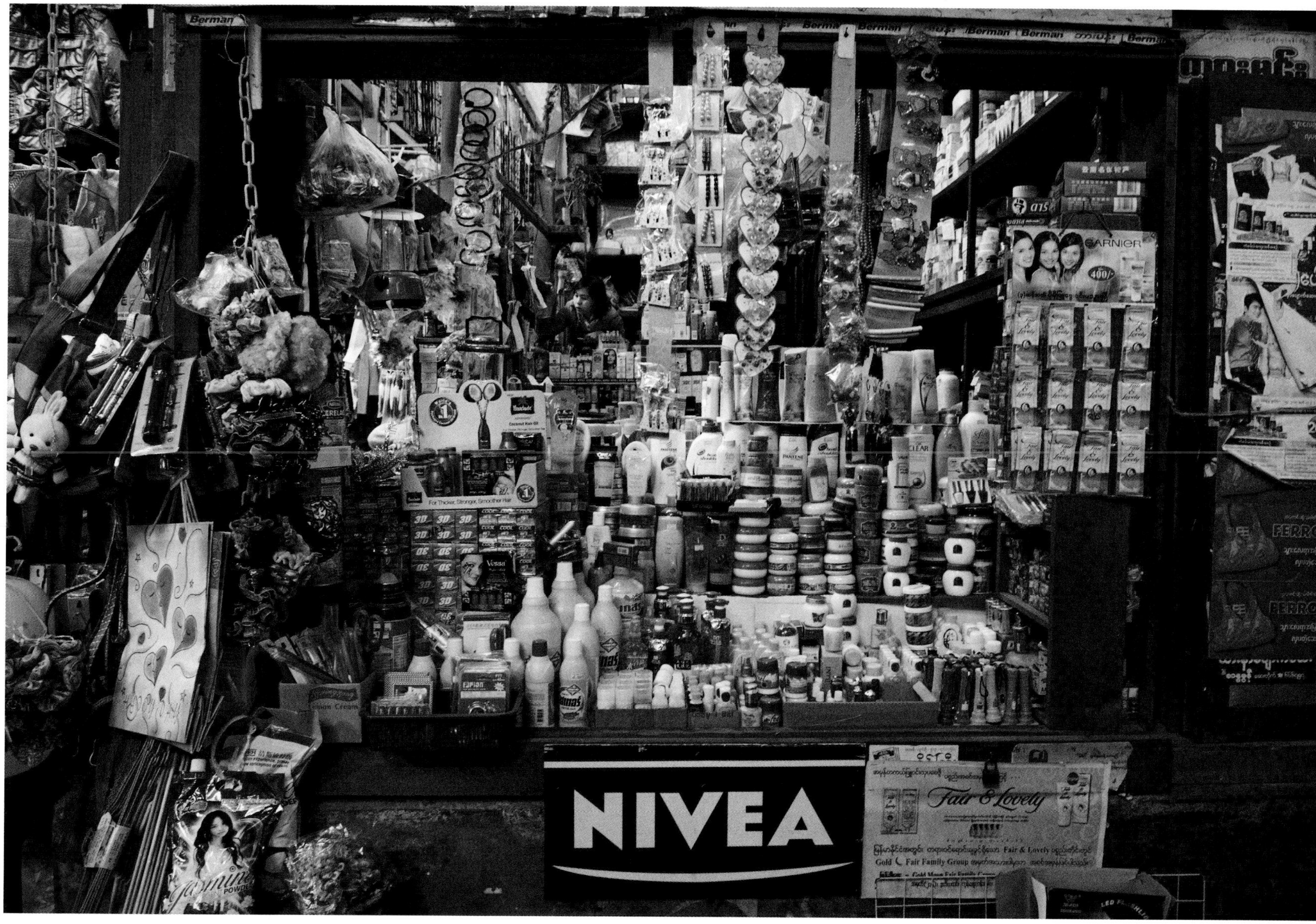

Market stall, Kyaukme, Shan State, 2012

With the help of vertical displays, the limited space available on this street-side shop front does not restrict the variety of products on offer, from Chinese detergents, Thai cosmetics, international brand-name shampoos, and local beauty potions to practical items such as hand torches, scissors, and clothes hangers.

Girl at a market, Bagan, Mandalay Region, 2010

When you are balancing a tray of fruit on your head, only your eyes can convey your mood.

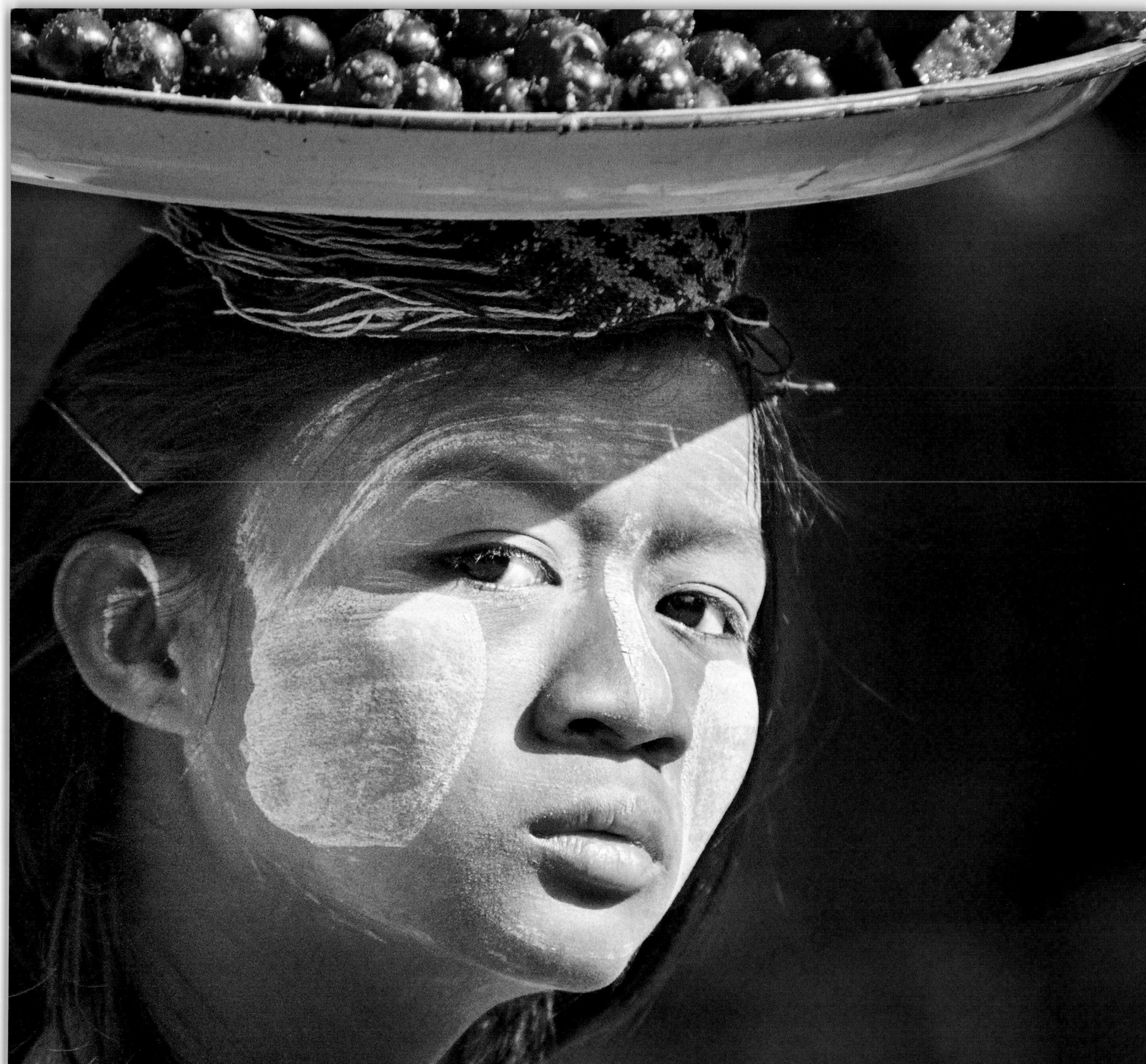

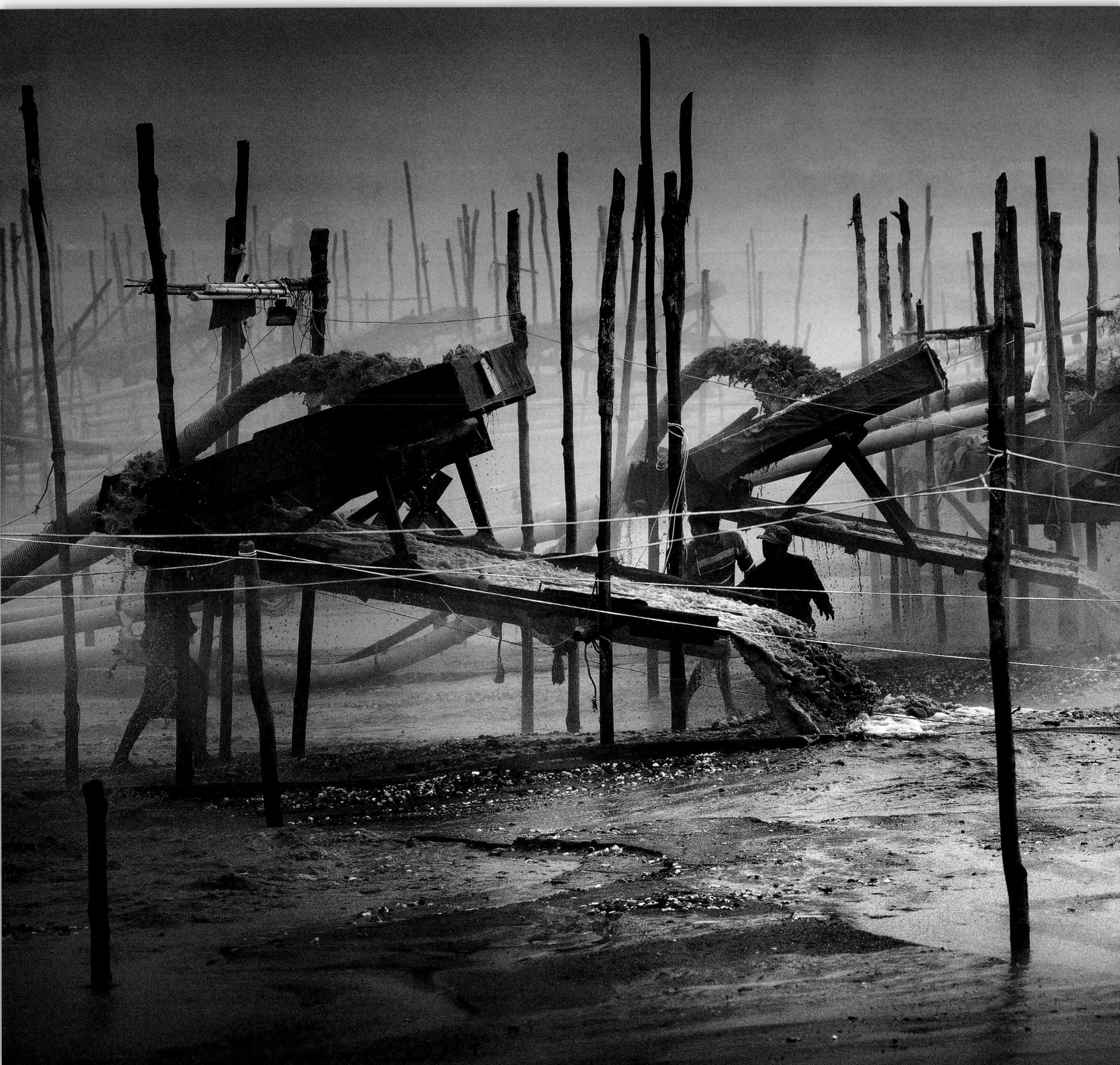

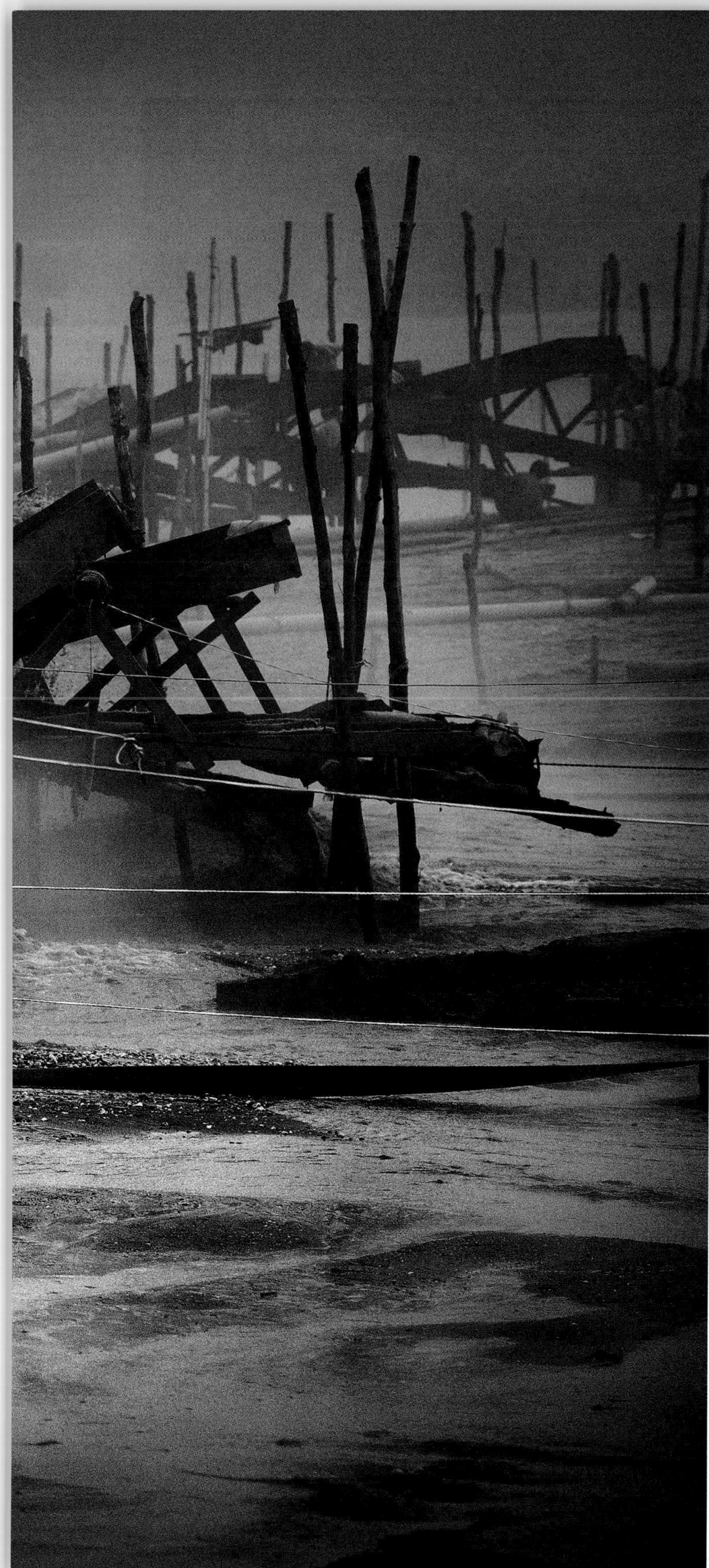

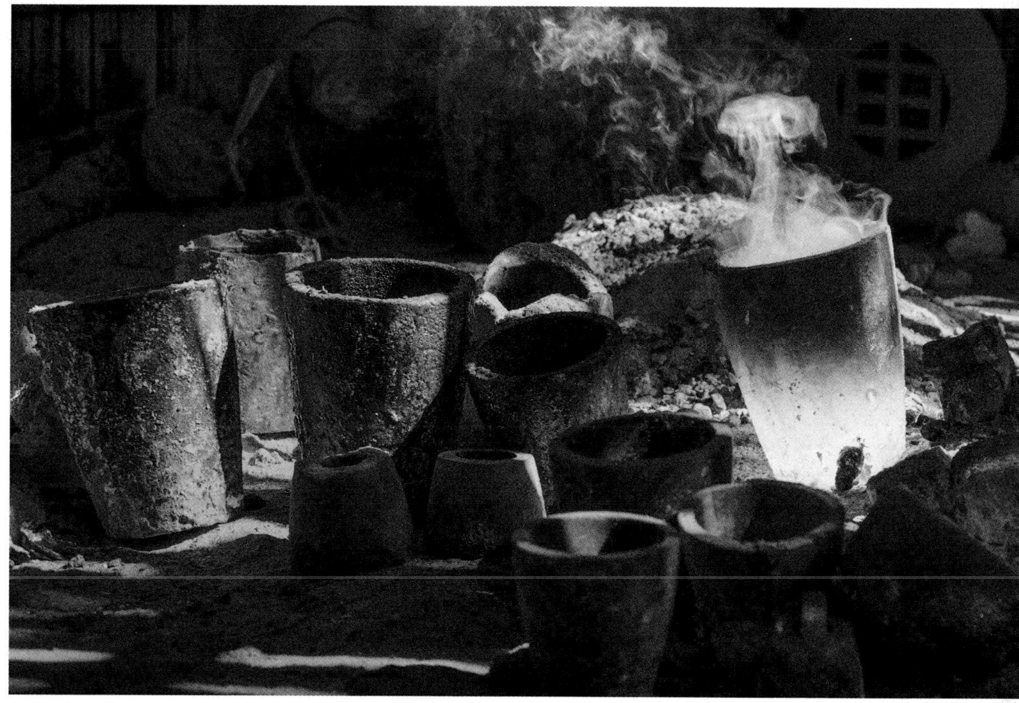

ABOVE: MELTING POTS FOR GOLD ORE, NORTHERN SHAN STATE, 2012

Myanmar is famous for its raw materials. A large part of the population is involved in the hunt for riches, from the simple act of hand-carrying rattan over the mountains to China to the complex task of searching for gold. Only a few succeed. In lieu of big machinery to exploit these raw materials, most of the work is still done manually. The photograph opposite shows a gold washing facility with a mechanism often used on big rivers such as the Ayeyarwady or Chindwin rivers. With the help of engines on boats anchored alongside the riverbank, sand from the riverbed is pumped through pipes into the structures pictured here. The water and sand is run through filters which are then cleaned into basins where women pan for gold using large wooden bowls.

LEFT: GOLD WASHING FACILITIES TO EXTRACT GOLD FROM THE RIVERBED, CHINDWIN RIVER, SAGAING REGION, 2010

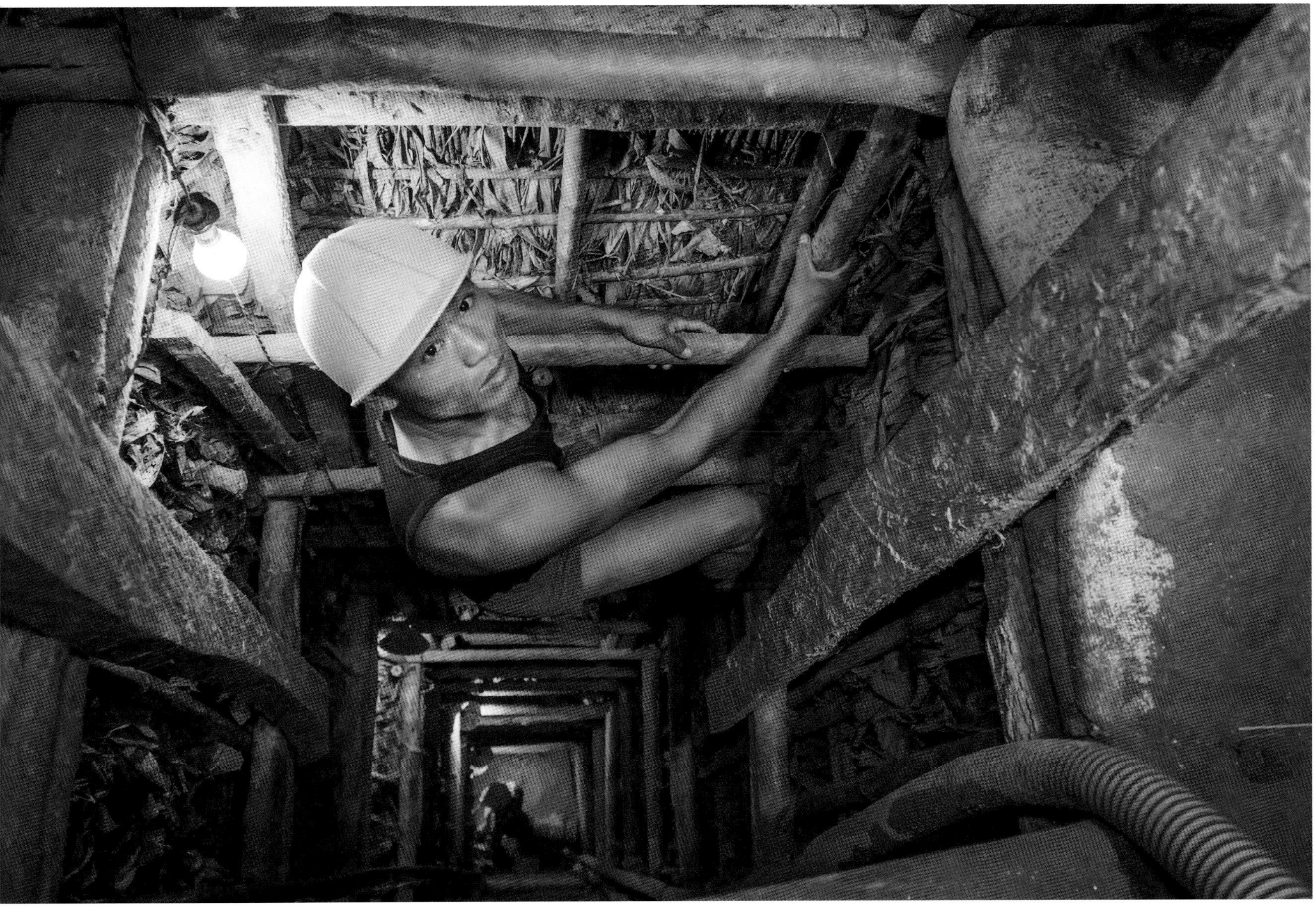

An underground quartz and topaz mine near Mogok, Mandalay Region, 2014

Myanmar has countless underground mines containing gold, topaz, quartz, rubies, and sapphires. Some mines are large enough for small pickup trucks to enter, others are narrow holes in the ground that can be 100 metres deep and into which miners climb down to search for an artery in the side walls. The amazing skill and daring of the workers is a counterbalance to the lack of modern technology in use.

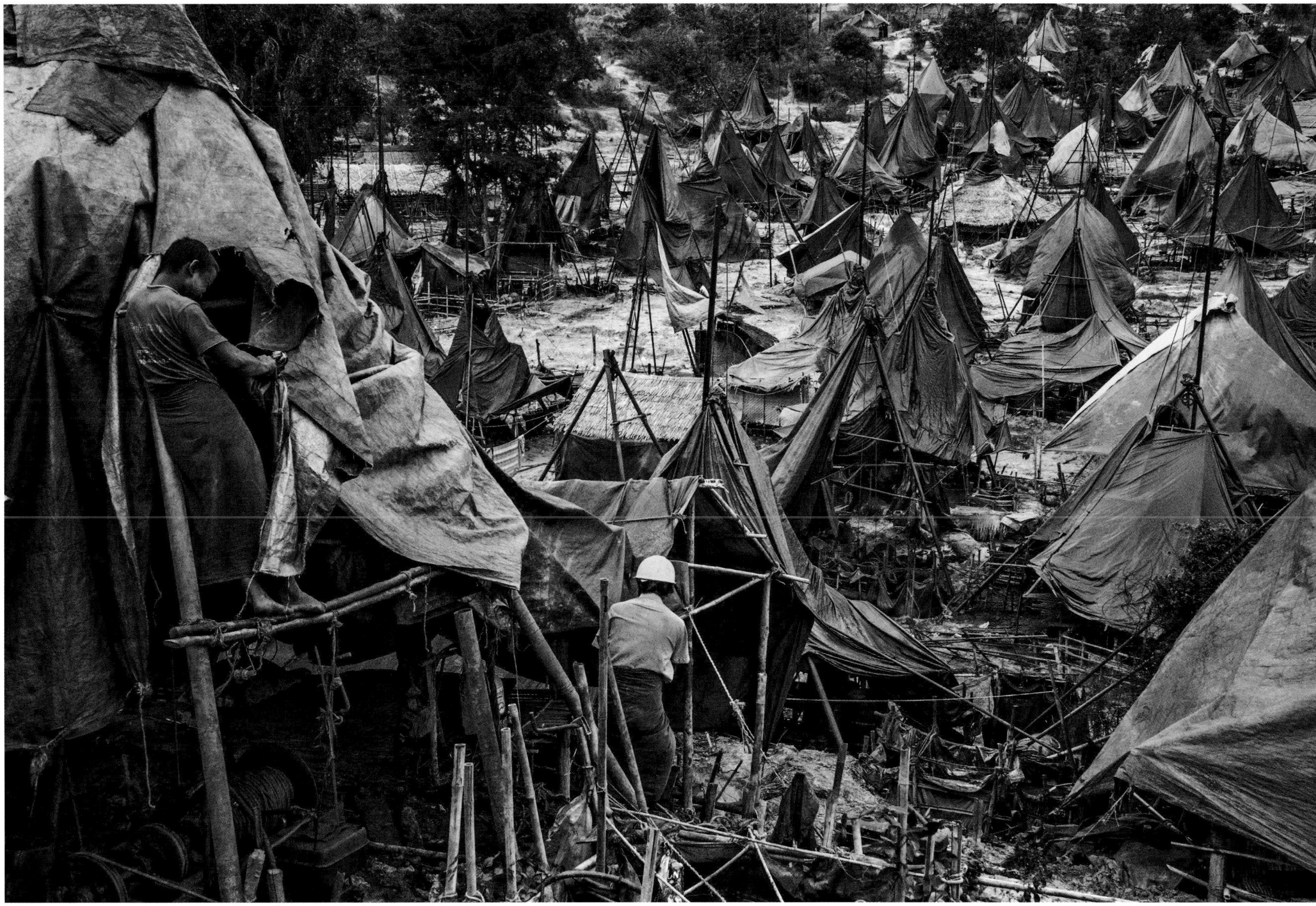

Private oil extraction, Minhla, Magway Region, 2015

In some areas of the country, oil is discovered very near the earth's surface. Entire villages are transformed or spring up around these sites as people drill for black gold using pipes winched down through small holes in the ground. Tarps erected over the holes provide some protection from the blistering sun. Once a field has been completely exploited, the village moves on to the next promising location.

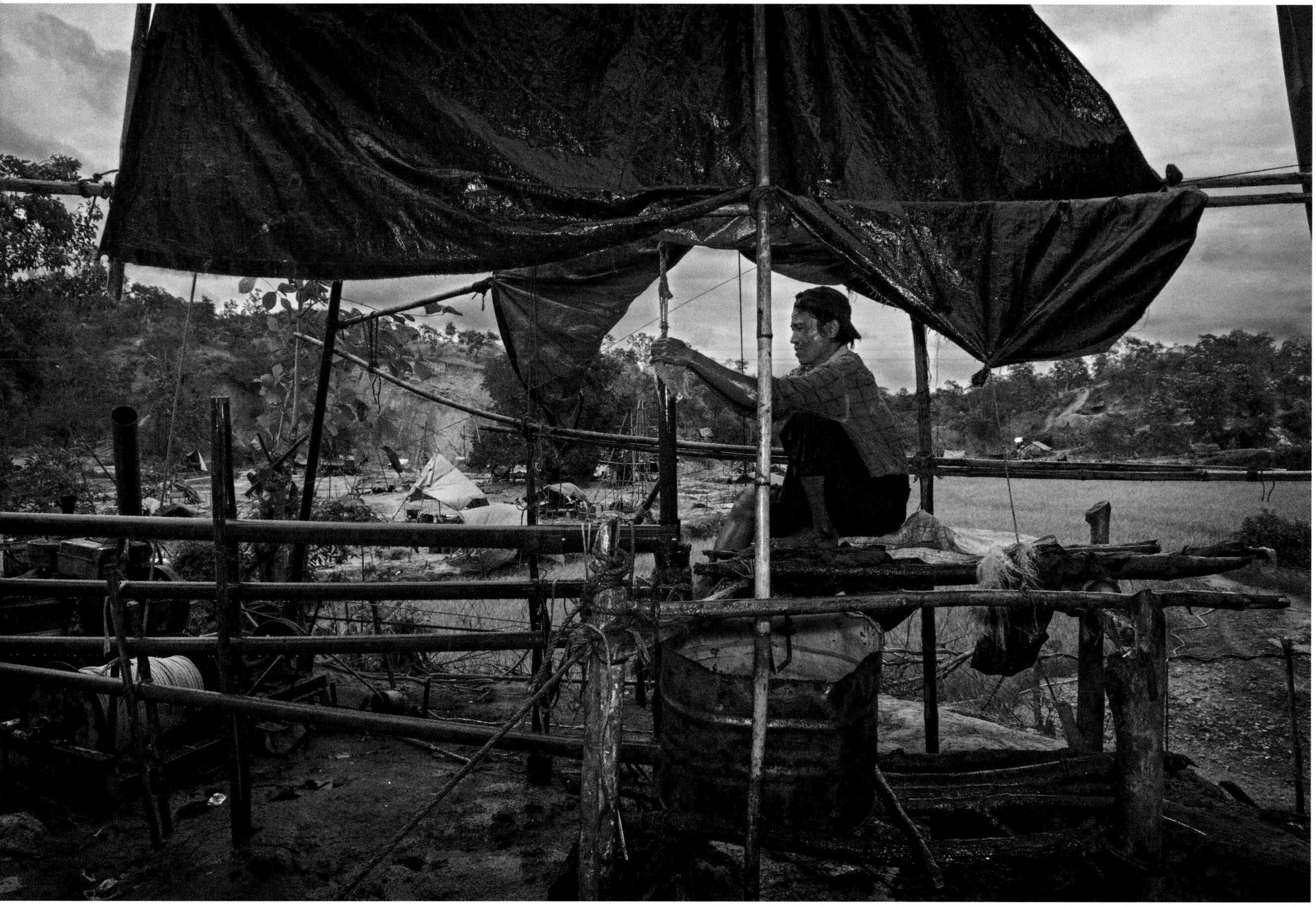

Oil worker winching a pipe to extract oil from the ground, Minhla, Magway Region, 2015

Oil has only just been discovered in this part of the Minlha region. The first drills have started production and no doubt soon the rice fields in the background of this photograph will be replaced by a pop-up oil village.

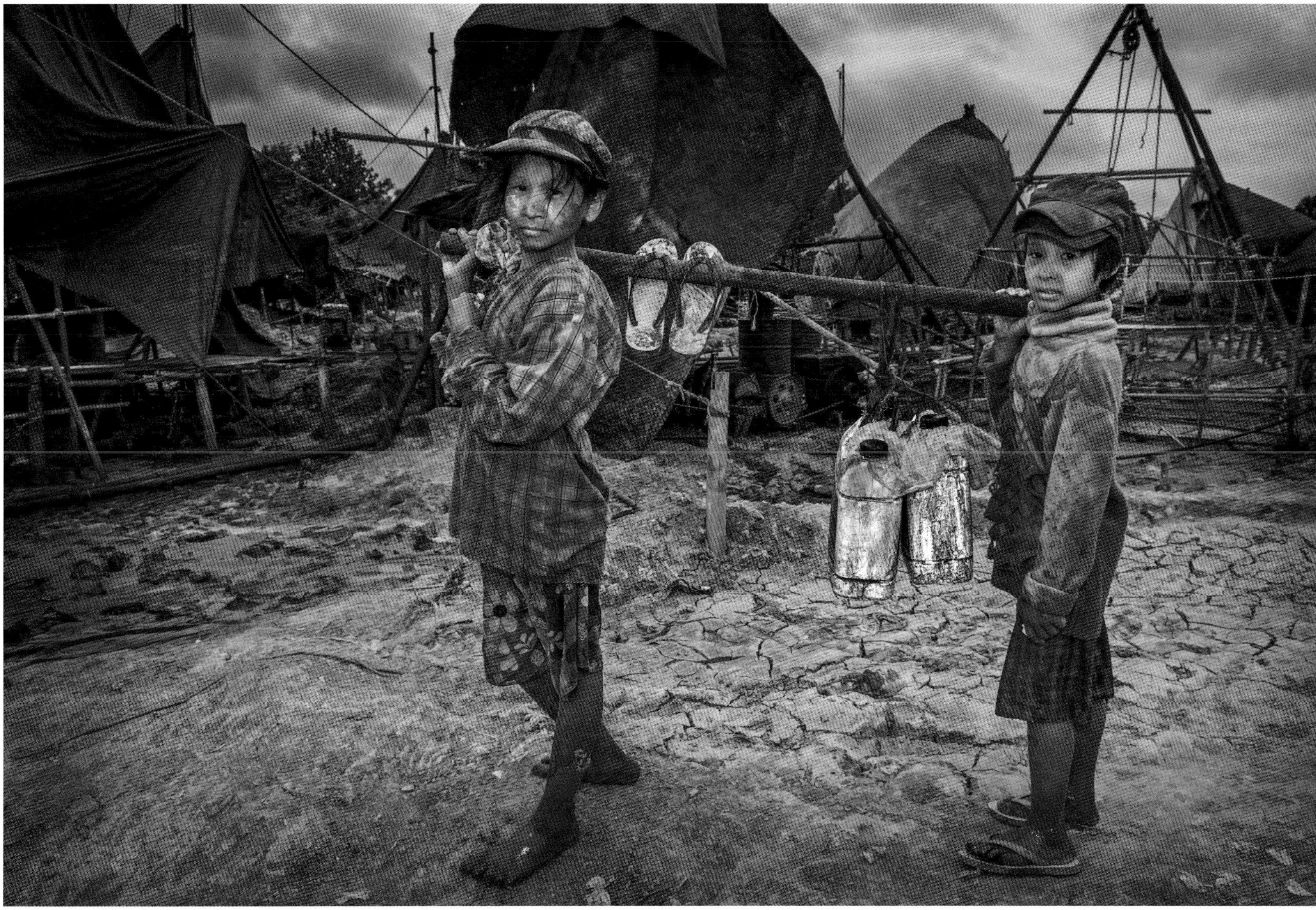

Children carrying oil canisters, Minhla, Magway Region, 2015

In temporary oil extraction villages, the whole family contributes to making a living from a single well while its supplies last.

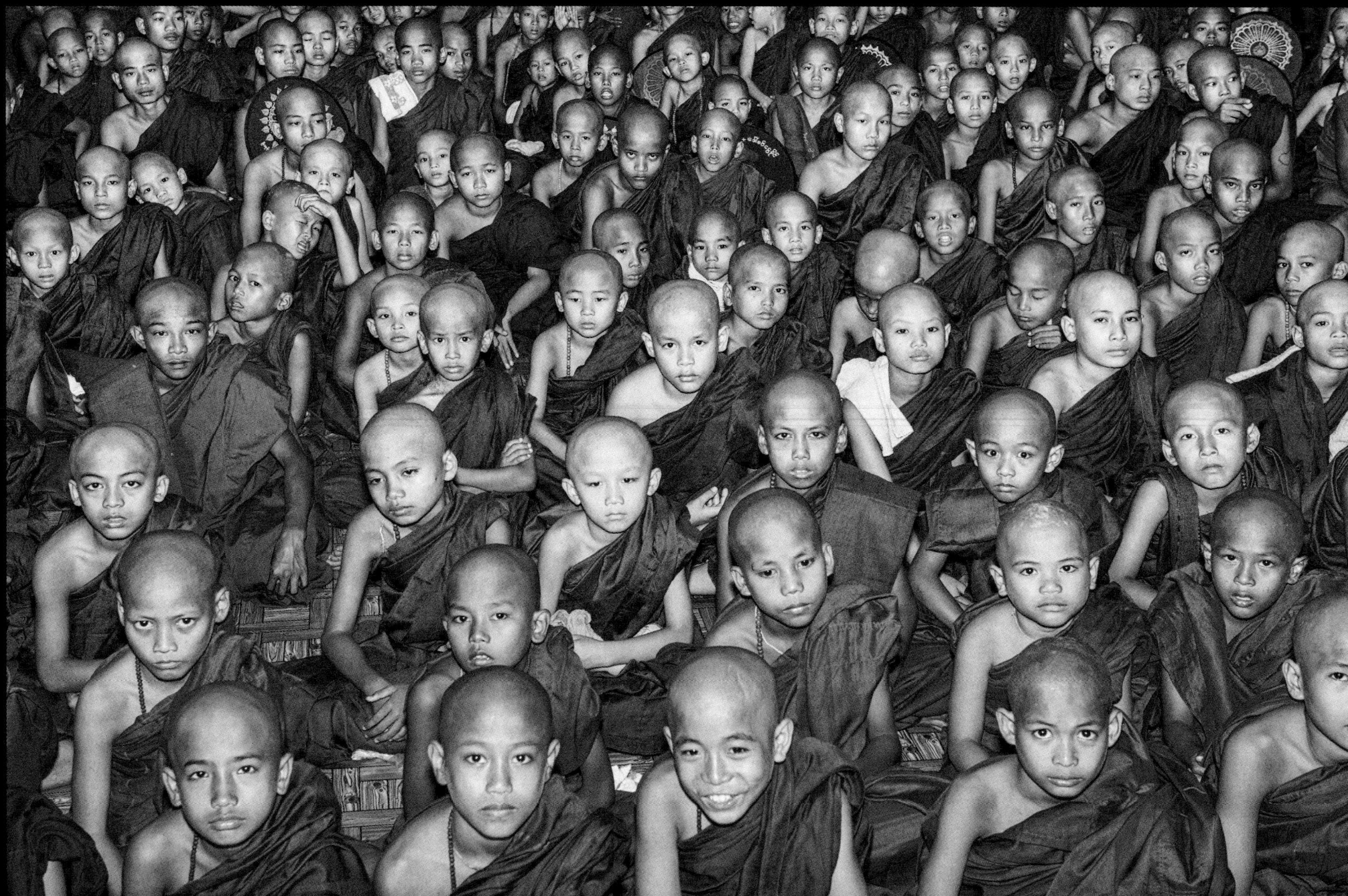

Novice monks waiting for lunch, Taungoo, Bago Region, 2013

When generous donors sponsor lunch at a monastery all the monastery residents must attend a special ceremony before they can partake of the meal – a delay that must be especially difficult on the young and hungry.

Right: Monks putting on their robes, Sittwe, Rakhine State, 2011

The method of wrapping a monk's robes differs according to whether he is preparing for the morning alms round, a monastic class, or football.

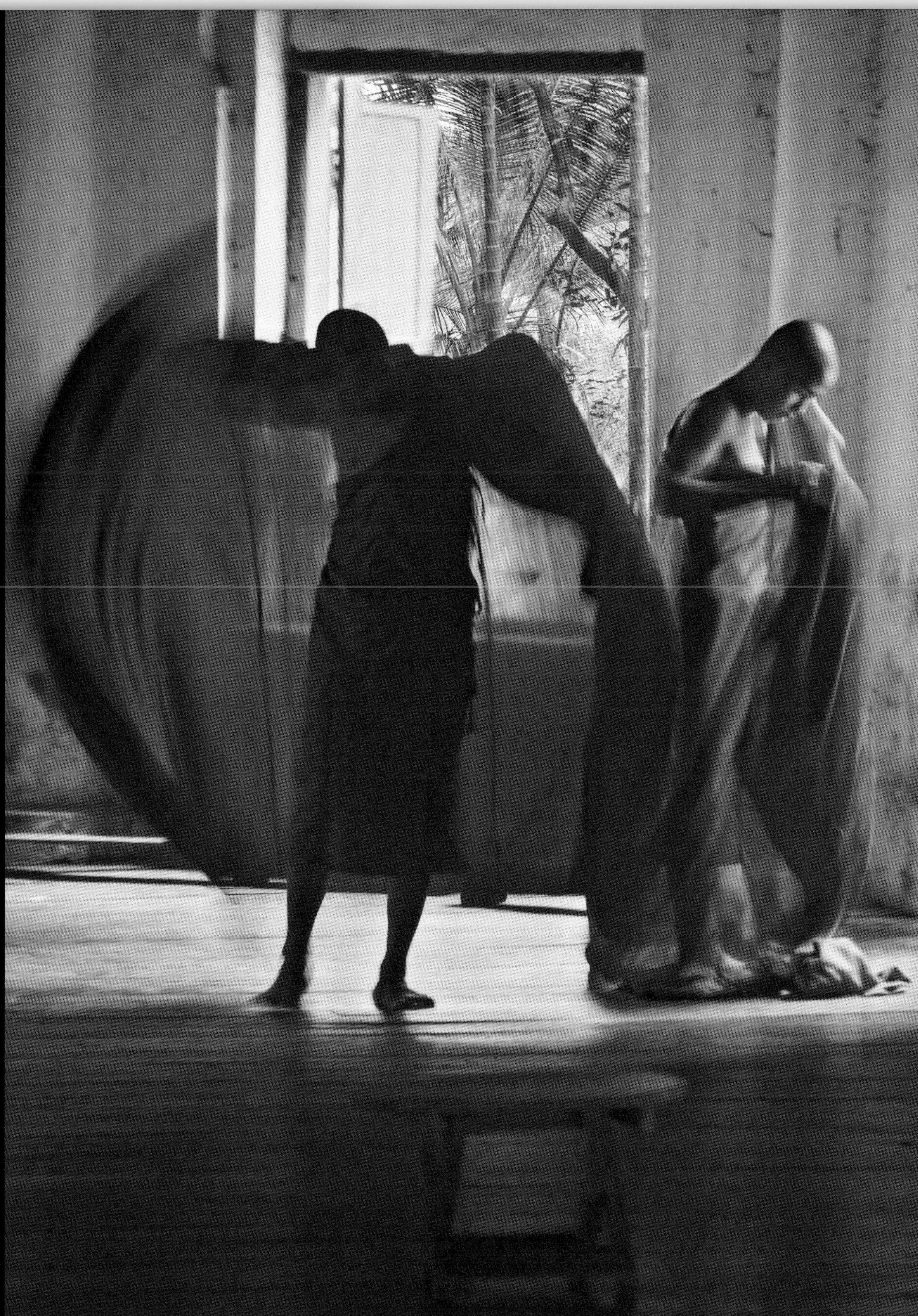

Nuns line up to receive their exam certificates, Loikaw, Kayah State, 2011

Just like monks, nuns must pass an annual examination to attain a higher ordination, though they will always rank lower than monks. Unlike men in Myanmar, not all women will spend time in a monastery; while the novitiation ceremony is an important rite of passage in the lives of boys, girls often have an ear-piercing ceremony instead.

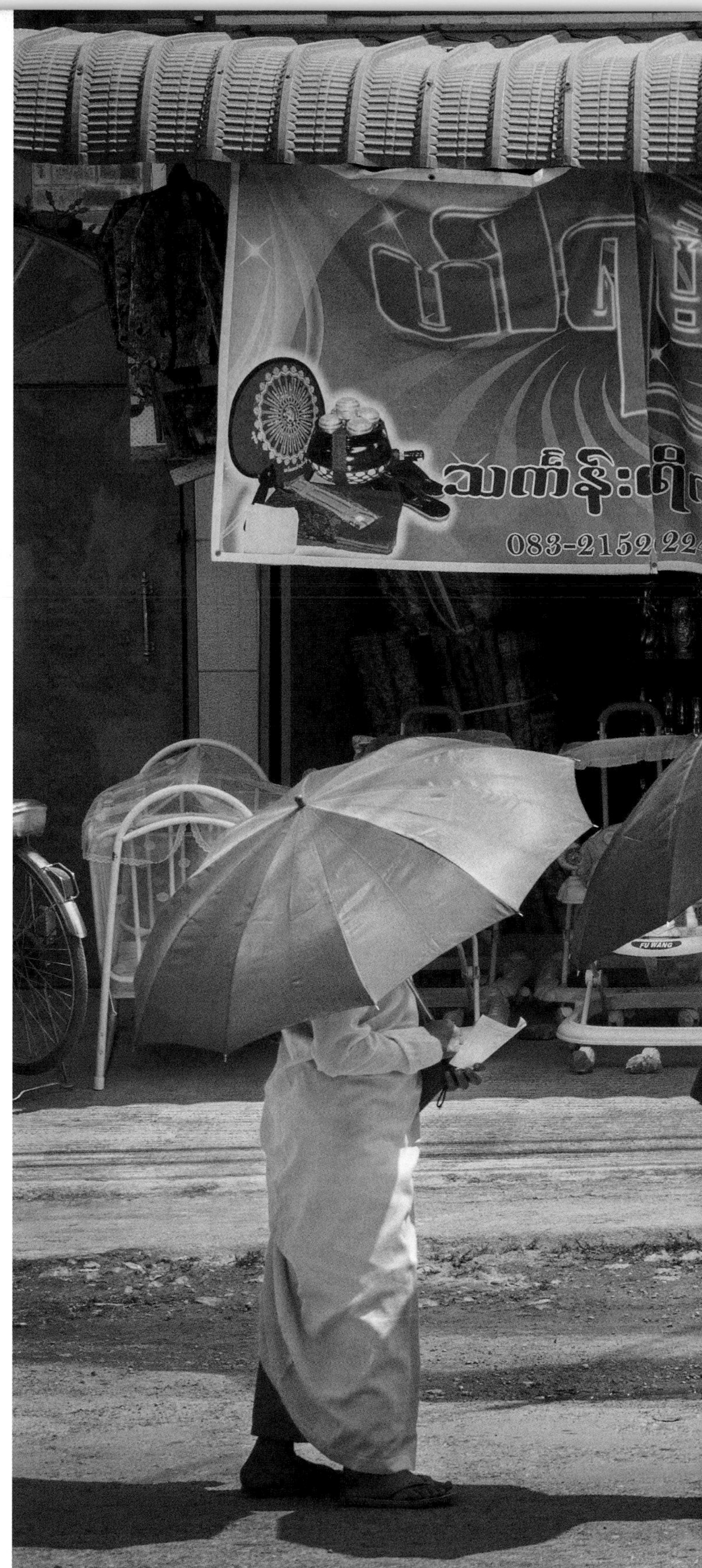

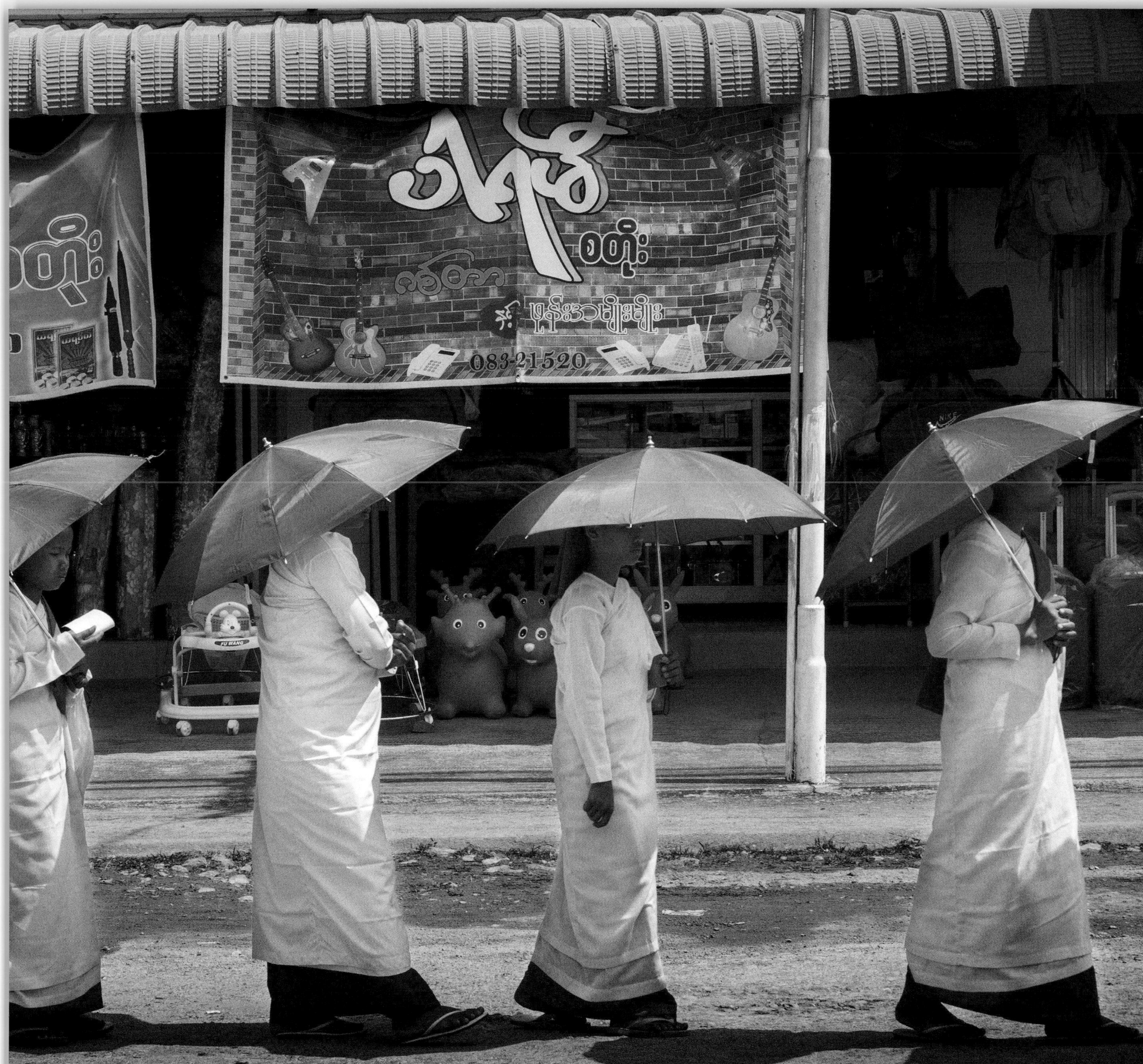
083-21520

Donation procession, Mawlamyine, Mon State, 2011

At the end of Buddhist Lent, a donation procession takes place so that monks can receive the food and goods they need for daily monastic life. Offerings include rice, sweets, soap, towels, and pots and pans. Monks lead the procession as they are the first group in the hierarchy of alms recipients. They are followed by nuns, lay nuns, and the poorest people in the community – all of whom receive their share.

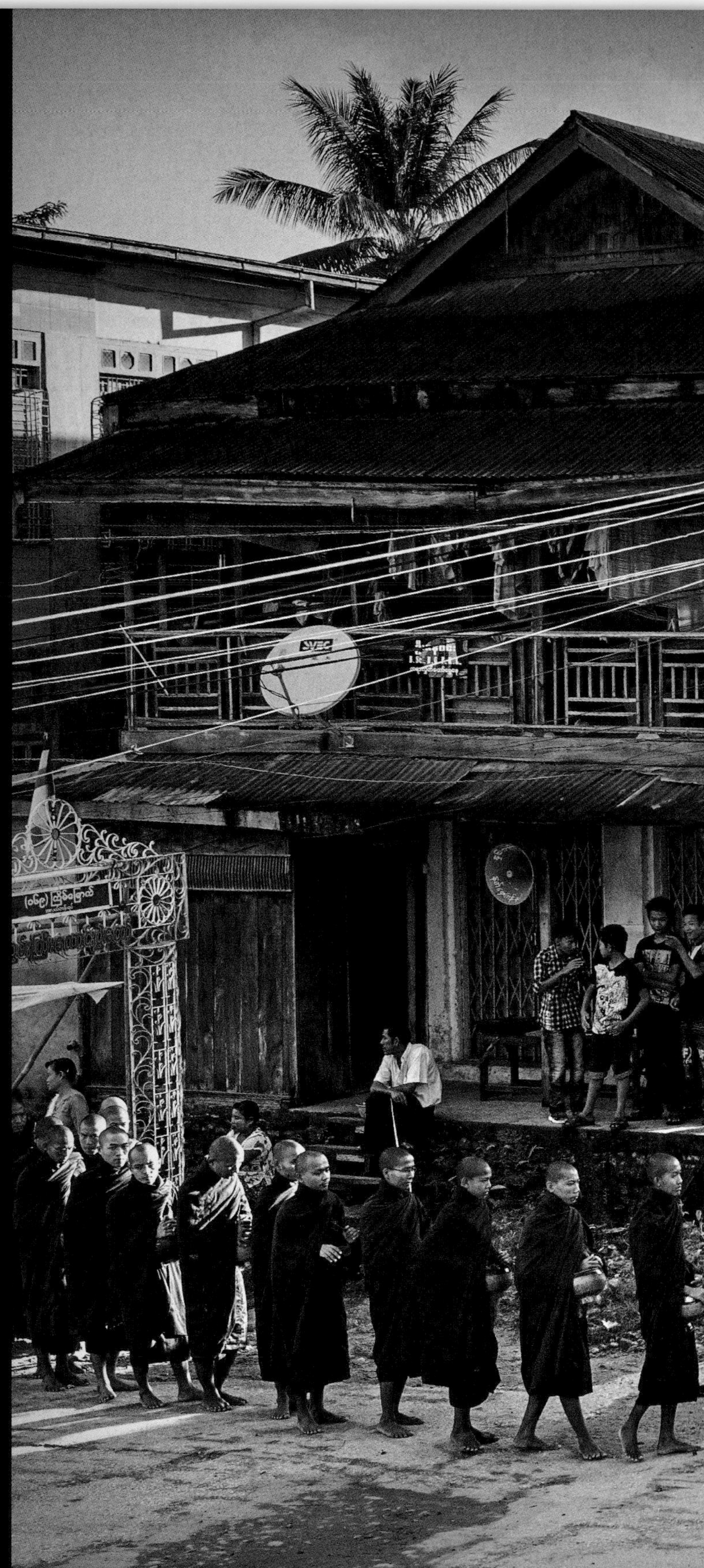

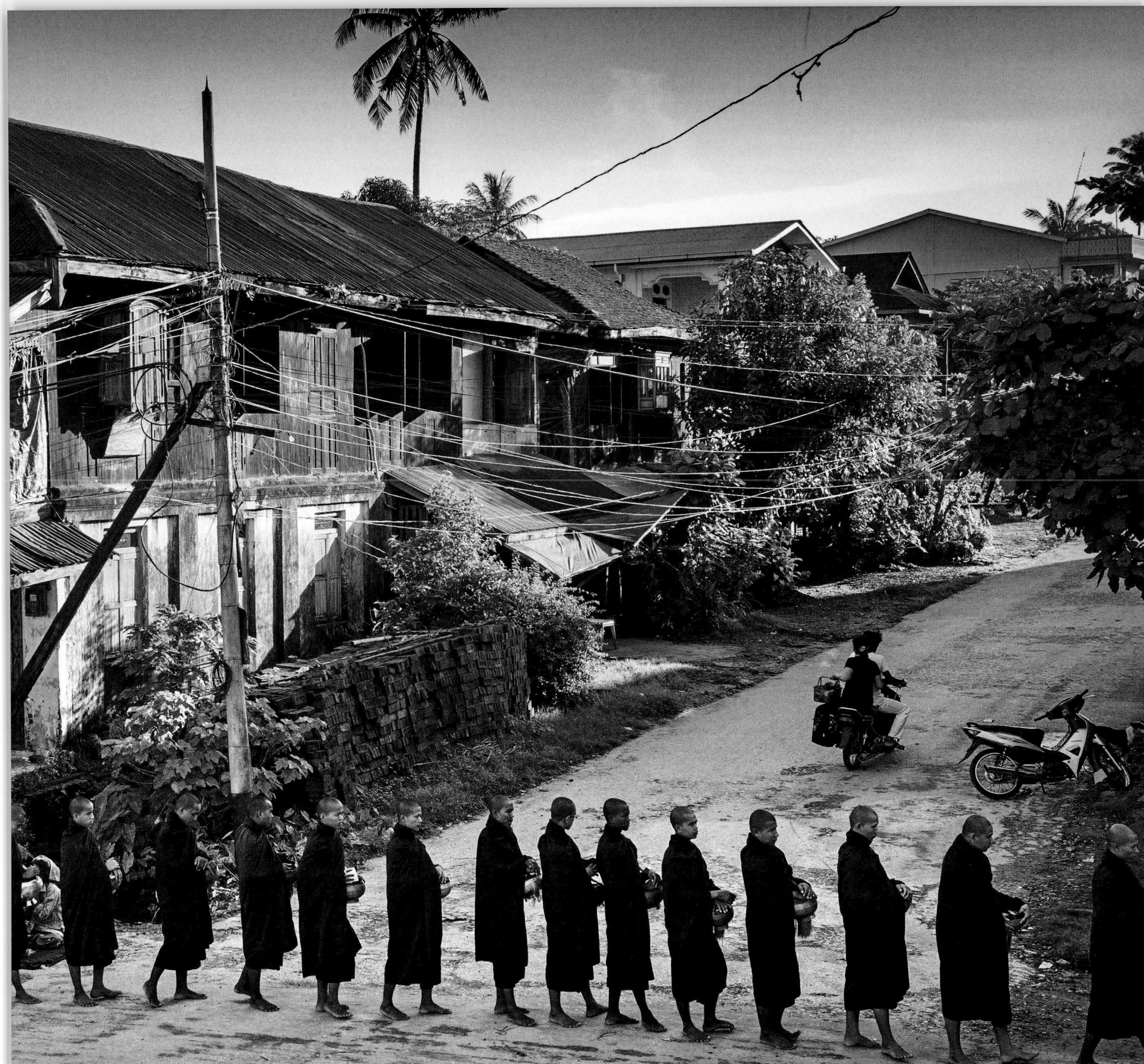

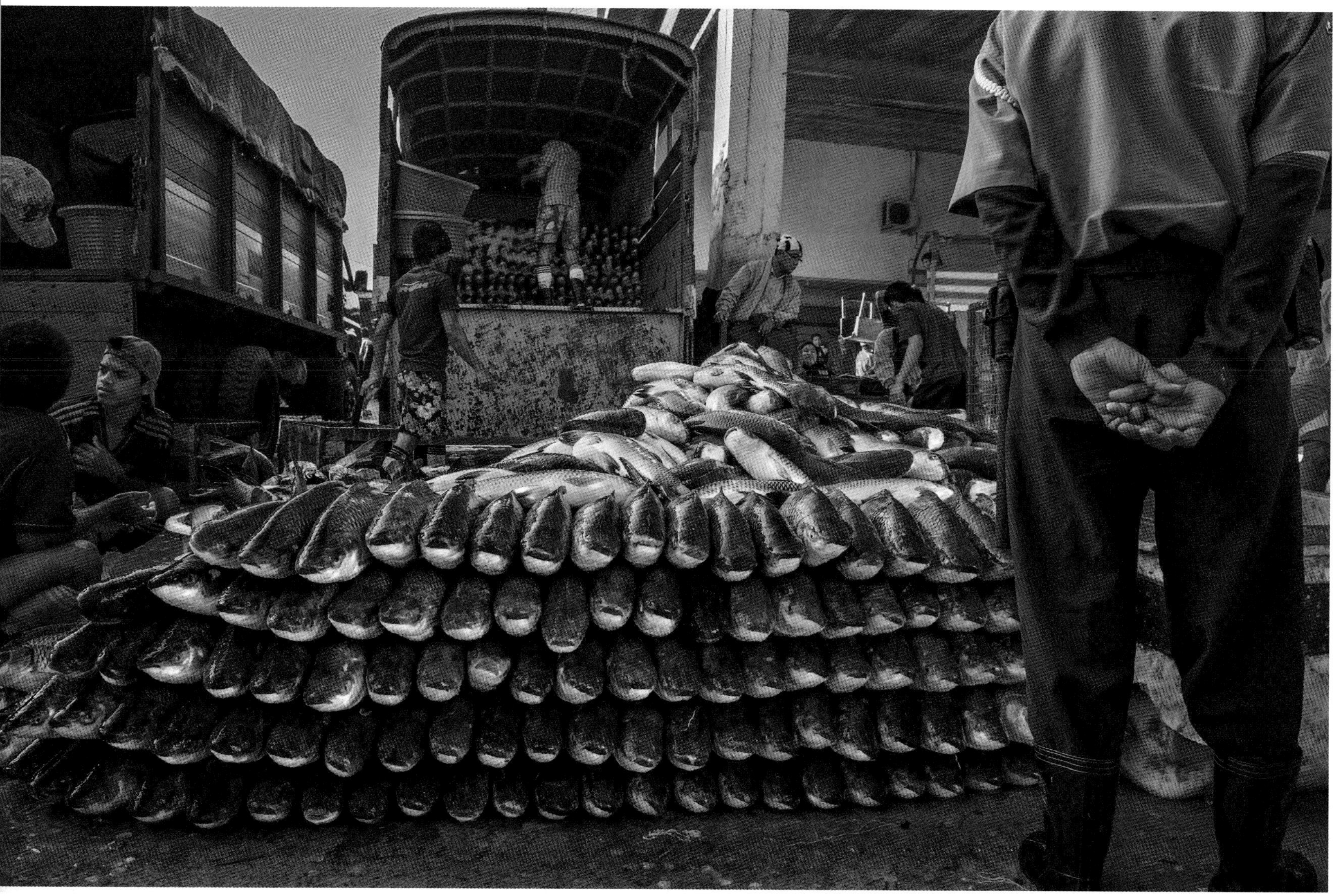

San Pya Fish Market, MMG Jetty, Yangon, 2012

The Yangon fish market is a very special and busy place. Porters run around transporting their loads on wheelbarrows, in baskets on their heads, or by hand. Buyers buzz around looking for the best quality at the lowest price. Noisy diesel-operated ice crunchers prepare ice to pack the fish. This photograph shows an unexpected oasis of tranquility where I could admire the way workers had stacked the fish so neatly and in such an aesthetically pleasing manner.

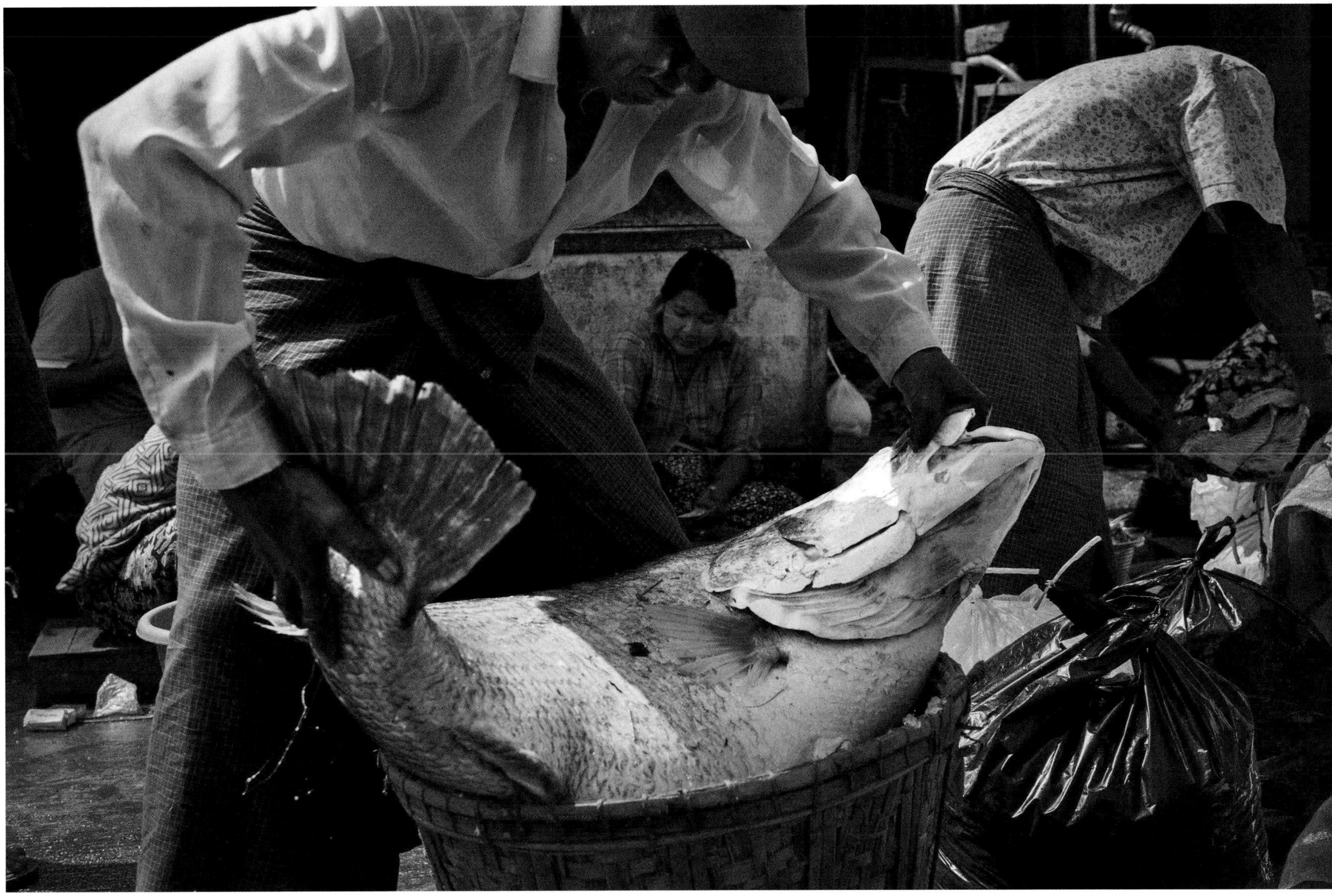

San Pya Fish Market, Yangon, 2011

This man is struggling to pack an extraordinarily large purchase into a basket for transportation.

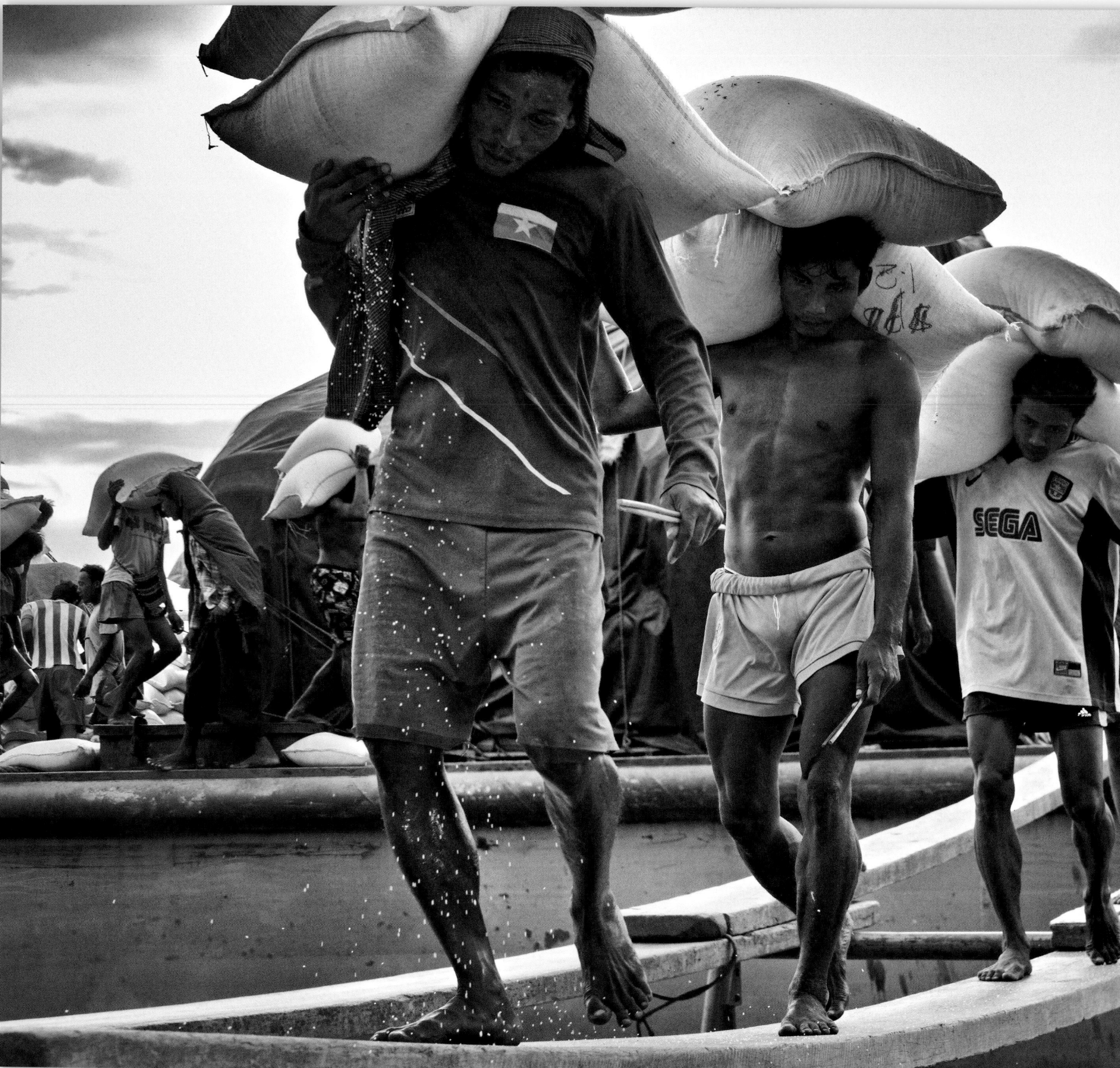
SEGA

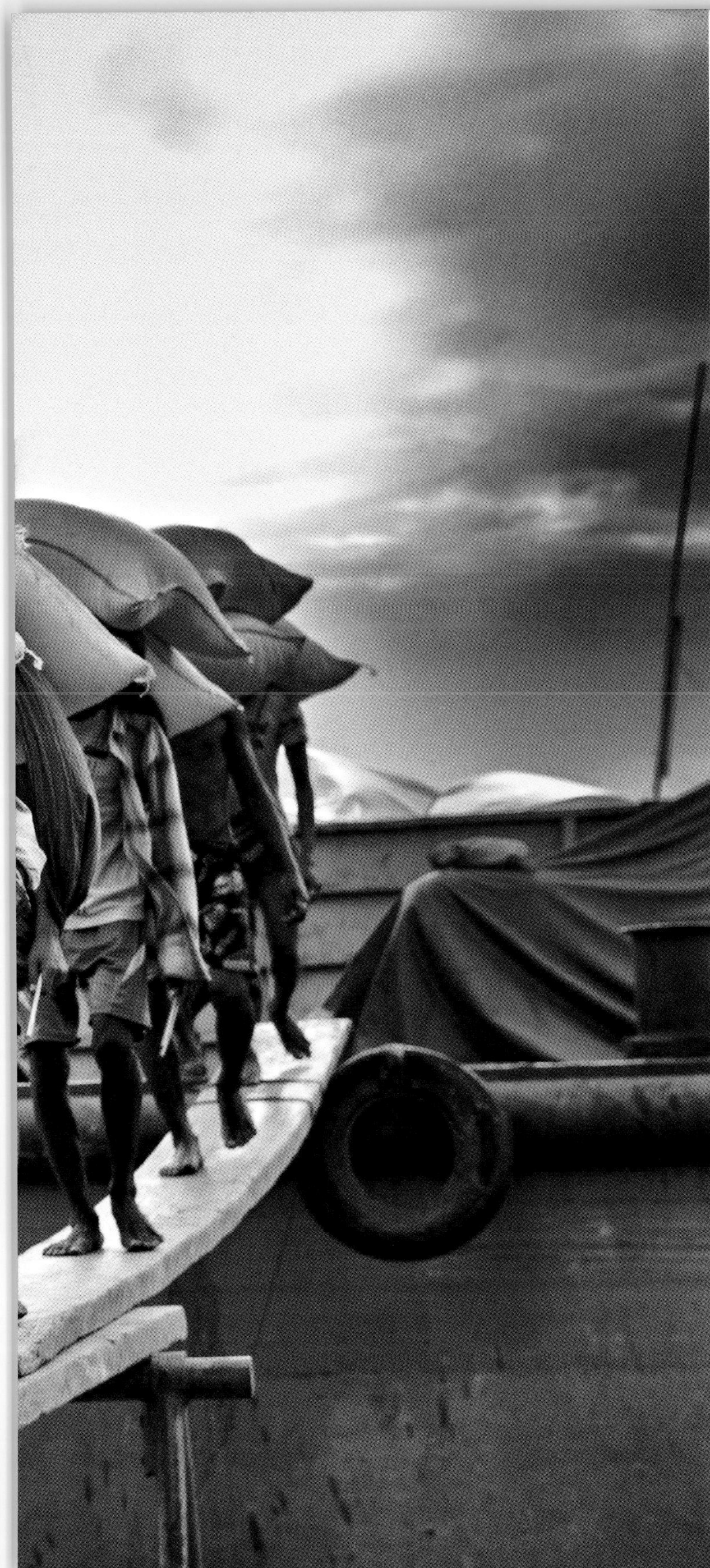

AT THE JETTY, MANDALAY, 2015

Rice bags are unloaded manually from a rice freighter on the Ayeyarwady River. The workers practically run along the planks laid down between the vessel and truck. Their rounds are counted using a tally system with each worker receiving one stick for every bag he delivers to the truck. Once the freighter has been unloaded, the workers exchange their sticks for cash. They all keep the same rhythm and even take their breaks together, jumping into the river to cool off, laugh, and splash around.

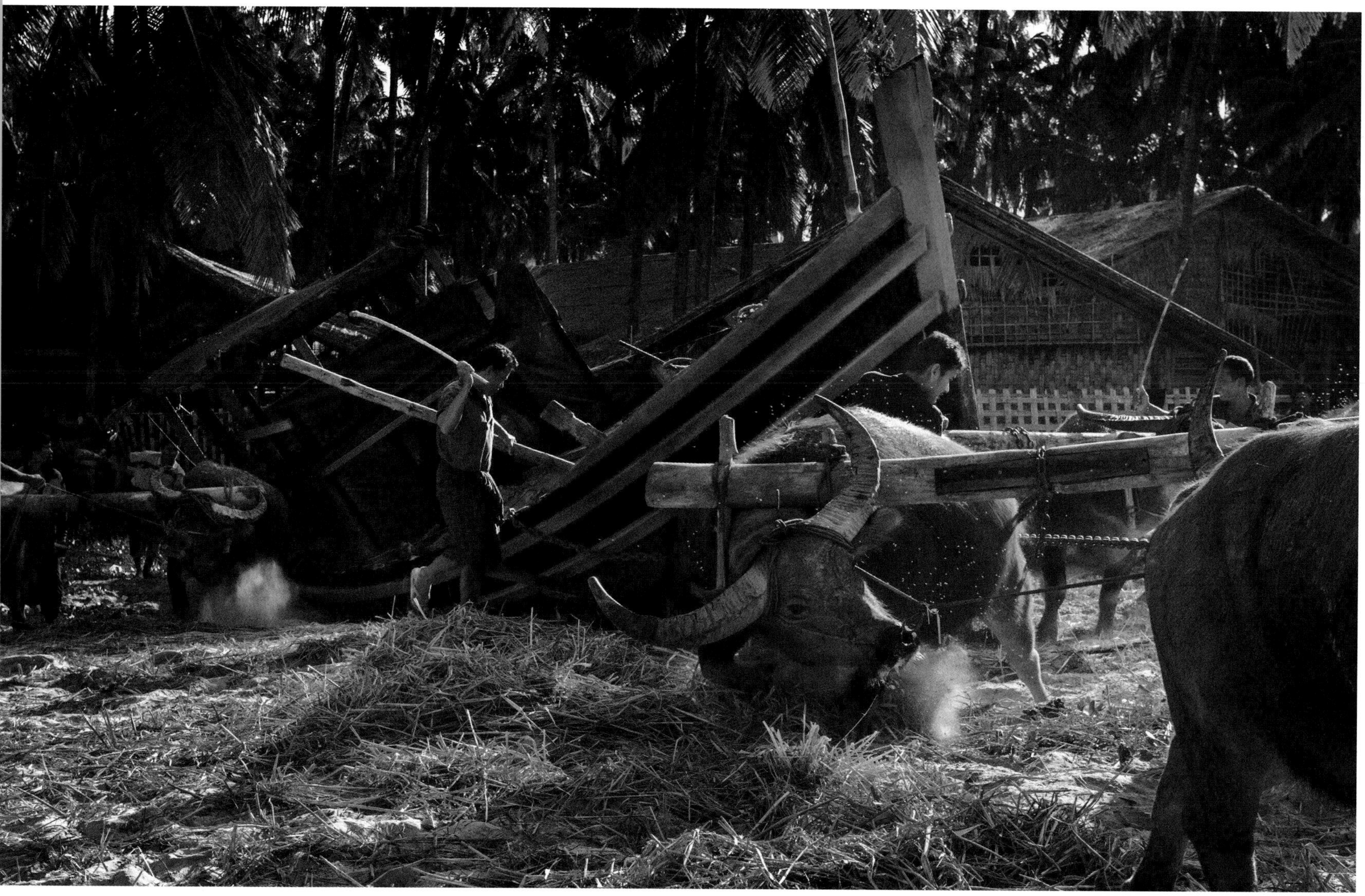

Oxen pulling boats, Ngapali Beach, Rakhine State, 2012

Ox, rather than horse, power is being used to drag this fishing boat back to the sea after repairs. The first attempt with 12 oxen had to be abandoned until more help could be found. The boat finally made it back to the sea pulled by 16 oxen.

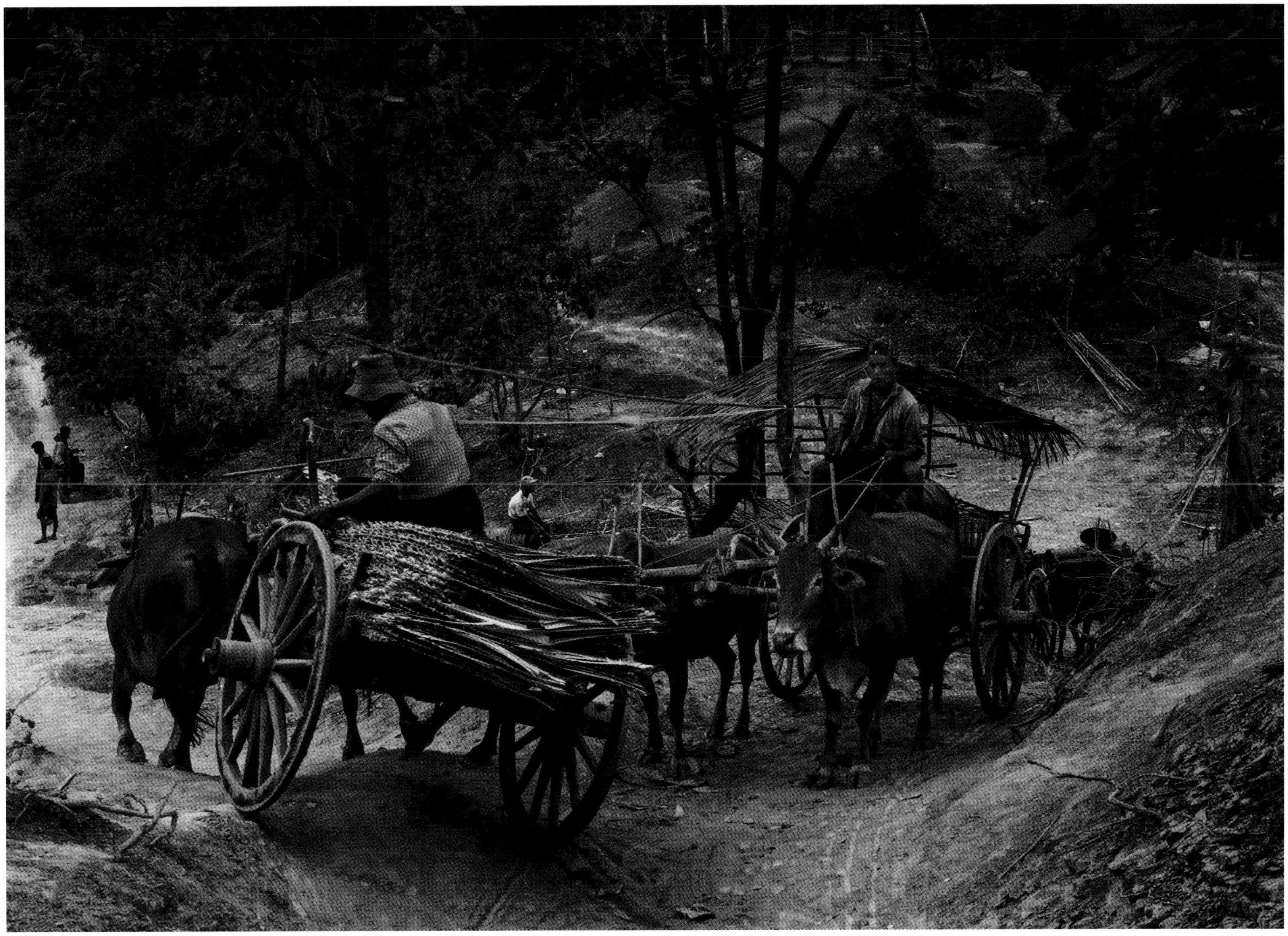

Ox carts near Minhla, Magway Region, 2015

As has been the case for hundreds of years, ox carts are a useful and versatile means of transporting nearly everything. Here, carts laden with building material and oil barrels converge at a crossroads in an area where there are no roads, let alone traffic signs.

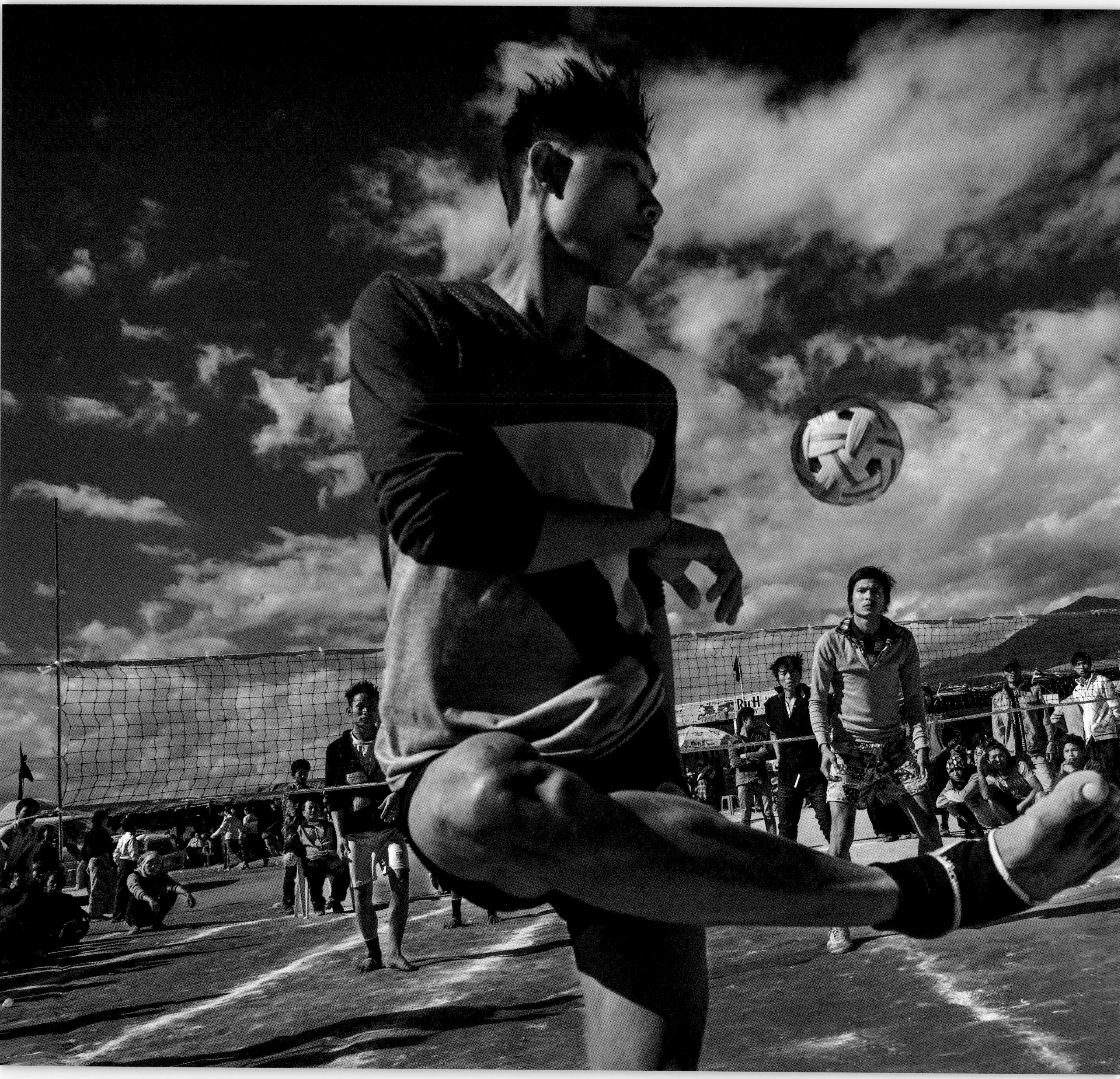

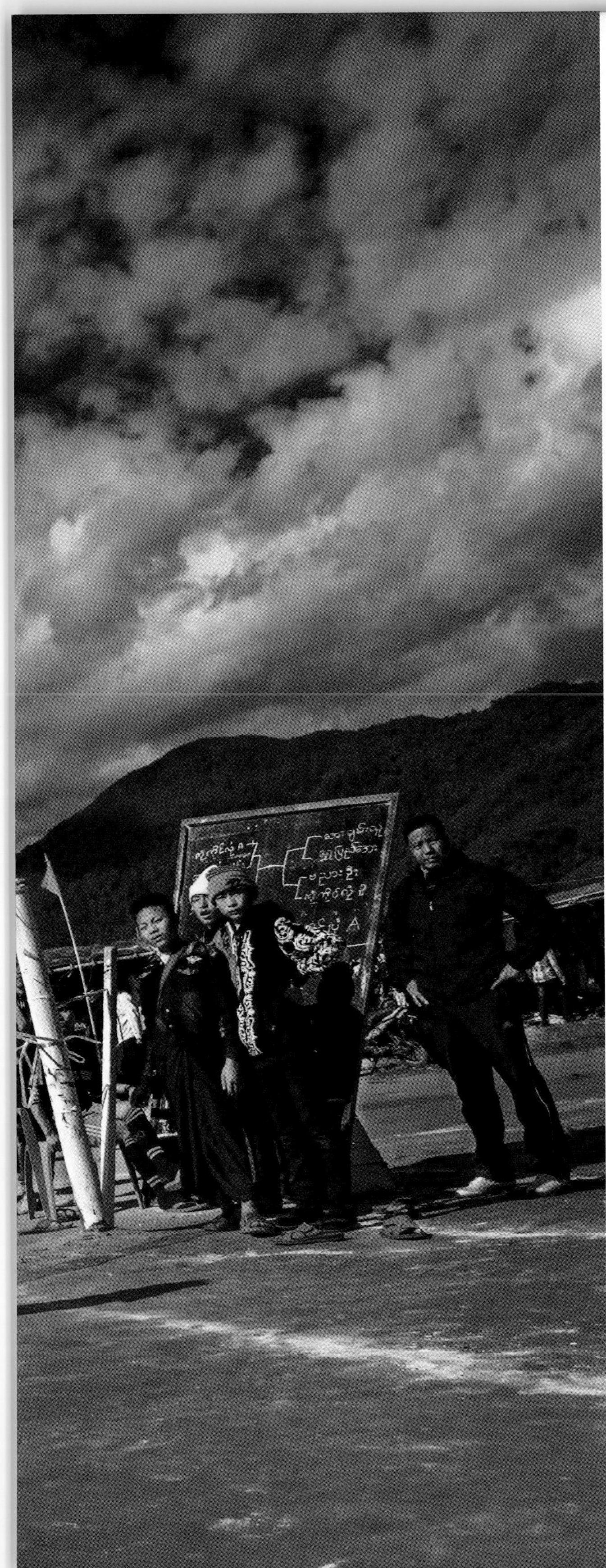

A game of *chinlone*, Layshi, Sagaing Region, 2015

Chinlone is a national game traditionally played with a light rattan ball. It is a favourite pastime of young men in Myanmar and doesn't require much space or equipment. The rules can be either those of volley ball or – more commonly – simply to keep the ball in the air for as long as possible without any of the players using their hands. It is always a delight to watch the agile players show off their tricks.

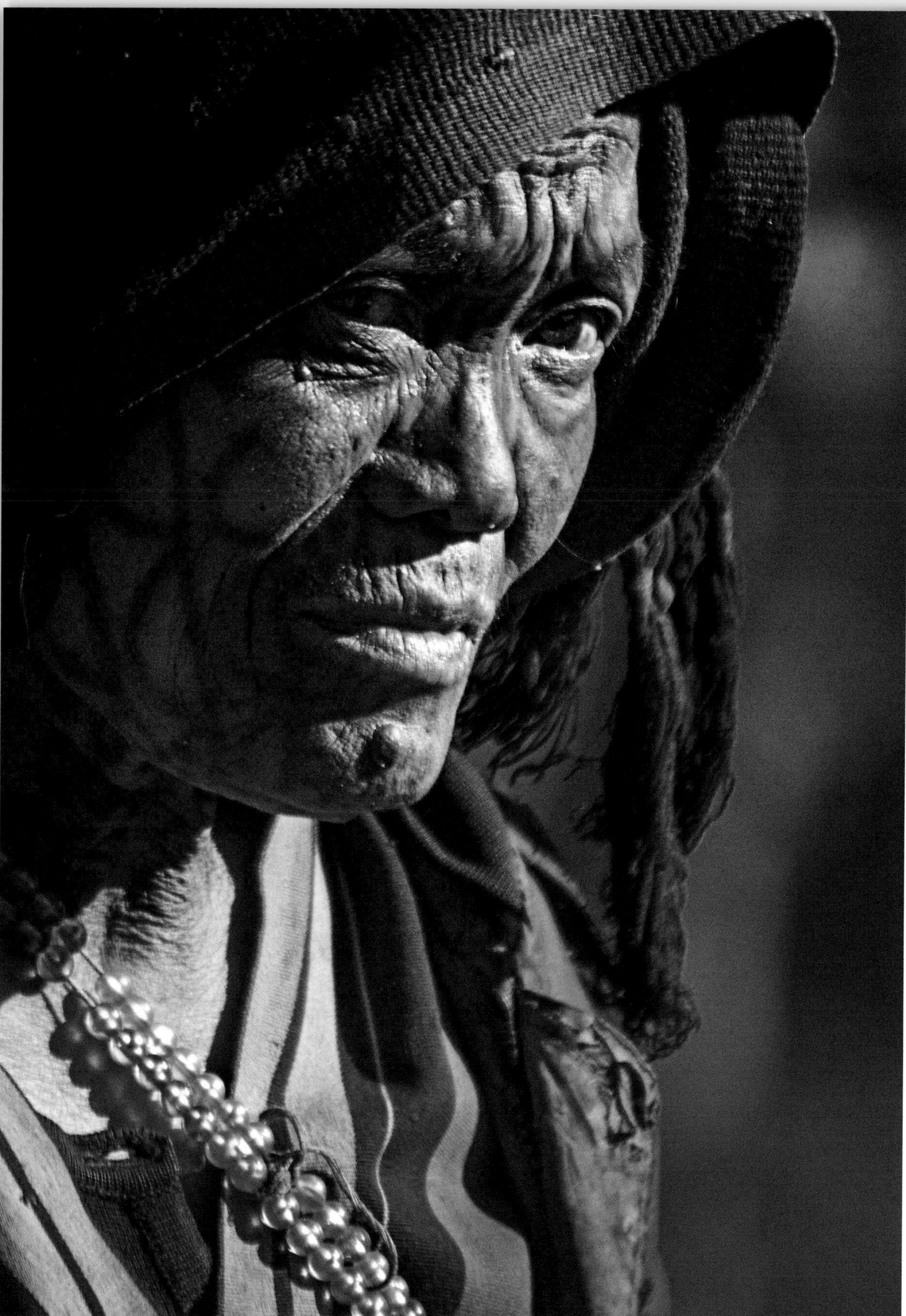

Tattooed woman, Mindat, Chin State, 2011

Opposite: Tattooed women, Mindat, Chin State, 2013

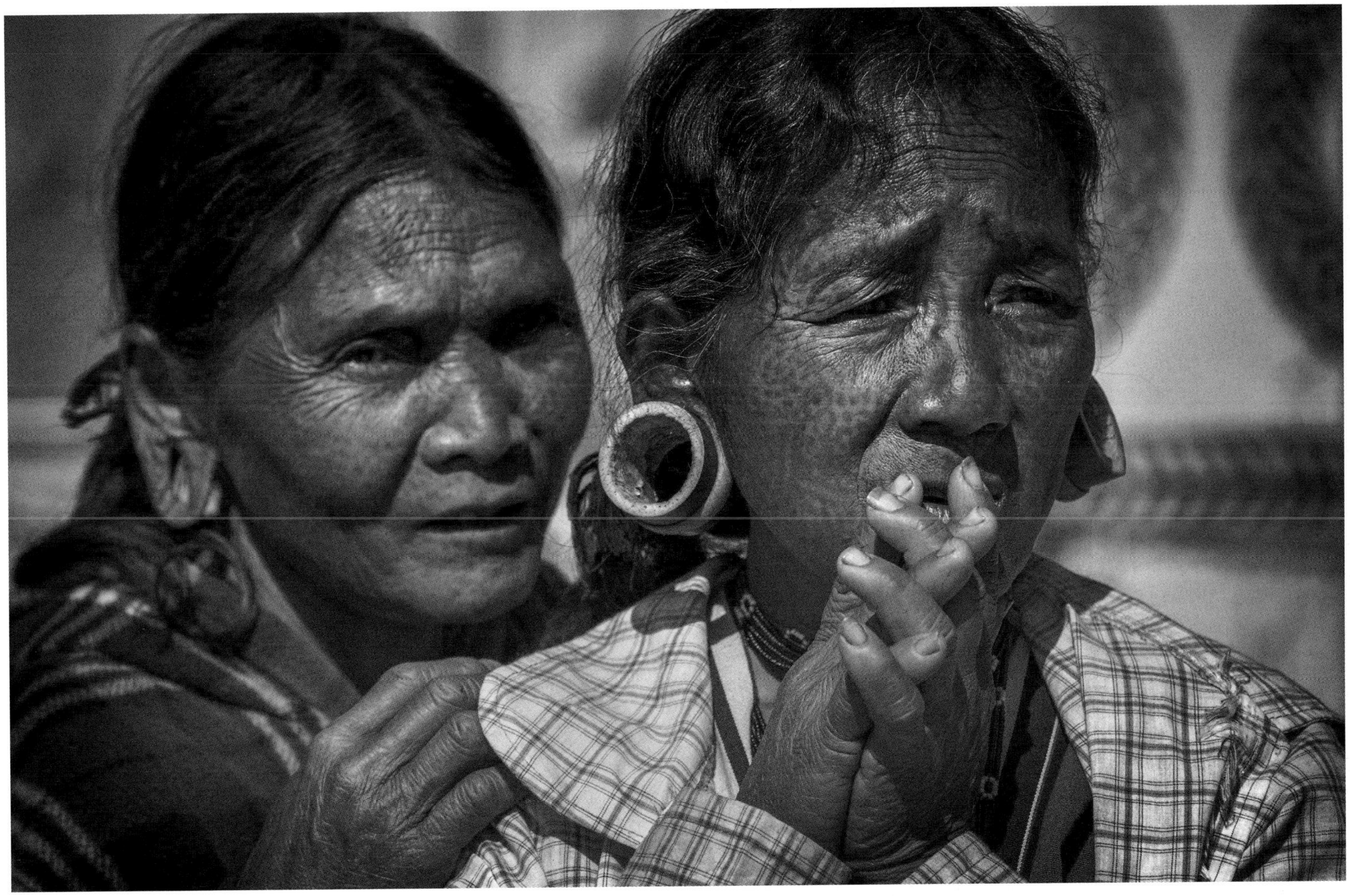

Face tattoos for women in Chin State are a vanishing custom. The origin of this extremely painful practice is unclear. According to legend, the tattoos may have served as a deterrent so that the Burmese king wouldn't demand any pretty young girls from Chin State for his court; rendered less desirable by their facial tattoos, the women were able to stay home with their families. One old man gave me an alternative explanation and told me that, since each sub-tribe has a different patterned tattoo, a woman's face identified where she came from and ensured she would be escorted safely home to her husband if she got lost in the woods.

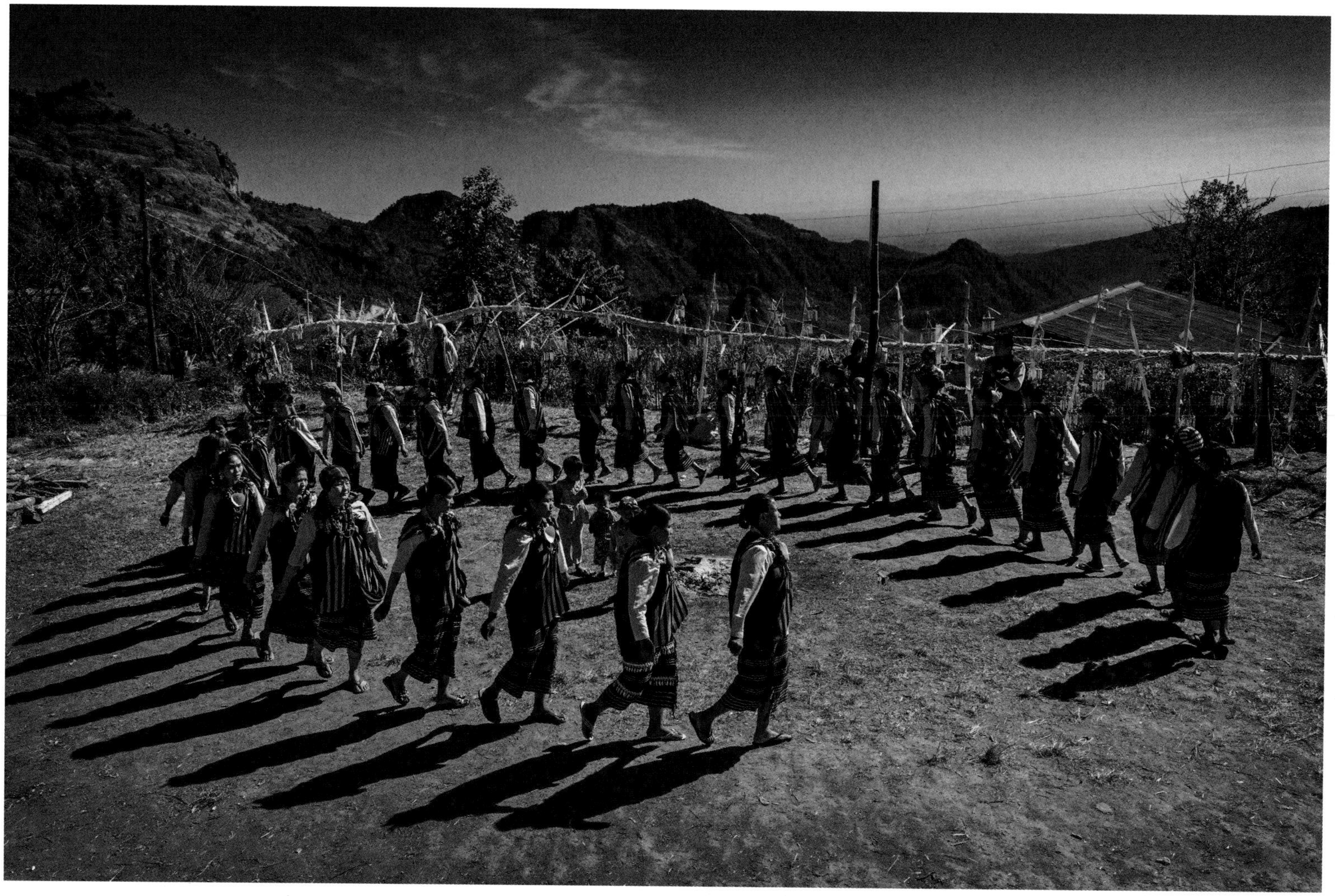

Above and right: Naga festival dance, Layshi, Sagaing Region, 2015

The Naga are a tribe living in the northwest of Myanmar and also across the border in India. An annual Naga festival is held in Myanmar each January. The dances, competitions, markets, and social gatherings enable distant members of the tribe to stay in contact and exchange goods and ideas. In this sparsely populated mountainous region, the festival can also lead to fortuitous meetings that result in marriage. Some tribe members walk up to three weeks just to attend the festival.

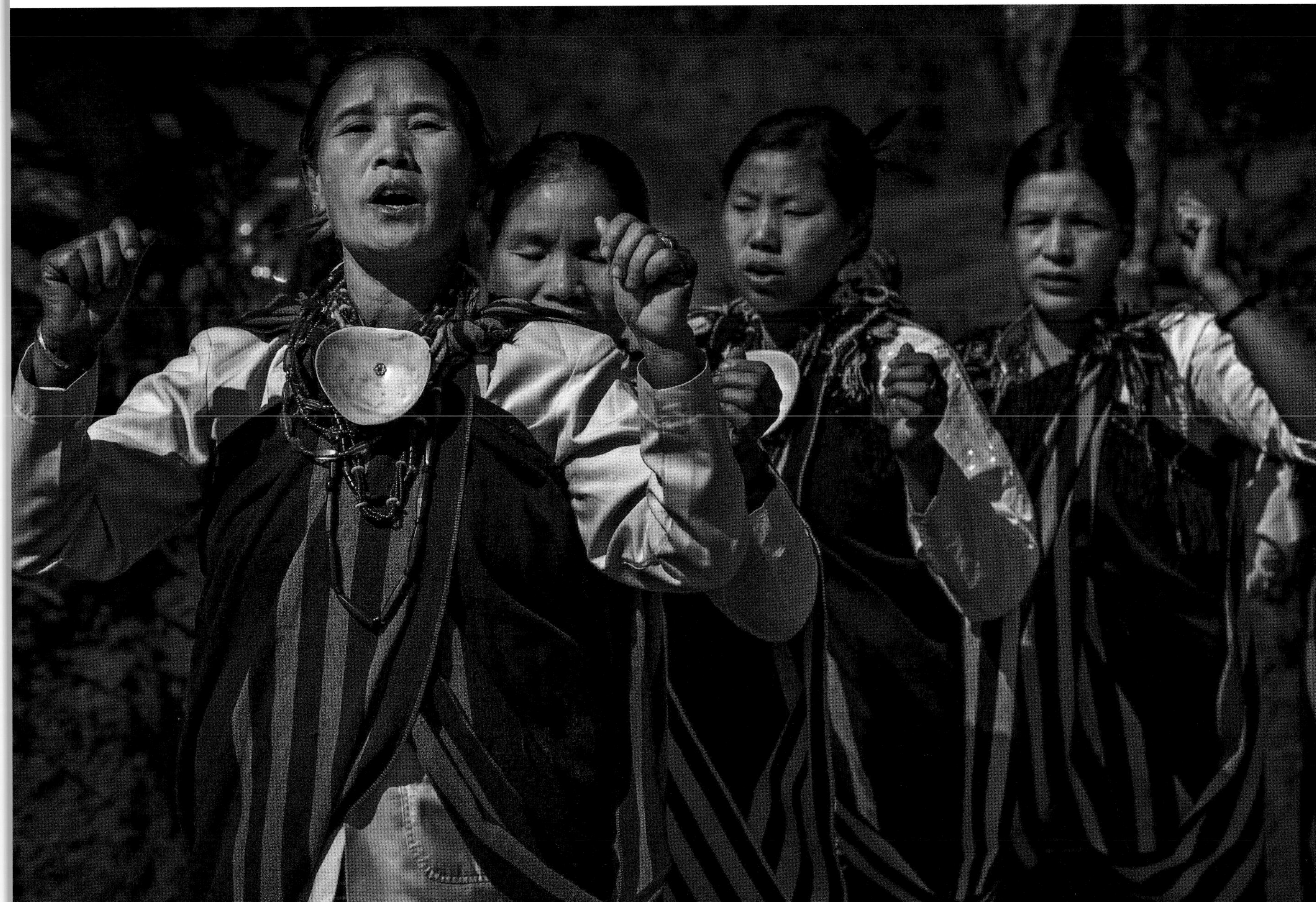

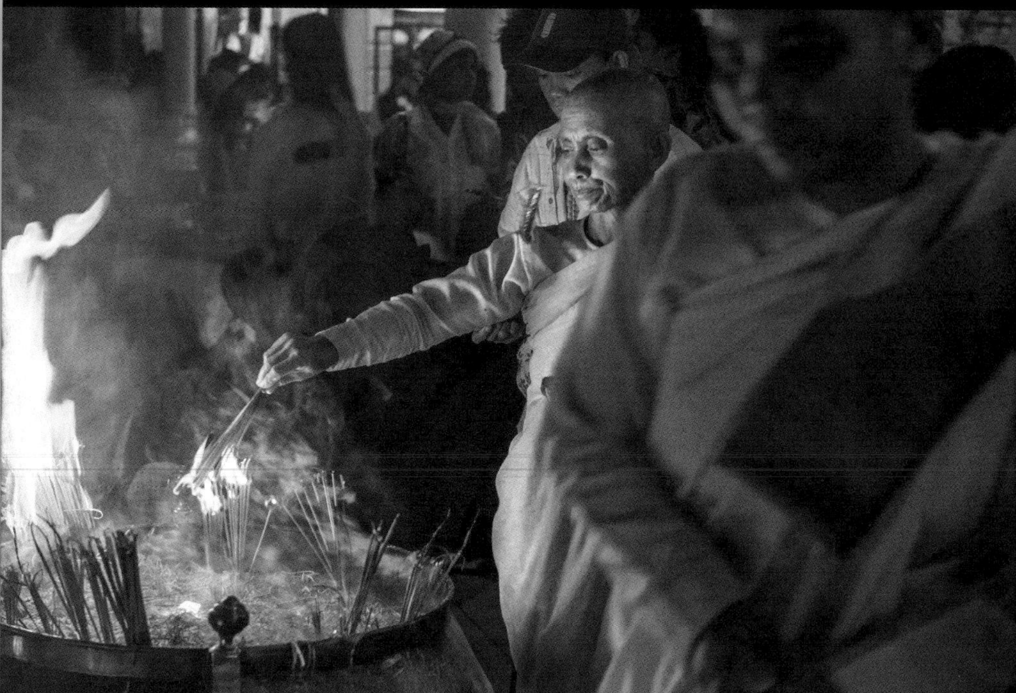

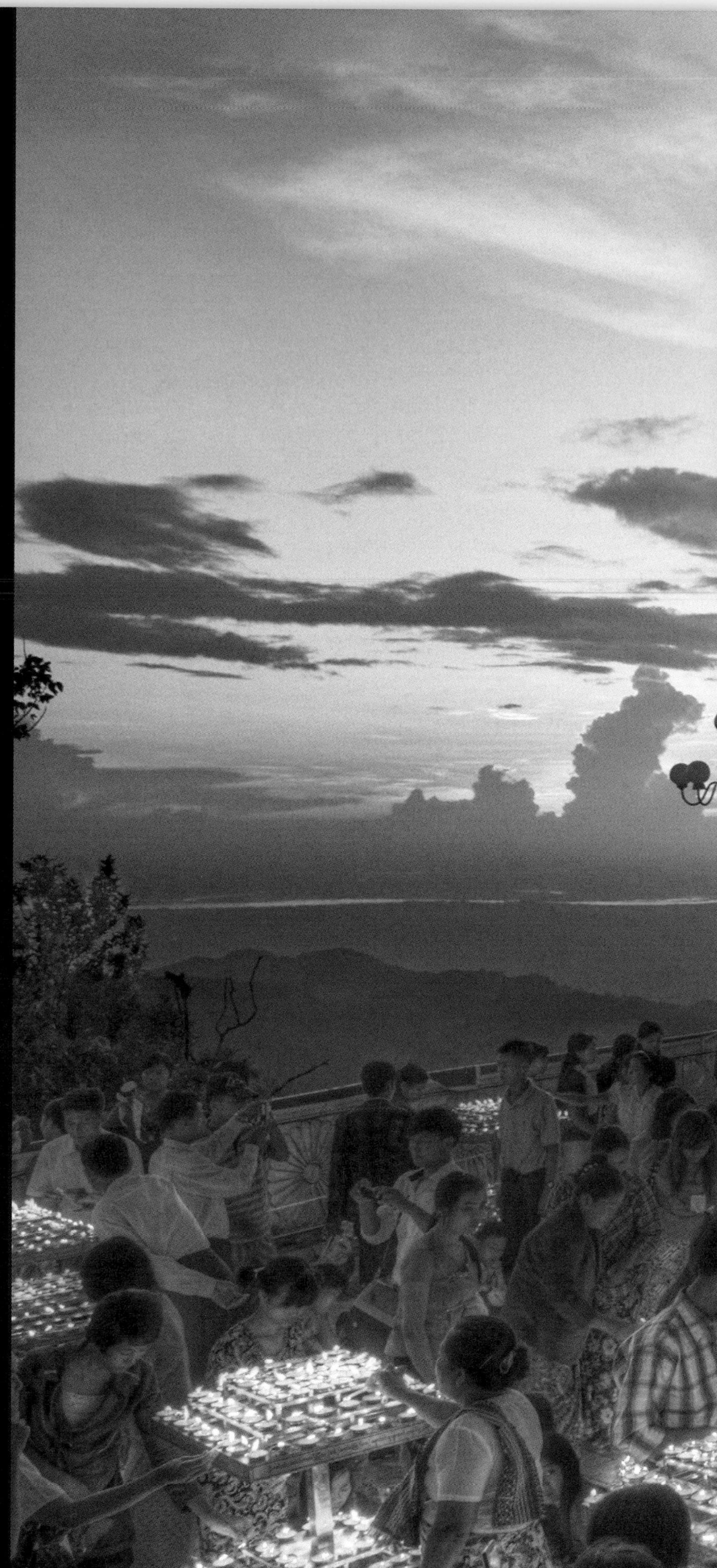

ABOVE AND RIGHT: FESTIVAL OF LIGHTS AT THE GOLDEN ROCK, KYAIKTIYO, MON STATE, 2011

Thadingyut, the Festival of Lights, is celebrated in different ways across Myanmar. At the Golden Rock, one of Myanmar's most important sacred sites, tens of thousands of pilgrims gather from all over the country to worship, pray, and celebrate. They eat and sleep on the grounds of Kyaiktiyo Pagoda. Various ethnic groups perform traditional dances, donation ceremonies are held, and millions of candles are lit with many laid out to form intricate patterns. On this occasion, an approaching thunderstorm adds drama.

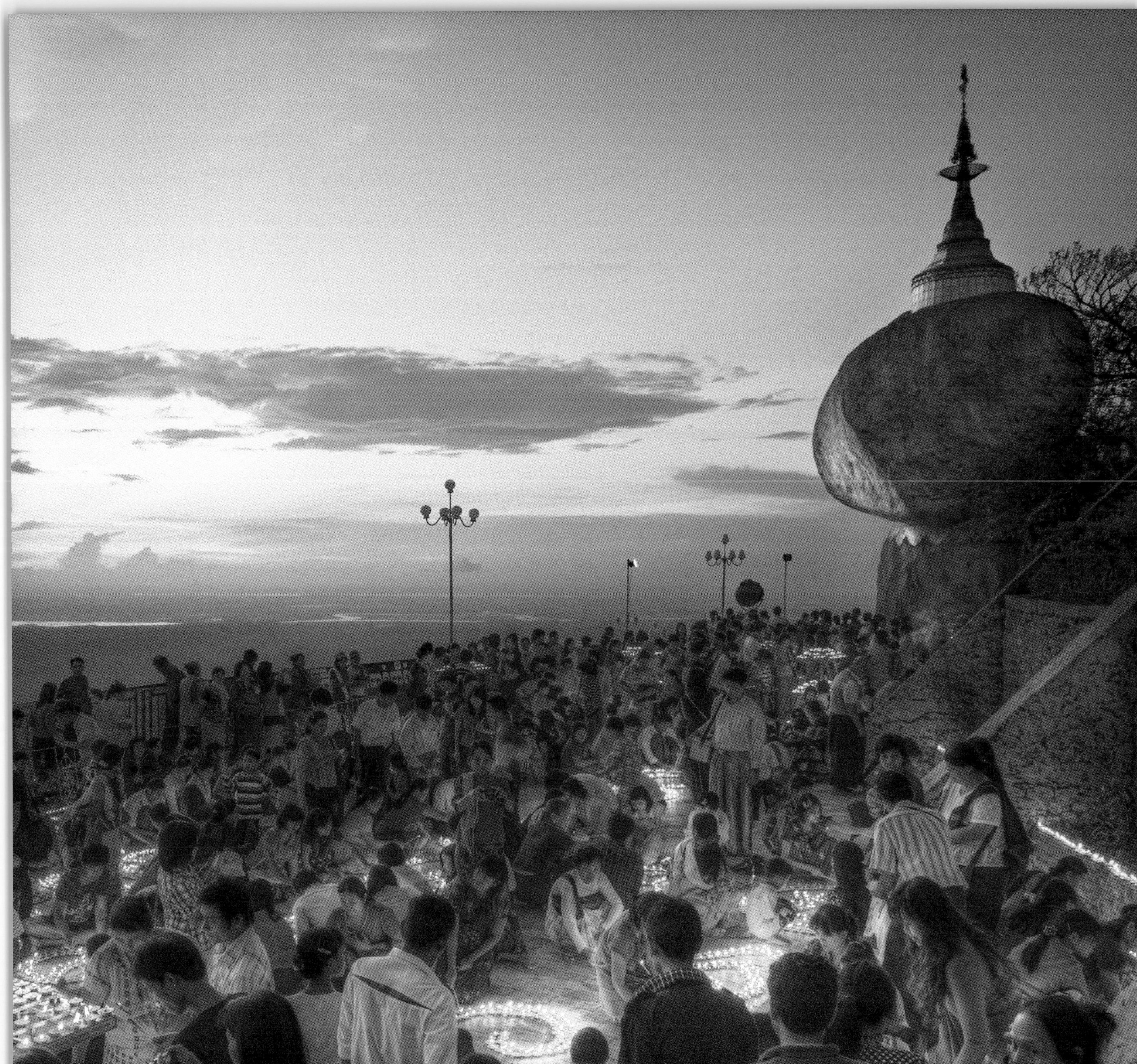

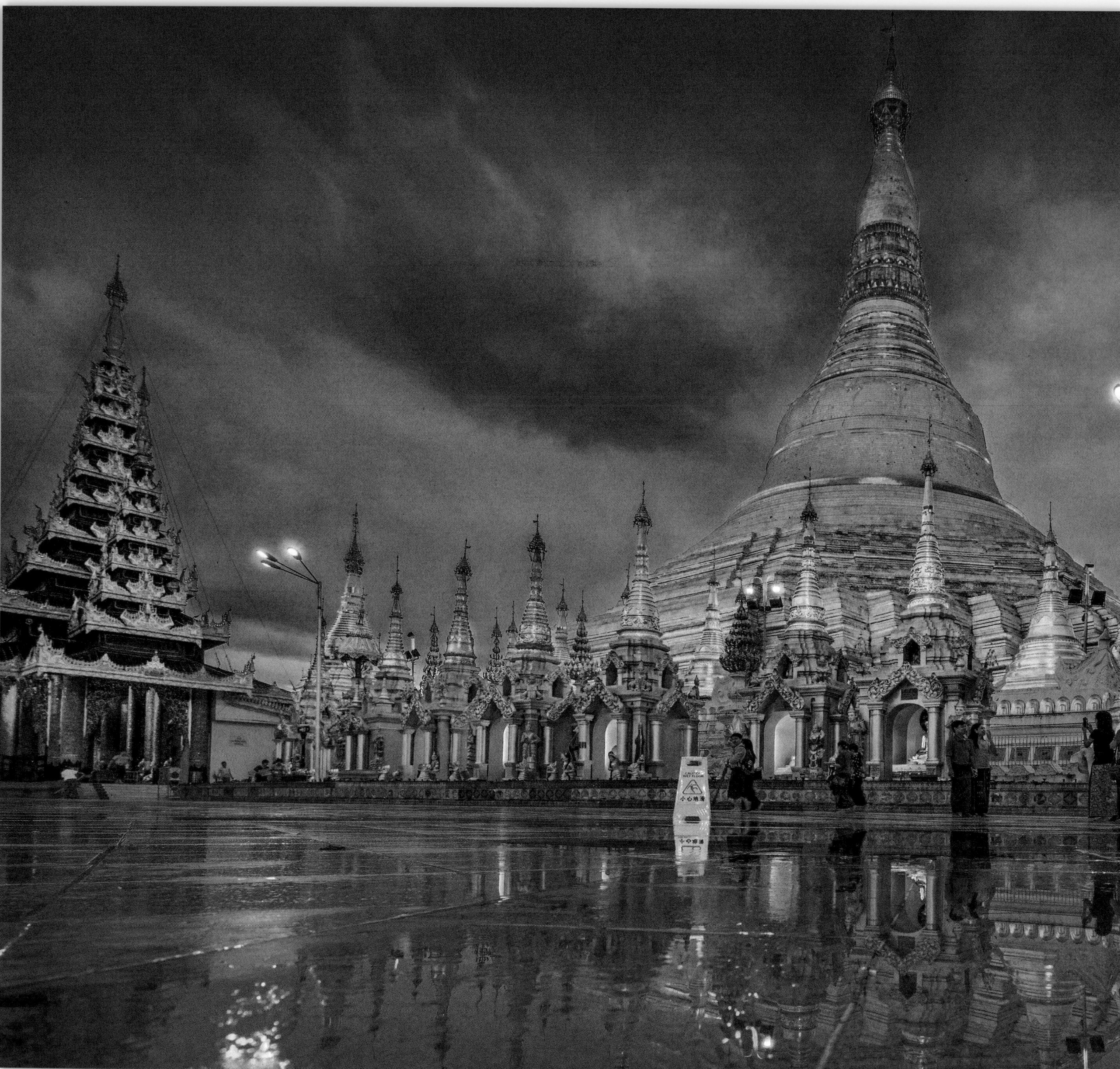
小心地滑

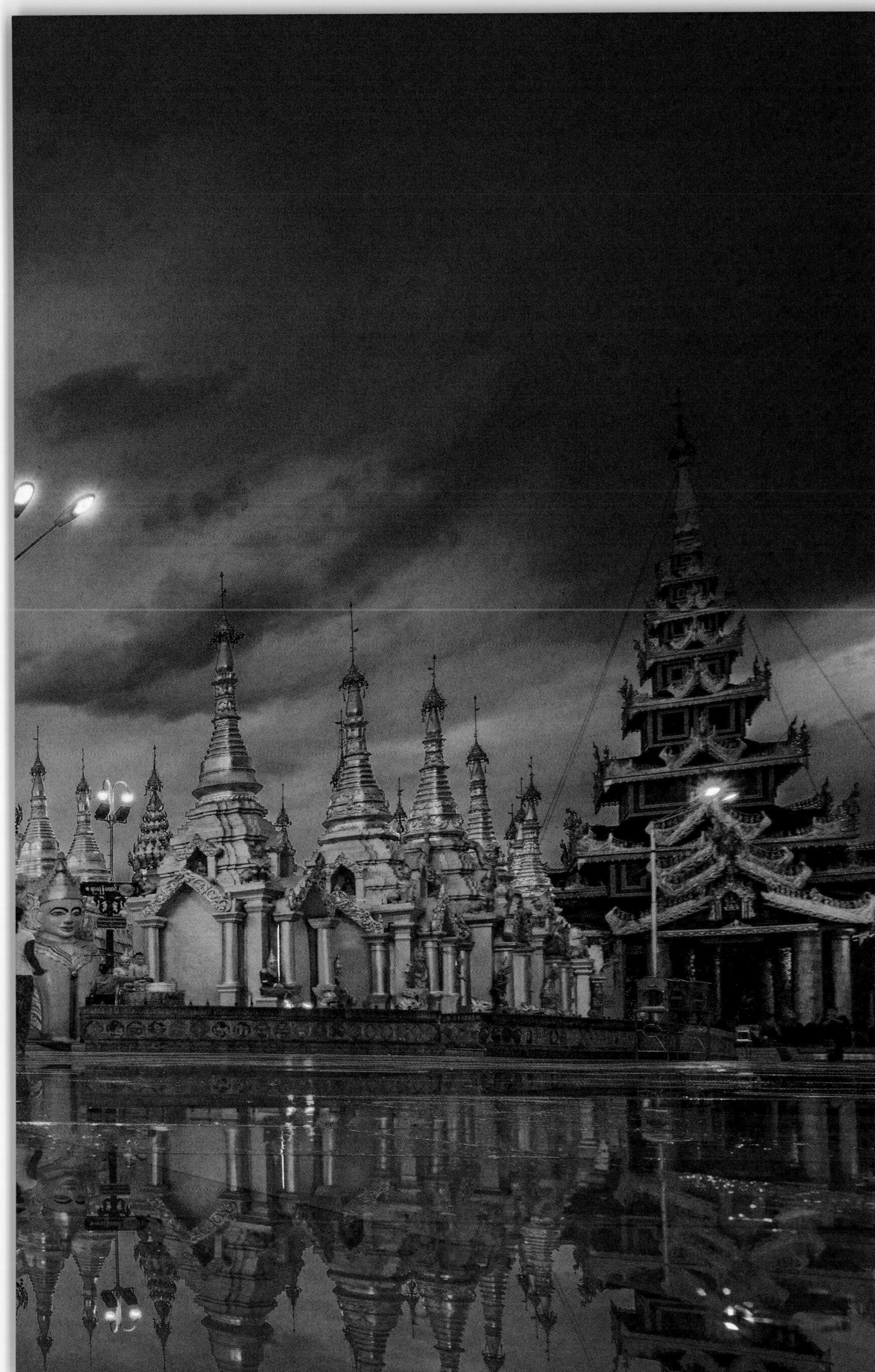

Shwedagon Pagoda, Yangon, 2014

During the rainy season, tourists are rarely seen at the Shwedagon Pagoda. The pagoda platform becomes very slippery but, if you join the locals in one of the numerous pavilions and wait for the rain to end (also a convenient opportunity for meditation), the pooled reflections on the platform make both the visit and the wait worthwhile.

THE SHWEDAGON PAGODA COMMEMORATES 2,600 YEARS, YANGON, 2012

For this significant event, the Board of Pagoda Trustees chose an array of colourful blinking lights to accentuate the silhouettes of the various structures on the pagoda platform. As the use of LED lights becomes more common in Myanmar, more and more Buddha statues are adorned with bright, blinking halos.

OVERLEAF: RECLINING BUDDHA, MUDON, MON STATE, 2011

This Buddha statue is more than 100 metres long and was commissioned by a very generous donor in order to improve his karma. The statue's interior is painted with vivid and expressive dioramas depicting scenes from the life of Buddha. Some of the figures on display look quite scary to me but this is probably intentional so that devout visitors will fully understand the difference between good and evil.

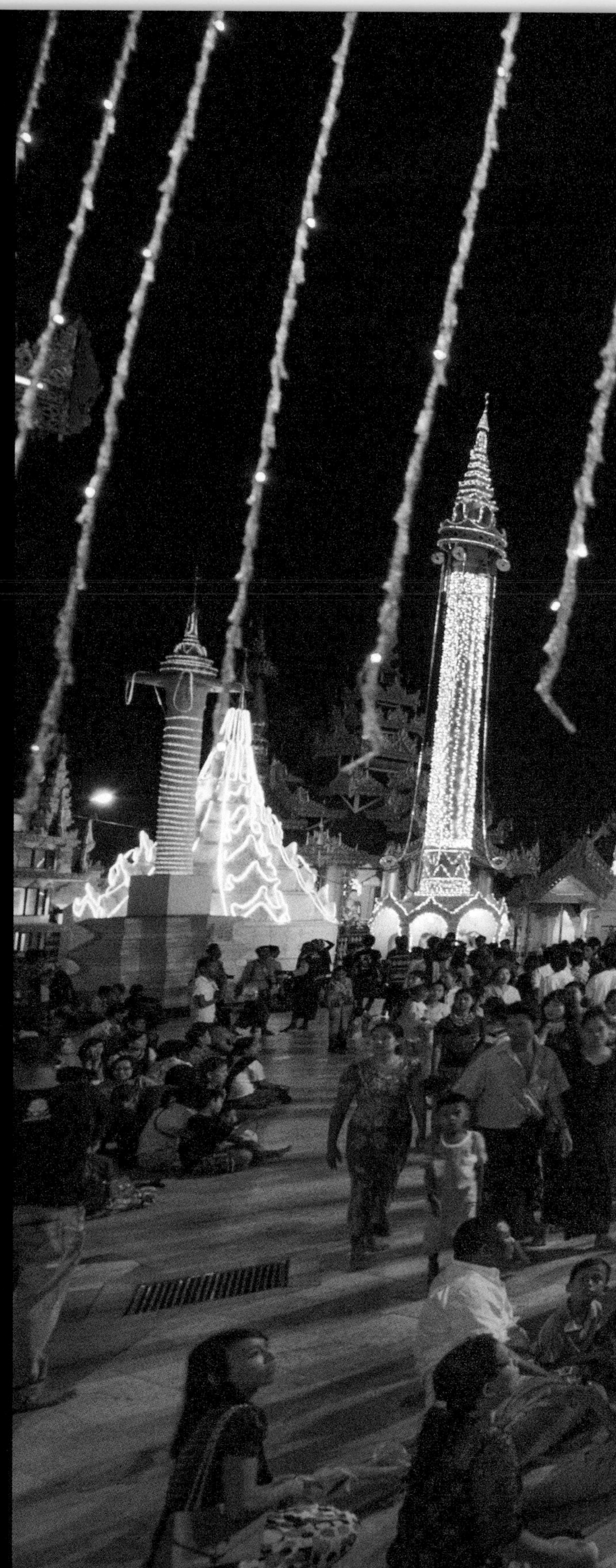

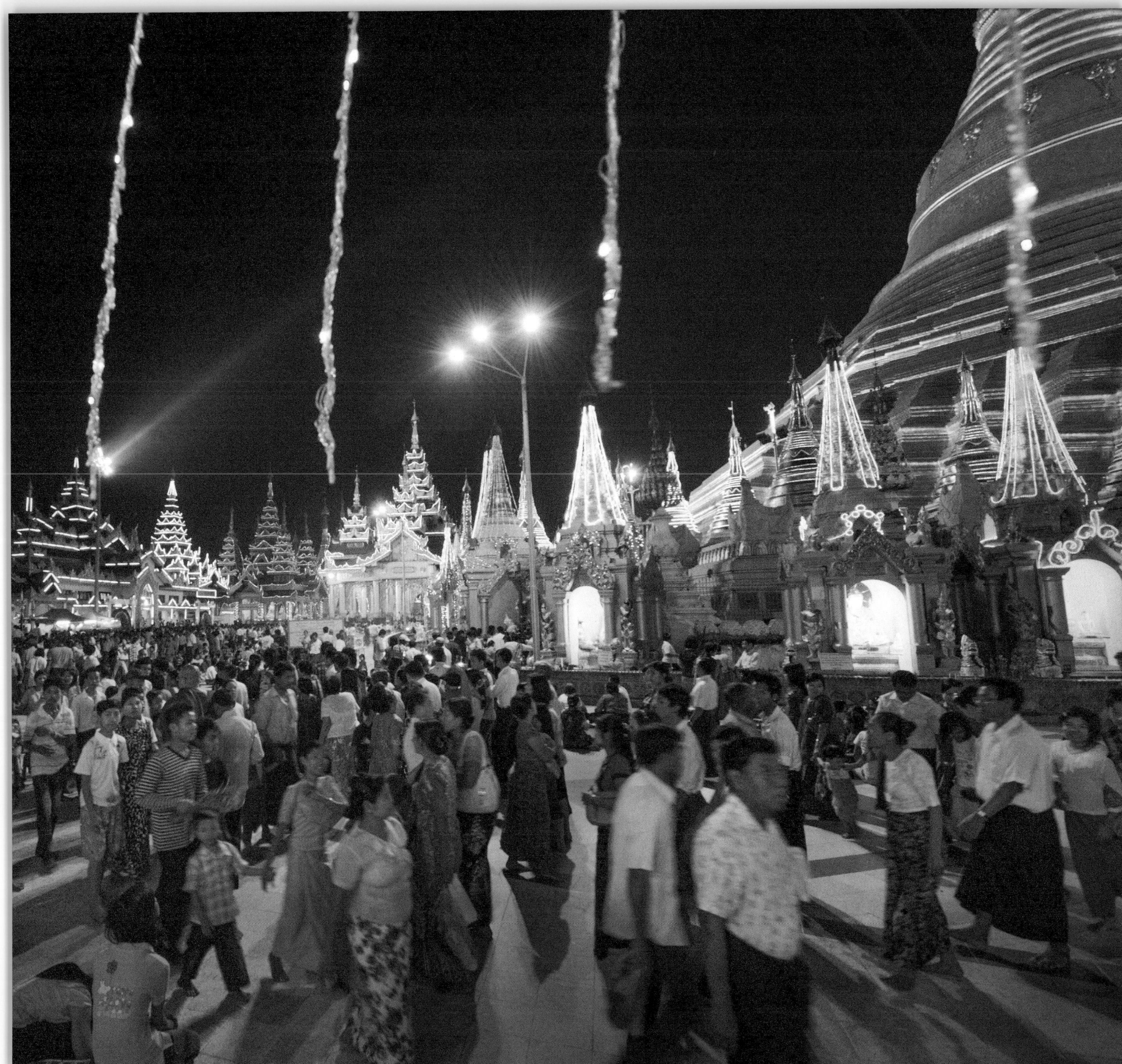

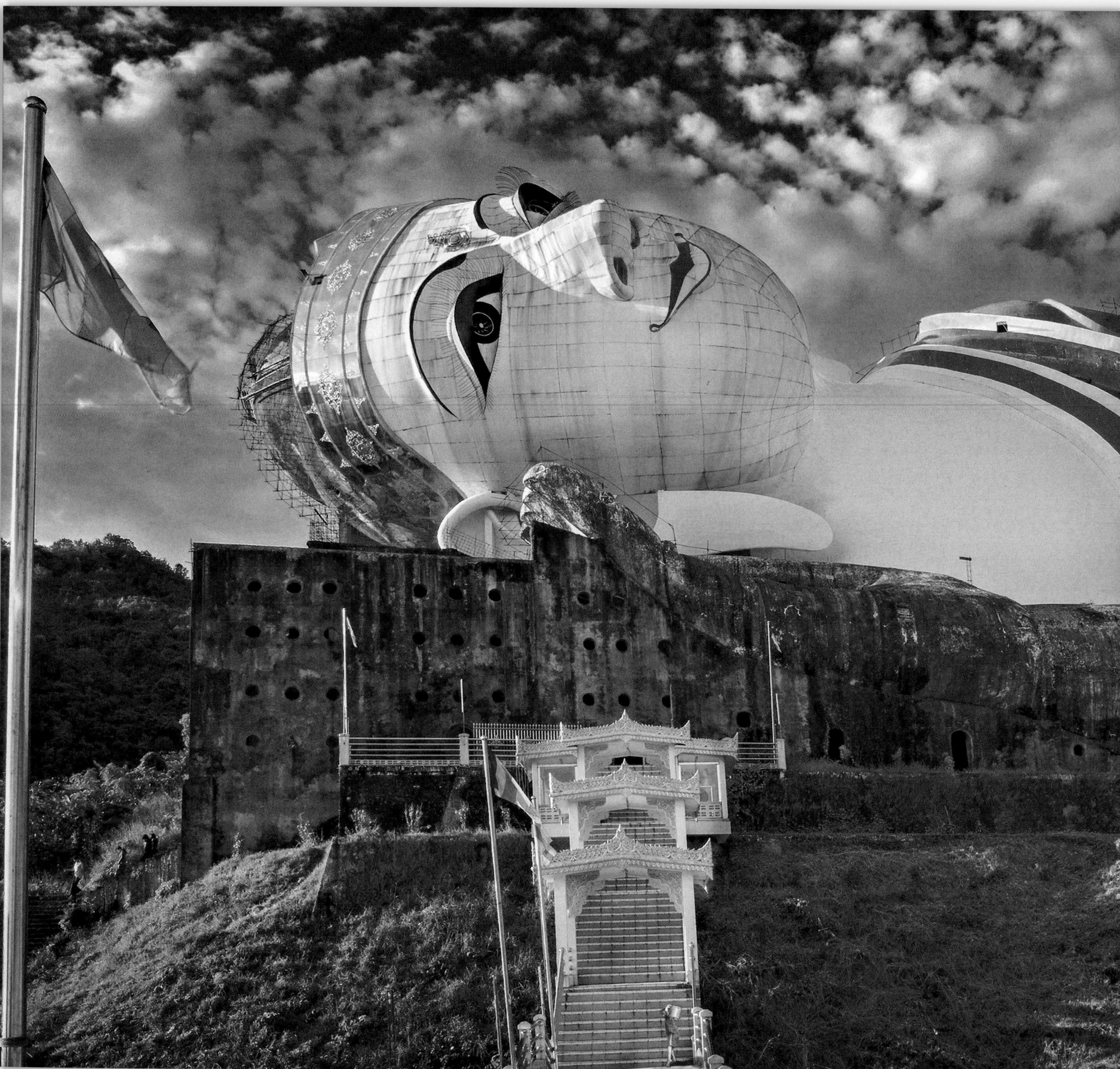

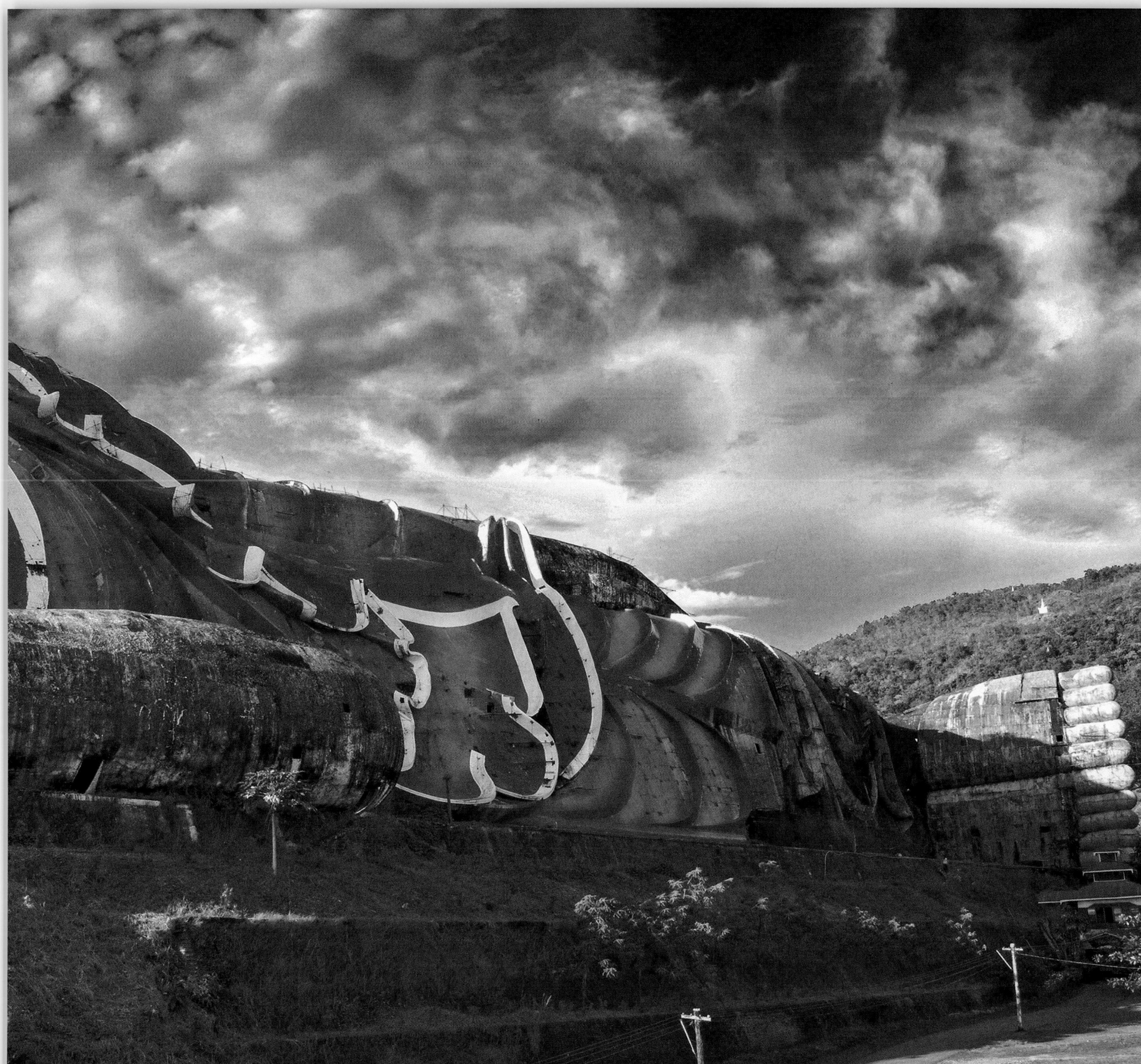

Right and opposite: Pauk Par Village on Inle Lake, Shan State, 2010

Originally from the Dawei region in southern Myanmar, the Intha people arrived at Inle Lake a long time ago. So as not to usurp any farmland from earlier settlers, they were only allowed to settle on the lake itself. Though the Intha can now live on the land there are still many villages located in the middle of the lake; they are built on stilts and accessible only by boat. The villagers make a living from fishing, agricultural floating gardens, and various crafts. Today, most of their income comes from tourists.

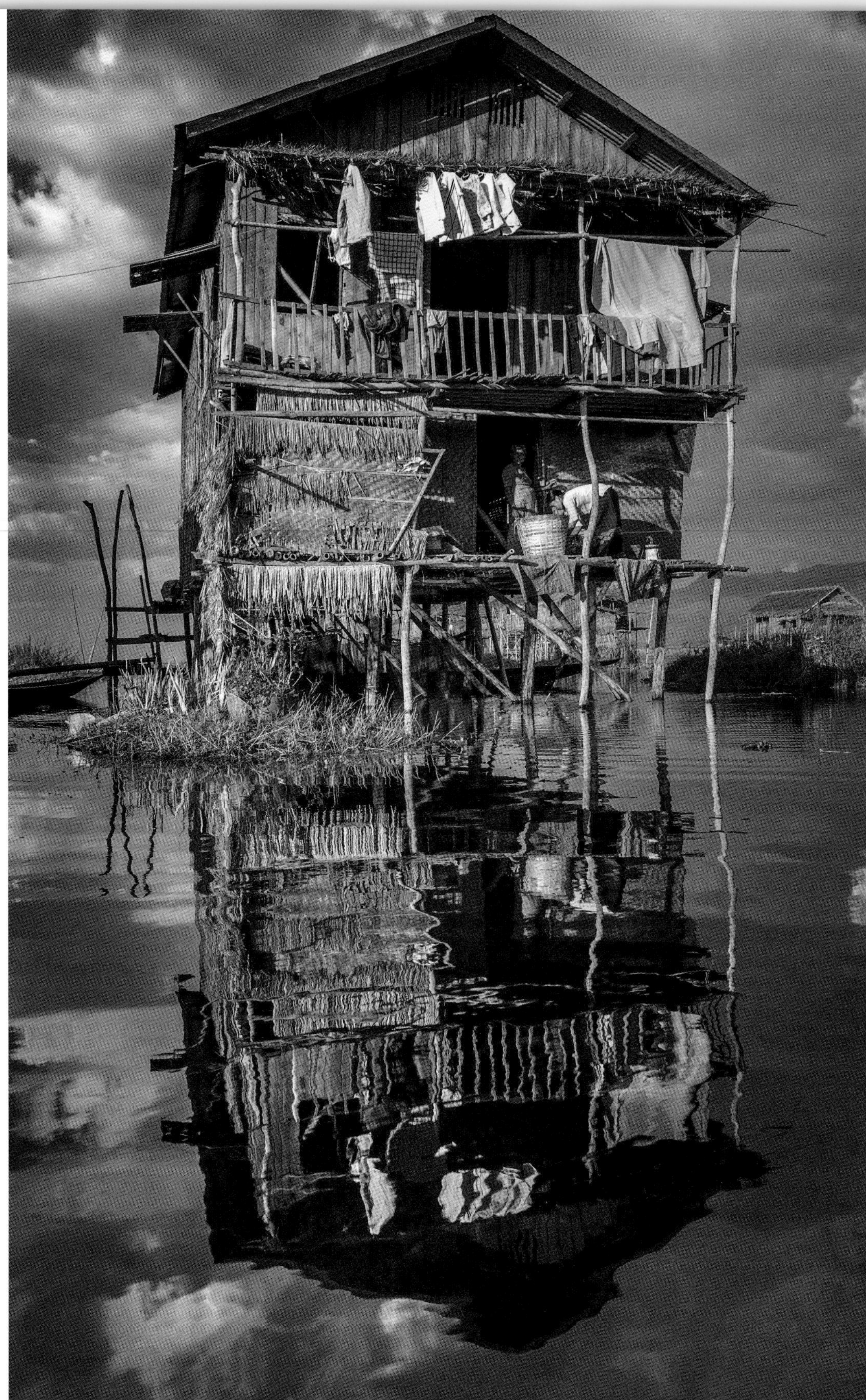

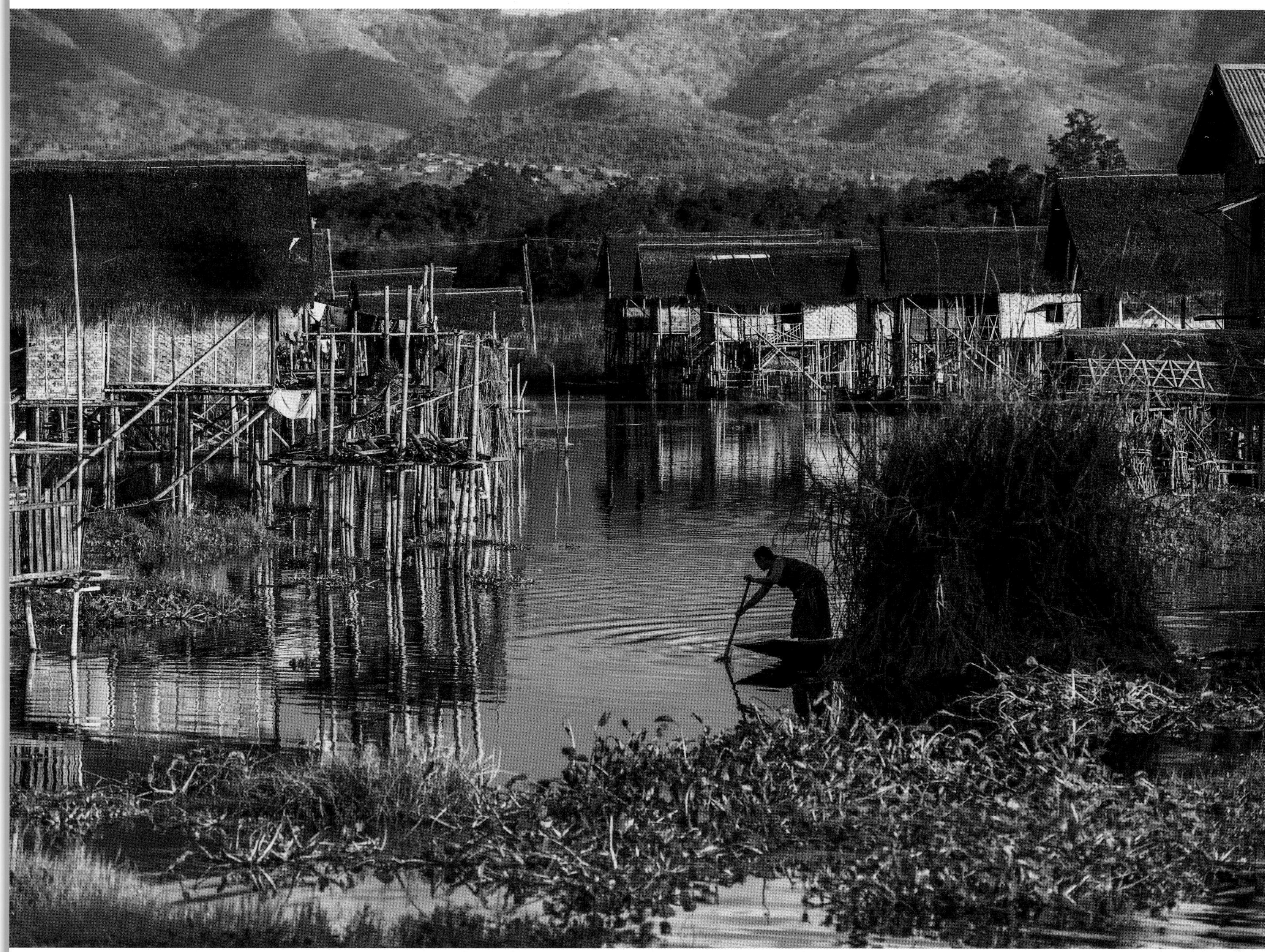

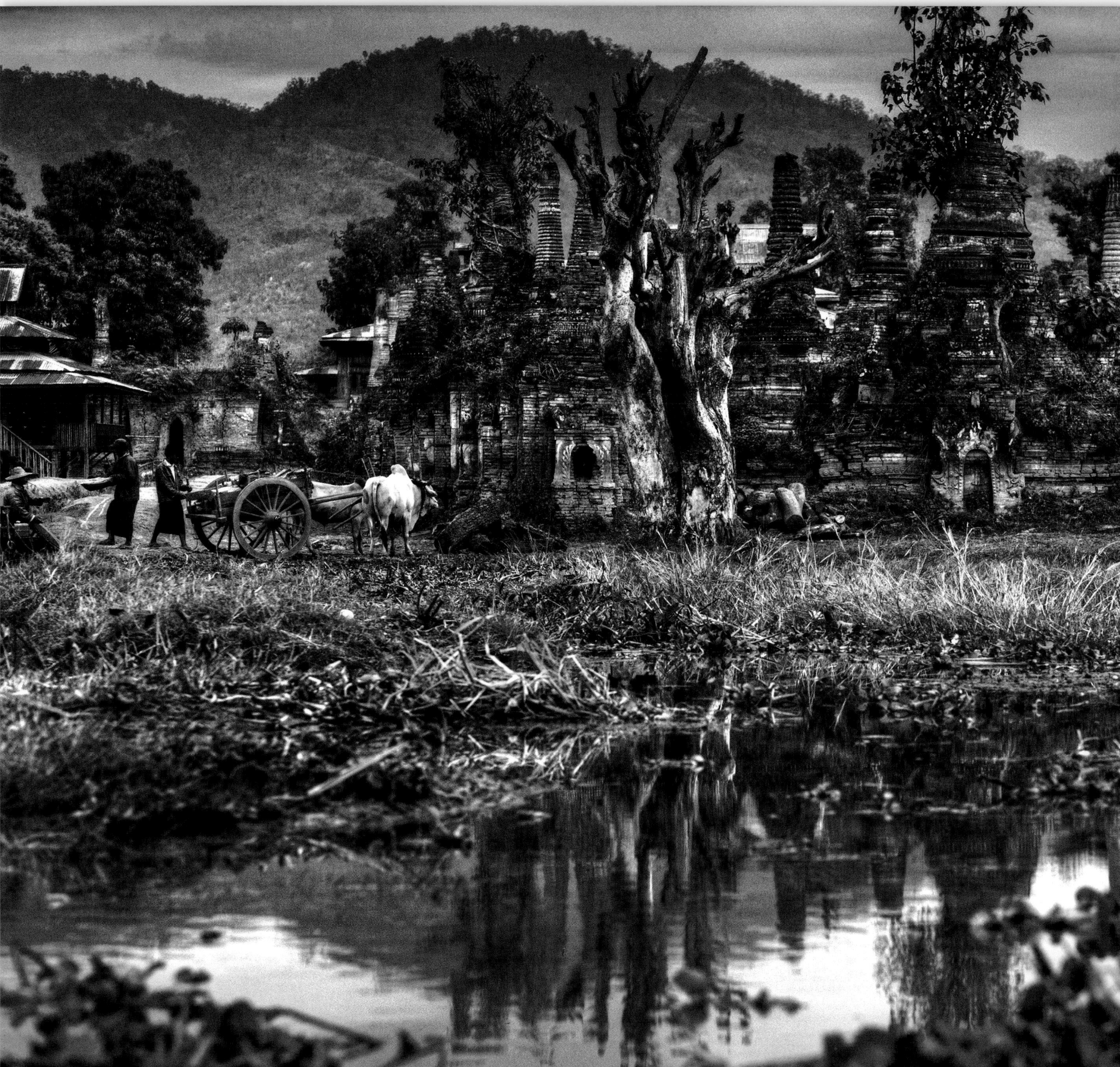

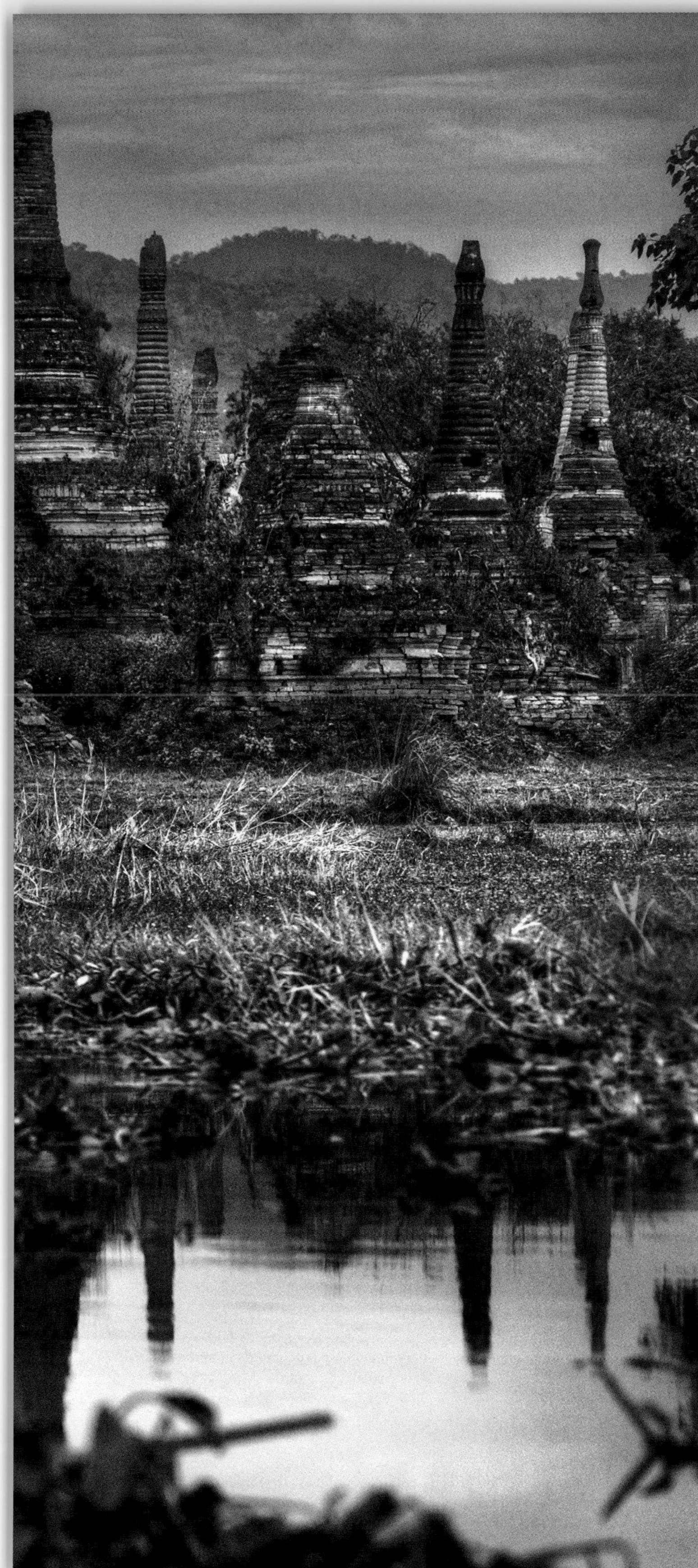

Pagoda ruins in Samka Village, Inle Lake, Shan State, 2010

As it is believed karma can only be accrued through the construction of new Buddha statues and pagodas, old structures do not attract donors for renovation and are often left to the elements. Native flora – including whole trees – works its way into crevices and, over time, organically integrates abandoned structures with nature.

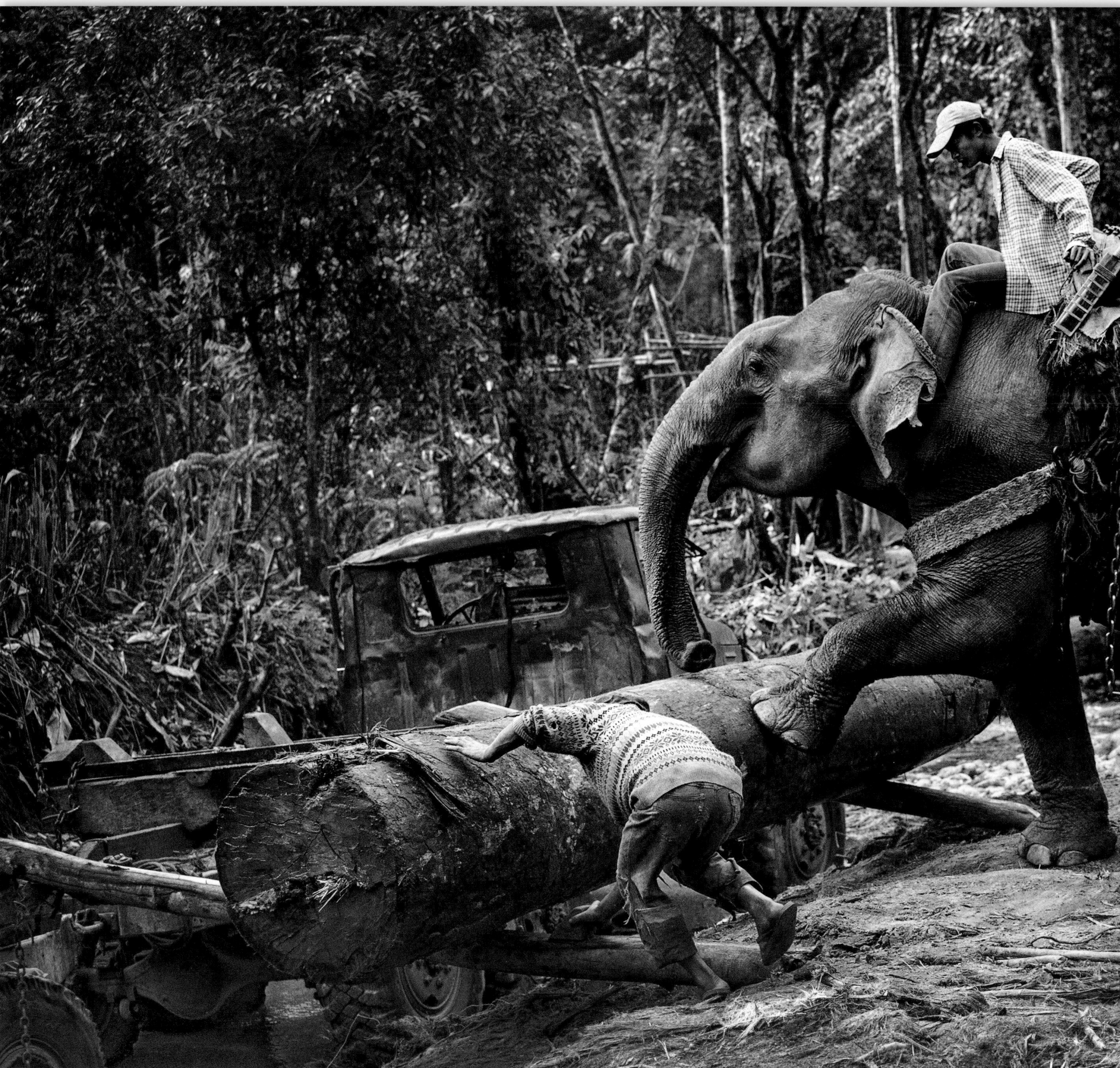

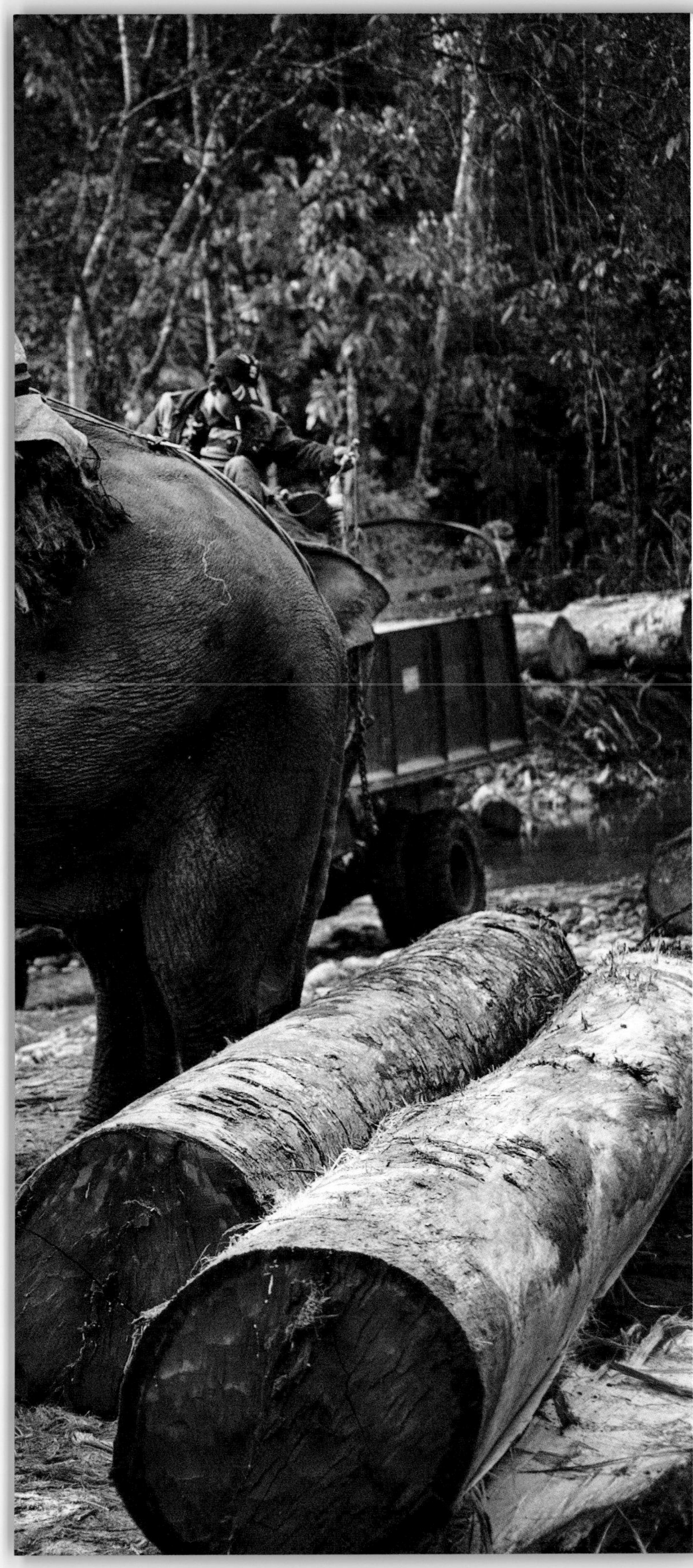

Elephant at work in the forest near Putao, Kachin State, 2011

To reach this working elephant camp outside Putao, I had to swap my vehicle for the timber truck pictured here. We drove for hours along a shallow riverbed that led deep into the forest. A group of women washing gold in the river had to clear their equipment so we could pass. At the camp, the elephants work hard to pull timber out of the forest and push it onto the truck from an elevated embankment. They are highly skilled and intuitive; when one log was close to rolling off the truck, they immediately tried to stop it from falling with two elephants working as a team to grab the log and heave it back onto the truck. The elephants seemed to enjoy the challenges they faced and I interpreted in their eyes the same proud look I saw on their mahouts at the end of the day. Navigating our return journey back along the riverbed on a truck now fully loaded with logs presented its own challenges.

Working elephant given a helping hand, Putao, Kachin State, 2011

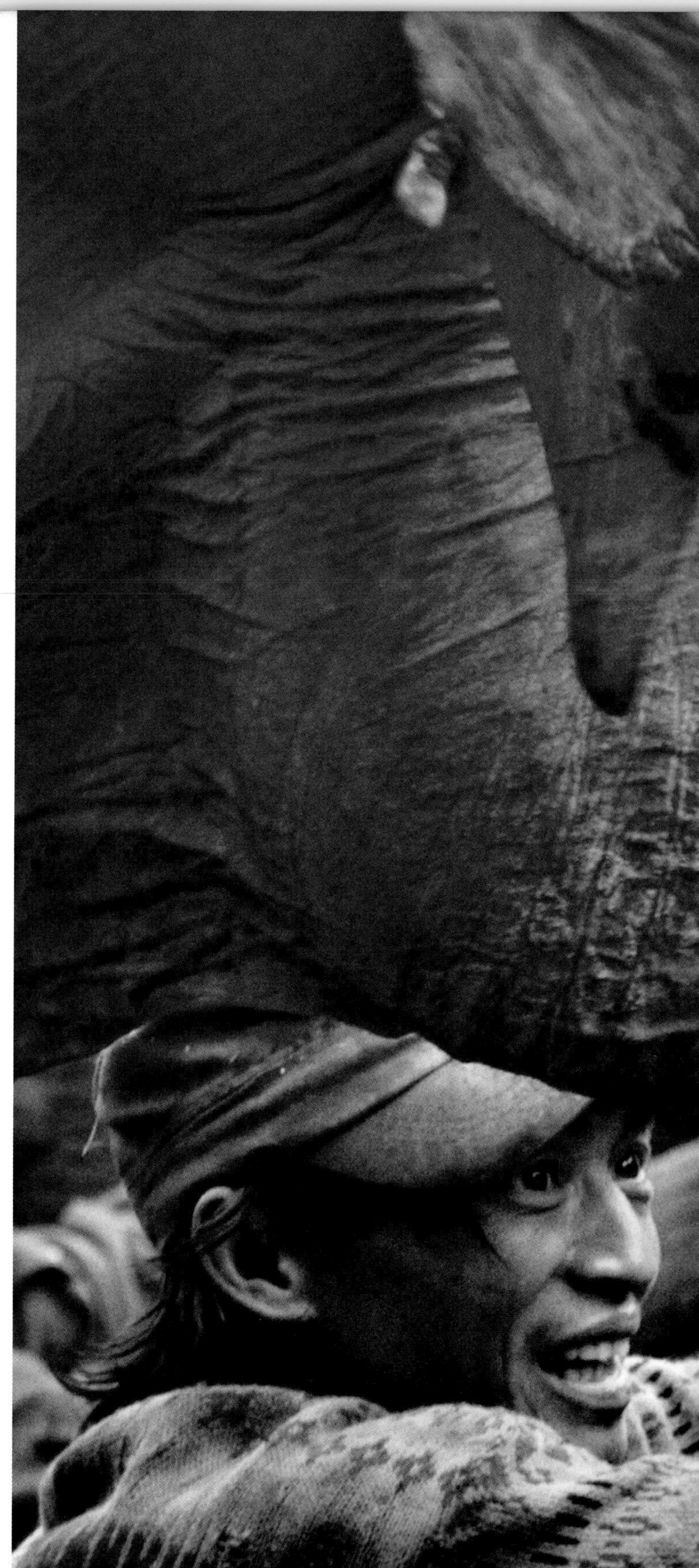

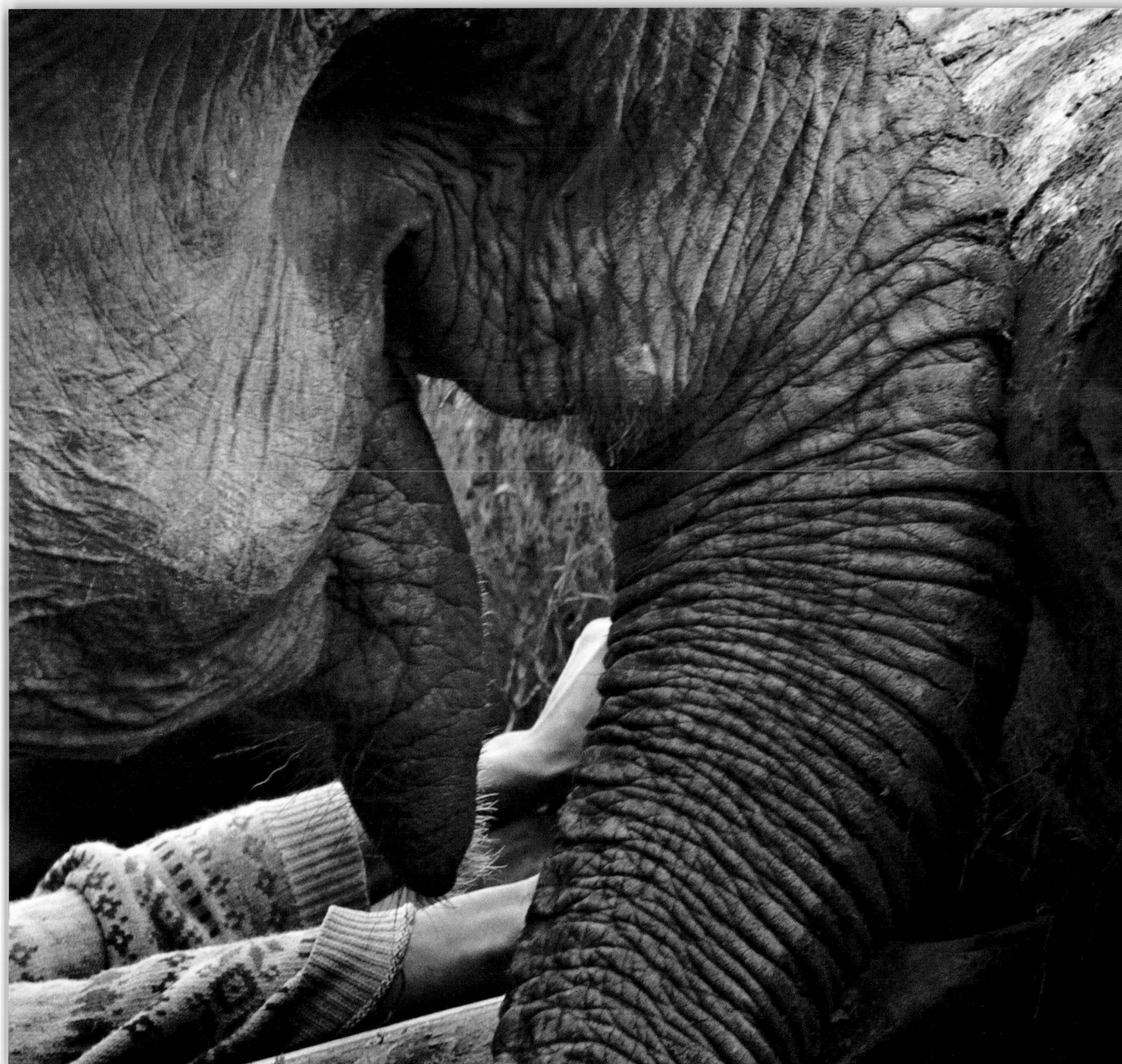

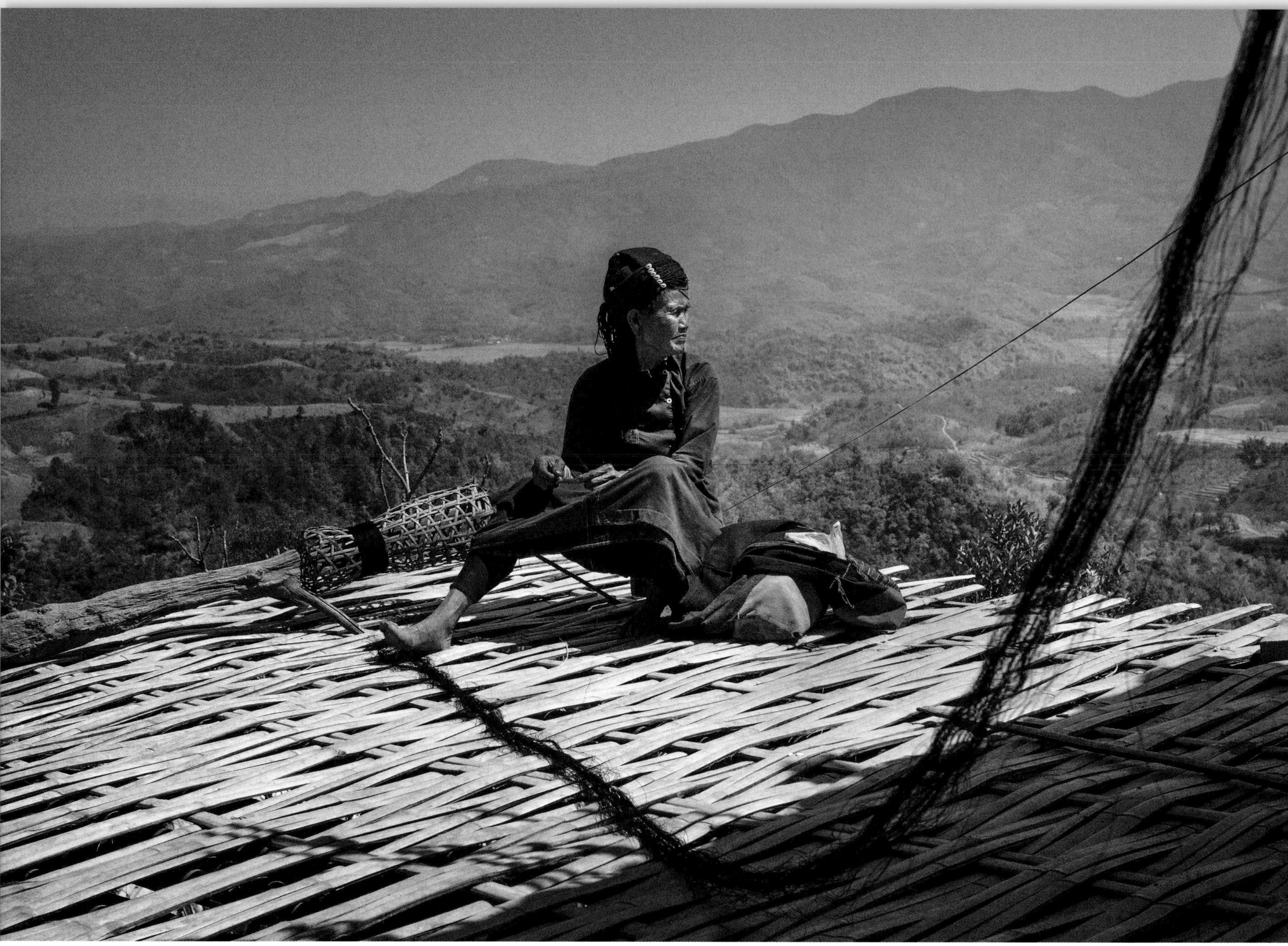

A WEAVER OF THE ANN TRIBE, PON LAY VILLAGE, SHAN STATE, 2011

The Ann tribe lives in the mountains of eastern Shan State. Their houses are constructed from timber and bamboo with terraces that extend from the hillside, following the topography of the terrain. On these terraces, women spend their time weaving, chatting, and enjoying the stunning view.

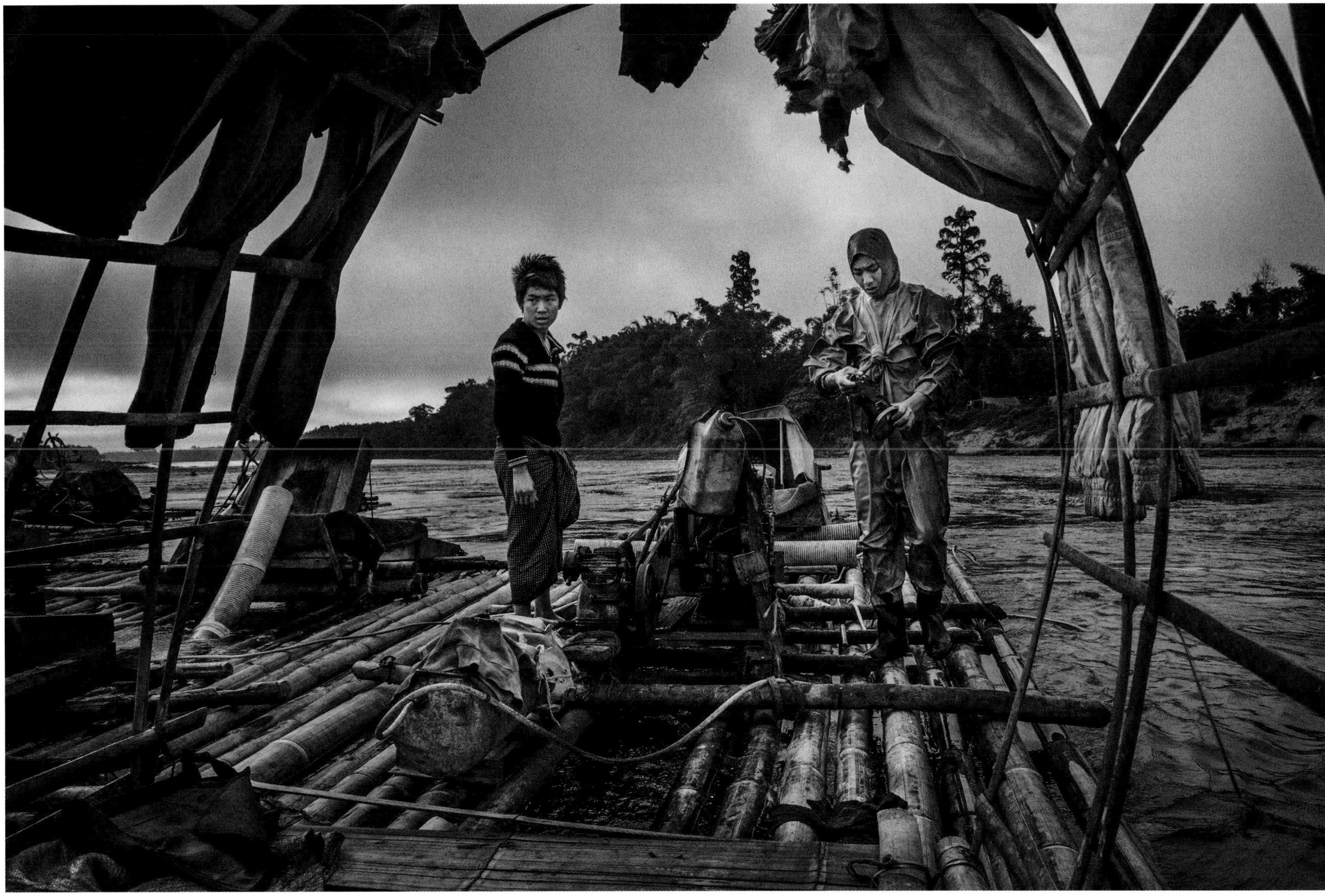

Looking for river gold, Putao, Kachin State, 2011

The preferred method of finding river gold in this region is from bamboo rafts anchored in the shallow rivers. People dive for gold wearing homemade wetsuits with rocks strapped to their backs for weight and a tube attached to the raft for oxygen. They dive down with a large hose through which sand from the riverbed is sucked up by a pump on board the raft and then flushed out over mats to filter out the gold.

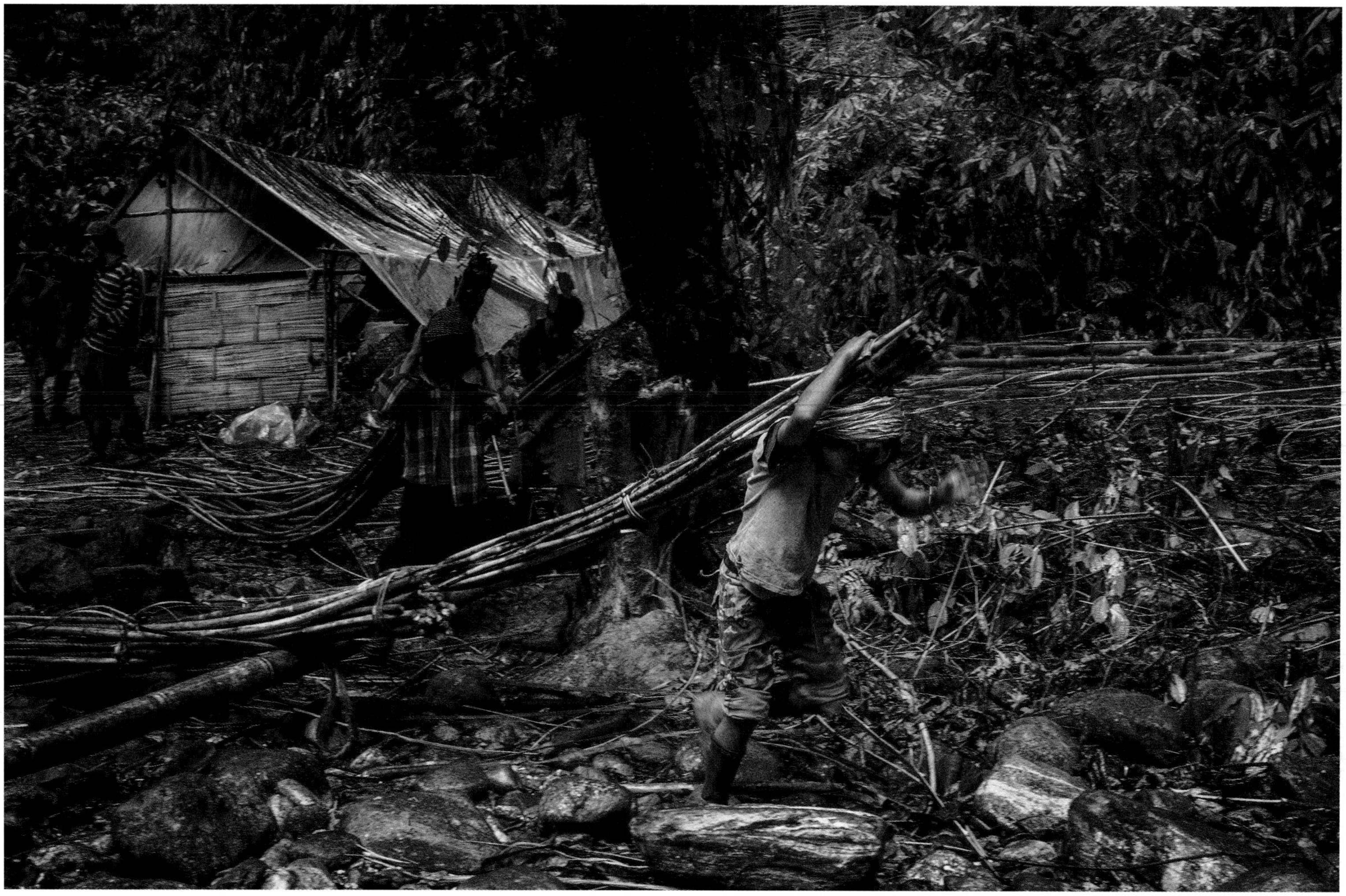

Carrying rattan over the mountains near Putao, Kachin State, 2011

In the mountains around Putao, rattan is grown for export. Porters cross the mountains to China a few times a day. As each delivery counts towards their income, they move at running speed and tie several bundles together to increase their earnings. While trekking in the area, I frequently had to jump aside to get out of their way. To move at such speed, they must be familiar with every step of a steep and often slippery trek that is arduous even without any cargo.

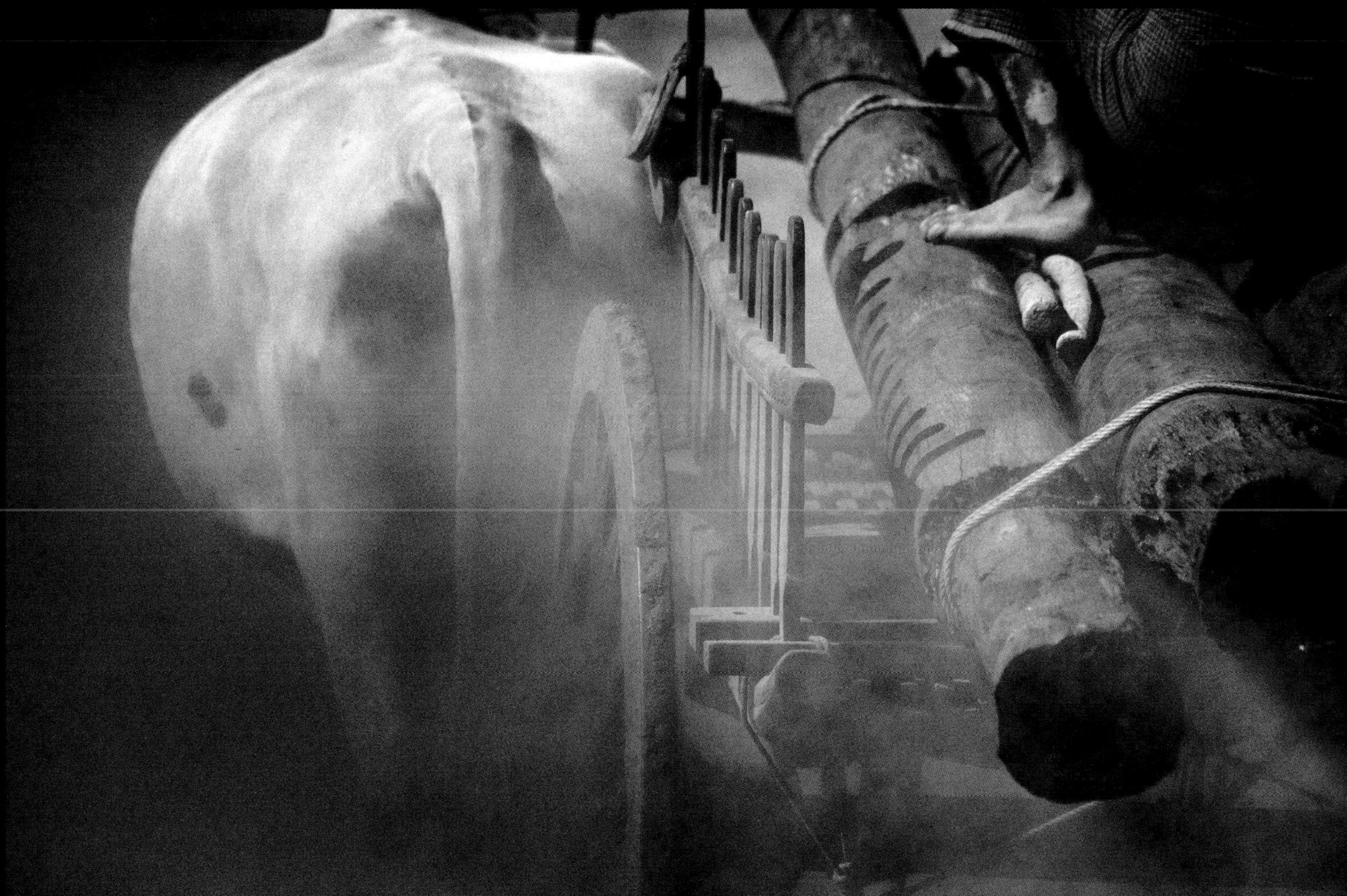

Above and overleaf: Ox carts transporting teakwood, Bagan, Mandalay Region, 2012

Teakwood is expensive, durable, and can be re-used many times. In this image, a villager upstream of Bagan had dismantled his house and sold the timber to someone further downstream along the Ayeyarwady River. The timber was shipped downriver on small boats and then manually loaded onto this caravan of ox carts to be transported to the new site.

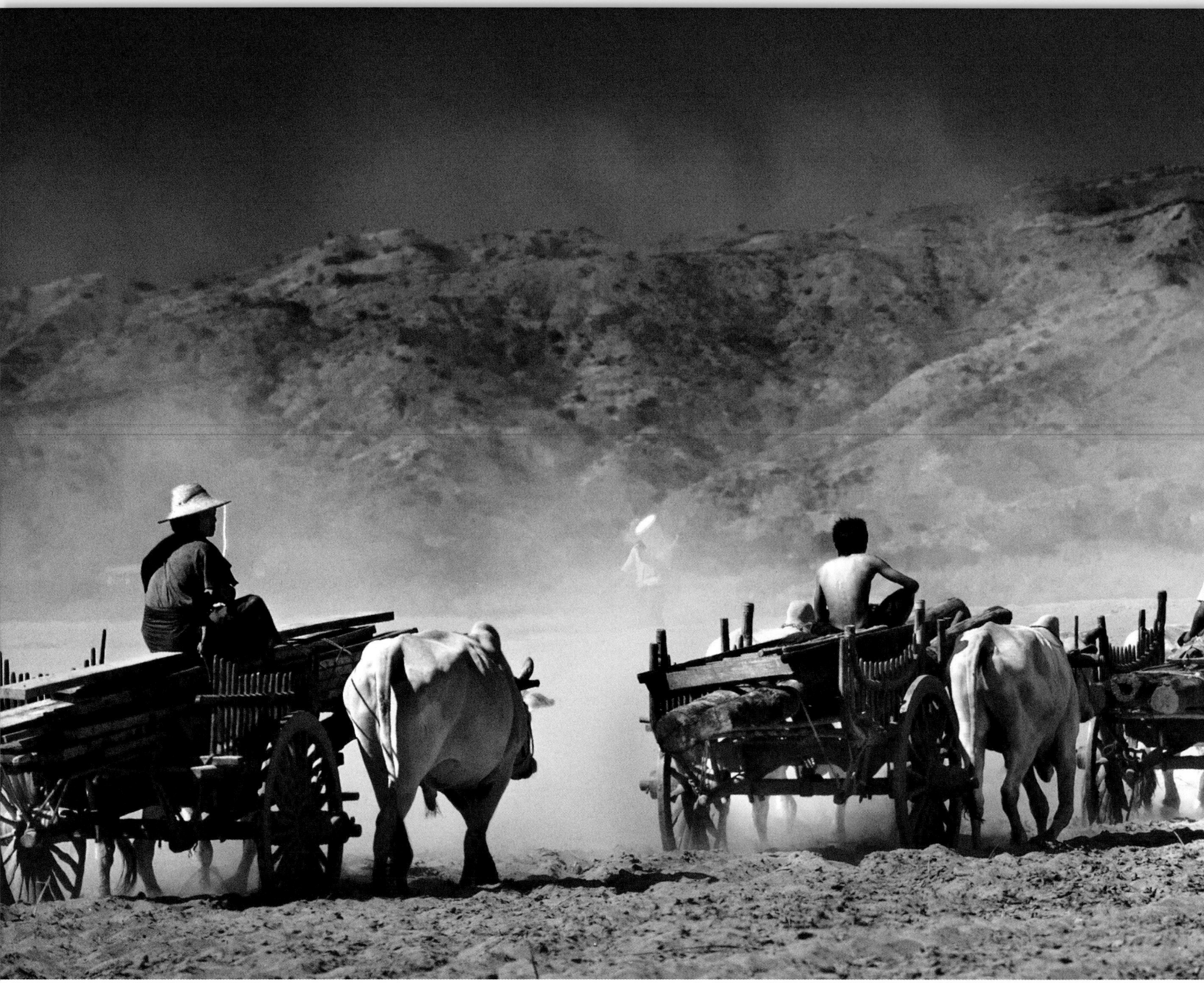

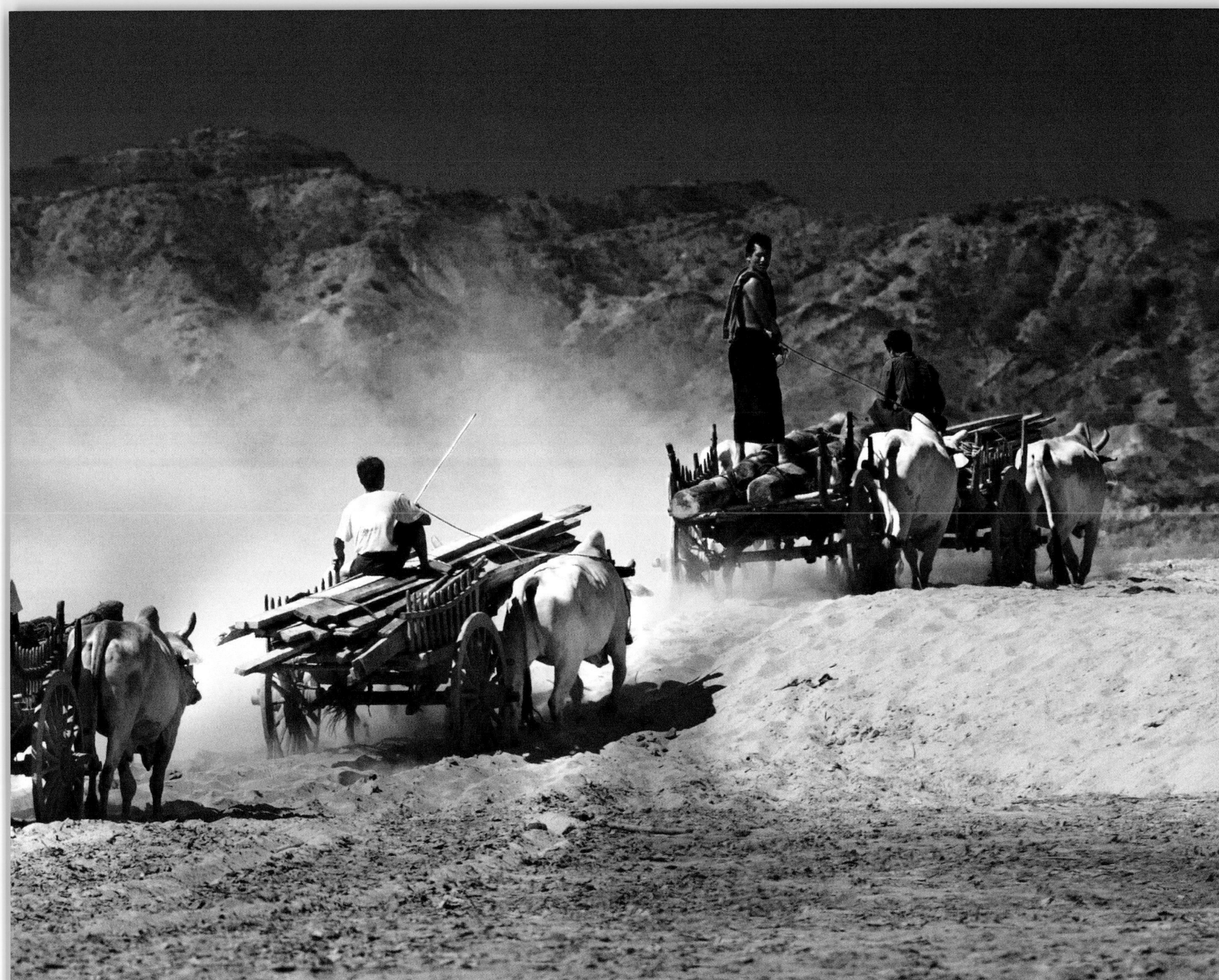

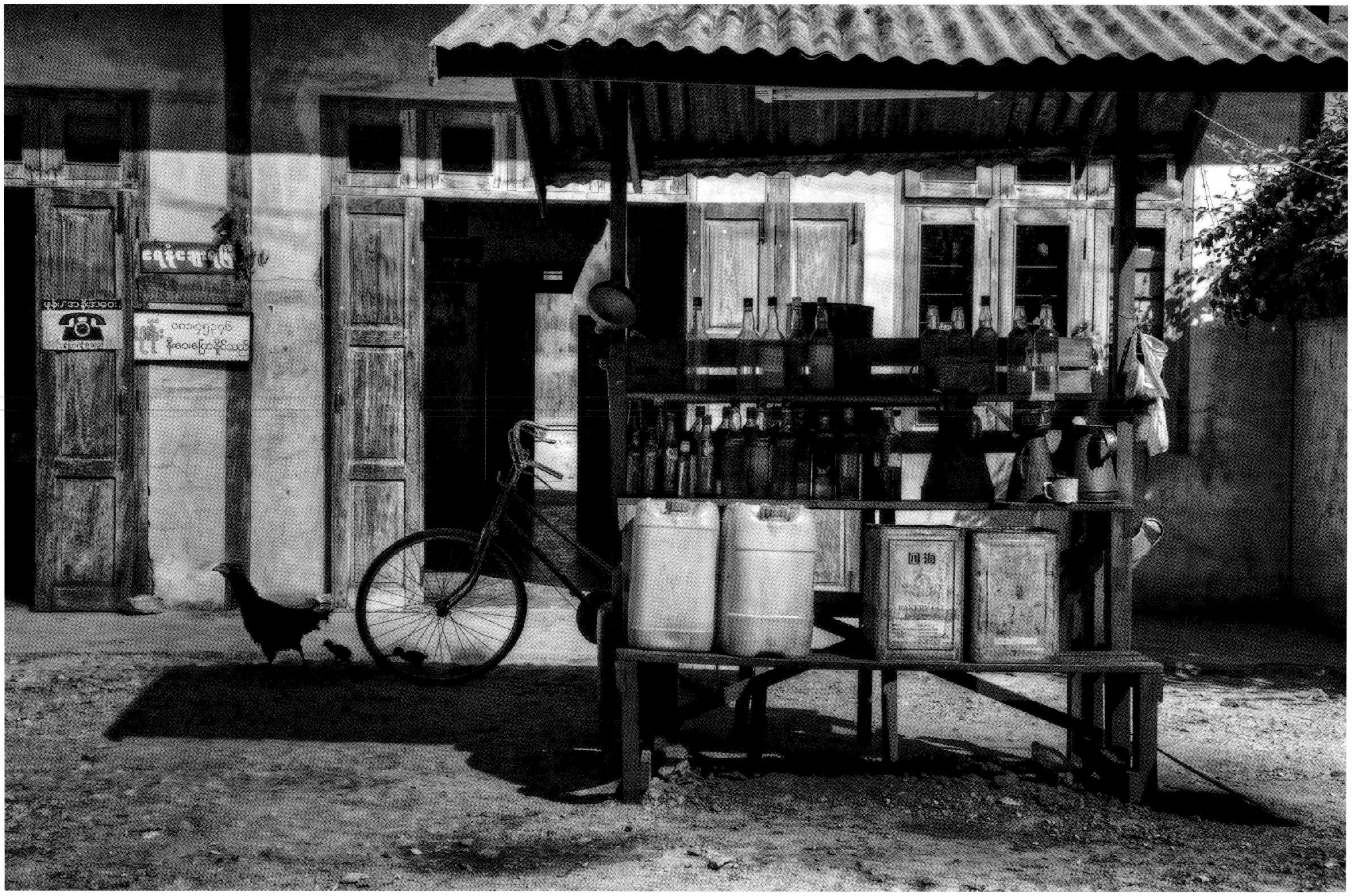

Petrol station near Kalaw, Shan State, 2010

In rural areas, gasoline for motorbikes and cars is often sold in old bottles or canisters. What looks at first glance like a roadside bar selling bottles of whisky or rum is in fact a petrol station.

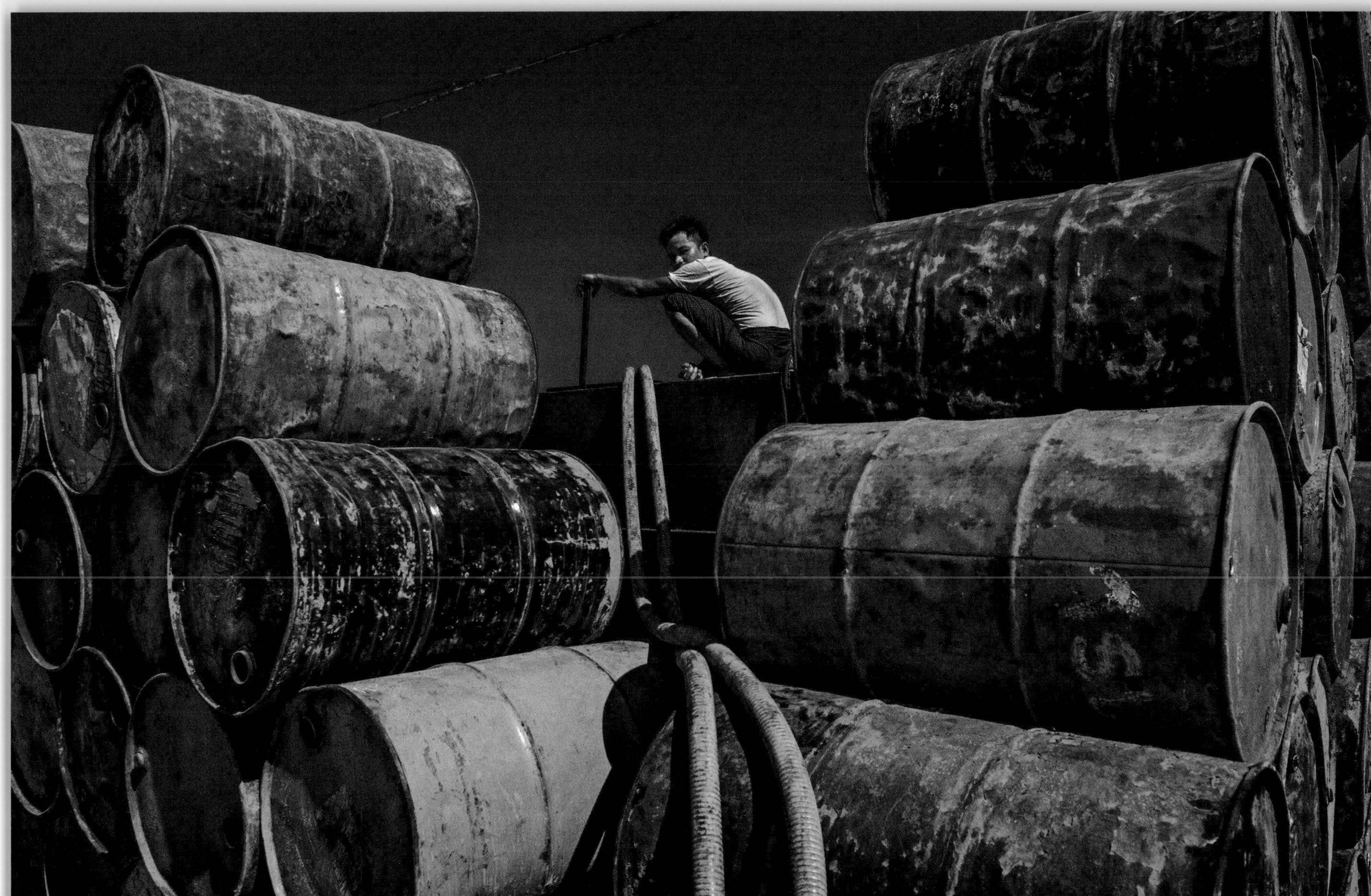

Oil barrels, Kaukha, Sagaing Region, 2015

Though private oil exploration and small-scale oil refineries are technically illegal, they are often tolerated by the authorities. These barrels of gasoline and diesel have been sold to brokers and are waiting to be loaded onto trucks.

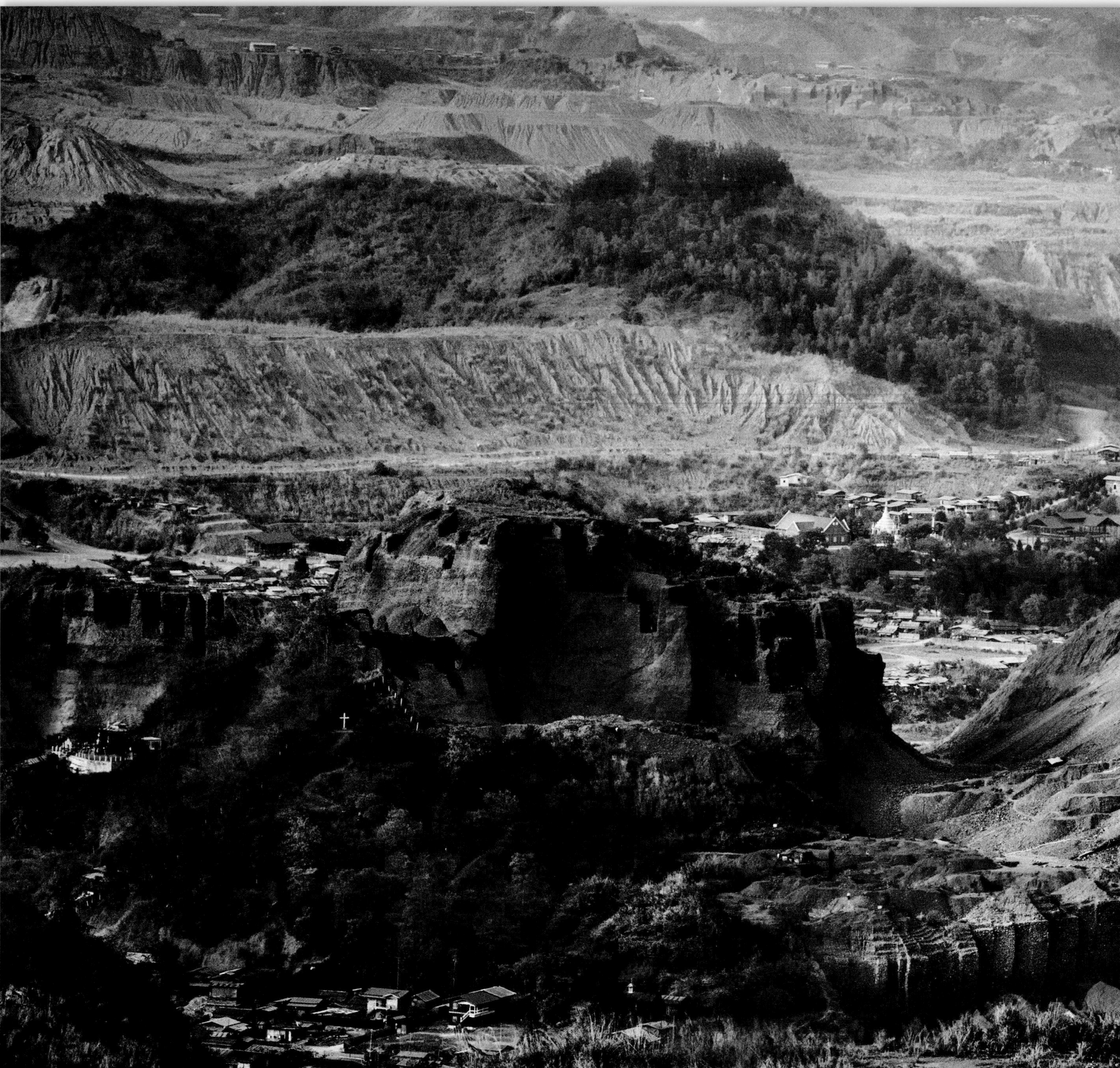

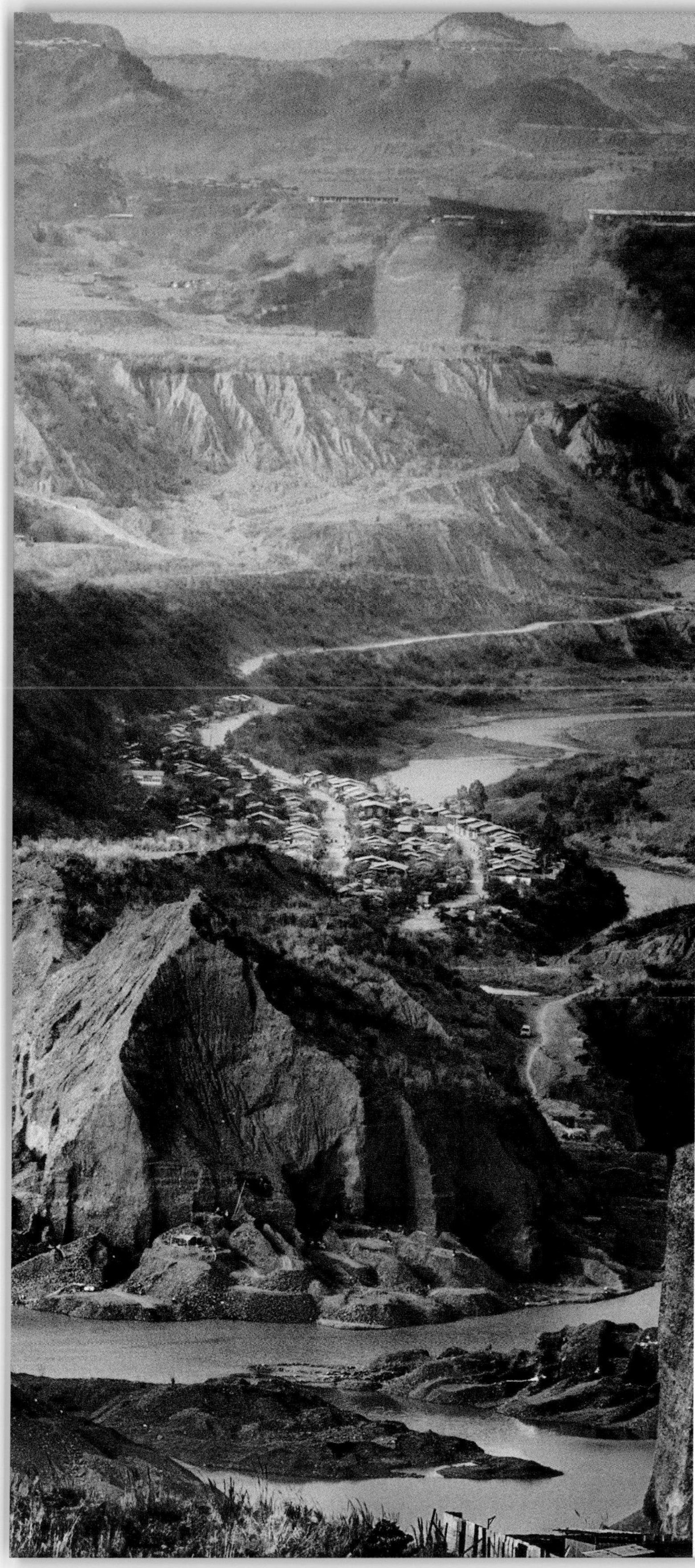

Jade mine, Hpakant, Kachin State, 2014

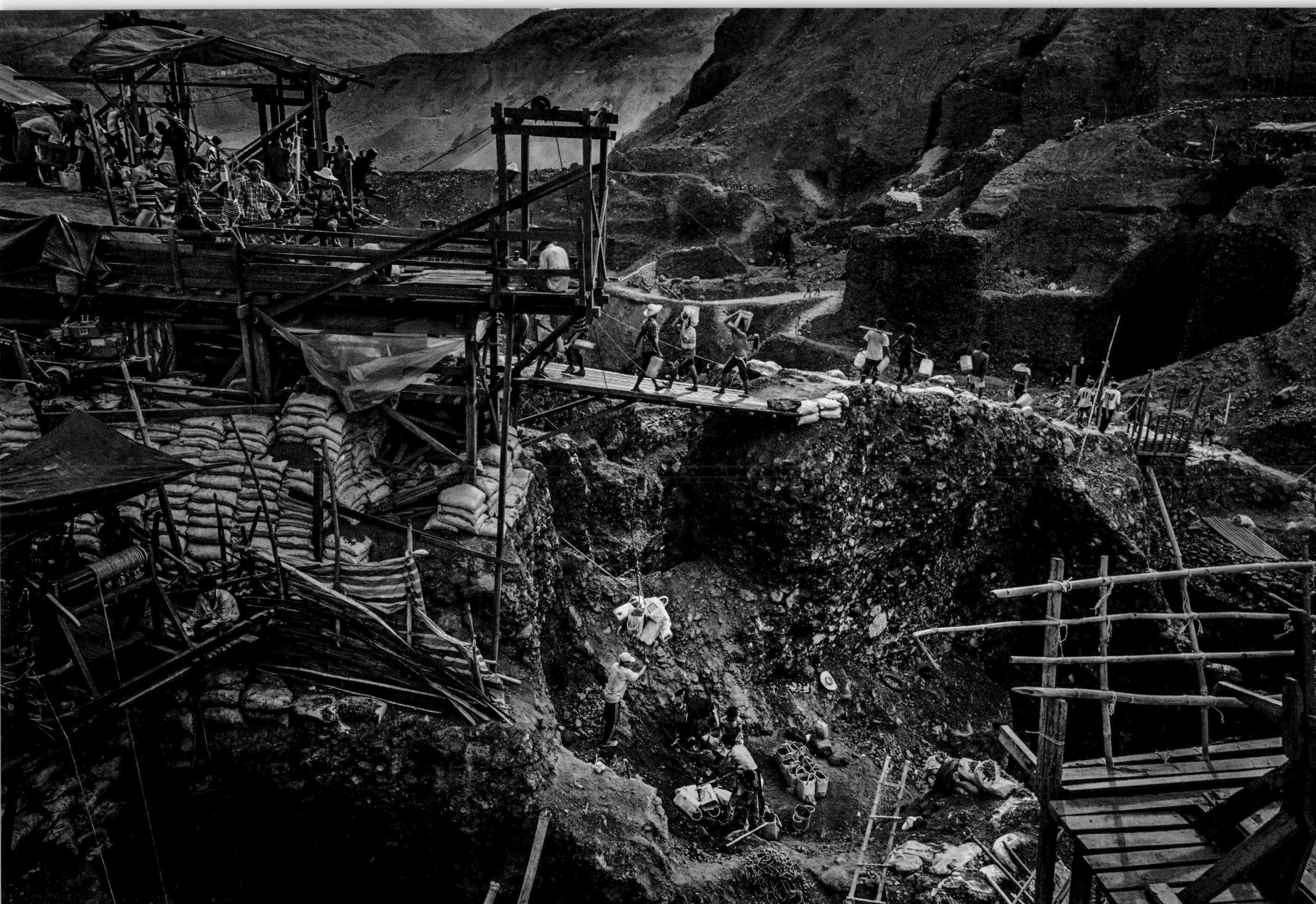

Jade mine, Hpakant, Kachin State, 2014

The Hpakant area is renowned for its jade. When there is fighting between the Kachin rebels and government troops, the mines are closed. During those times, villagers and adventurers comb the area hoping to find the lucky stone that will help them escape poverty. The stones can be sold to China, where there is an insatiable appetite for the so-called "Royal Jade". In Hpakant, I had the chance to mingle with miners and photograph their daily work. They use only hand tools and old canisters to collect any stones they find. Due to the lack of safety standards and the coordinated mining, the area's hills and freestanding towers of earth are prone to collapse and the workers are always in danger of being buried by landslides.

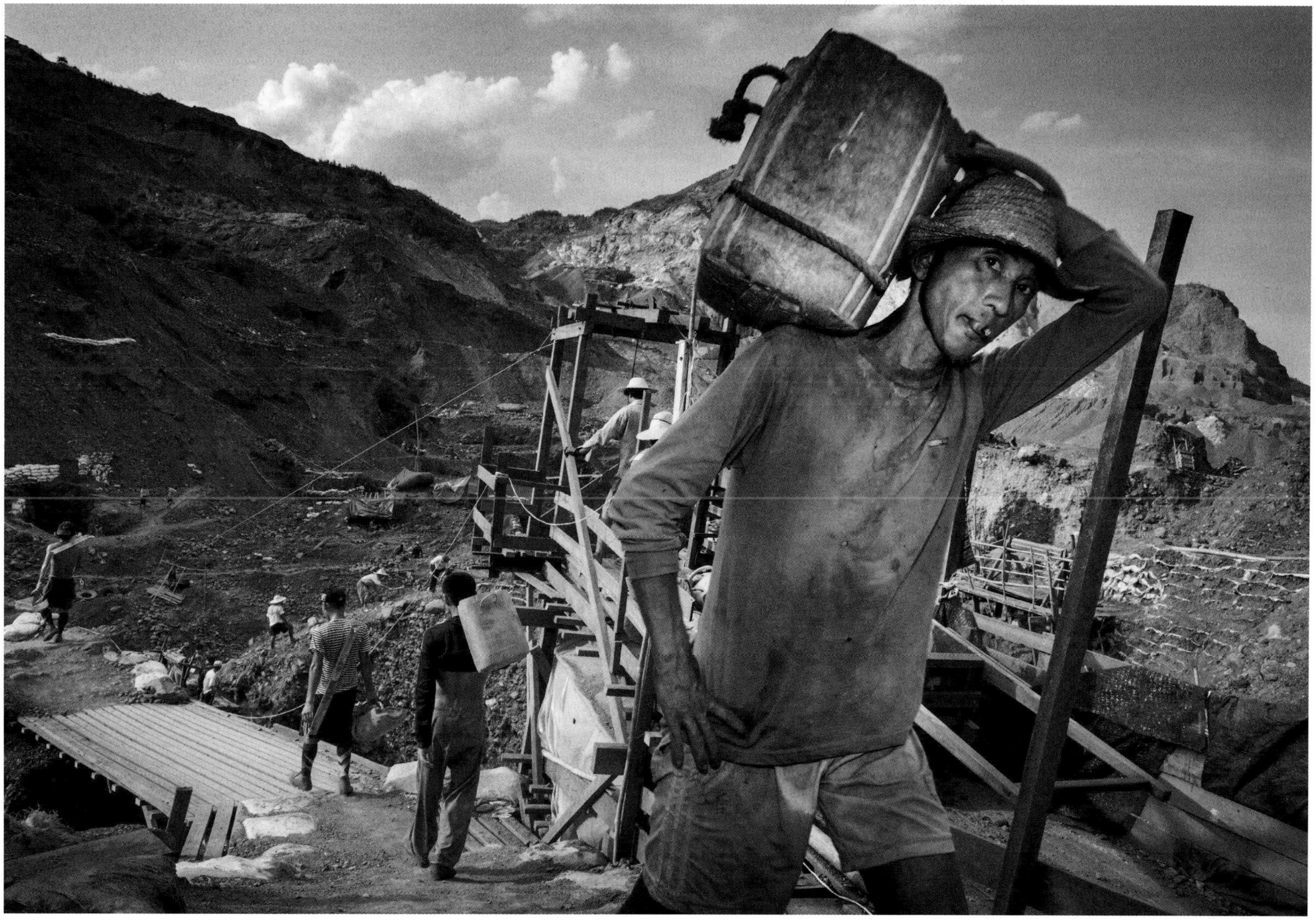

Jade miner, Hpakant, Kachin State, 2014

Individual miners either work for themselves or as day labourers. Most workers who come here leave their families at home and everyone is hoping to find a big, high-quality piece of jade that will make them rich. The negligible income from the small stones they regularly find is just enough to make a living, sometimes with a little leftover to gamble in the evenings in Hpakant.

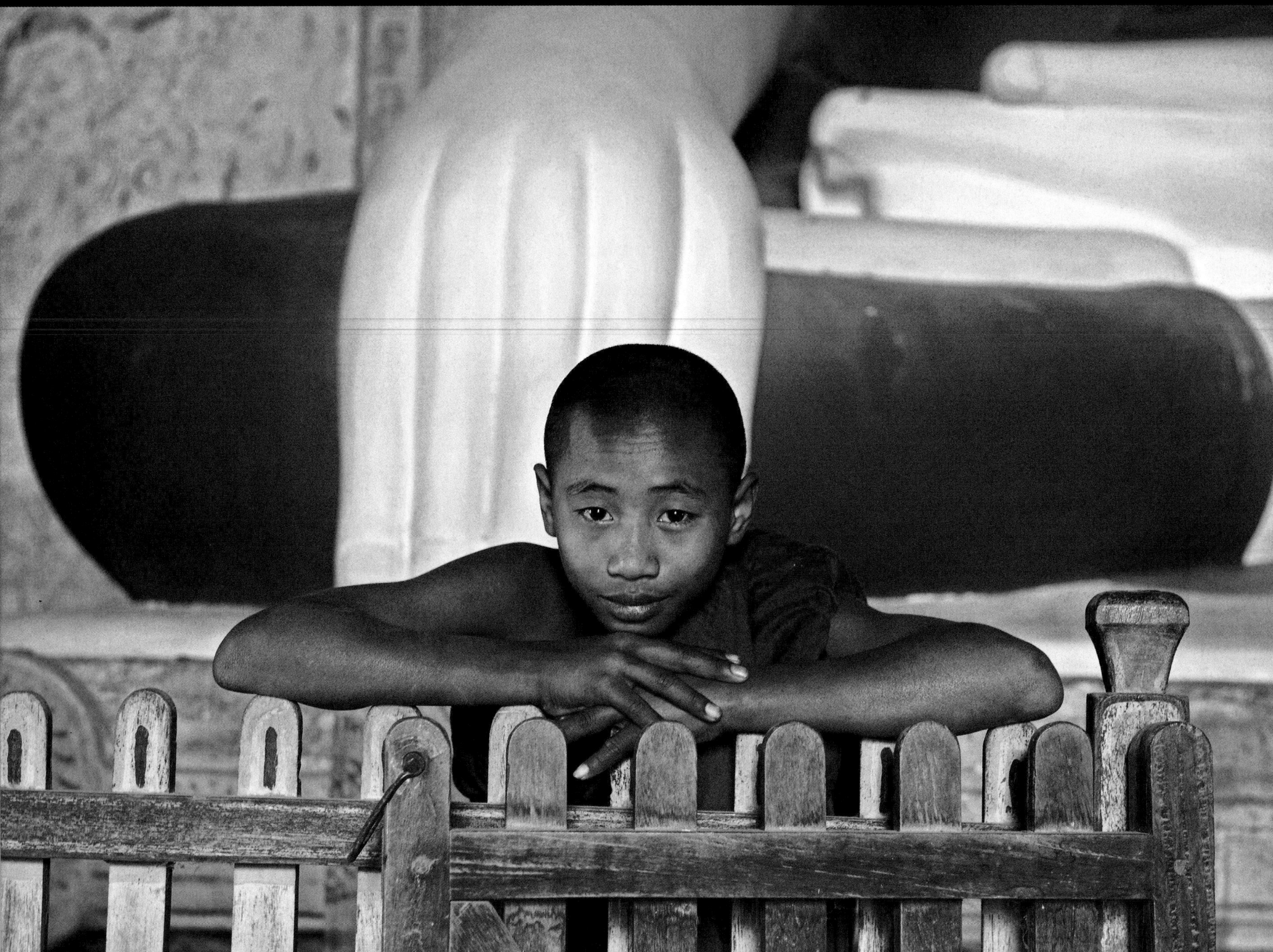

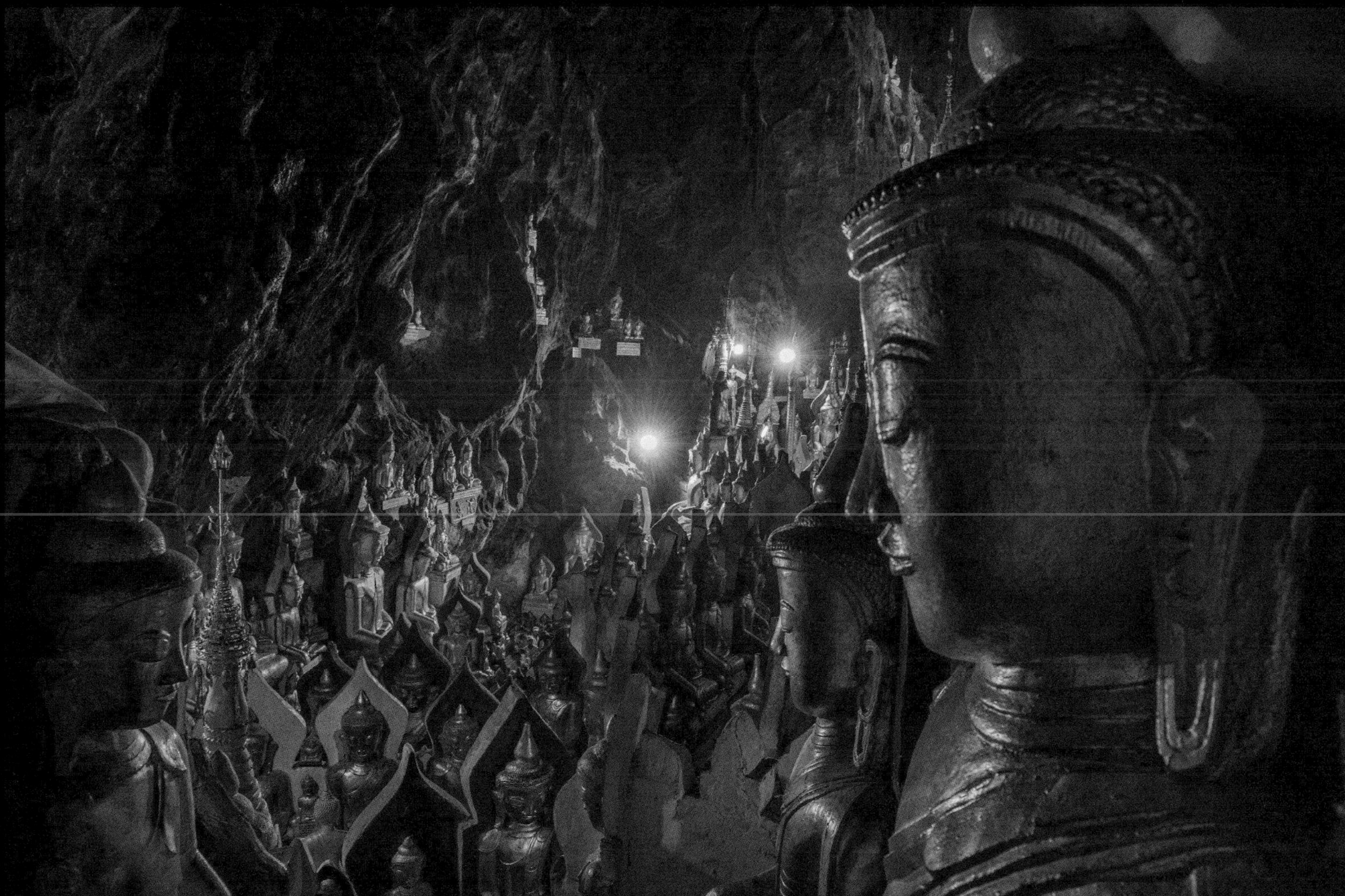

Pindaya Caves, Pindaya, Shan State, 2013

Since the eighteenth century, people have been bringing Buddha statues to the Pindaya caves. Today, the caves are an important pilgrimage site in Myanmar. They are filled with thousands of Buddha statues that have been placed not only on the floor but also in niches on the rock walls.

Opposite: Young monk in the Sala Mani Temple, Bagan, Mandalay Region, 2010

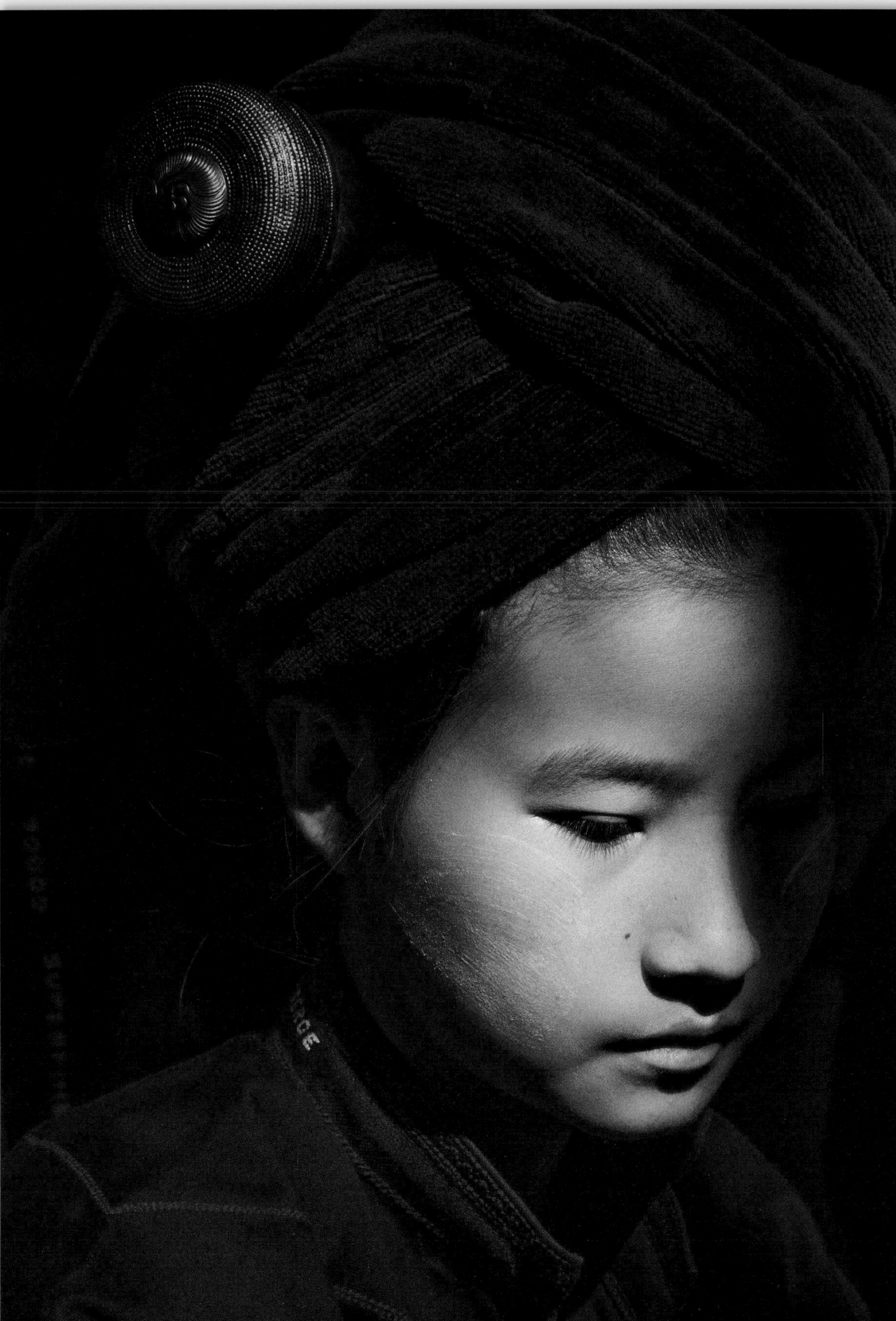

Pa-Oh girl praying, Kekku, Shan State, 2011

The Pa-Oh tribe gathers once a year at the Mwetaw Pagoda complex in Kekku. Terrycloth towels are used as headdresses and incorporate a "dragon's eye" sticking out one side – a symbolic reference to the tribe's belief that its members are descended from a dragon.

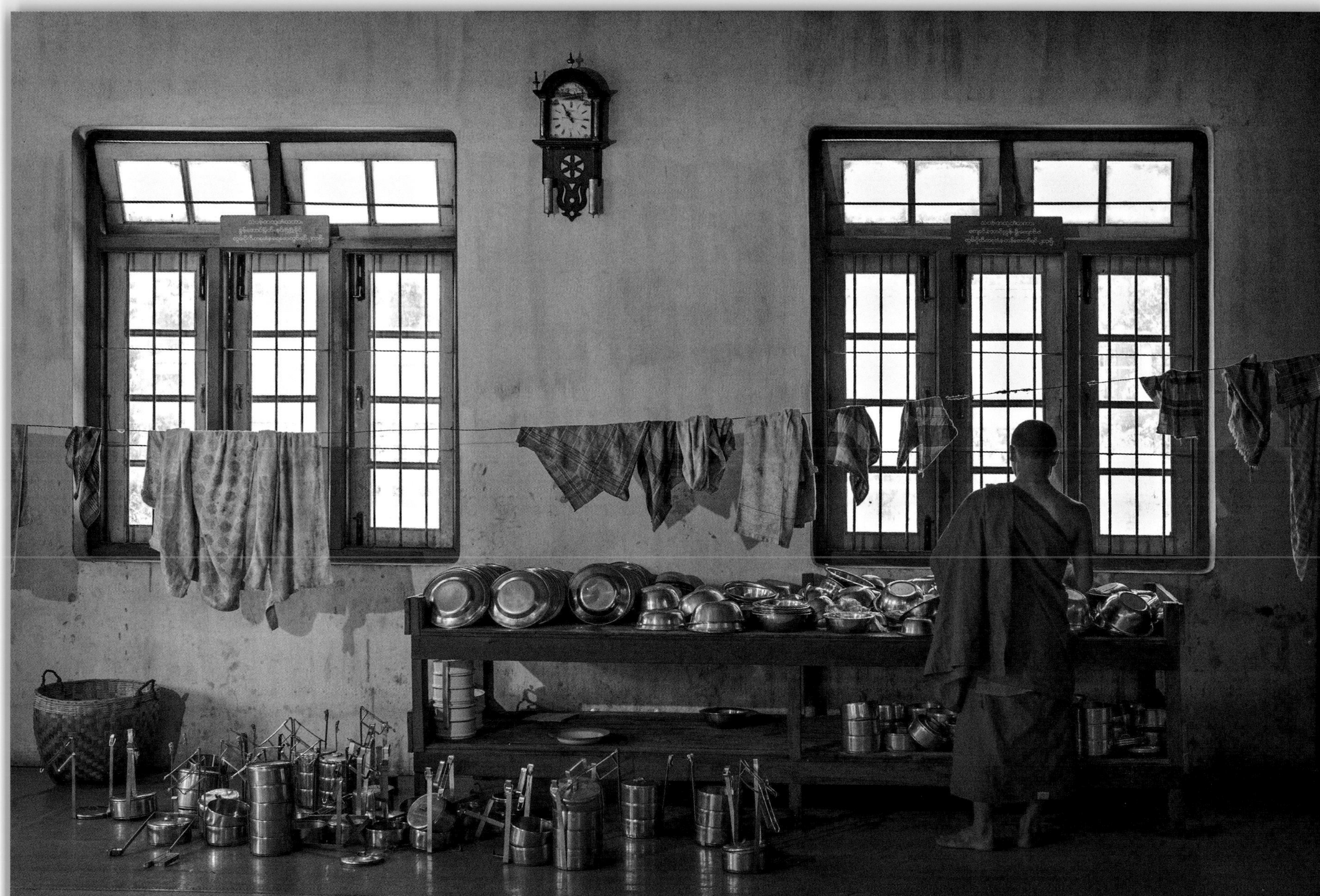

Dining hall in the Taung Khaung Kyi Monastery, Taunggyi, Shan State, 2011

Young monks take turns to prepare and serve meals, set out the dinnerware and crockery, and make sure everything is clean.

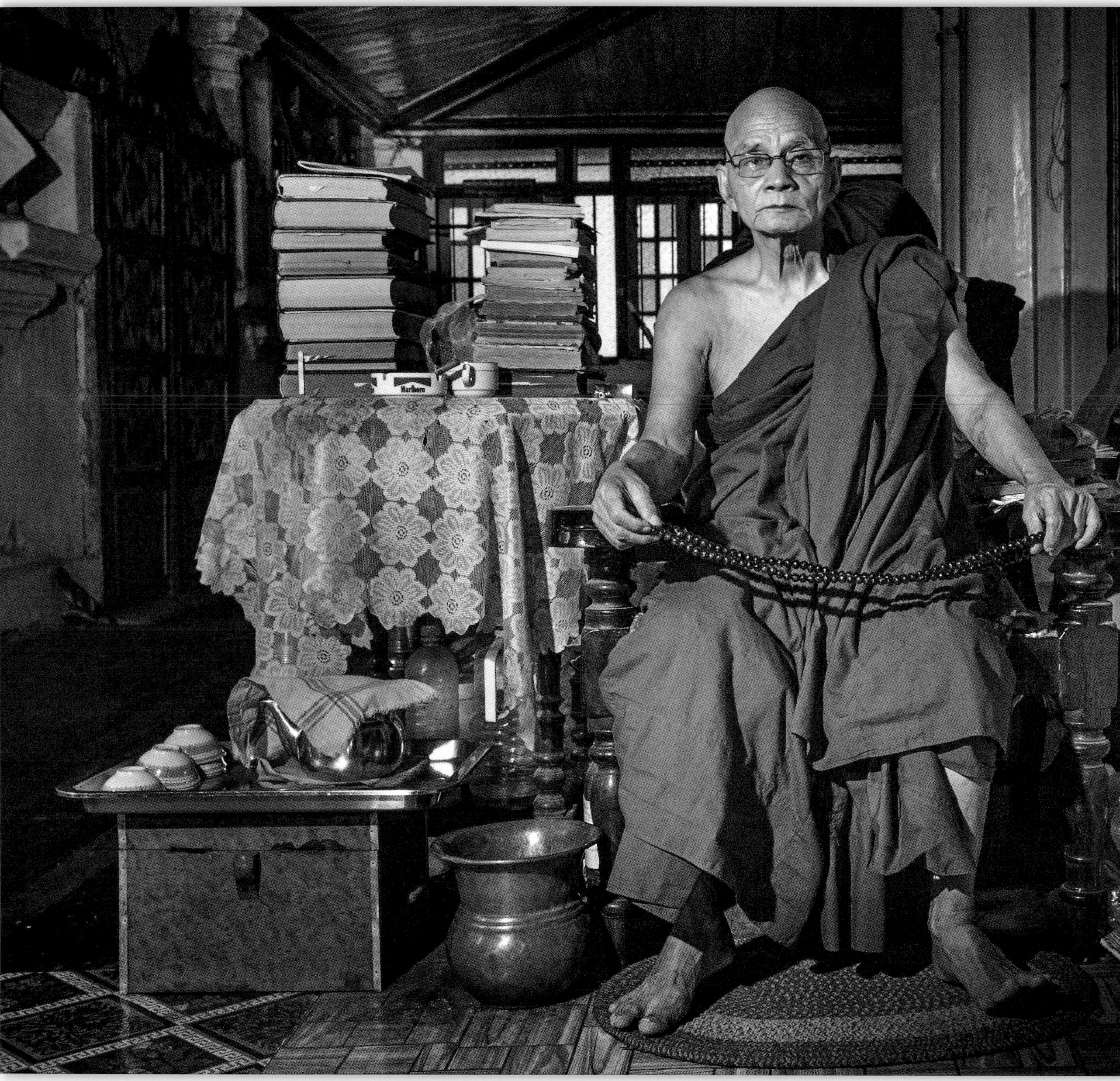
Marlboro

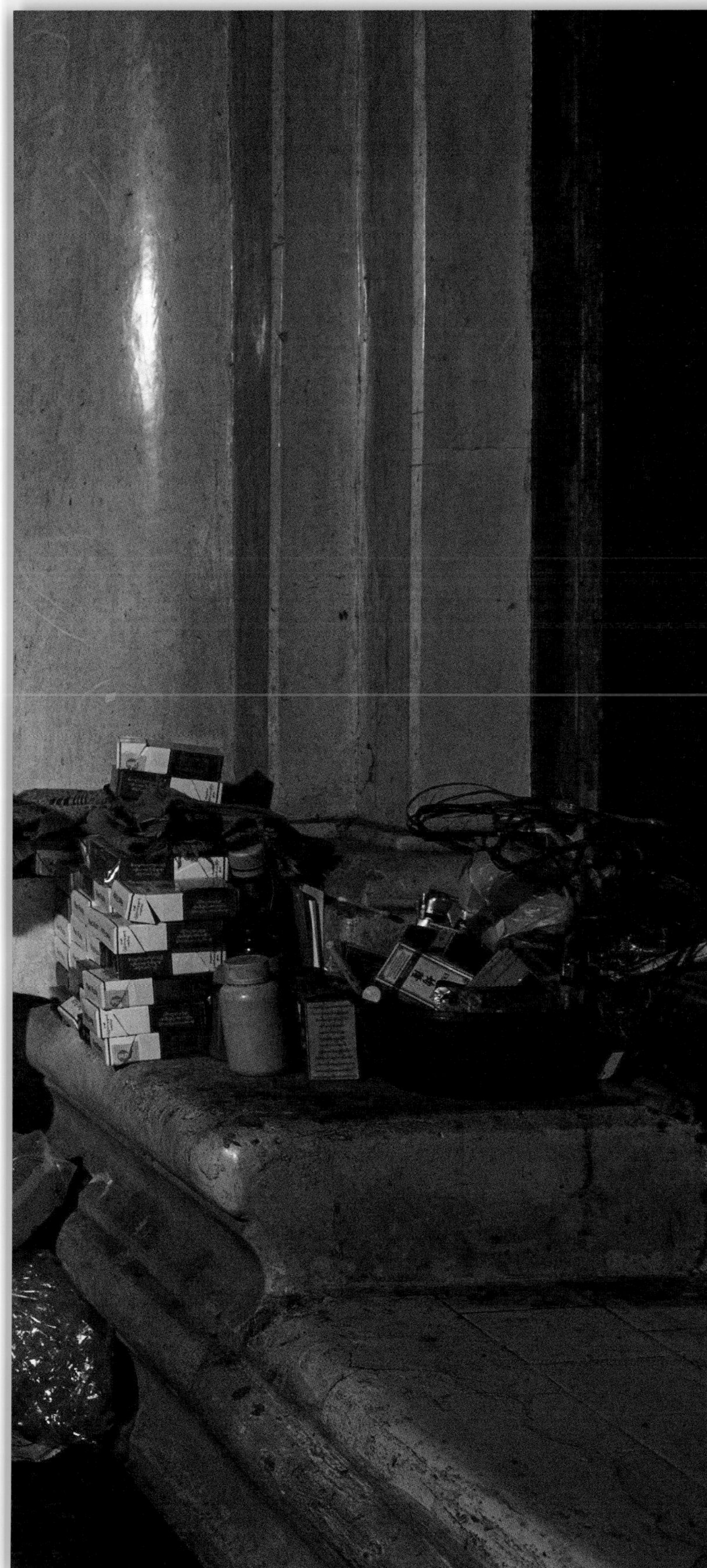

Abbot U Kaymarwara of the Sein Don Monastery, Mawlamyine, Mon State, 2011

Though the abbot was happy to have his photograph taken, to show too much enthusiasm would have been unbefitting of his high position. He maintained his serious expression throughout the process, holding this pose with the rigorous stillness of a subject in a photographic studio.

Overleaf: Pagoda festival at the Shwe Myit Zu Pagoda, Indawgyi Lake, Kachin State, 2012

This pagoda is situated in the middle of Indawgyi Lake. During the festival, tens of thousands of pilgrims come to worship at the pagoda, approaching via a narrow pathway above the shallow water. It is said that the pathway, which remains above water during the festival, is submerged again the day after the festival ends. I wanted to wait a day longer to see for myself but my guide was so insistent on getting home it seemed almost like she didn't want to invite disappointment if we stayed and the pathway remained above water. The phenomenon may actually be attributable to the area's weather patterns; held at the end of the dry season, the heavy rains that usually start at the end of the week-long festival can raise the water level in the lake and make the pathway disappear.

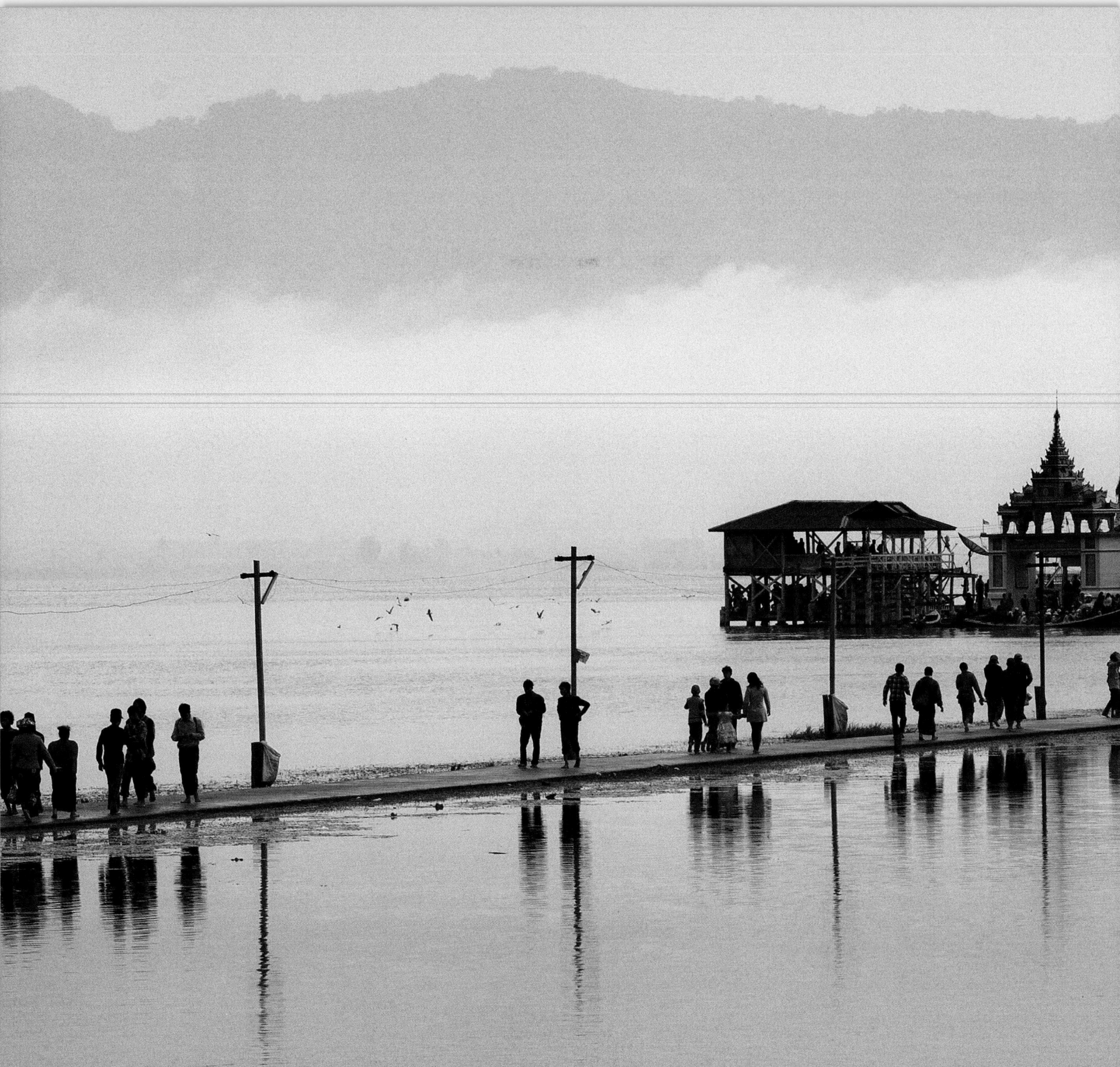

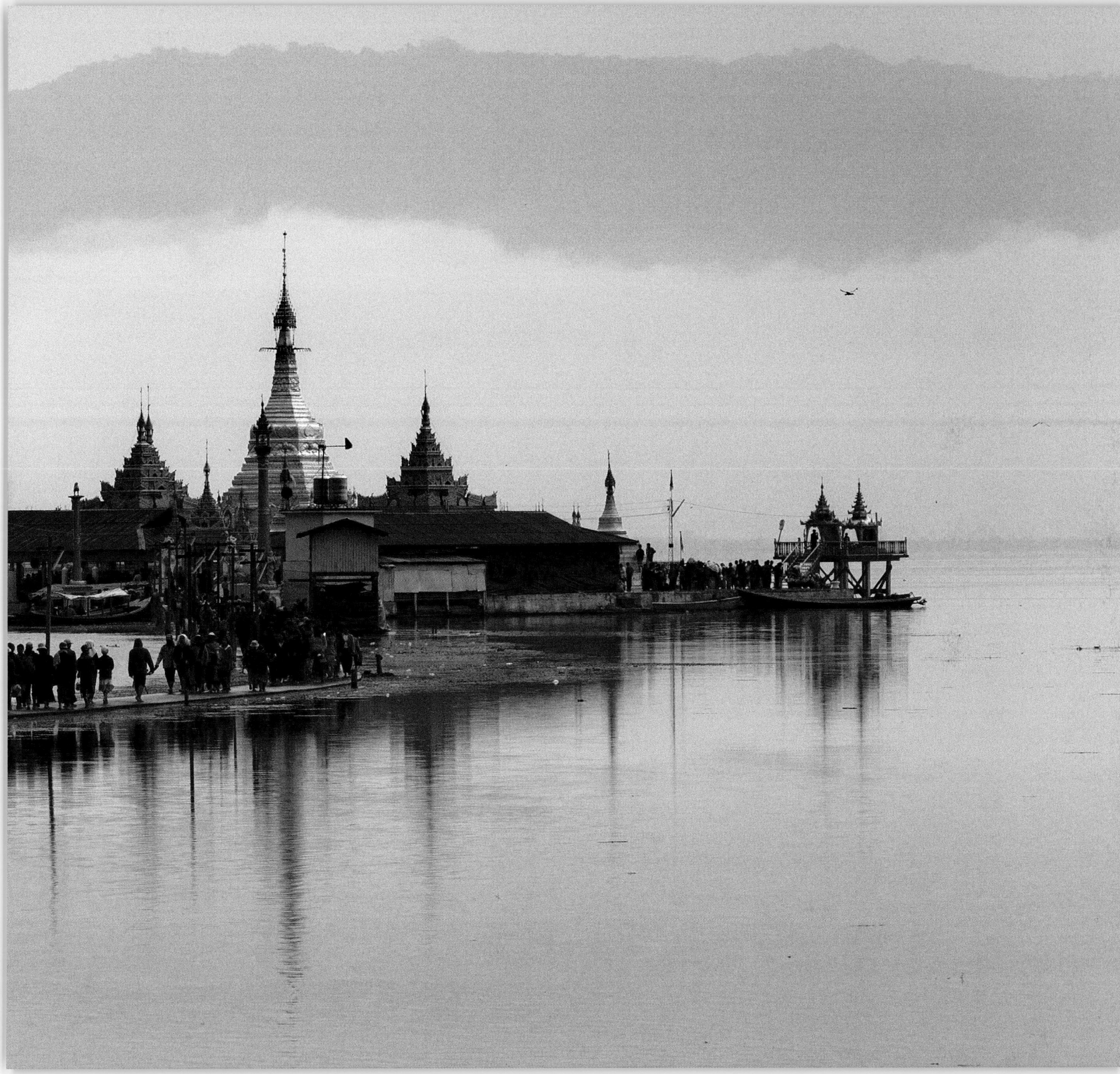

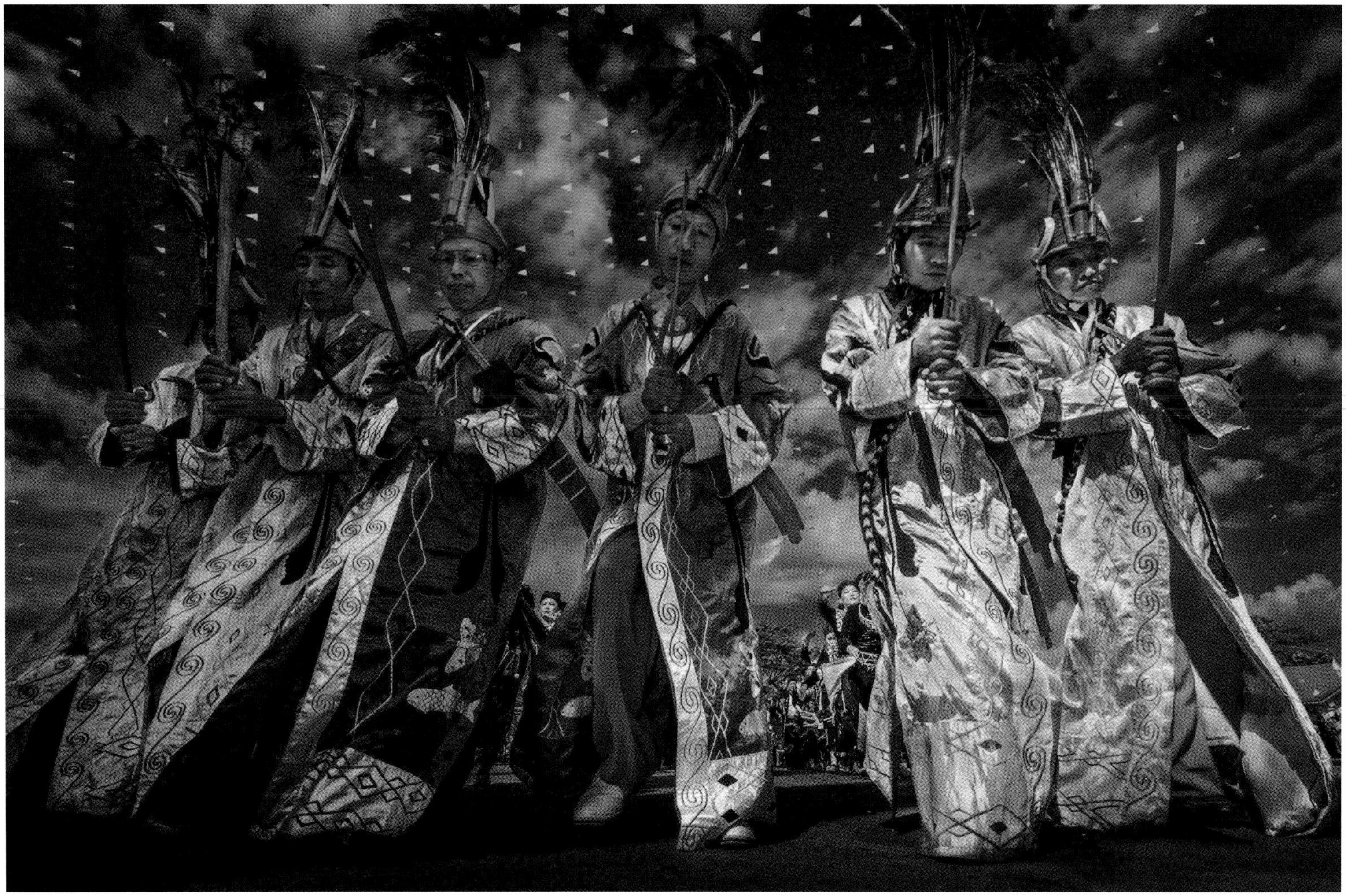

Manaw festival on Kachin State Day, Myitkyina, Kachin State, 2015

During the Manaw festival, dance performances are held by various Kachin tribes from both Myanmar and China – tribal borders don't always coincide with national borders. Ceremonial swords and costumes vary but the dances and music are the same for all participants. The meditative tunes and repetitive steps continue for hours as the dancers form a kilometre-long procession and proceed in a prescribed pattern across the large ceremonial ground.

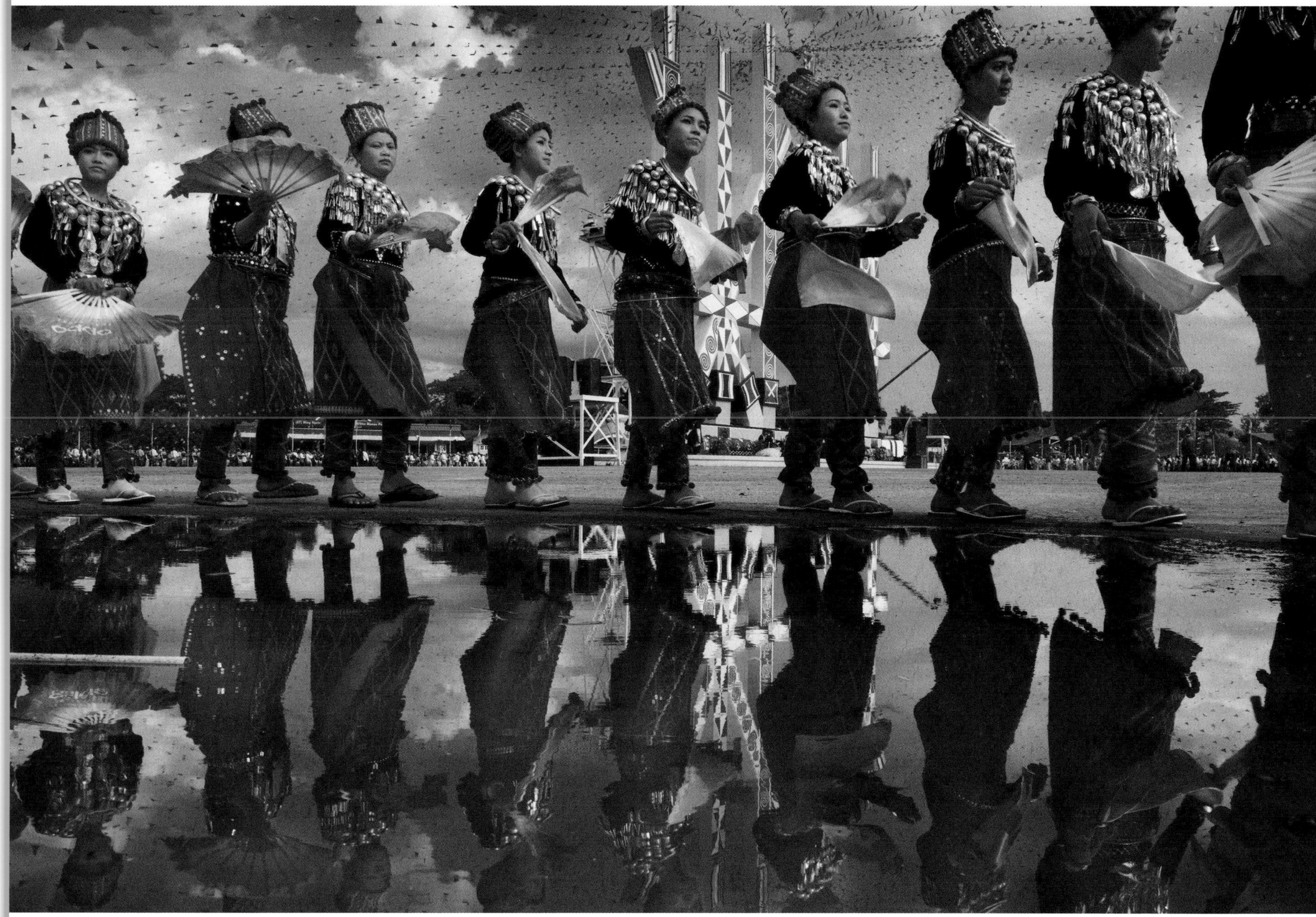

Manaw festival dancers at the Kachin State Day,
Myitkyina, Kachin State, 2015

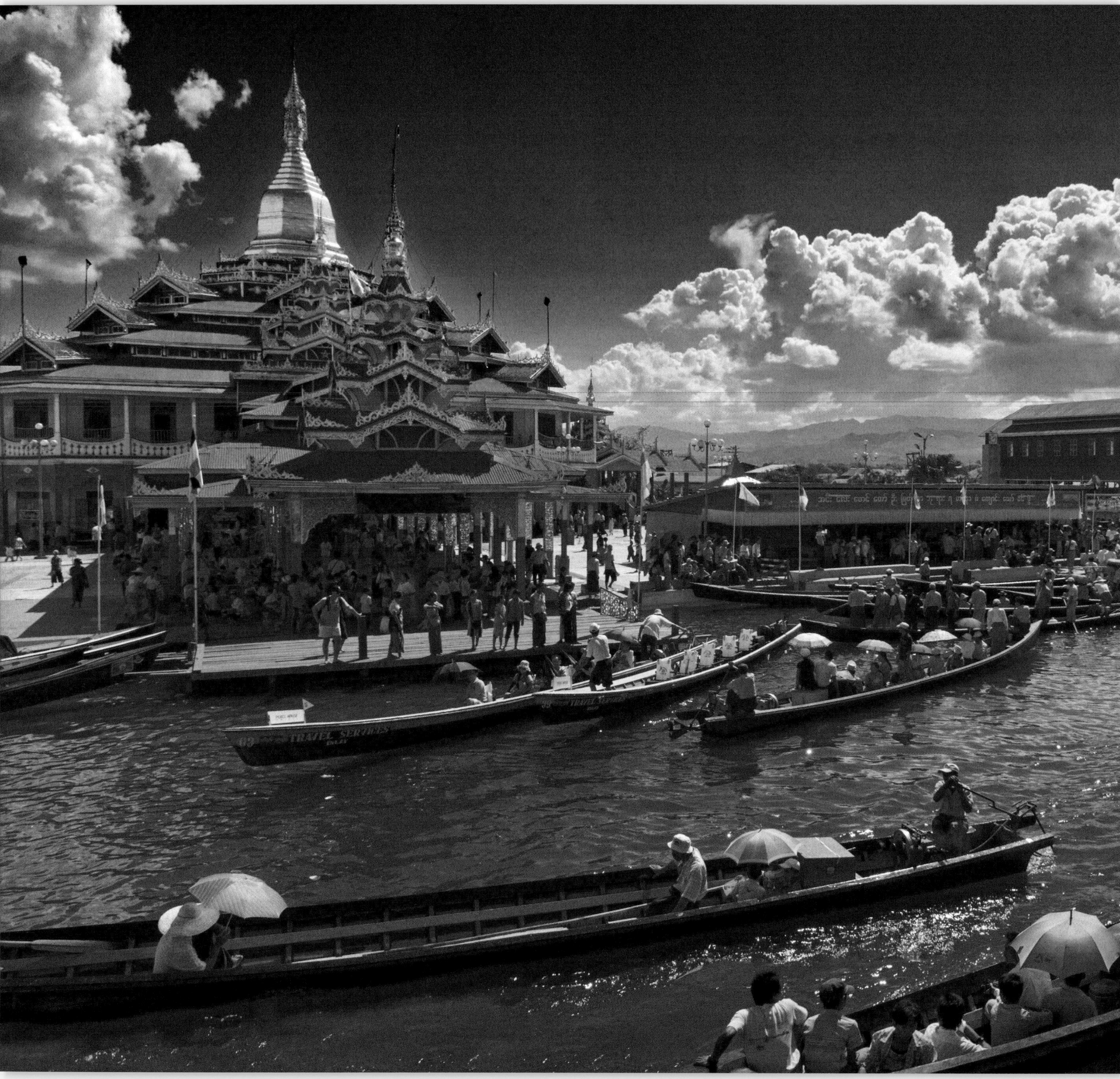
TRAVEL SERVICES

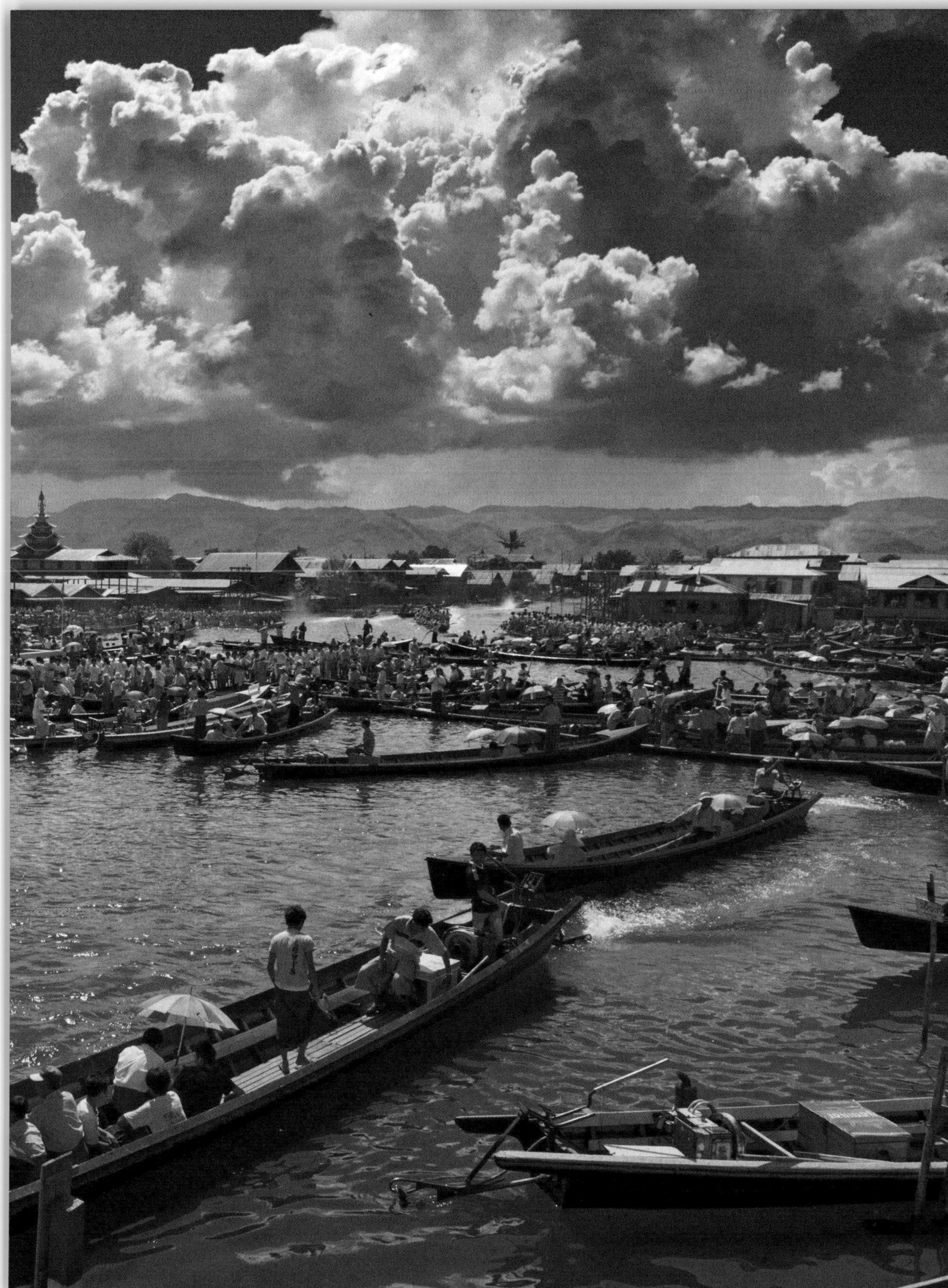

INLE LAKE, SHAN STATE, 2011

During the Phaung Daw U Pagoda Festival on Inle Lake, spectators come by boat to watch the processions and boat races. For those who live on the lake, boats are the only means of transport.

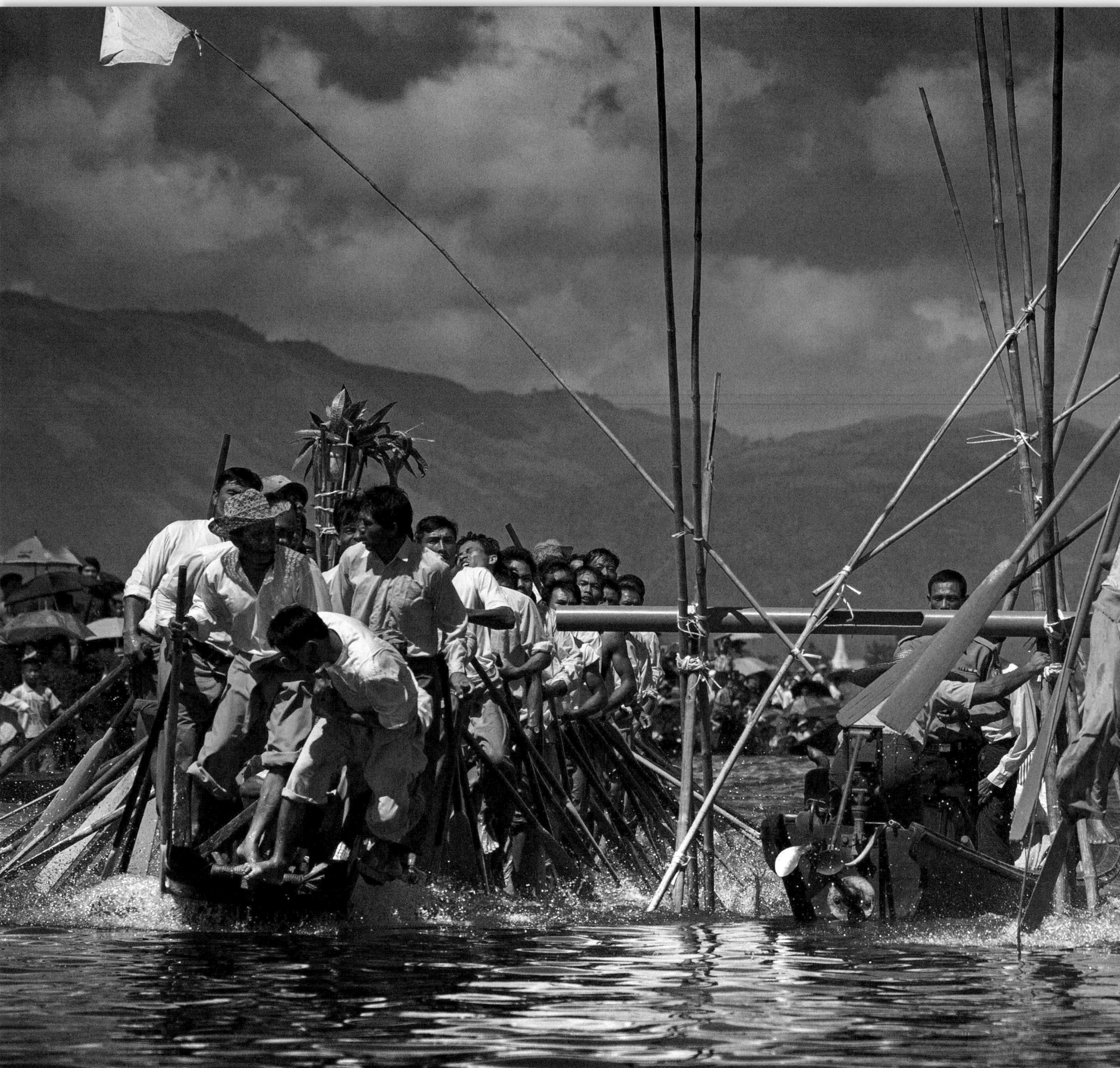

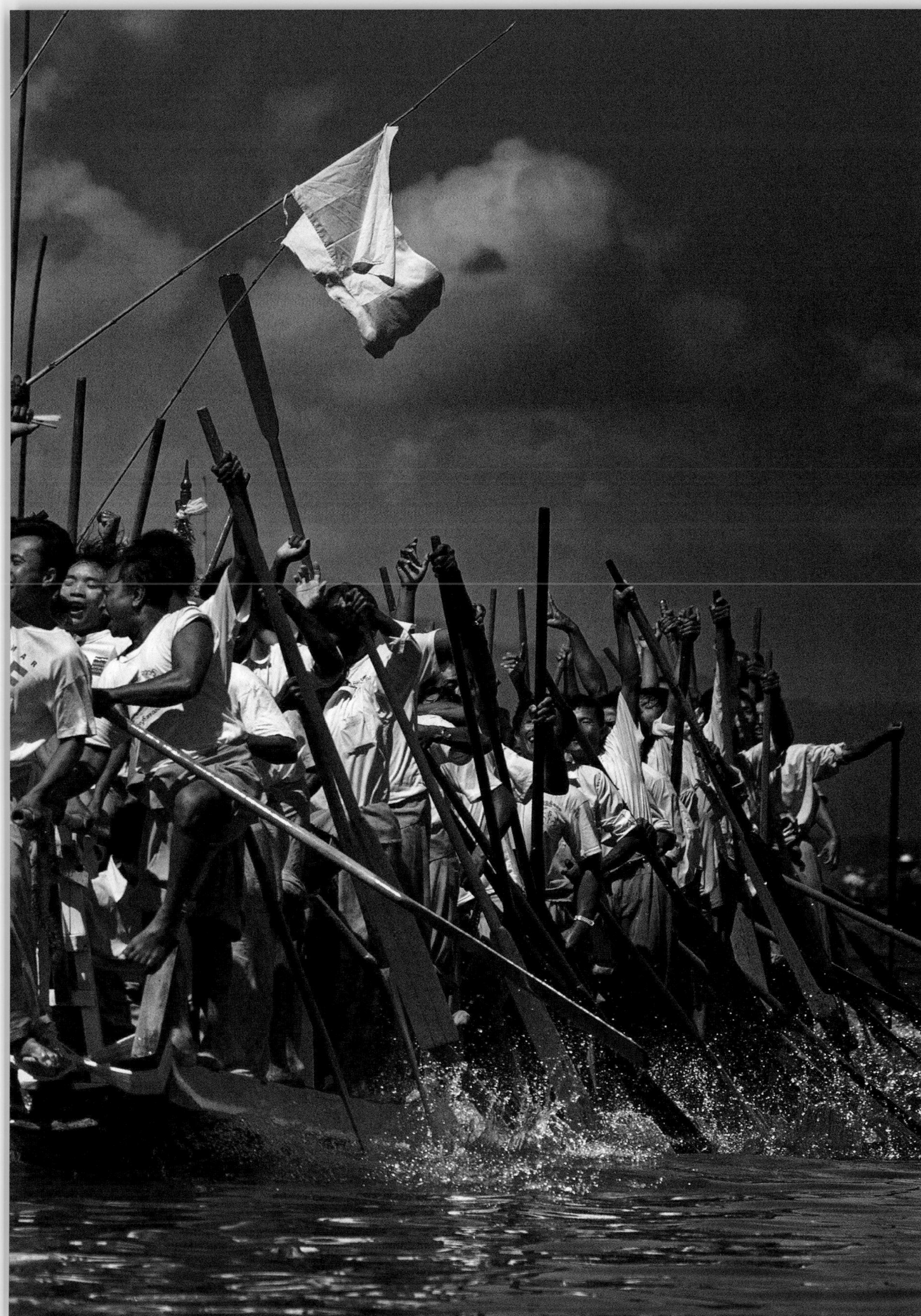

Boat races at the Phaung Daw U Pagoda Festival, Inle Lake, Shan State, 2011

The famous leg rowers of Inle Lake use their skills to propel the ceremonial barge during this festival. At the end of the day, they still have enough energy for a boat race. Each boat represents a different village and the rowers take the competition very seriously. A single boat can hold more than 30 men, including some whose job is to take up the necessary task of bailing out water that seeps into the boats and others in charge of beating the drums to help their team keep up a steady rhythm.

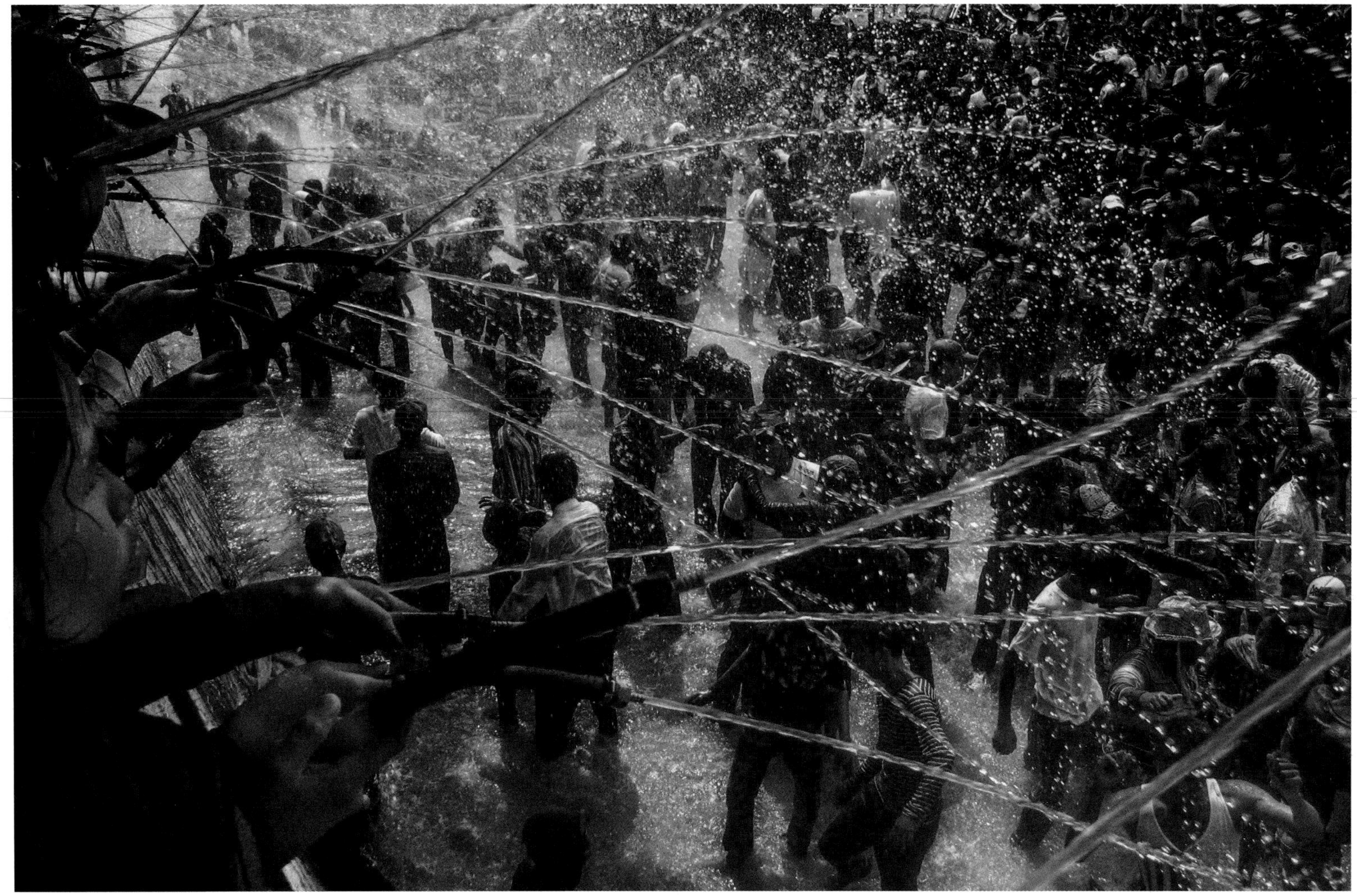

Water festival, Mandalay, 2013

Thingyan, the water festival, is the most important annual holiday in Myanmar and marks the Buddhist New Year in mid-April. As with most festivals in the country, the exact date changes each year in accordance with the lunar calendar. The holiday falls during the hottest period of the year just before the rainy season starts and water is splashed around to cool the temperature and wash away the past year. Buckets, water guns, or any suitable containers able to hold liquid are put to use. In Mandalay, grandstands are built around the moat of the former palace. While famous singers and bands perform, water from the moat is pumped through hoses to douse the public. I found an underwater camera helpful during the festival because no one is safe from getting soaked.

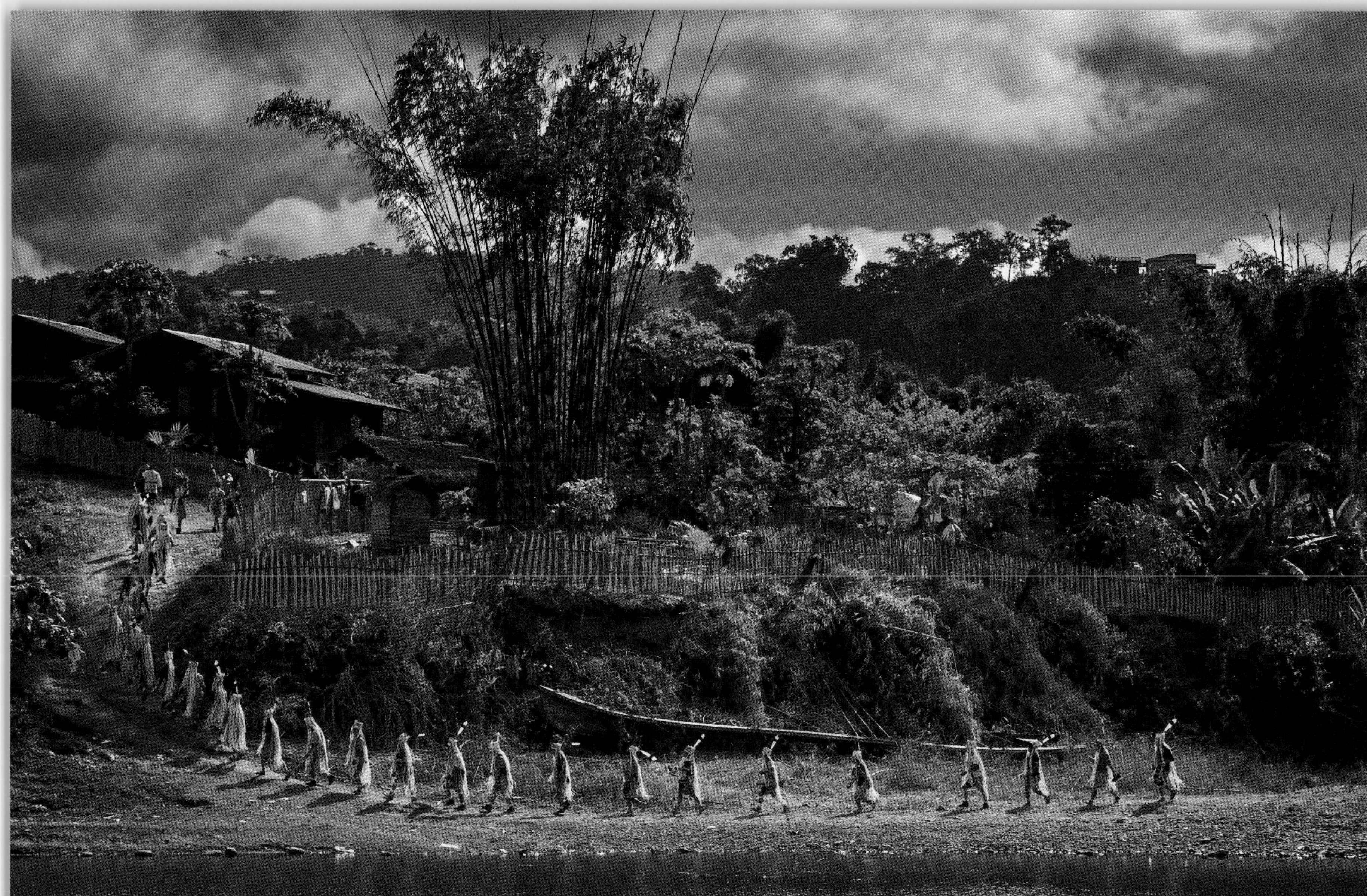

Group participating in the Naga festival, Namyun, Kachin State, 2014

Various Naga tribes from Myanmar and India gather for their annual festival, this time close to the Indian border in Namyun. The two countries have agreed that the tribespeople are allowed to cross the border without travel documents. During the festival, they perform dances, hold competitions, and buy and sell goods at the local market. The Naga in Myanmar sometimes find it difficult to sell textiles and other goods to the Indian Naga because the latter are only willing to use Indian rupees as currency.

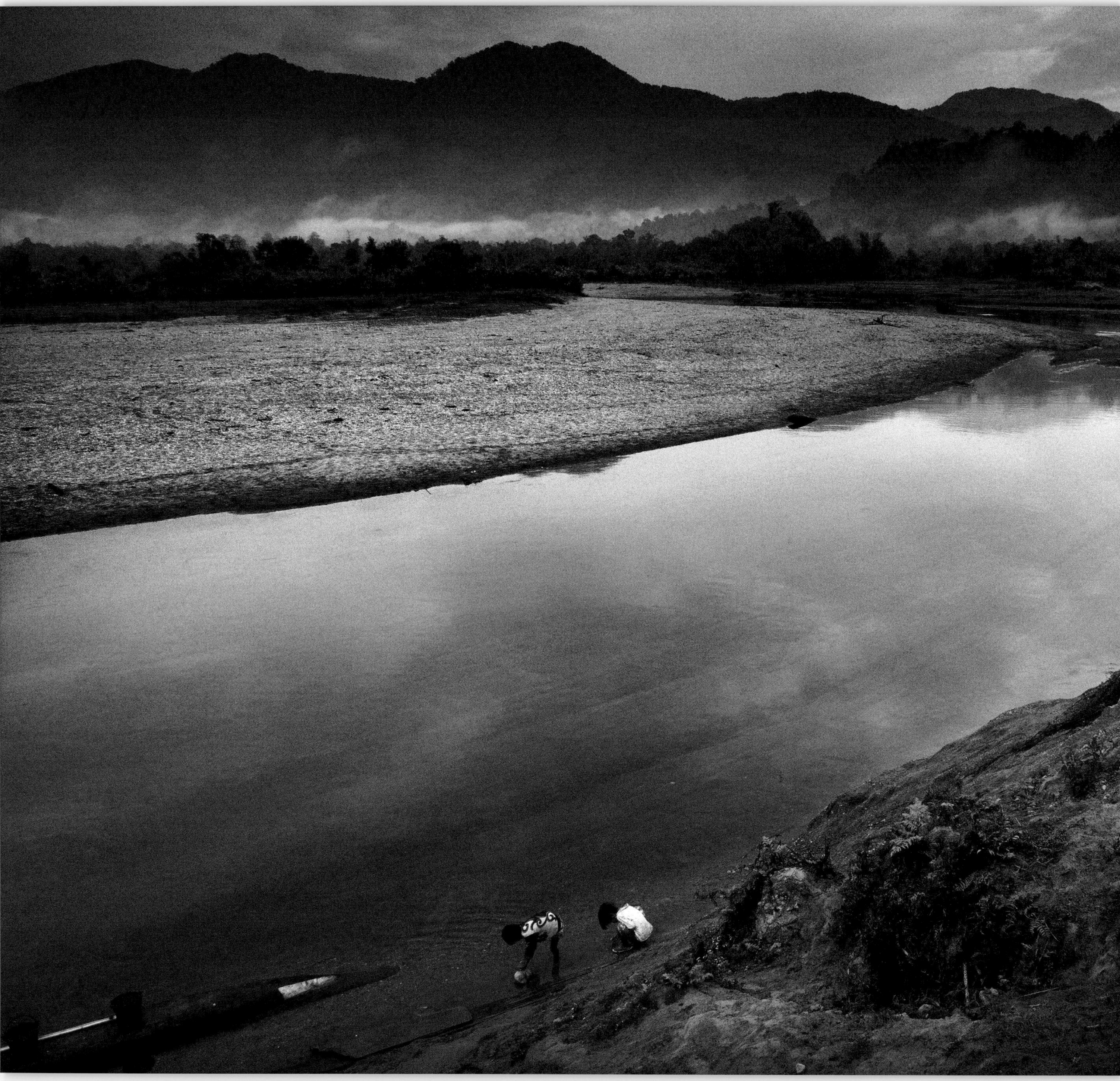

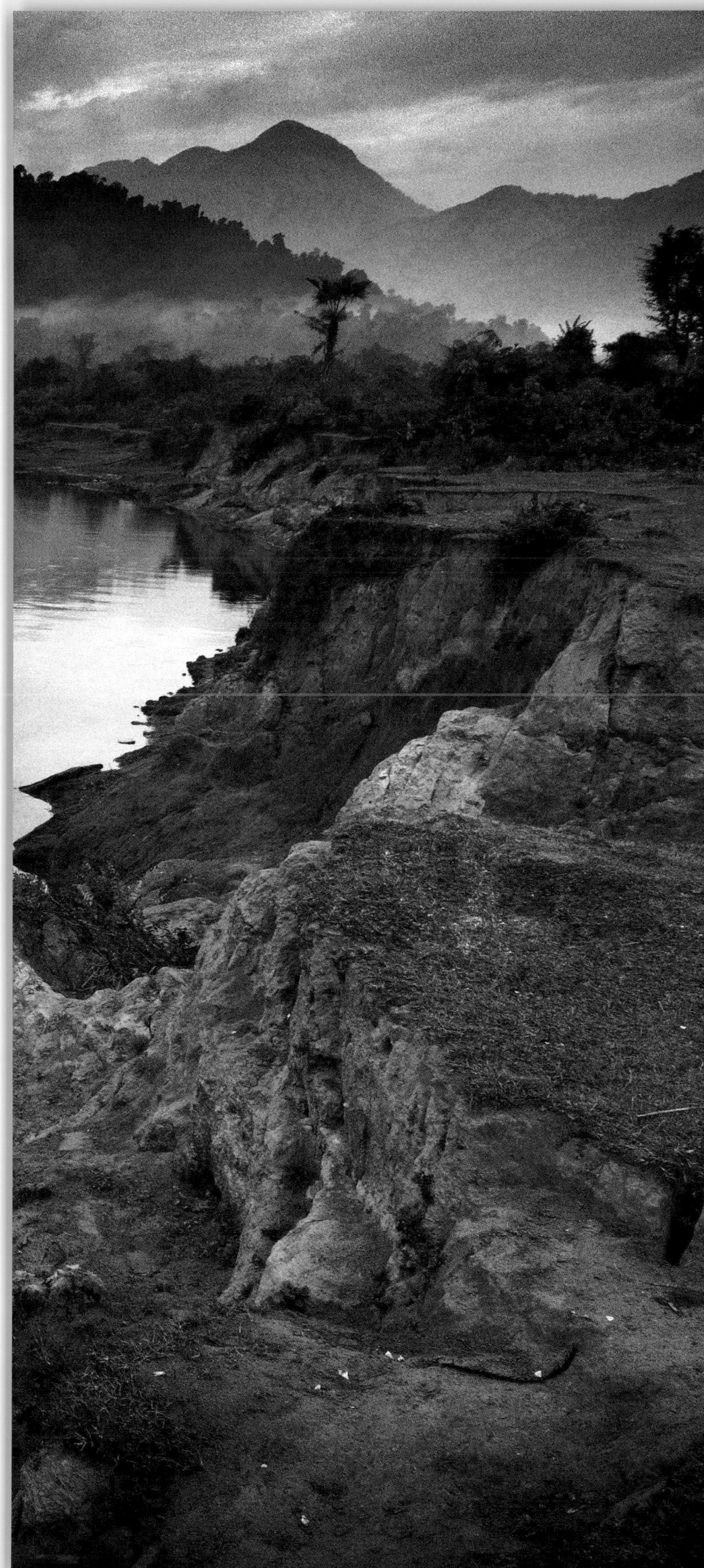

Landscape near Terain Dam village, Kachin State, 2011

In this mountain region at the foot of the so-called "Icy Mountains", or the Himalayas, the air is crisp and the water is freezing – cold but clean. As with all rivers in Myanmar, villagers gather at the riverside to fetch water, bathe, and do their laundry.

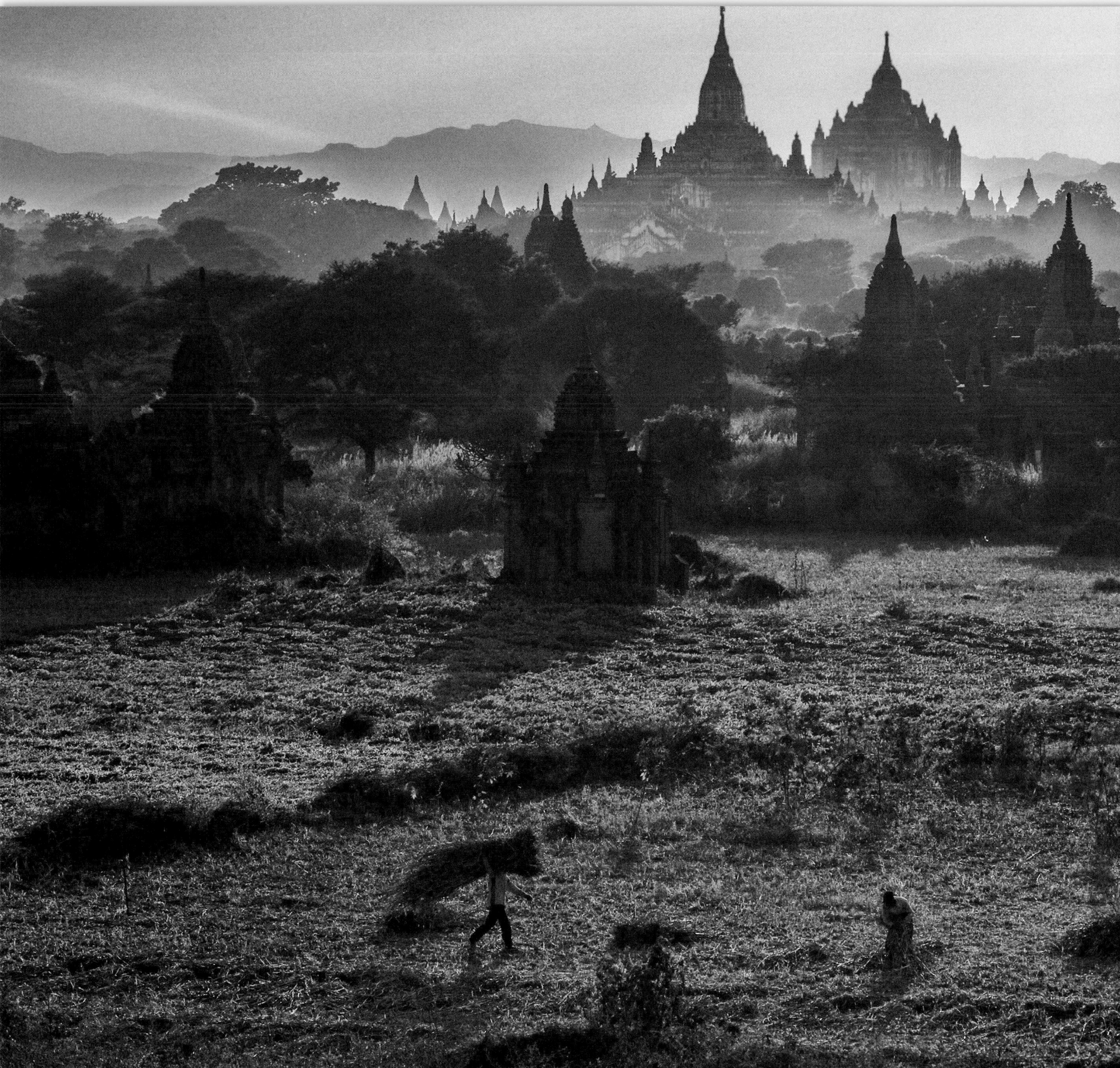

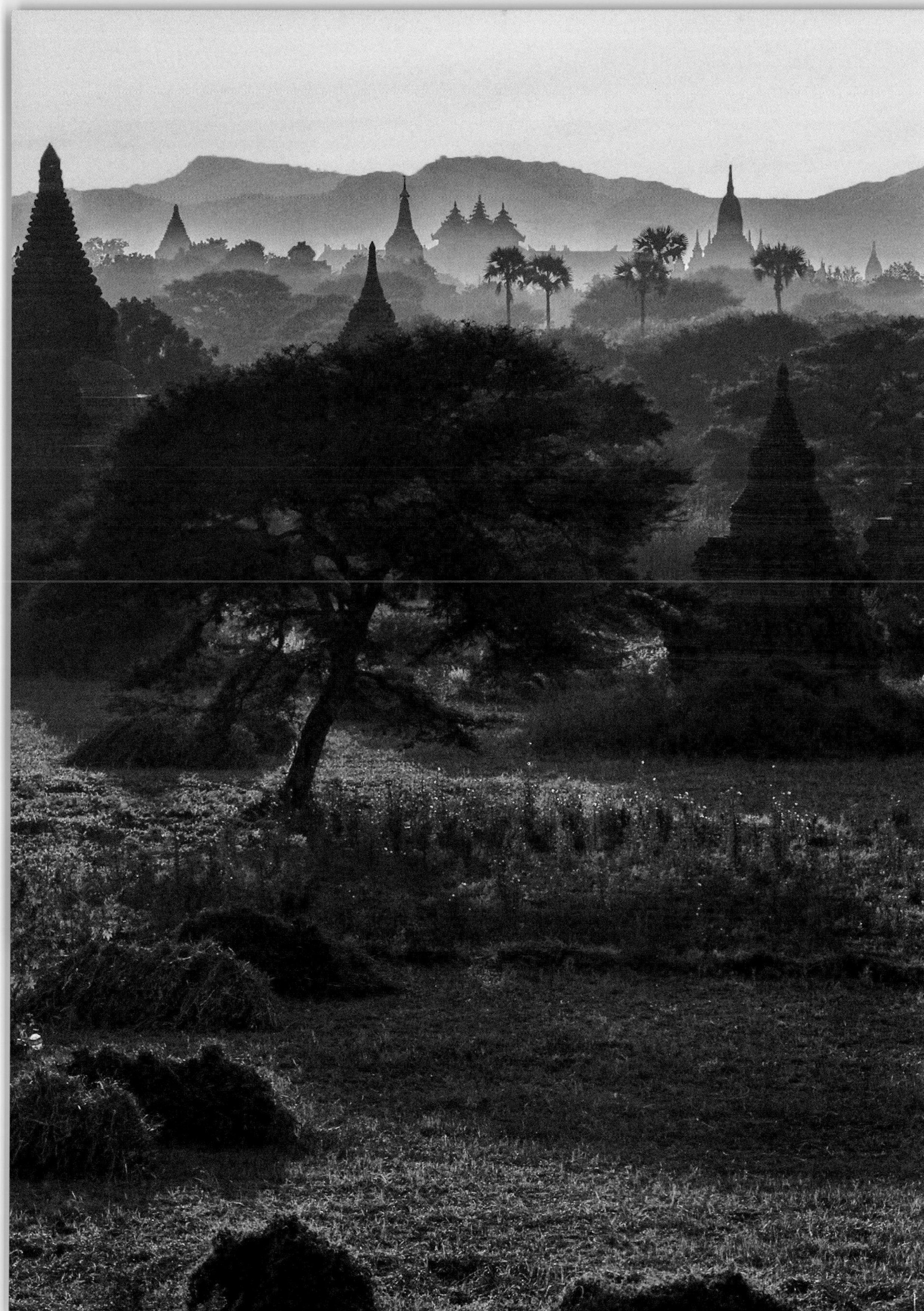

Sunset seen from the Khin Ma Kha Pagoda, Bagan, Mandalay Region, 2012

Sunsets in Bagan are spectacular from the top of any pagoda as the view stretches out over a landscape dotted with seemingly endless pagodas.

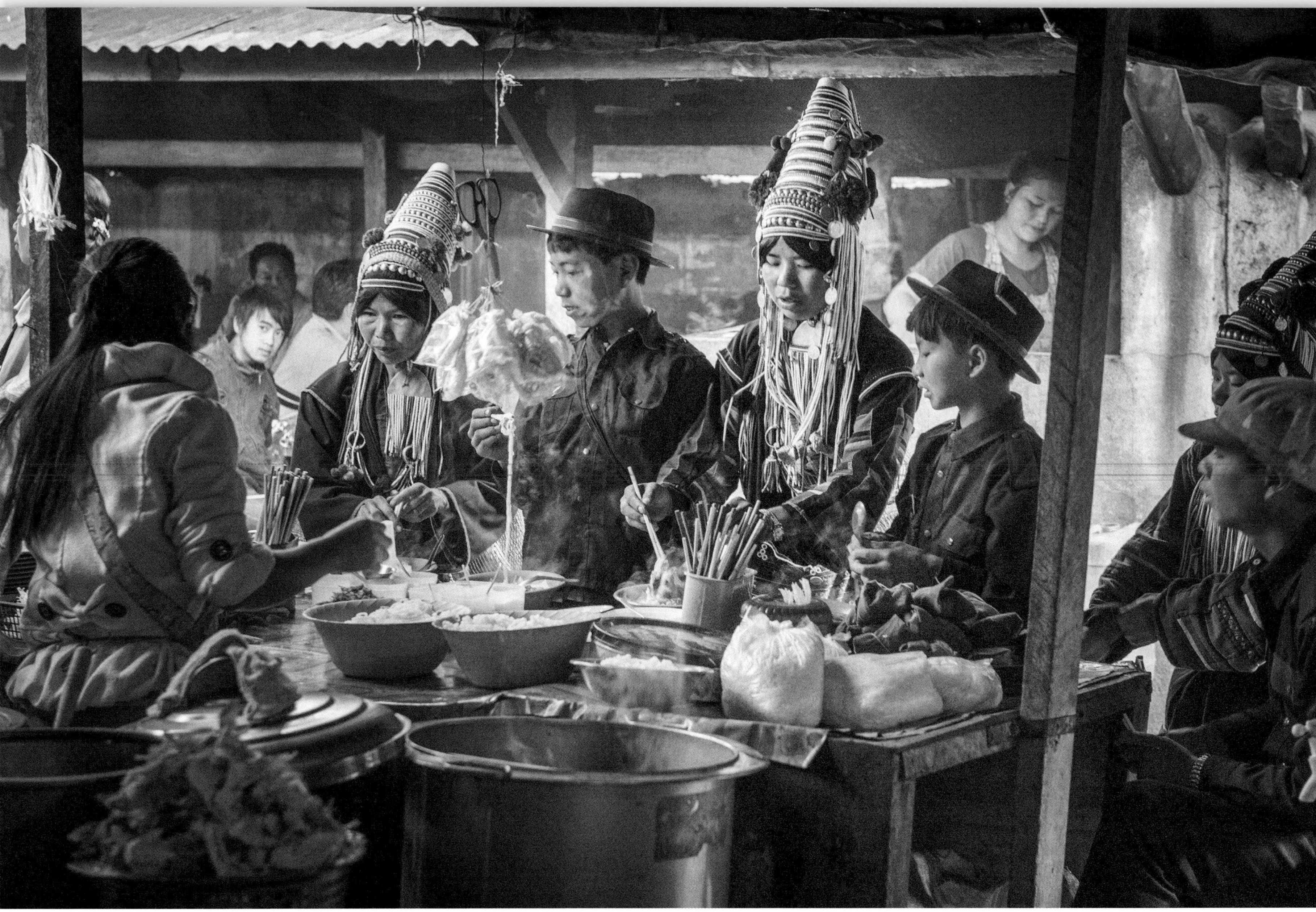

Food stall at the market, Kyaing Tong, Shan State, 2011

The Akha are one of many hill-tribes living in eastern Shan State. They often come down to the town of Kyaing Tong on market days. In the rural areas of Myanmar, ethnic costumes are still worn everyday even for work, despite their weight and irrespective of comfort.

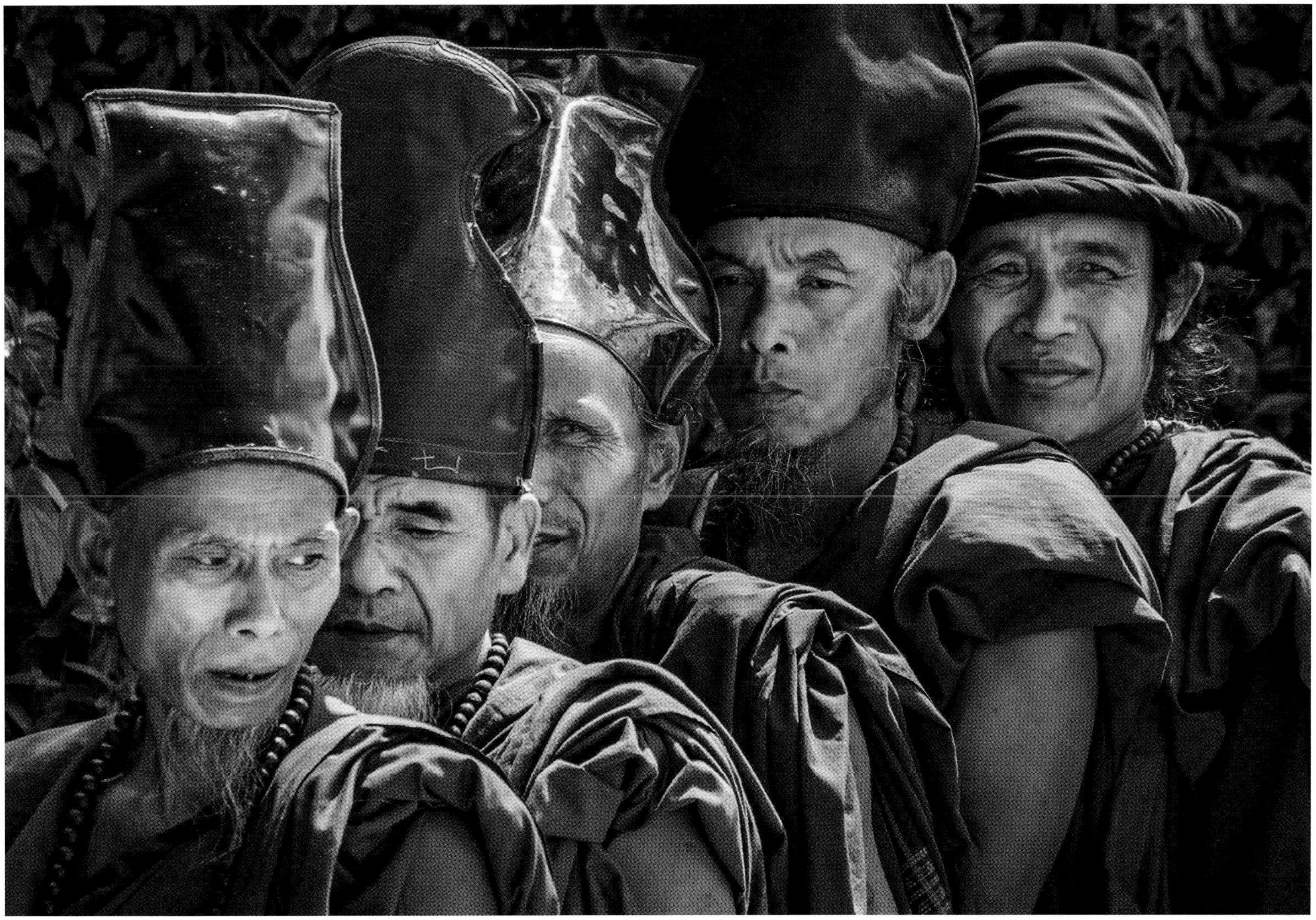

Hermits at a donation procession, Kyaiktiyo, Mon State, 2011

Held during the Festival of Lights at Golden Rock, this donation procession follows a prescribed procedure. Donors stand in line waiting to hand out their donations, which can include money and various useful items such as blankets, towels, soap, cooking oil, rice, or radios. Monks lead the procession, followed by nuns and lay nuns. The hermits are the last group to receive donations.

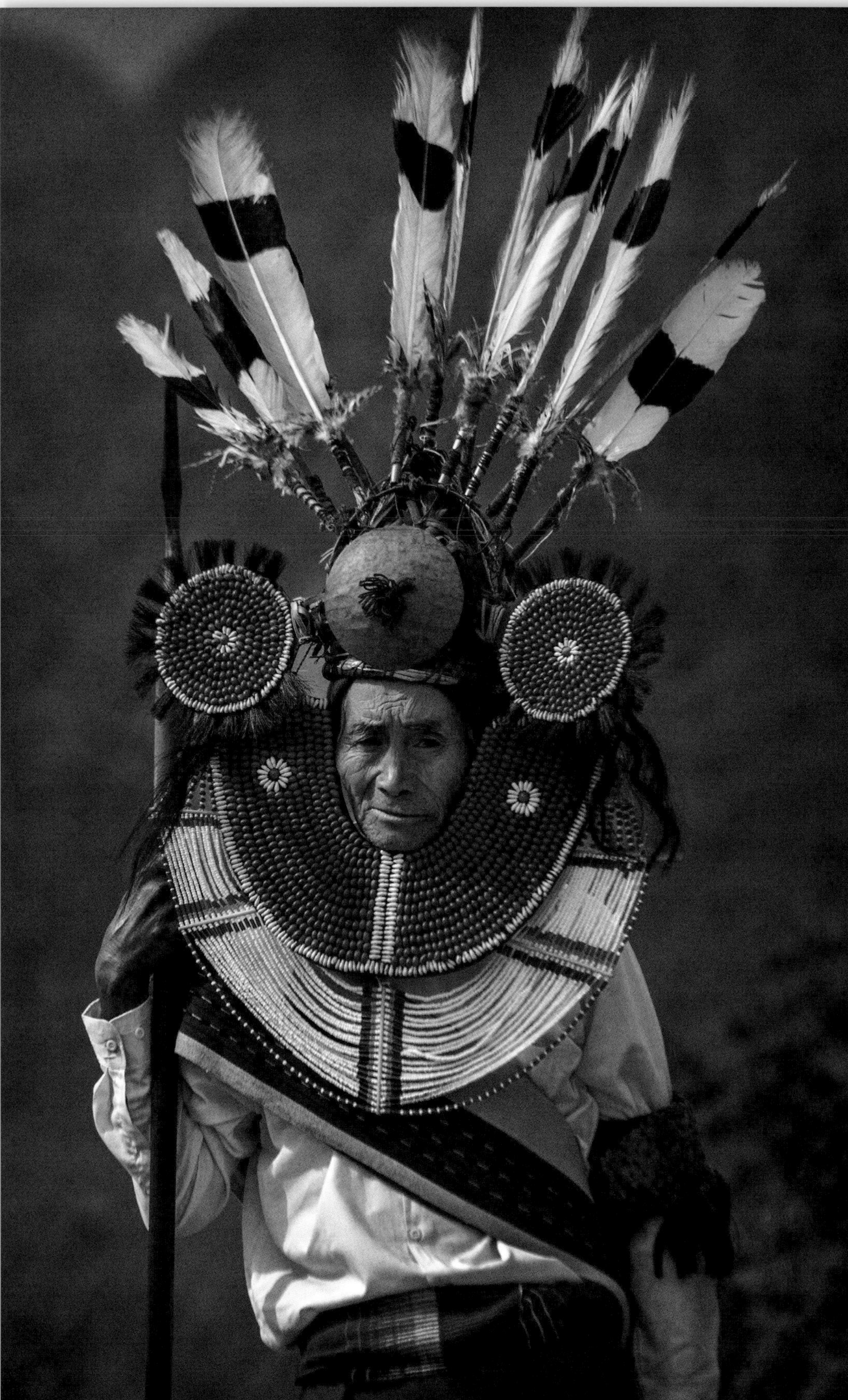

Taungkul Naga elder at the Naga festival, Layshi, Sagaing Region, 2015

The elders of the Taungkul Naga wear a special headdress made of a solid wooden plate and ornamented with beads. The size and number of hornbill feathers reflect the importance of the wearer. Assistance is usually required to don the headdress as it is very heavy and the elderly men must walk and dance with a very upright posture to ensure that it stays in place. Finely woven blankets are worn as sashes. The costume is completed by an armband, which used to be made from ivory, and an essential spear.

Opposite: Female *nat kadaw* at a *nat* festival, Lae Gyi village, Sagaing Region, 2012

A widely spread animist belief in *nat* spirits coexists with Buddhism in Myanmar. A *nat kadaw* is a medium who contacts the *nat* spirits on behalf of the common people and is paid to request assistance from the spirits in business matters or relationships.

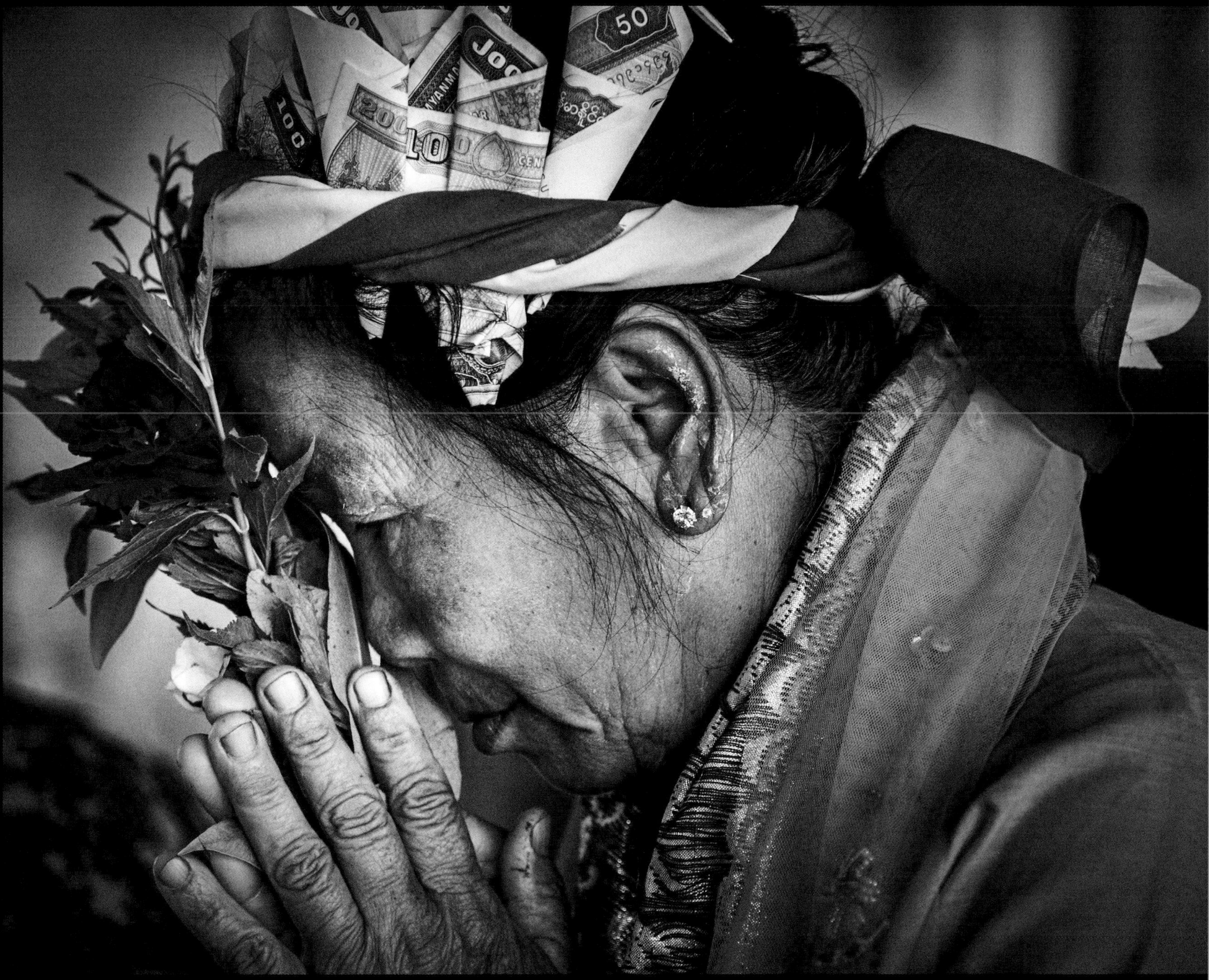

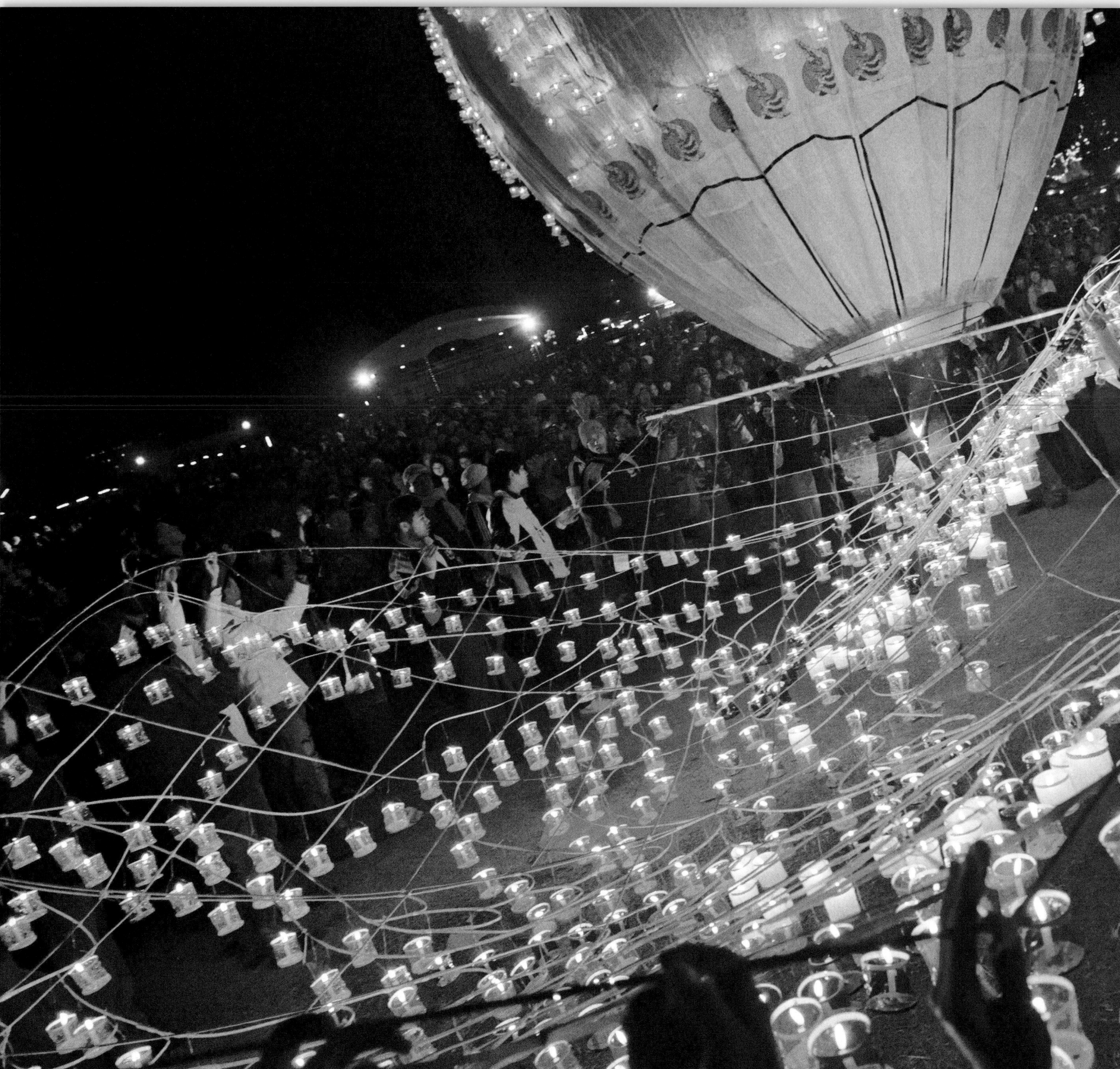

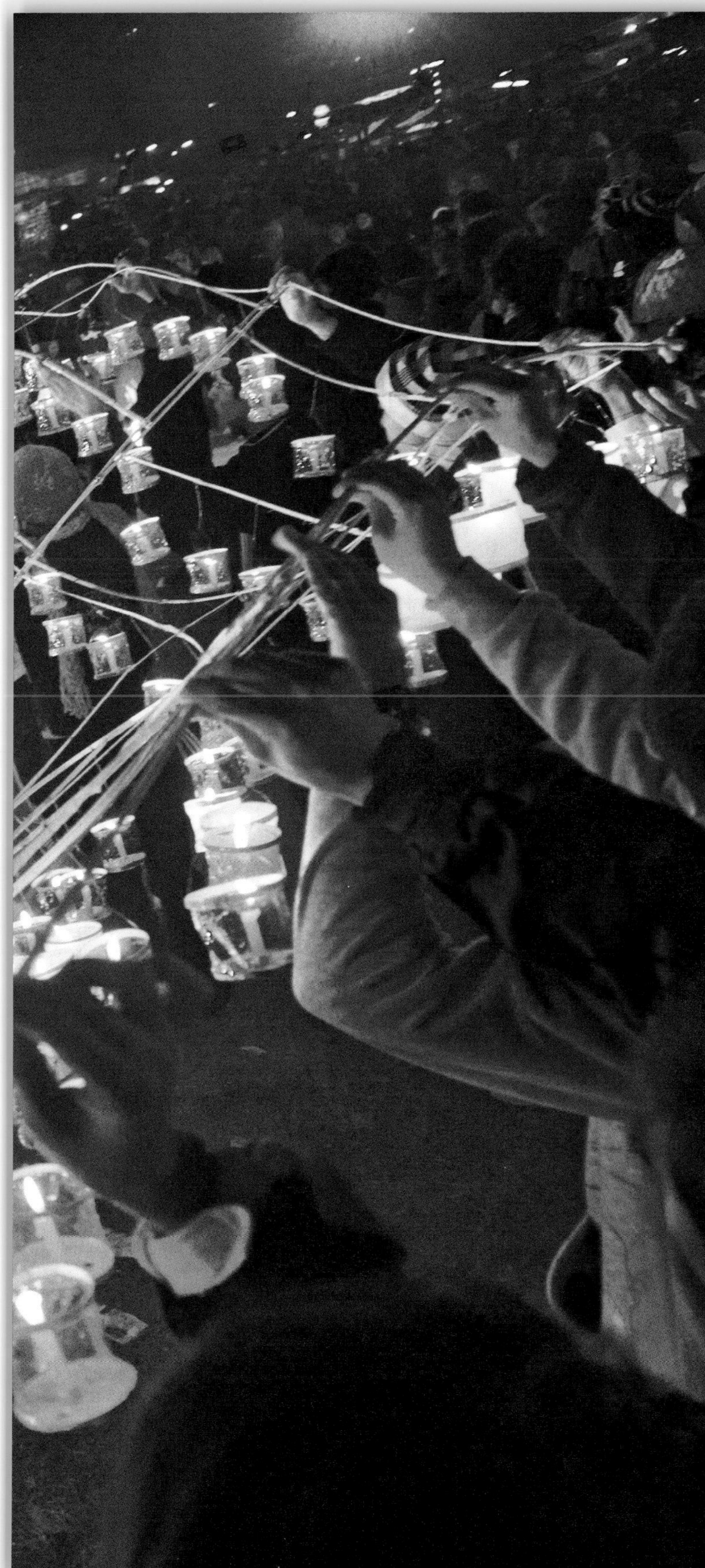

Balloon Festival, Taunggyi, Shan State, 2011

According to legend, the Buddha entered the heavenly realm to visit his mother during the time of Buddhist Lent, which coincides with the rainy season. When he returned to the earthly realm at the end of the rains, lights were lit to guide him safely home. In Myanmar, the end of Lent is marked by the full moon each October and celebrated with Thadingyut, or the Festival of Lights. I found myself wanting to be in a hundred places at once during the festival as every region, city, village, and pagoda celebrates the event with its own unique tradition. In some areas, small candles are placed in handmade paper cups and floated away upon a lake or river. In others, candles are arranged on the ground in artistic patterns such as a Buddhist *mudra* or even a gigantic Buddha statue that can only be seen properly from the air. In Taunggyi, a balloon contest is held and the tail of each balloon is hung with candles in small containers made of translucent paper. It takes months to construct these balloons and their luminous tails. Many hands are also needed to ensure a smooth take-off, which can easily go wrong. If all goes well, the night sky is filled with lights.

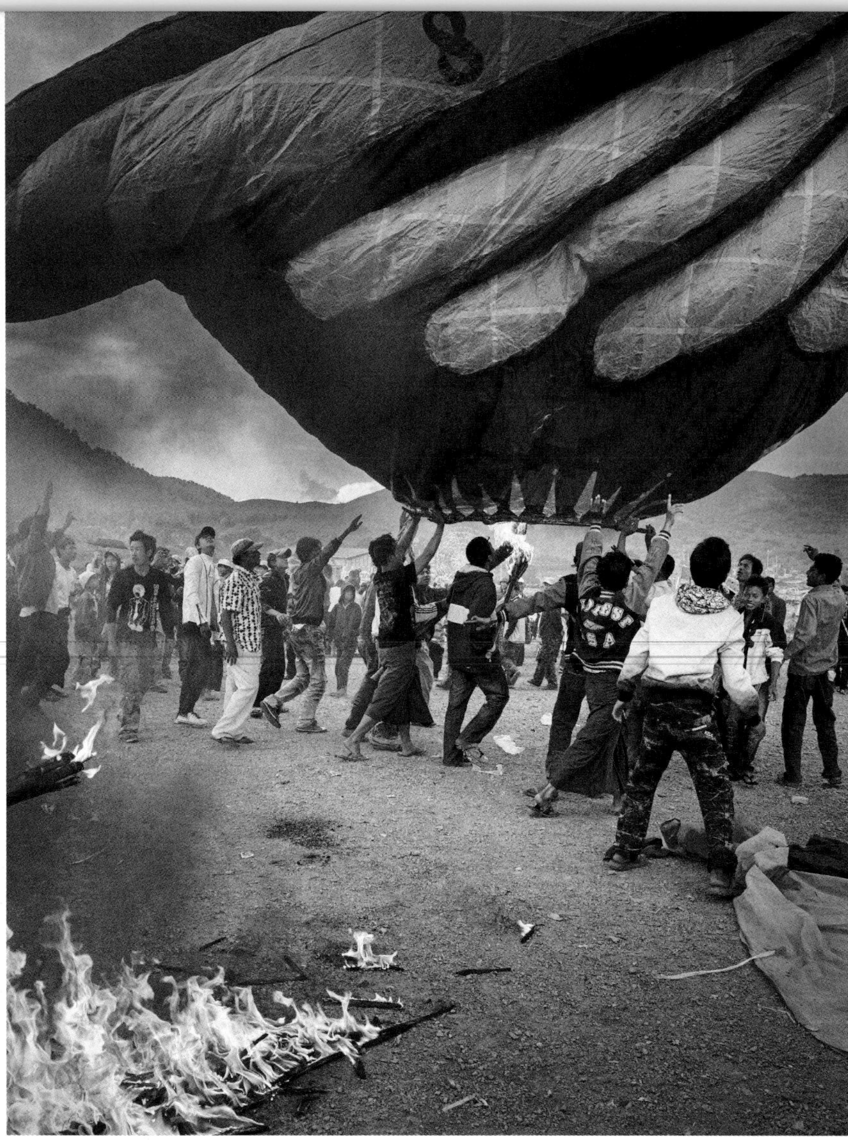

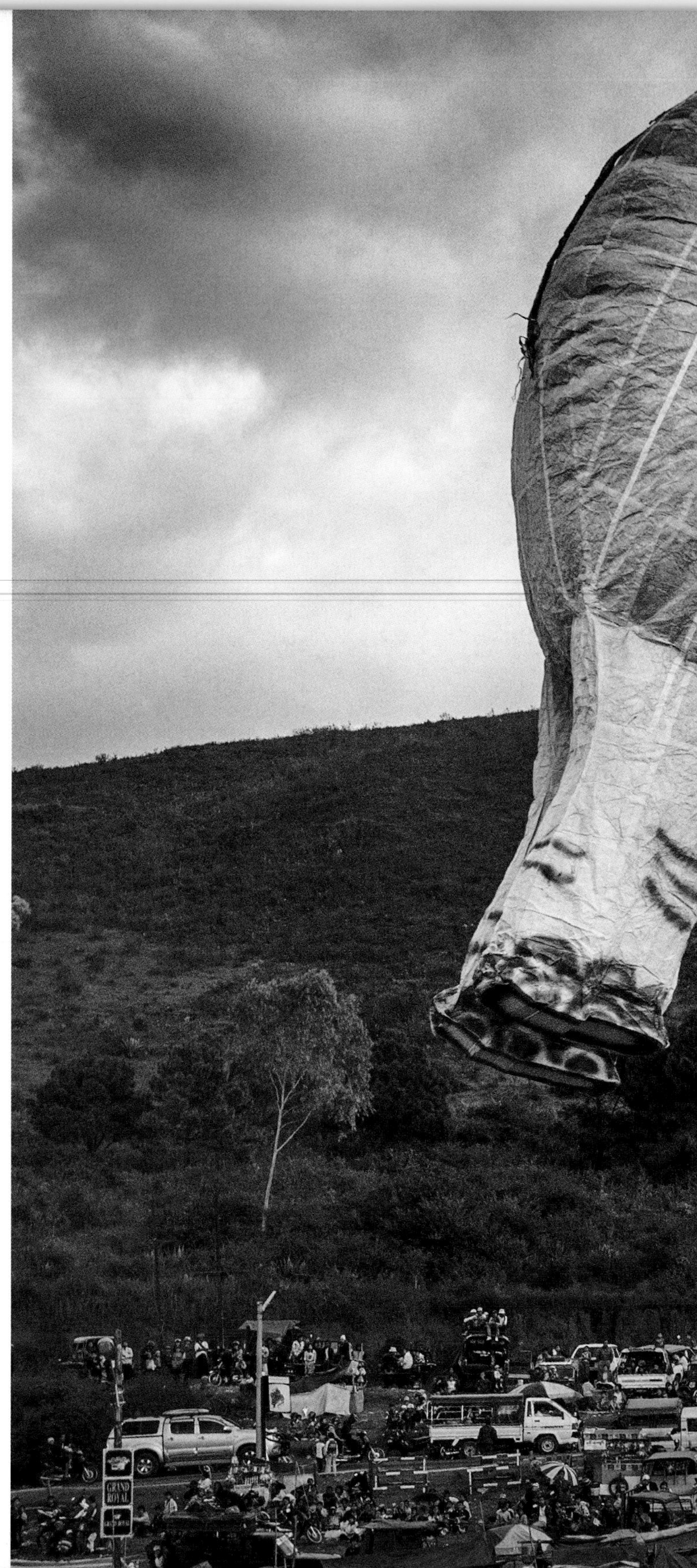

ABOVE AND RIGHT: BALLOON FESTIVAL, TAUNGGYI, SHAN STATE, 2011

In Taunggyi, Thadingyut, or the Festival of Lights, is celebrated with a balloon festival. Huge paper balloons are crafted over many months and take the form of various animal shapes such as elephants, zebras, dinosaurs, pigs, rabbits, or birds. The criteria for winning are the aesthetic appearance of the balloon, good teamwork during lift-off, and flight capability.

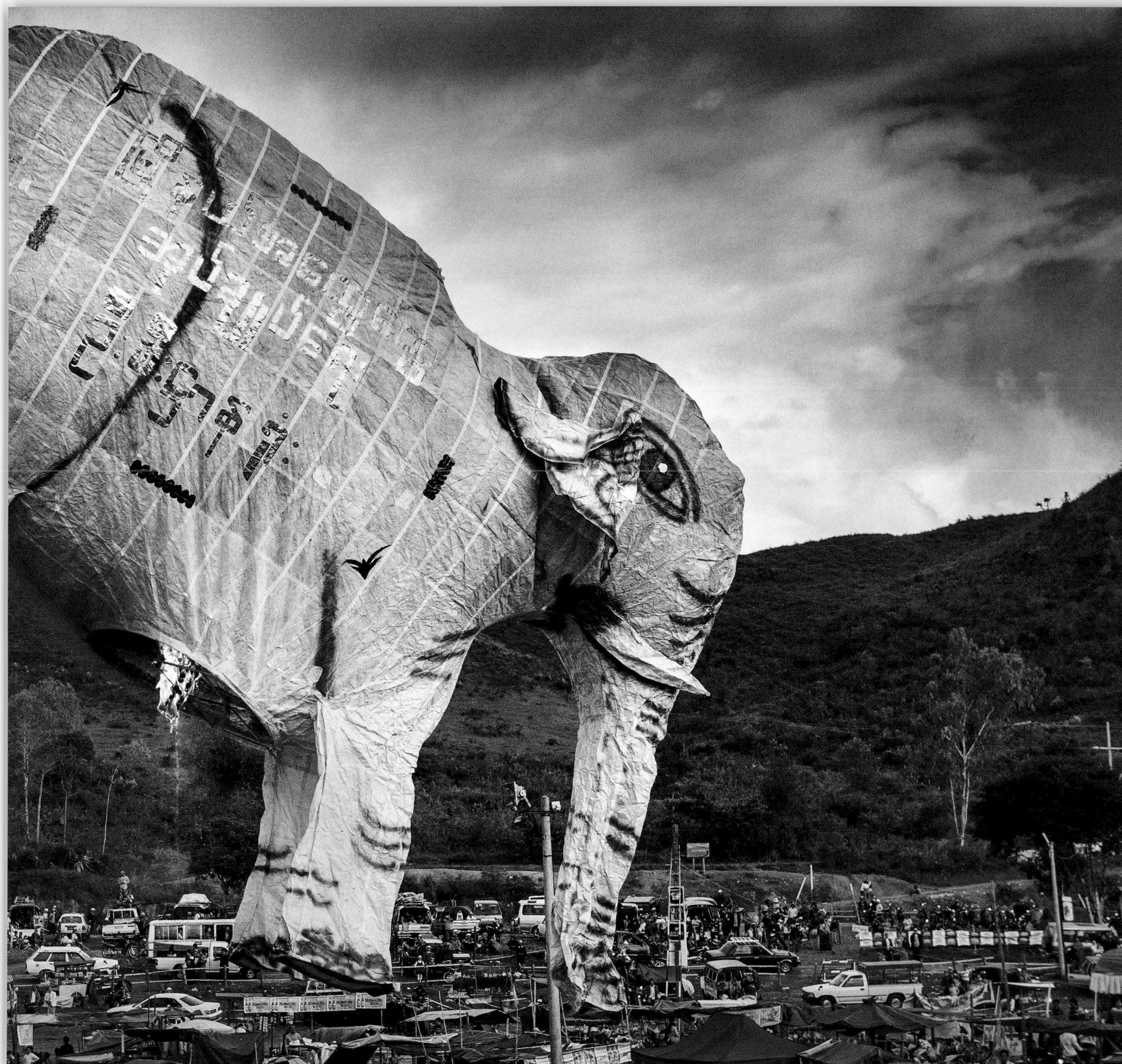

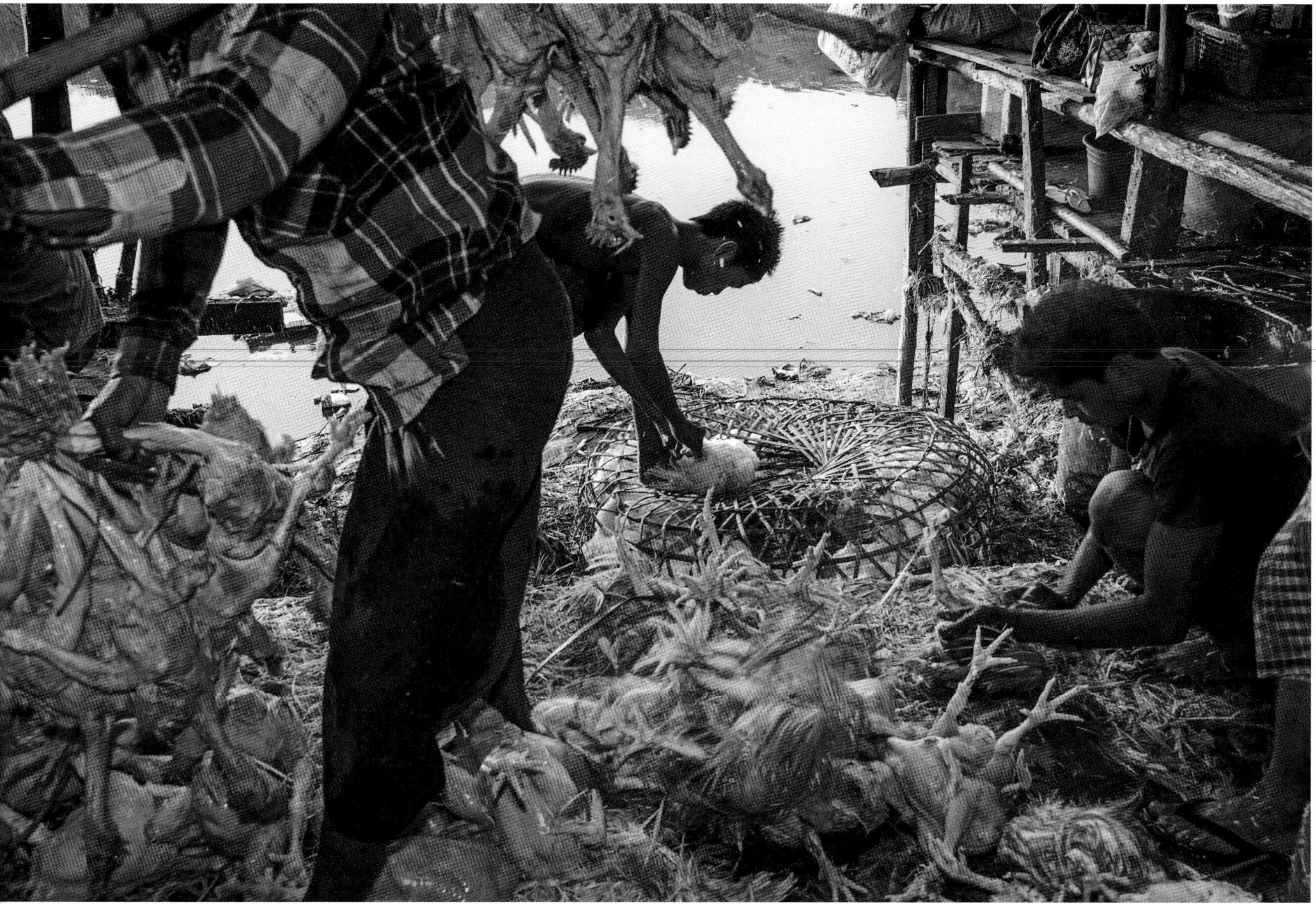

Chicken market, Yangon, 2013

Every morning thousands of chickens are delivered to this market to be slaughtered, plucked, and sold wholesale – chicken is an inexpensive staple meat in Myanmar. The workers are usually non-Buddhist and slaughtering methods vary depending on whether they are Hindu or Muslim.

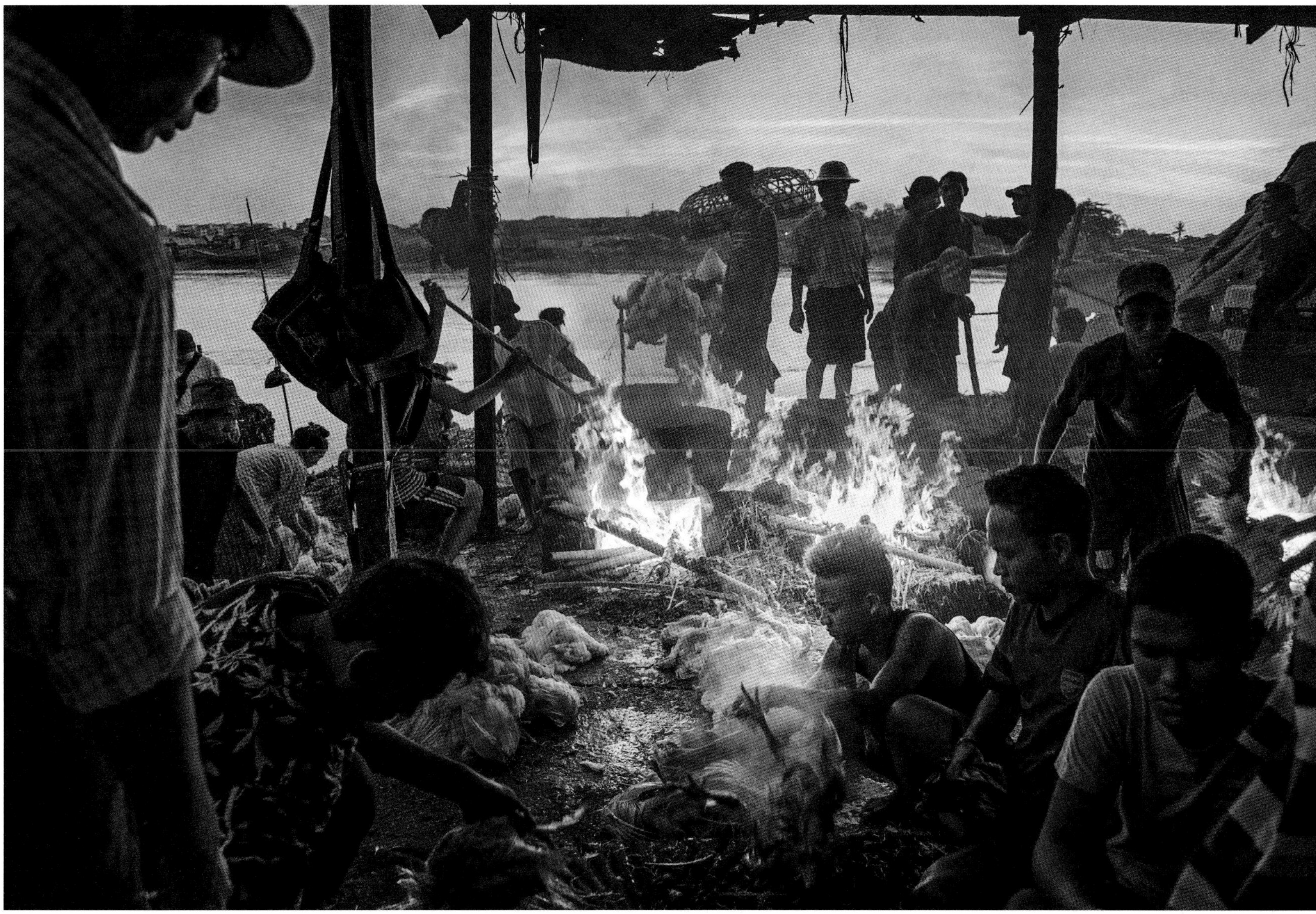

Plucking chickens at the chicken market, Yangon, 2013

In order to make plucking chickens easier, the dead chickens are dipped into pots of boiling water so that the feathers will come off more readily.

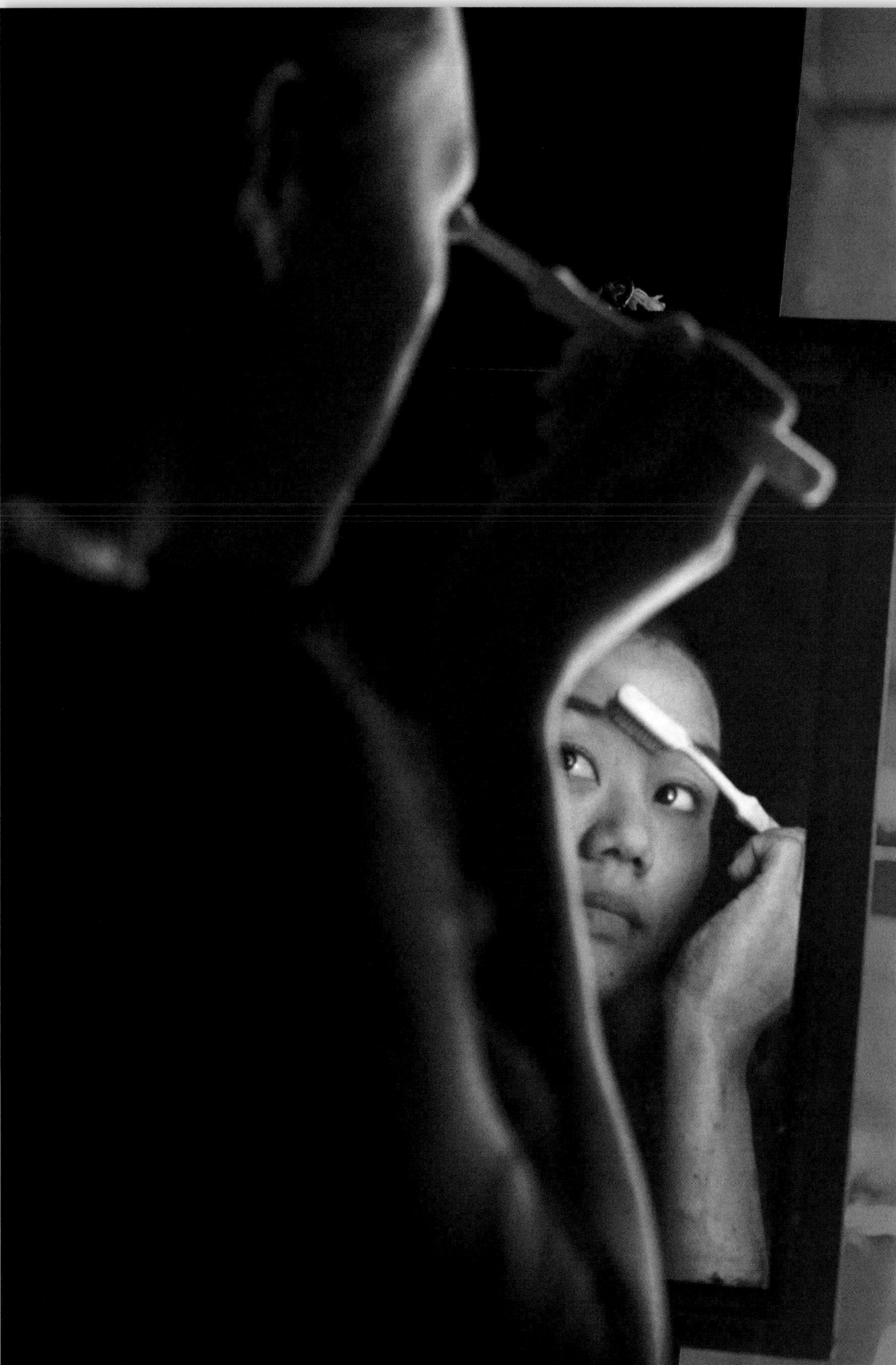

Left: Girl applying *thanaka*, Mindat, Chin State, 2013

Many people, especially women and children, put *thanaka* paste on their faces. Ground from the bark of the *thanaka* tree, the paste protects against the sun and also acts as a form of makeup. Applying the paste can be considered an art form as some users decorate their faces with intricate and elaborate patterns.

Opposite: Women doing laundry in the Ayeyarwady River, Monywa, Sagaing Region, 2015

To avoid the heat, women bring their laundry down to the river in the early morning or evening. This picture was taken in the early morning – my favourite time to go out photographing in Myanmar.

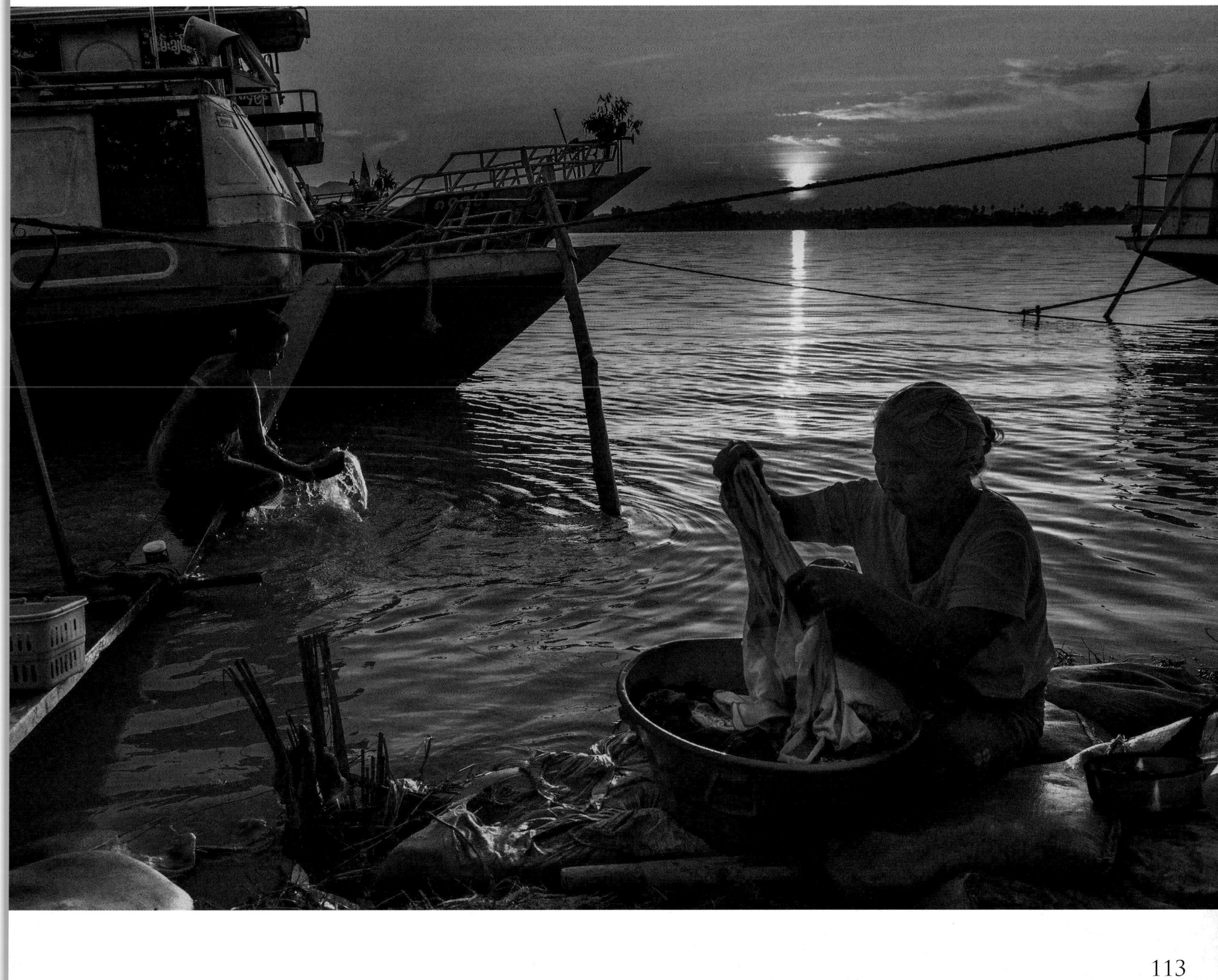

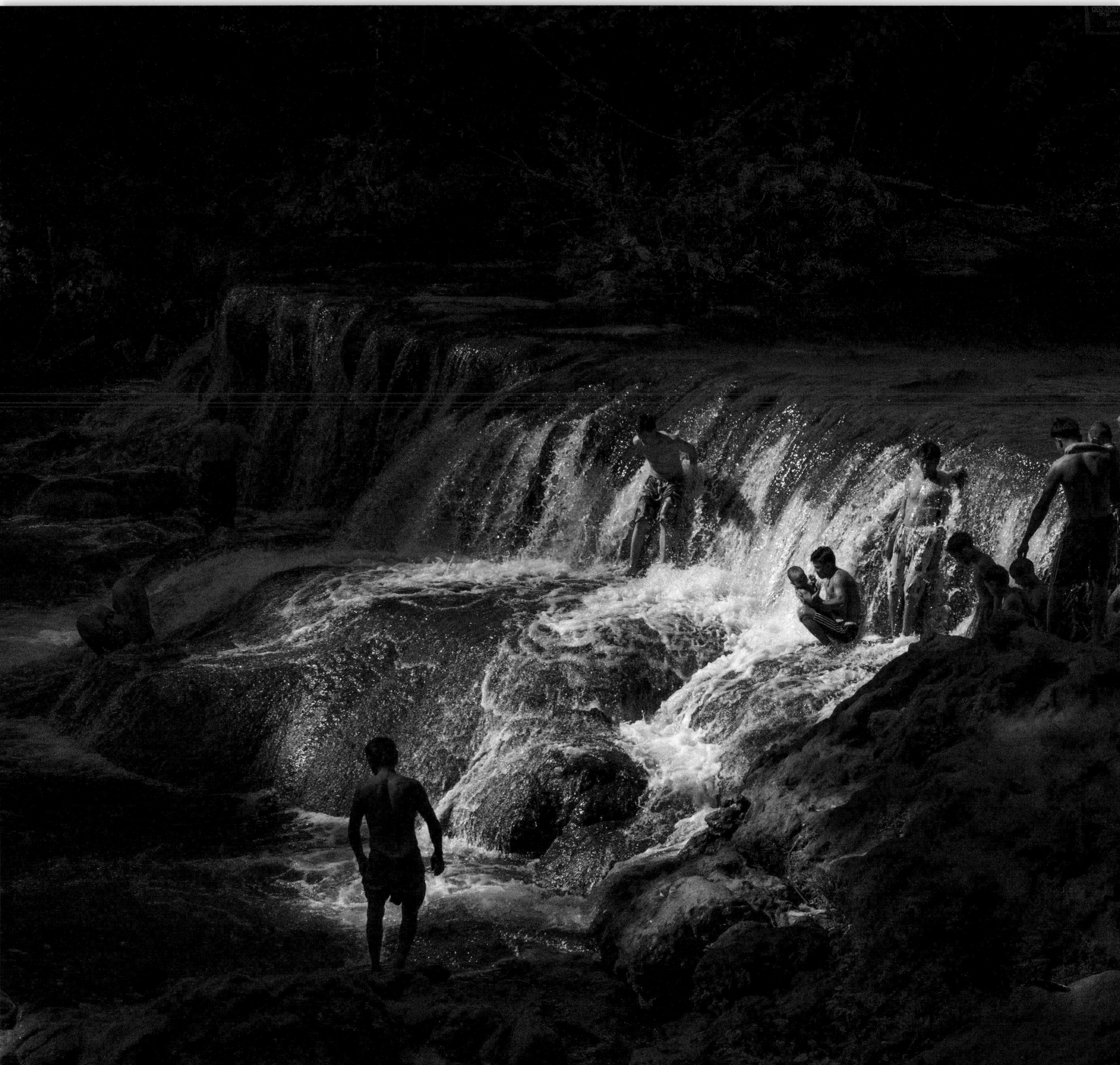

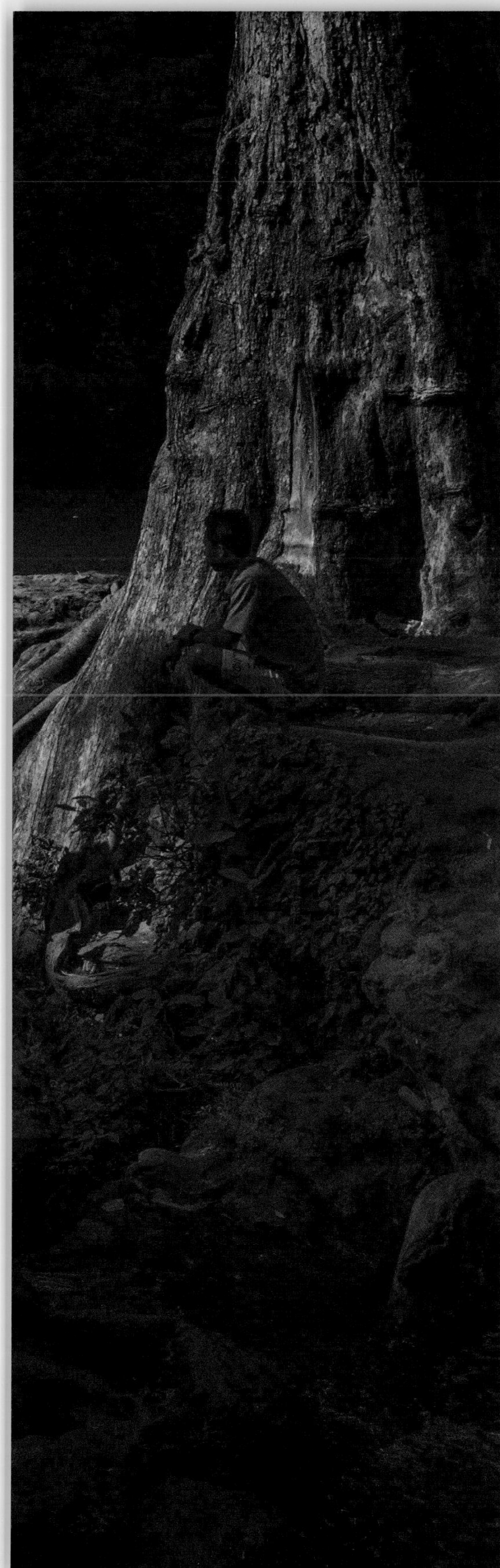

Left: At the Pwe Kauk Falls, Pyin Oo Lwin, Mandalay Region, 2012

This is a popular spot for people to come with friends and family to cool off and have fun on weekends or during their free time. The falls are located near the town of Pyin Oo Lwin, the former British hill-station of May Myo.

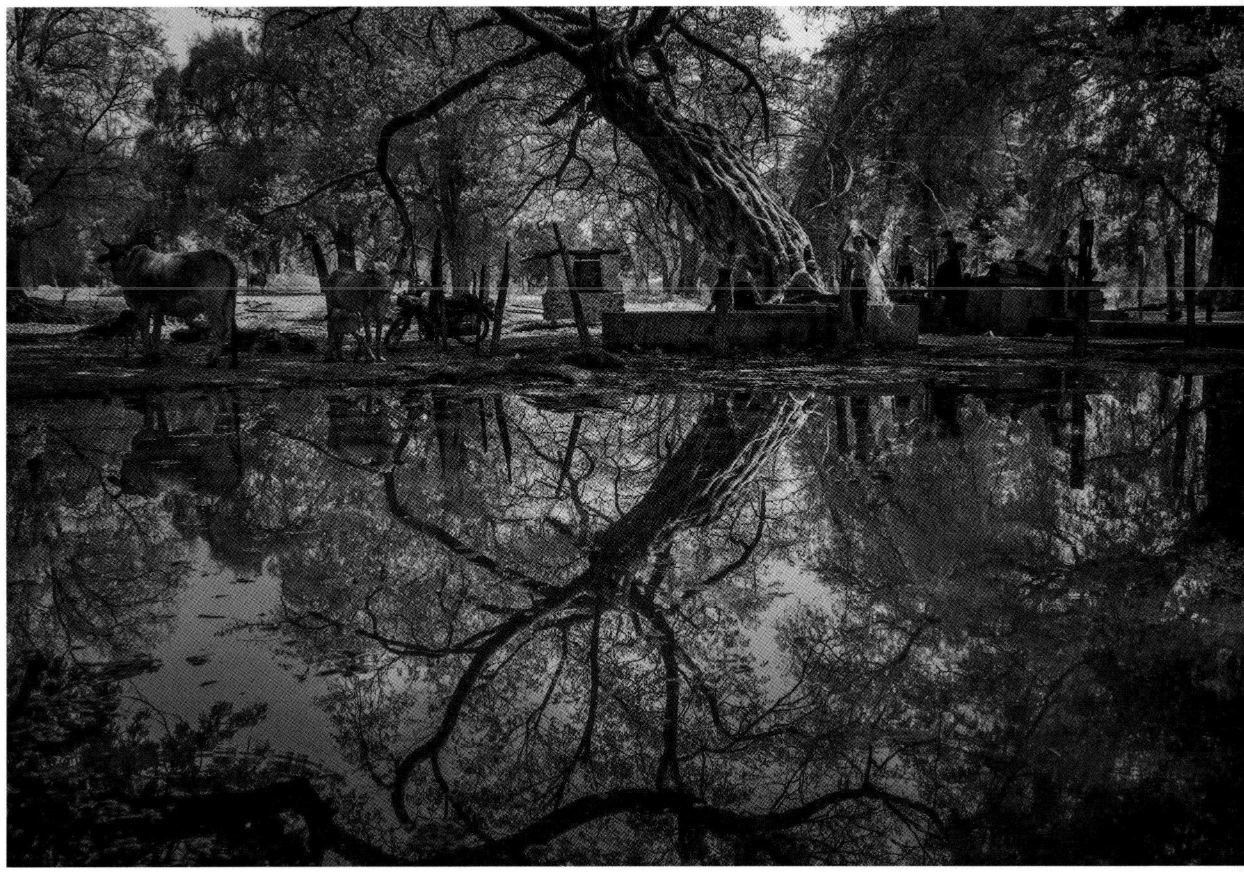

Daw Kattapha Park, Sagaing Region, 2013

Access to water is essential, whether it comes from a river, lake, or public well. Since there is no privacy when taking a bucket shower at the well, the *longyi* (sarong) is always kept on. This well is surrounded by magnificent trees that create shade and a peaceful atmosphere.

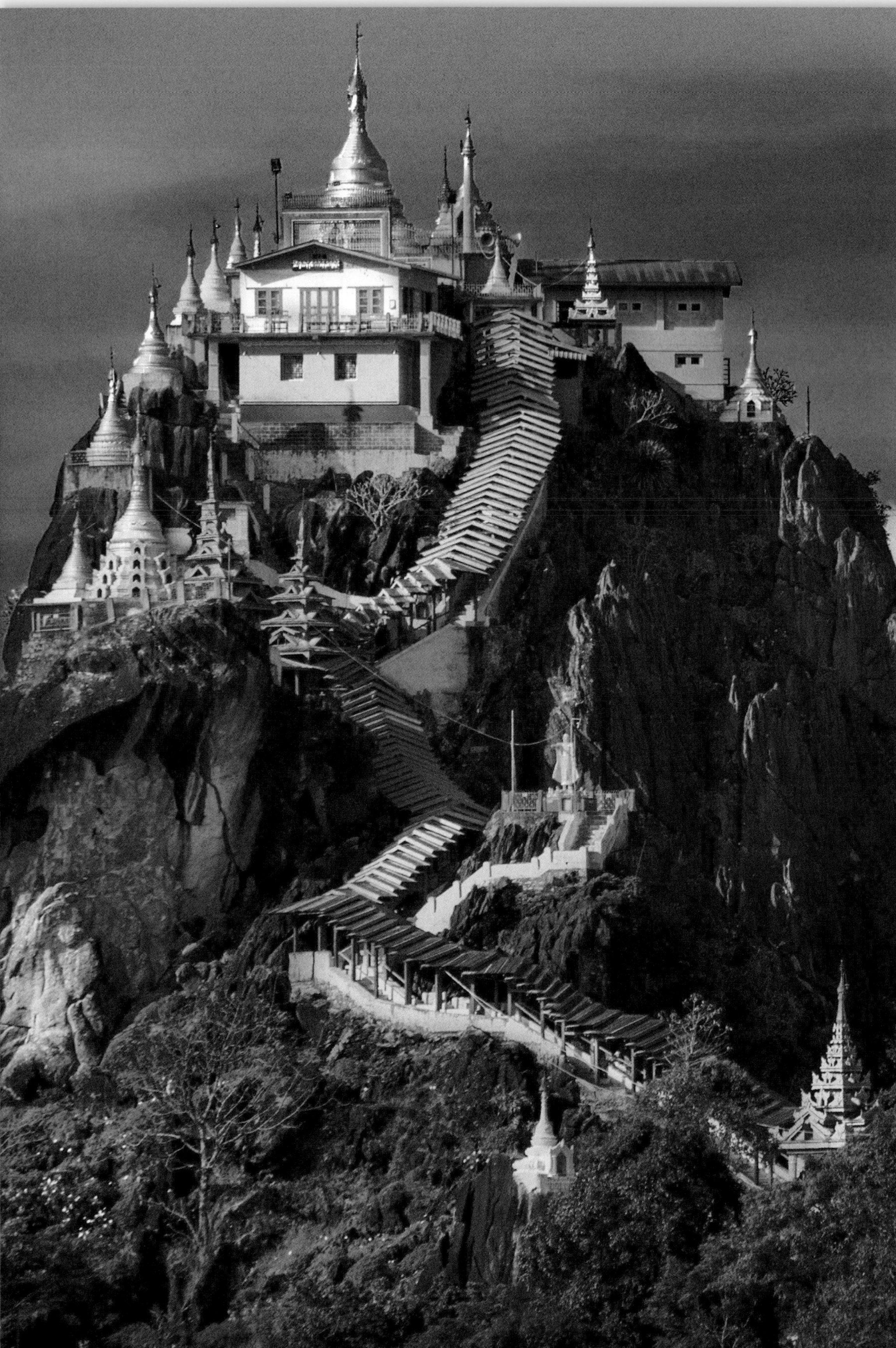

Kyang Pay That Pagoda, Kyang Pay That village, Mandalay Region, 2013

As many pagodas are built on top of hills and mountains, a visit often involves an upwards hike. In most places, covered staircases lead visitors to the summit.

Opposite: Early morning scene on the Chindwin River, Sagaing Region, 2010

On extended trips along the Chindwin River, the landscape is ever changing. Mornings are especially beautiful when the fog starts to lift.

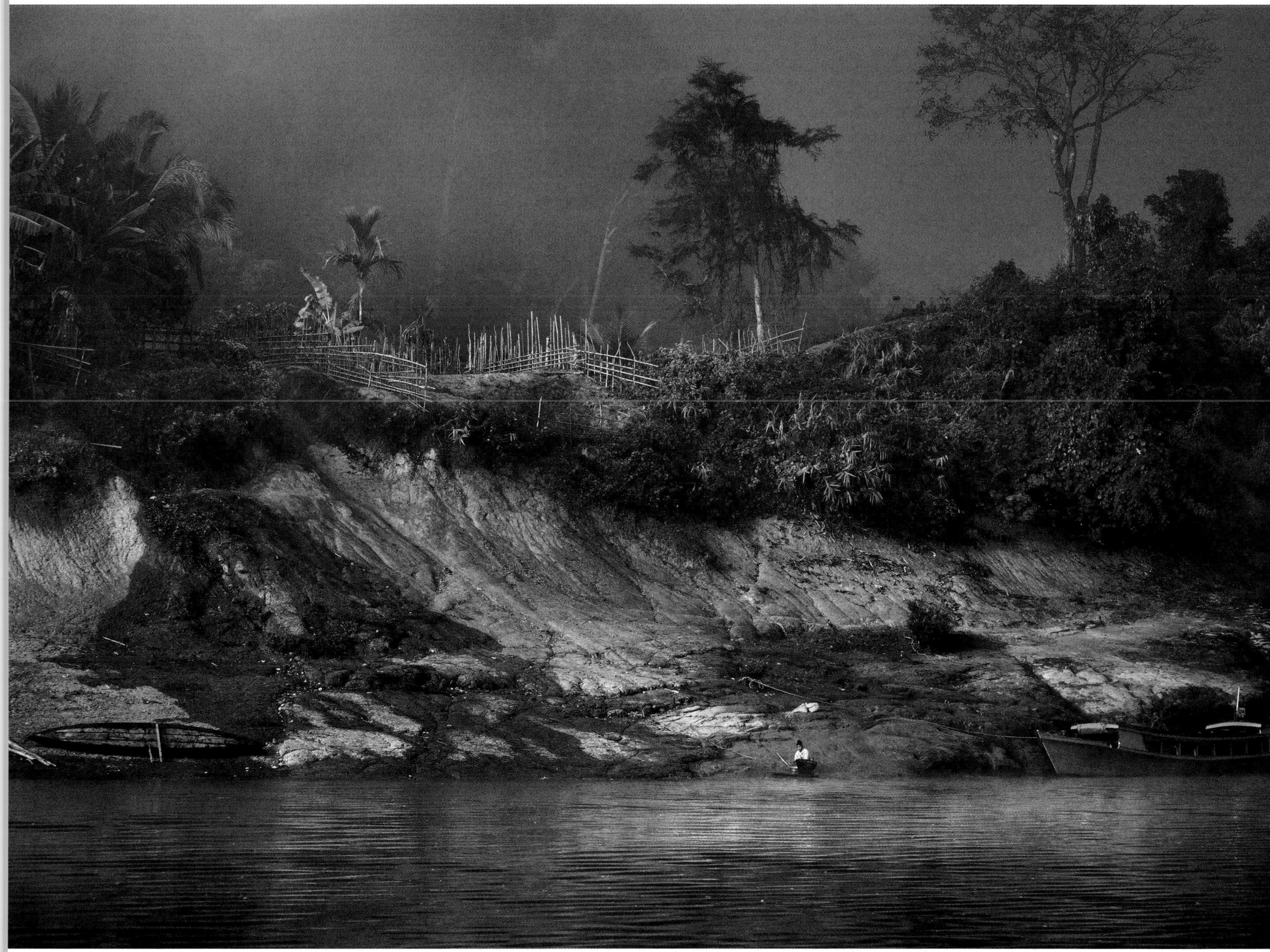

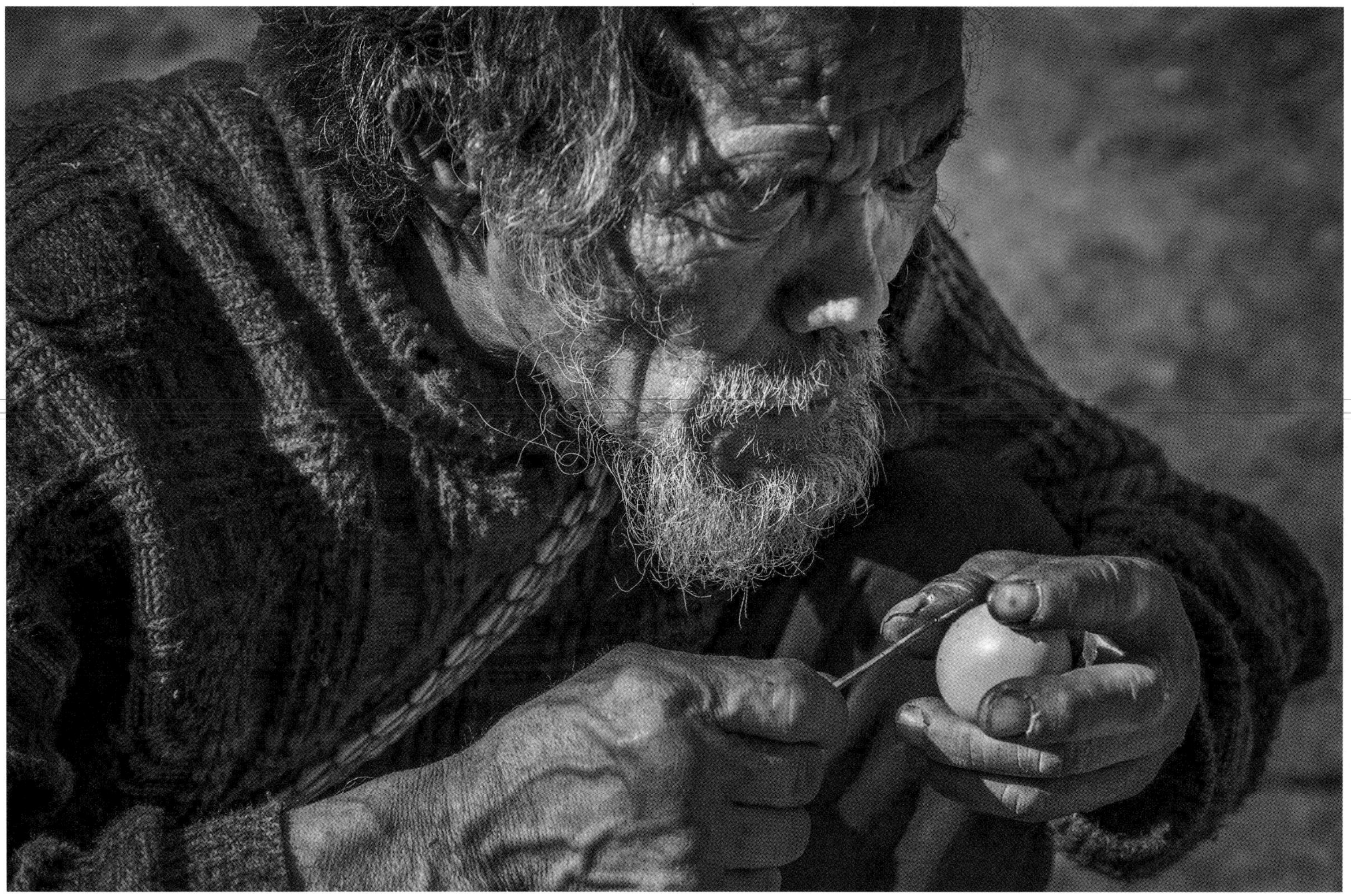

Astrologer Nein Aung, Mindat, Chin State, 2013

Many decisions in Myanmar, both political and individual, are made with the help of astrologers. Major national policies have been implemented following astrological consultations, such as the introduction of new currency denominations, a shift from driving on the left-hand side of the road to the right-hand side, and the decision to move the country's capital city to Naypitaw. On a personal level, astrologers help with business decisions, give advice on marriages, or select new names for sickly children to encourage their recovery. Various astrologers use different means and tools. In this case, Nein Aung blows out a raw egg and then places a hot stick on the shell to crack it; his advice will be based on the pattern of the cracks.

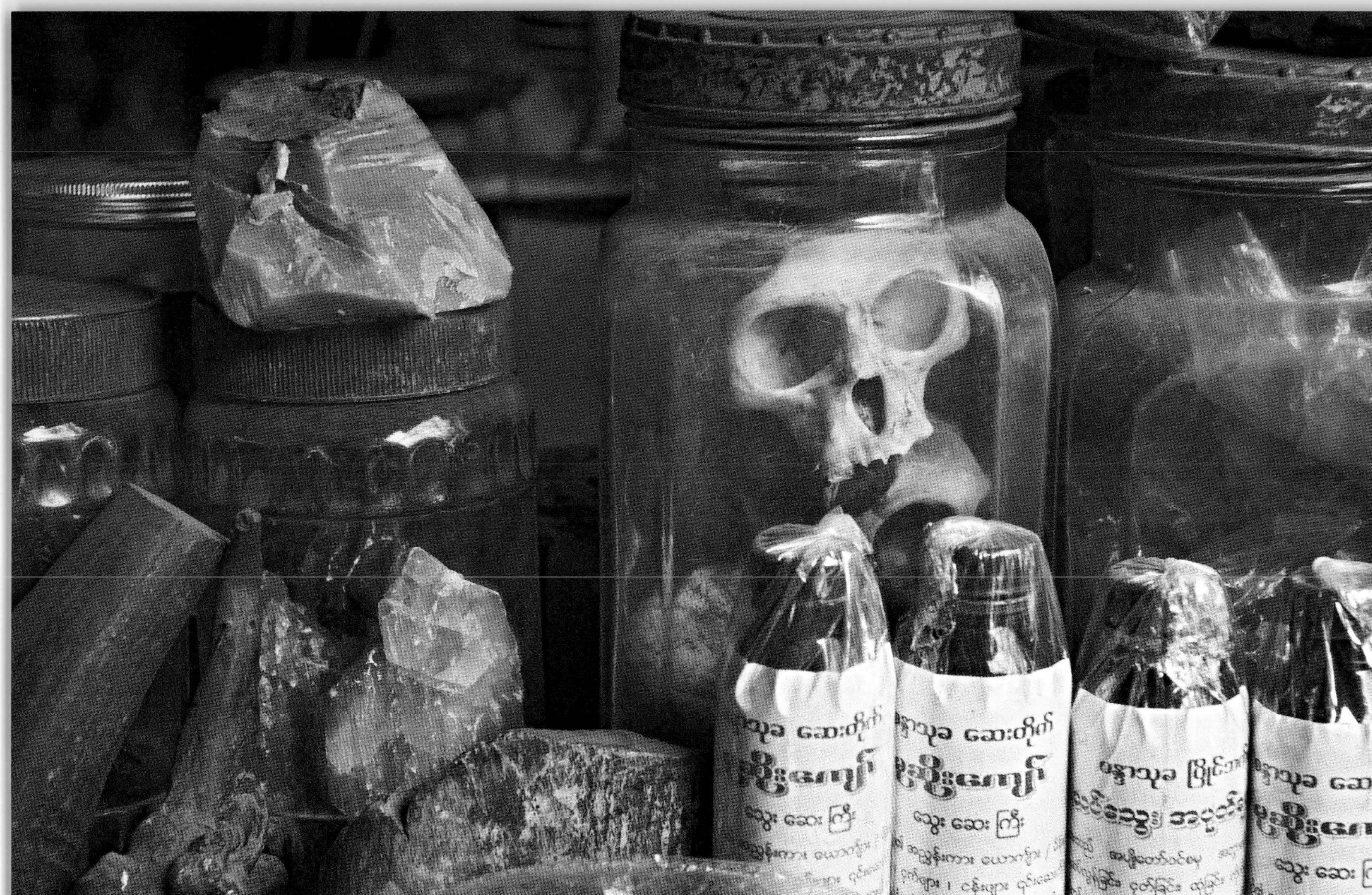

Traditional medicine stall at a market in Chauk, Magway Region, 2013

Dried plants, animal parts, and minerals are integral to traditional medicine. Snake skins, bear bladder, caterpillars, and all kinds of bones used in medicinal treatments are for sale at local markets.

Street-side book stall, Yangon, 2012

Until the economic sanctions imposed upon Myanmar were relaxed in 2012, it was very difficult to obtain foreign reading material. People in Myanmar love to read so the books and magazines that were available had long lives and were bought and sold multiple times. As can be seen in this photograph, street-side book vendors offer all types of written material, from a manual for a long-outdated software programme to a more recent German magazine (probably left behind by a tourist) with the cover headline *Alle Macht den Frauen*, or All Power to the Women. With sanctions now lifted and the local press much freer than before, a new bookstore opens almost every month.

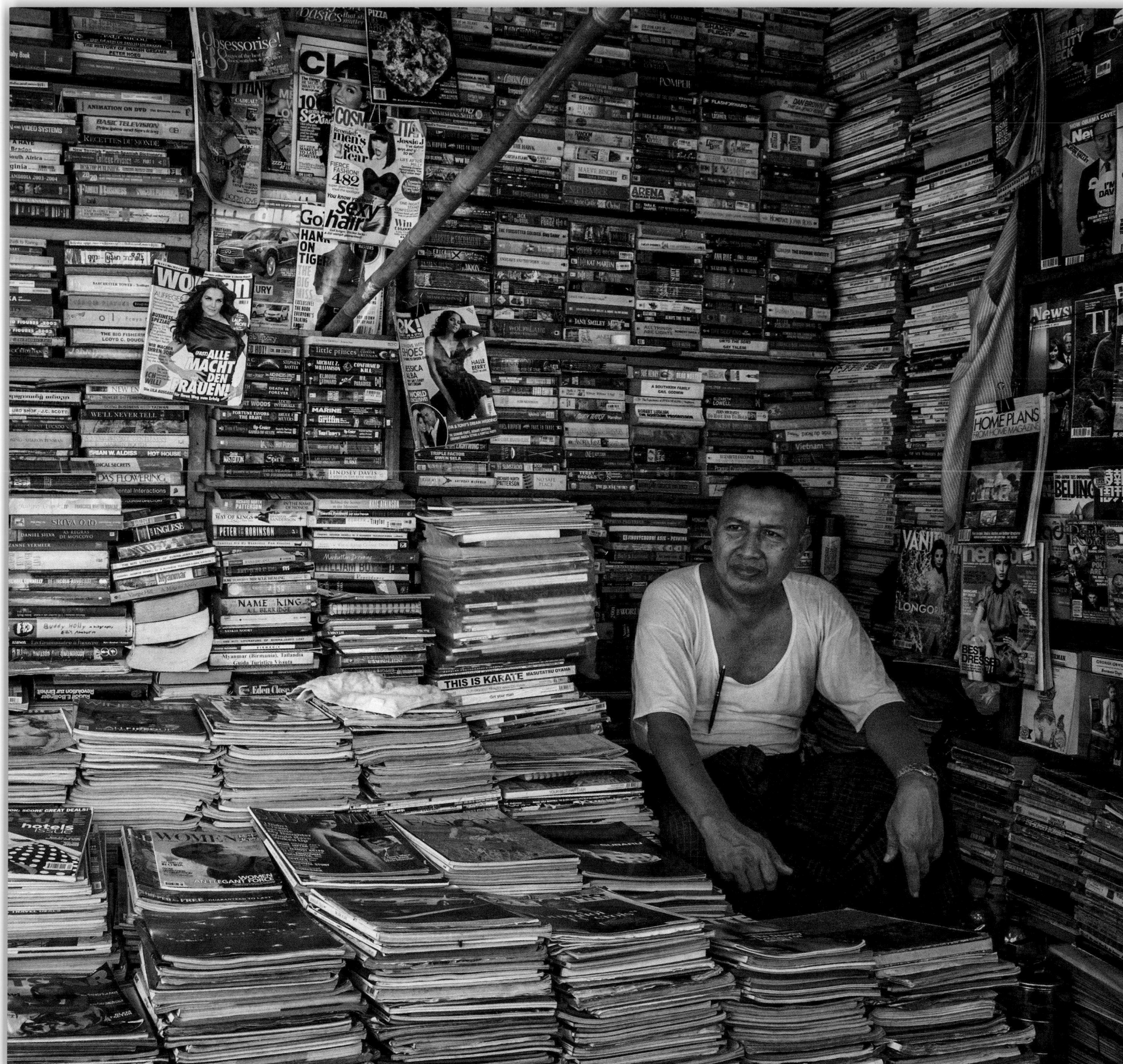
ALLE MACHT DEN FRAUEN!
sexy hair
HOME PLANS FROM HOME MAGAZINE
THIS IS KARATE MASUTATSU OYAMA
BEIJING
ANIMATION ON DVD
BASIC TELEVISION
RECETTES DU MONDE
ARENA
JANE SMILEY
LINDSEY DAVIS
PETER ROBINSON
Eden Close
Vietnam

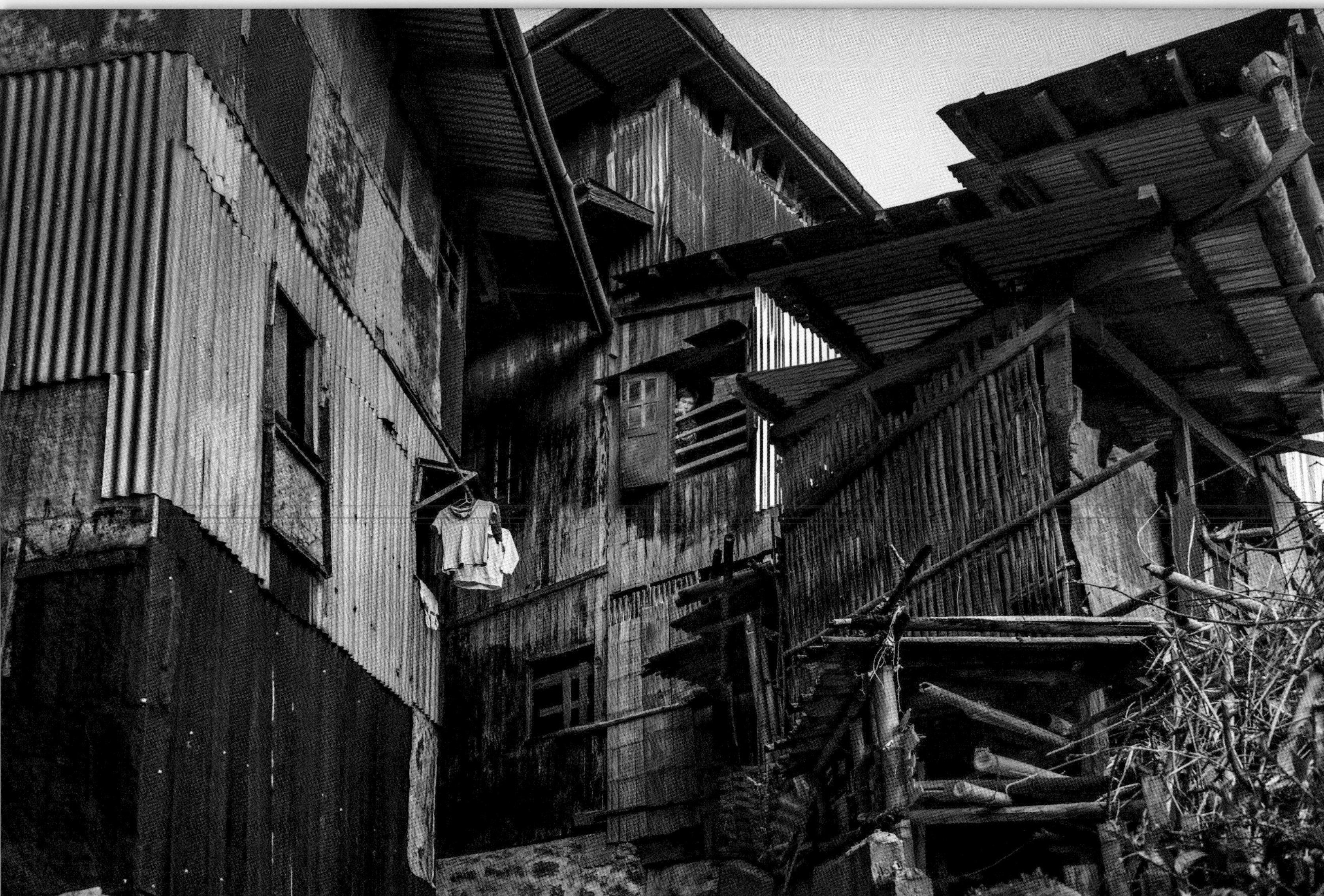

Houses in Namshan, Shan State, 2013

Traditional houses in the countryside are usually made only of natural materials. Those who can afford it now use corrugated iron sheets as building material.

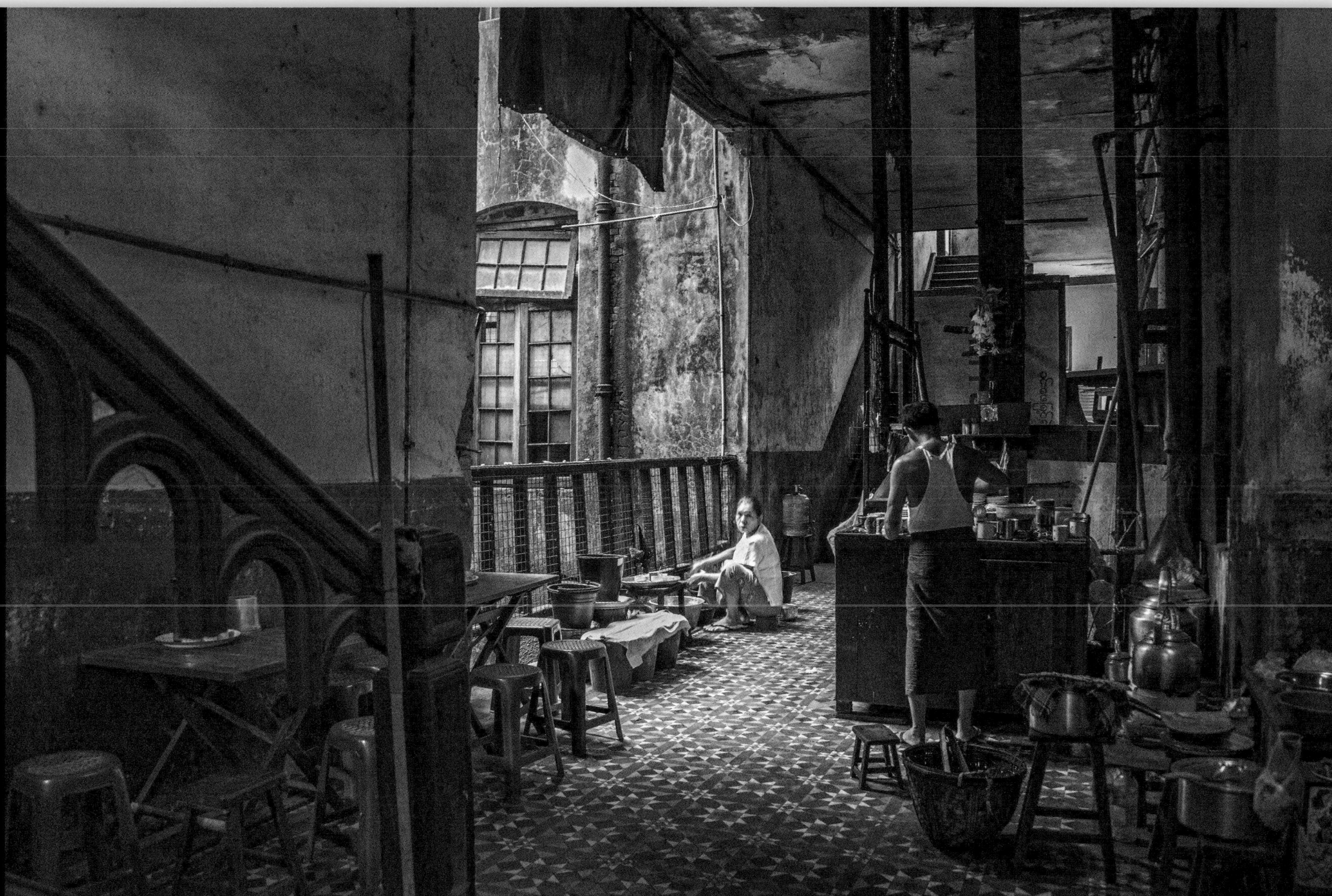

Interior of the Sofaer Building, Yangon, 2013

To make the most of limited and costly retail space in the heart of downtown Yangon, a large hallway on the first floor of this colonial-era building is being used as a corridor restaurant and tea shop. Downstairs in the same building, small photocopy shops are squeezed into the triangular spaces beneath the staircases. People in Yangon use every possible square metre to make a living.

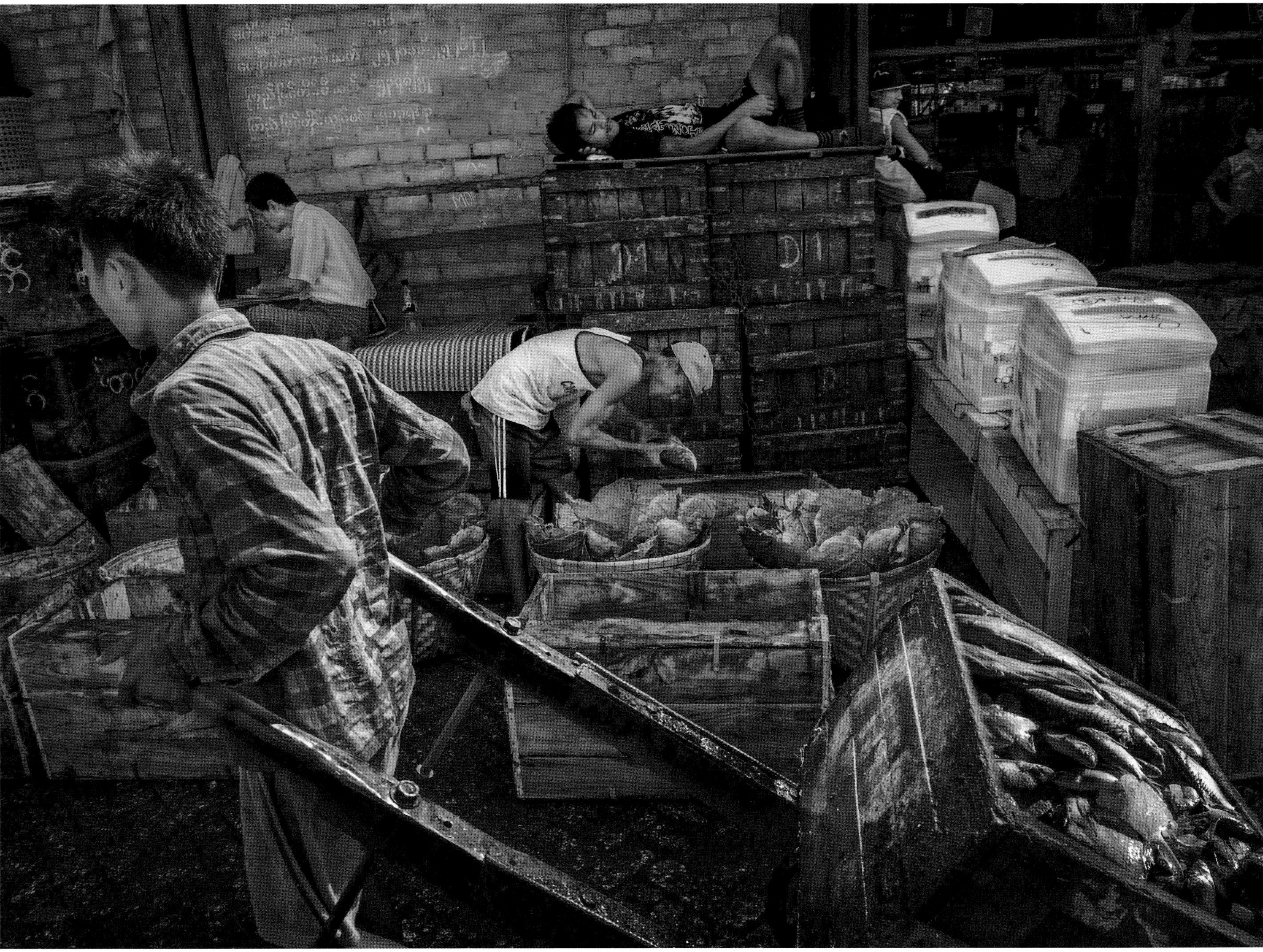

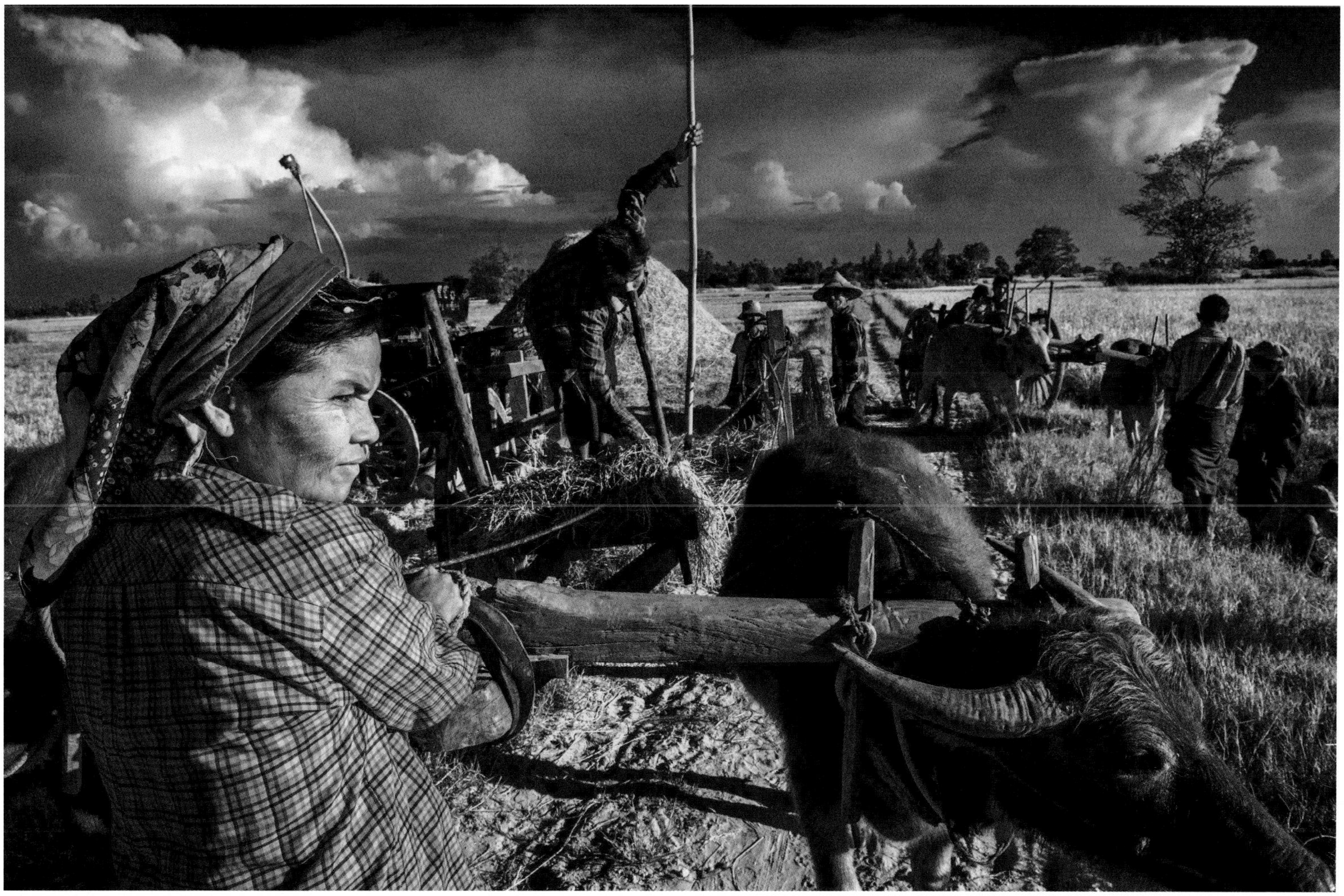

Farm workers, Taungoo, Bago Region, 2013

Ox carts and manual work still prevail during the harvest and neighbours help each other out with a system of bartered labour.

Opposite: San Pya Fish Market, Yangon, 2011

The busiest time at Yangon's fish market is the early morning. On this morning, some workers are already in need of a rest, traders are doing their paperwork, and porters are rushing to transport fish from vendors to buyers.

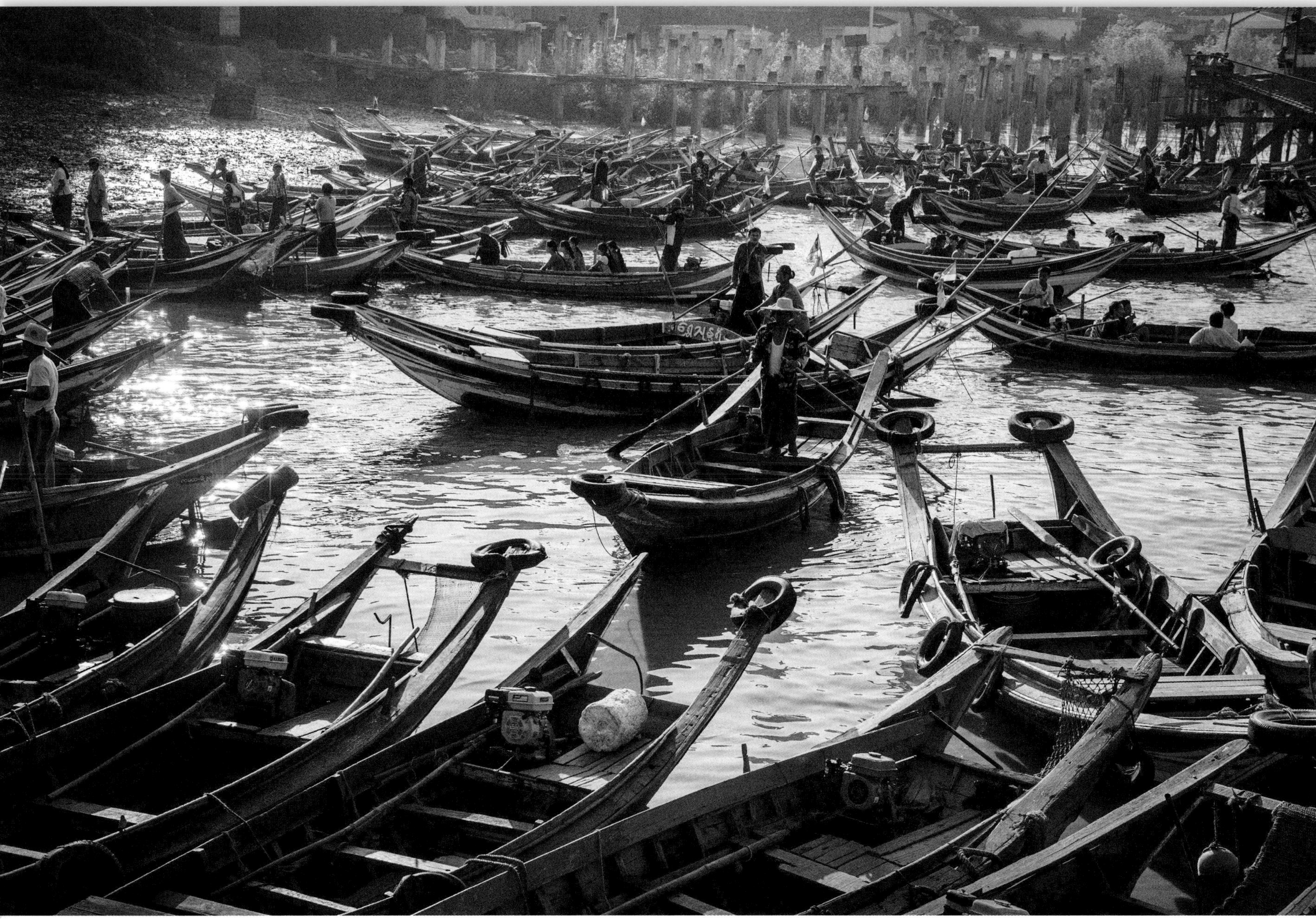

Boats arriving for market, Yangon, 2012

Rivers are still lifelines in Myanmar. The shores of the Yangon River are lined with container terminals, wharfs, piers, and markets. At this spot, people arrive by boat taxis from the opposite shore to shop at markets in the city.

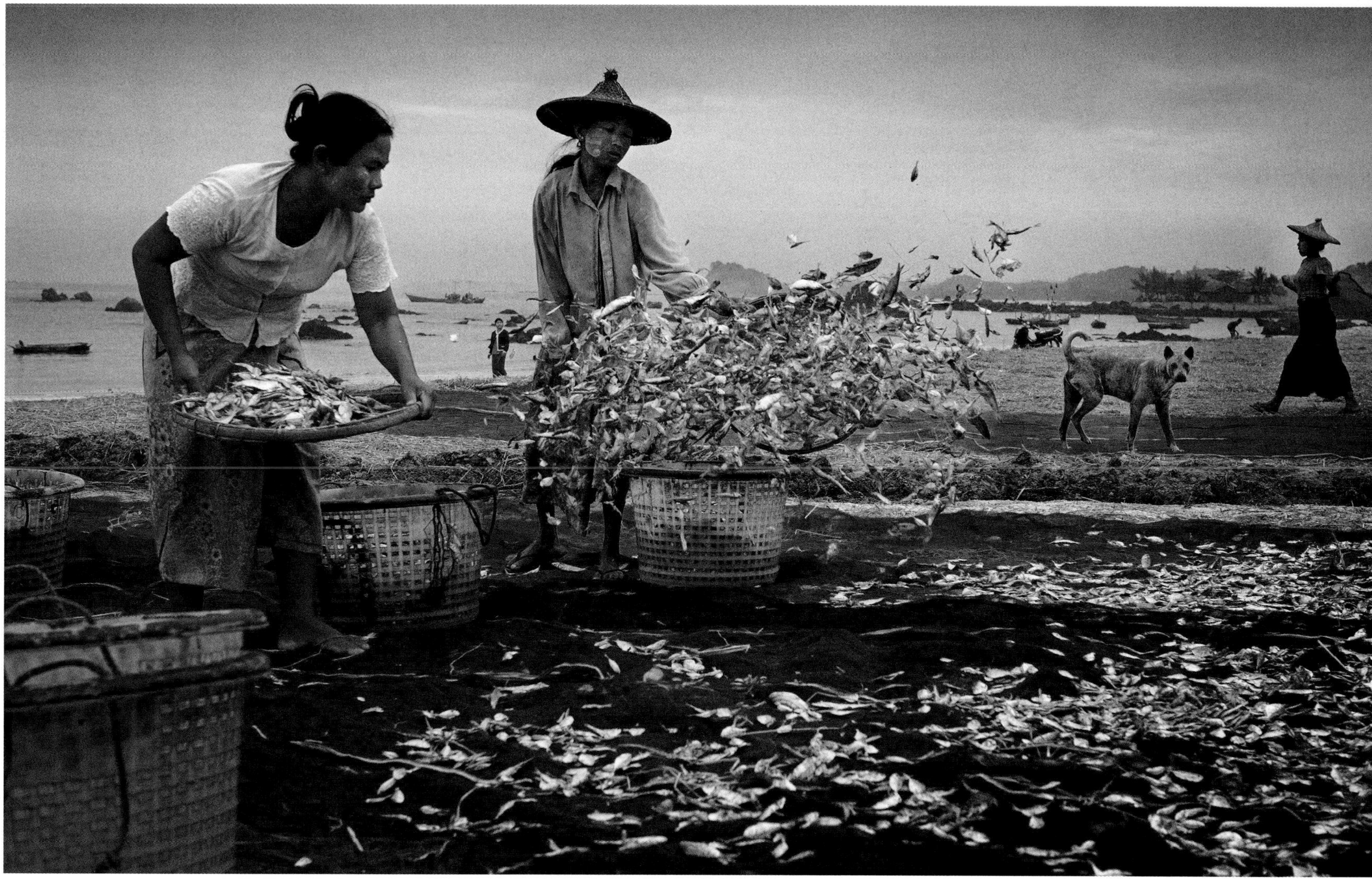

Drying fish, Ngapali Beach, Rakhine State, 2011

After a full night out at sea, fishermen return to Ngapali Beach in the mornings to unload their catch and women spread the small fish onto mats to dry in the sun. The dried fish is later sold at markets as the main ingredient of the local staple, *ngapi*, a fish paste eaten with rice and present at most meals.

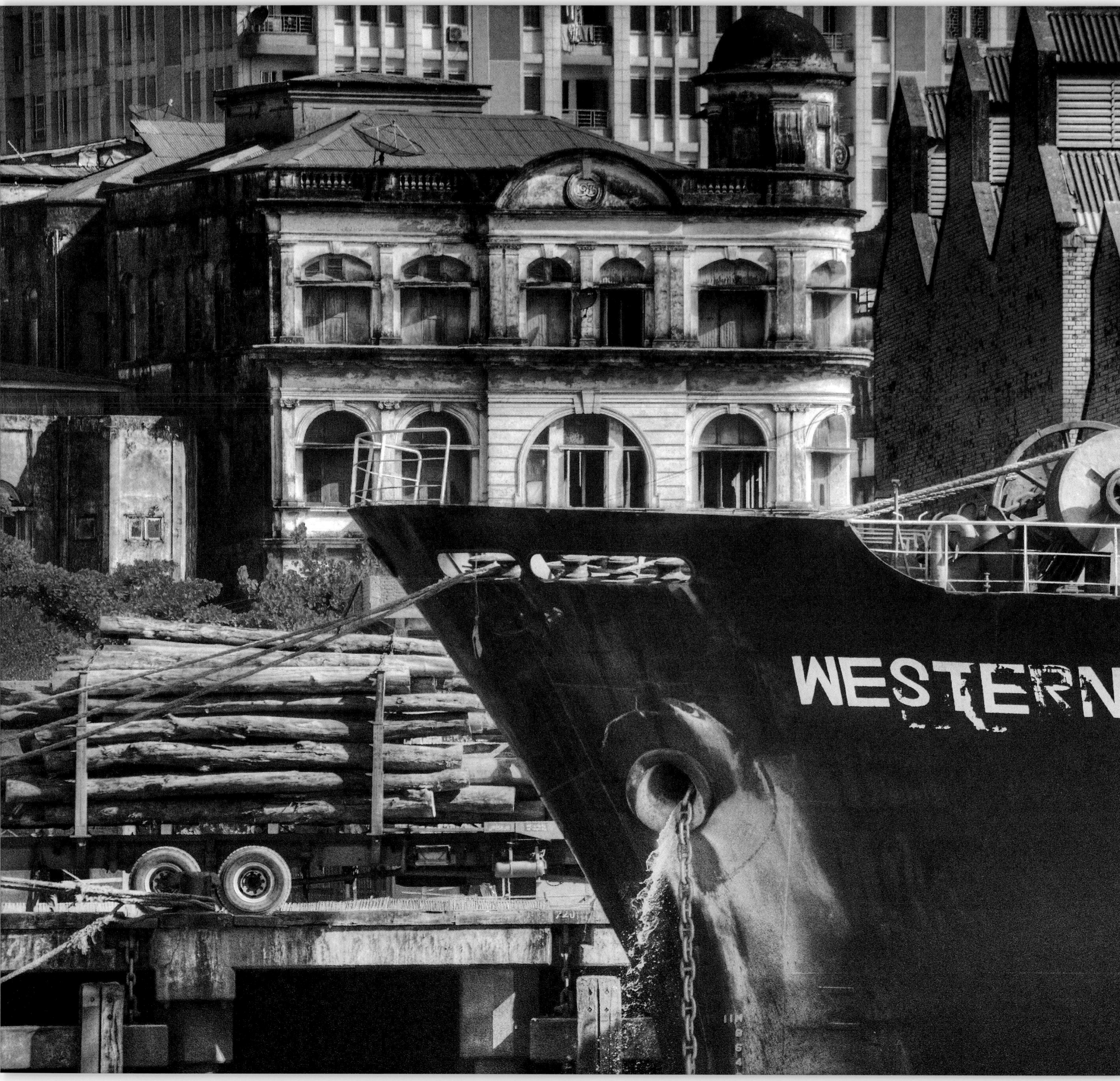
WESTERN

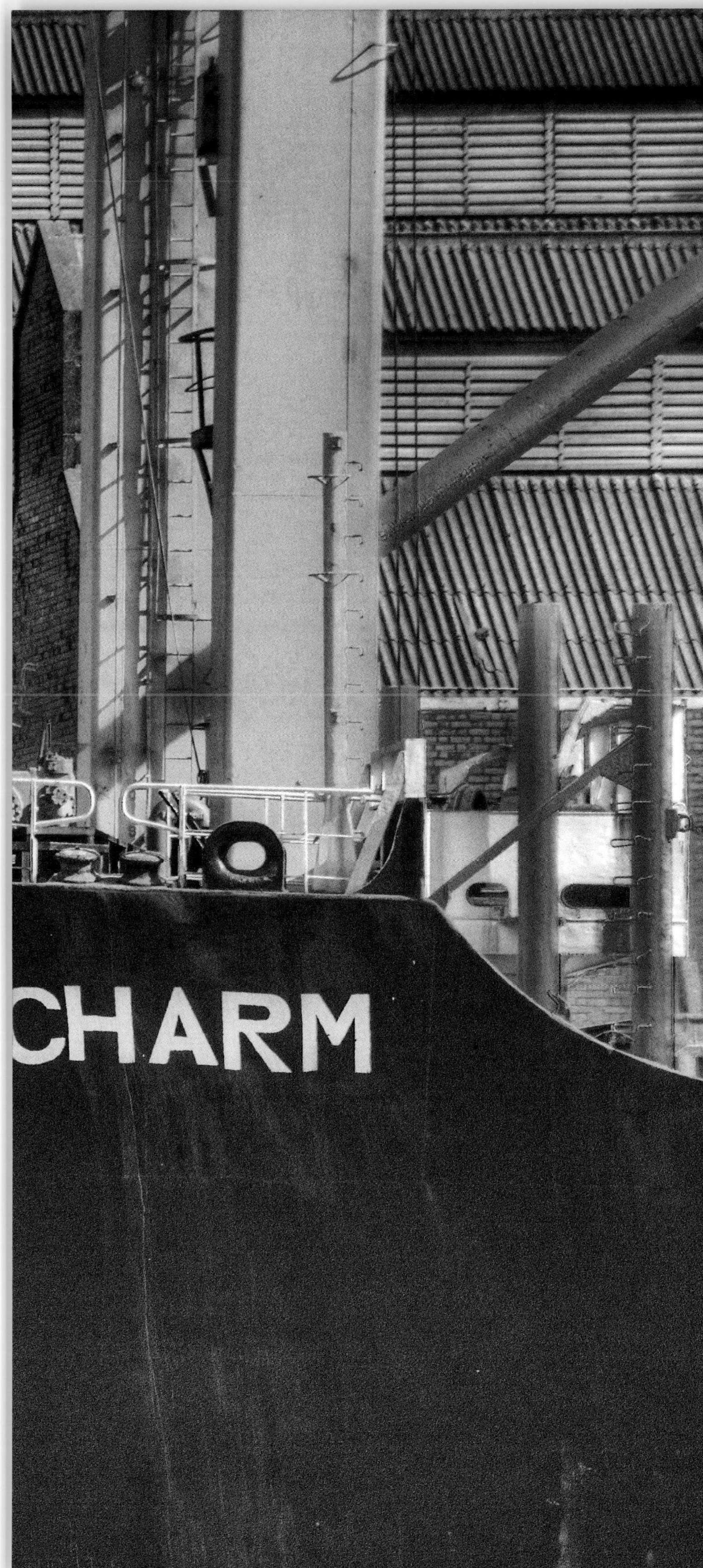

PORT OF YANGON, 2012

The port of Yangon is the biggest commercial port in Myanmar and most export goods leave the country by sea from here.

Boys at the water festival, Mandalay, 2013

Fashion in Myanmar is changing rapidly and the traditional *longyi* (sarong) is disappearing fast. It is being replaced by trendy new fashions inspired by South Korean soap operas that are viewed by more and more people as the number of televisions increases and broader programming becomes available.

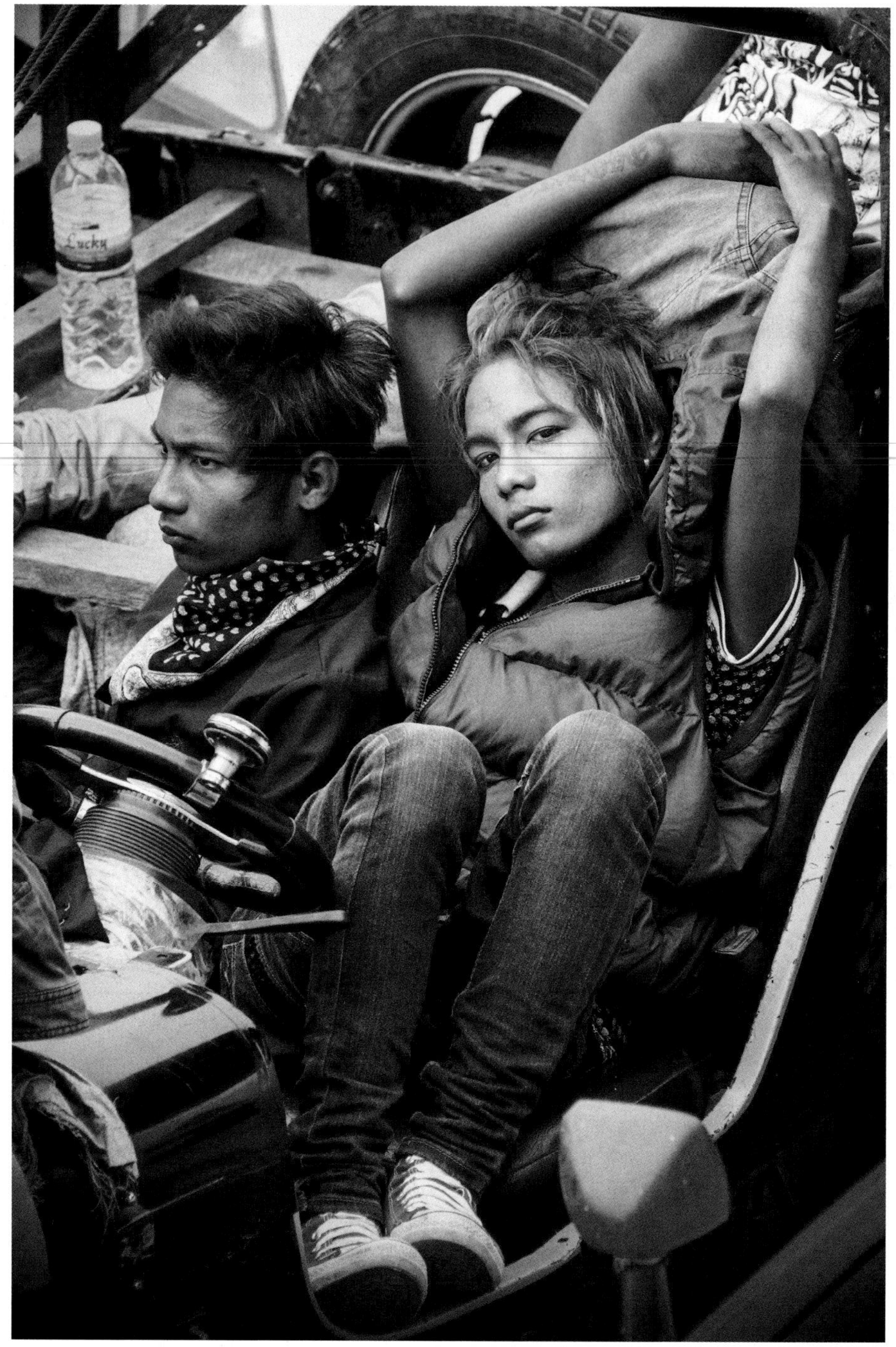

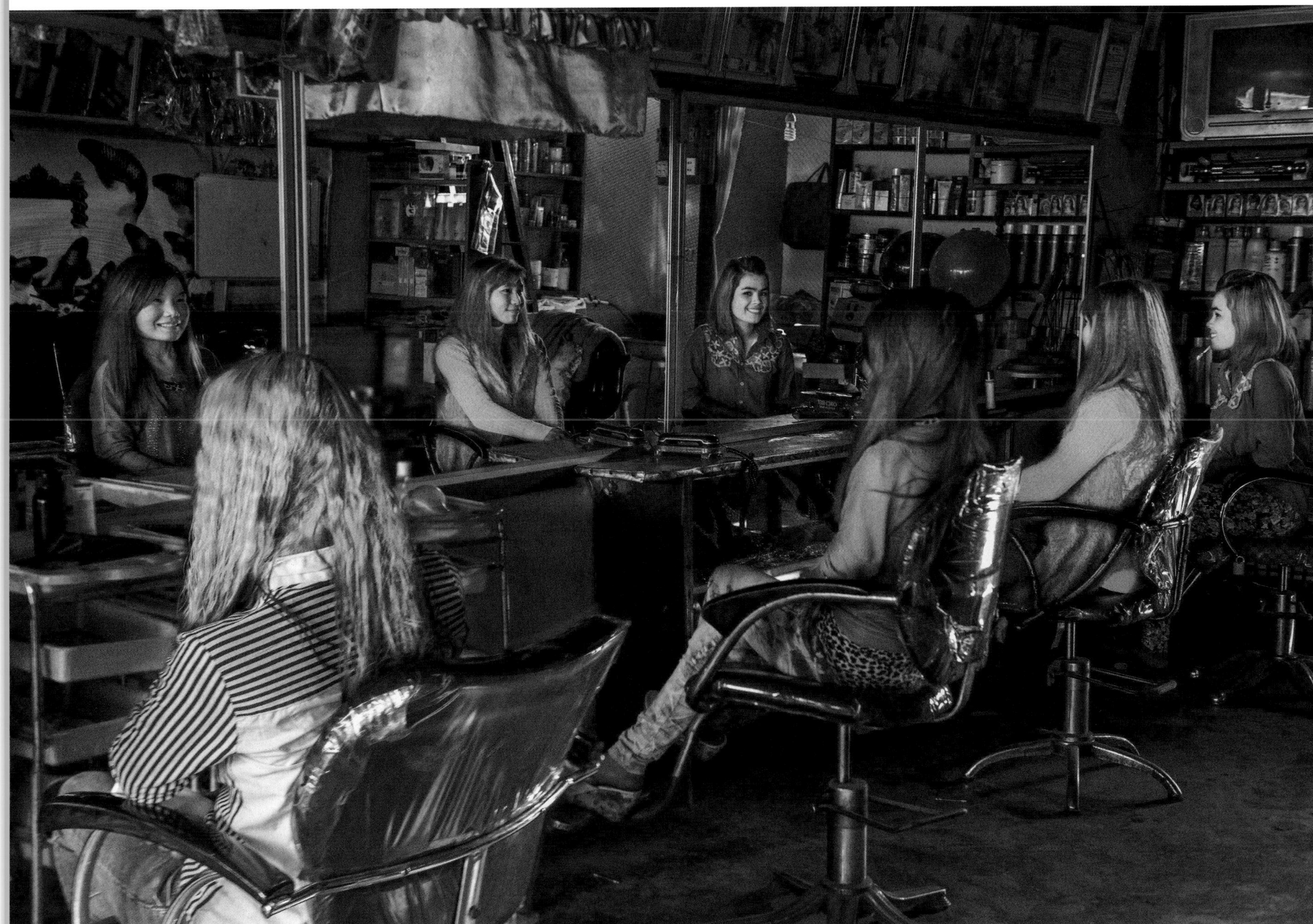

Girls at the hairdresser, Tanaing, Kachin State, 2013

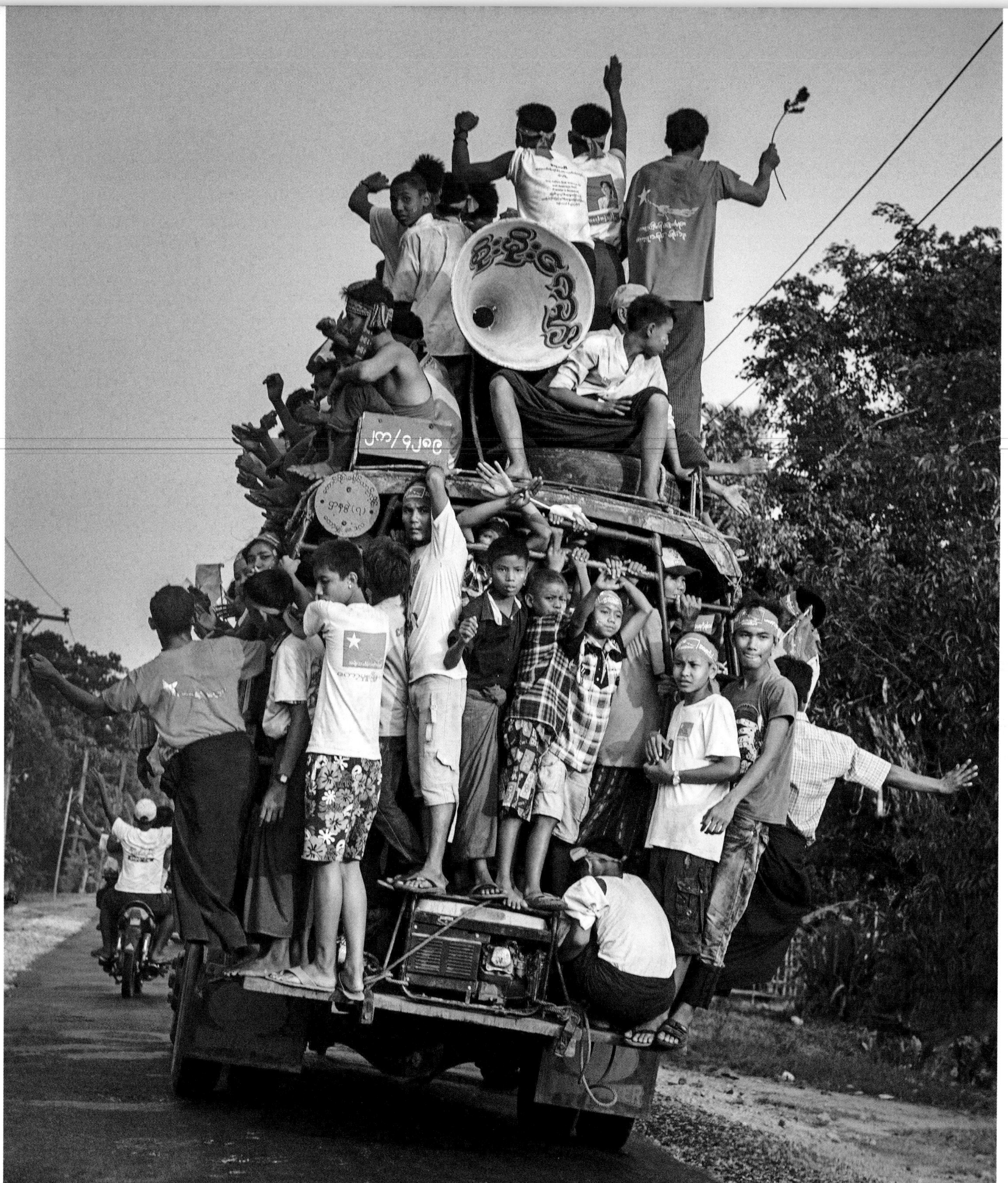

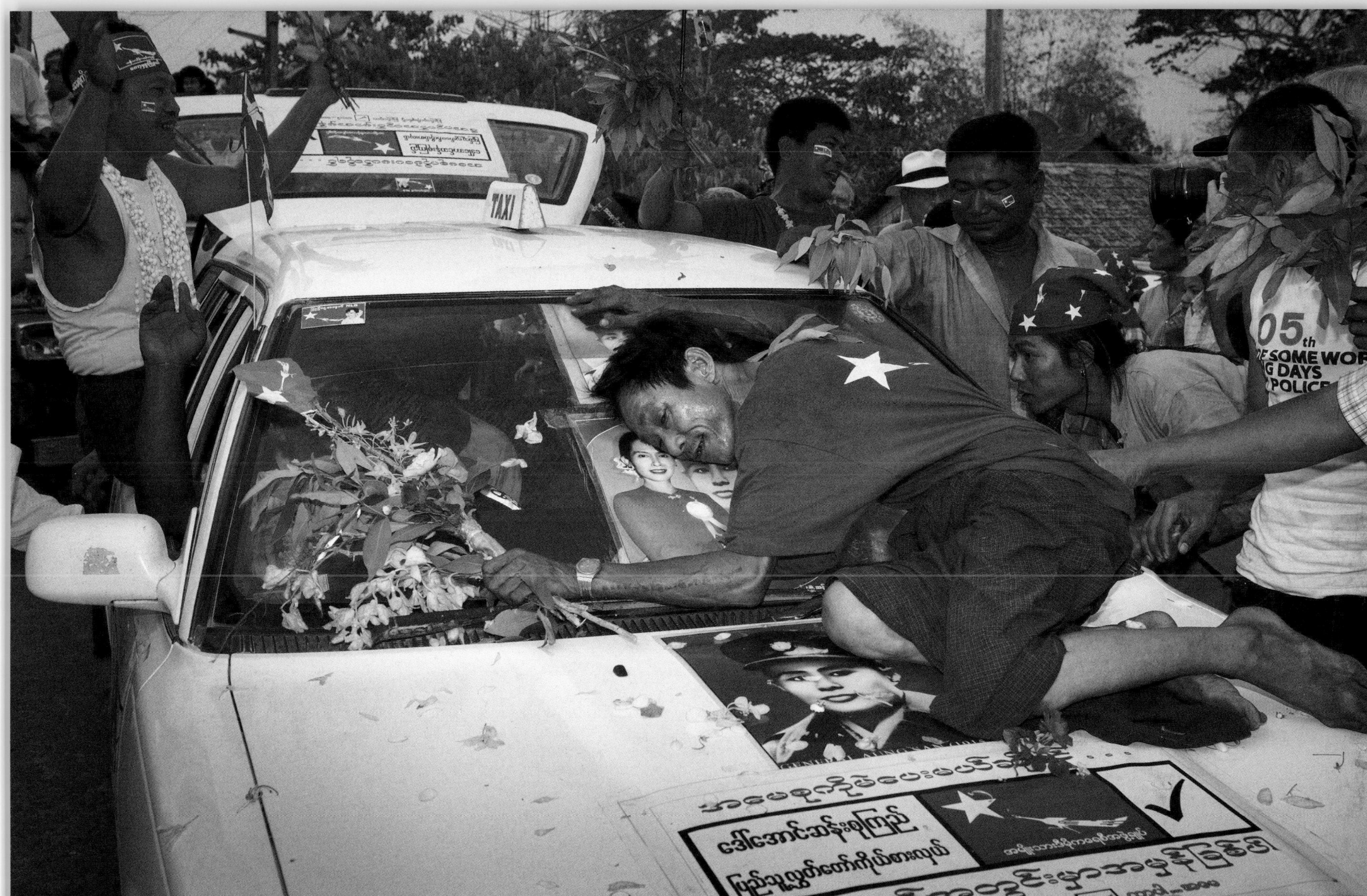

Above and opposite: Campaigning for the by-election in Aung San Suu Kyi's electorate, Kawhmu, Yangon Region, 2012

There was a lot of enthusiasm during the by-elections and the National League for Democracy (NLD) campaign was a joyous affair, with many people out in the streets showing their support. The election resulted in the NLD being represented in parliament for the first time.

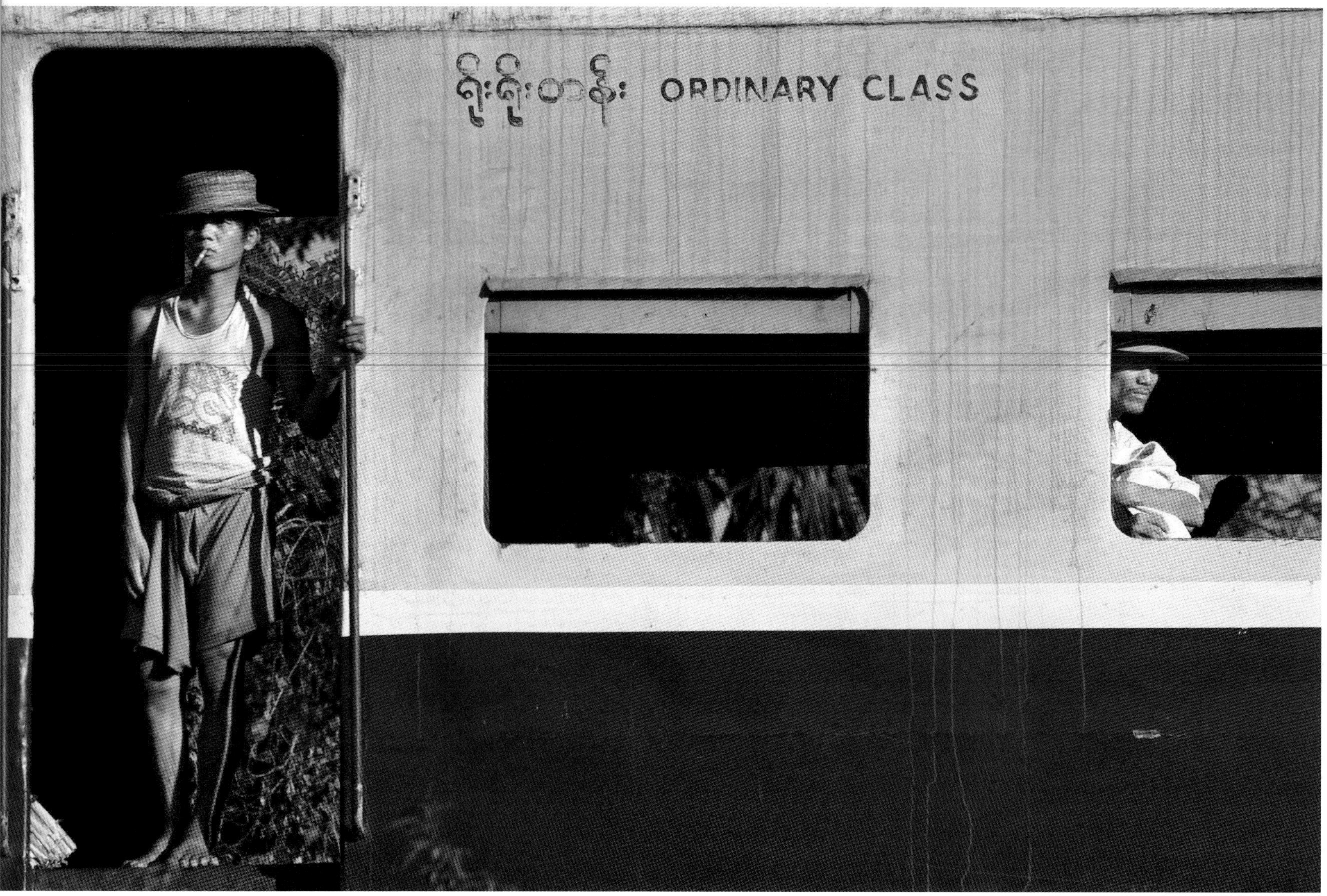

"ORDINARY CLASS" TRAIN, YANGON, 2012

Trains and wagons from British colonial times are still in use in Myanmar. This carriage is part of the Circular Line, a railway service that loops through Yangon.

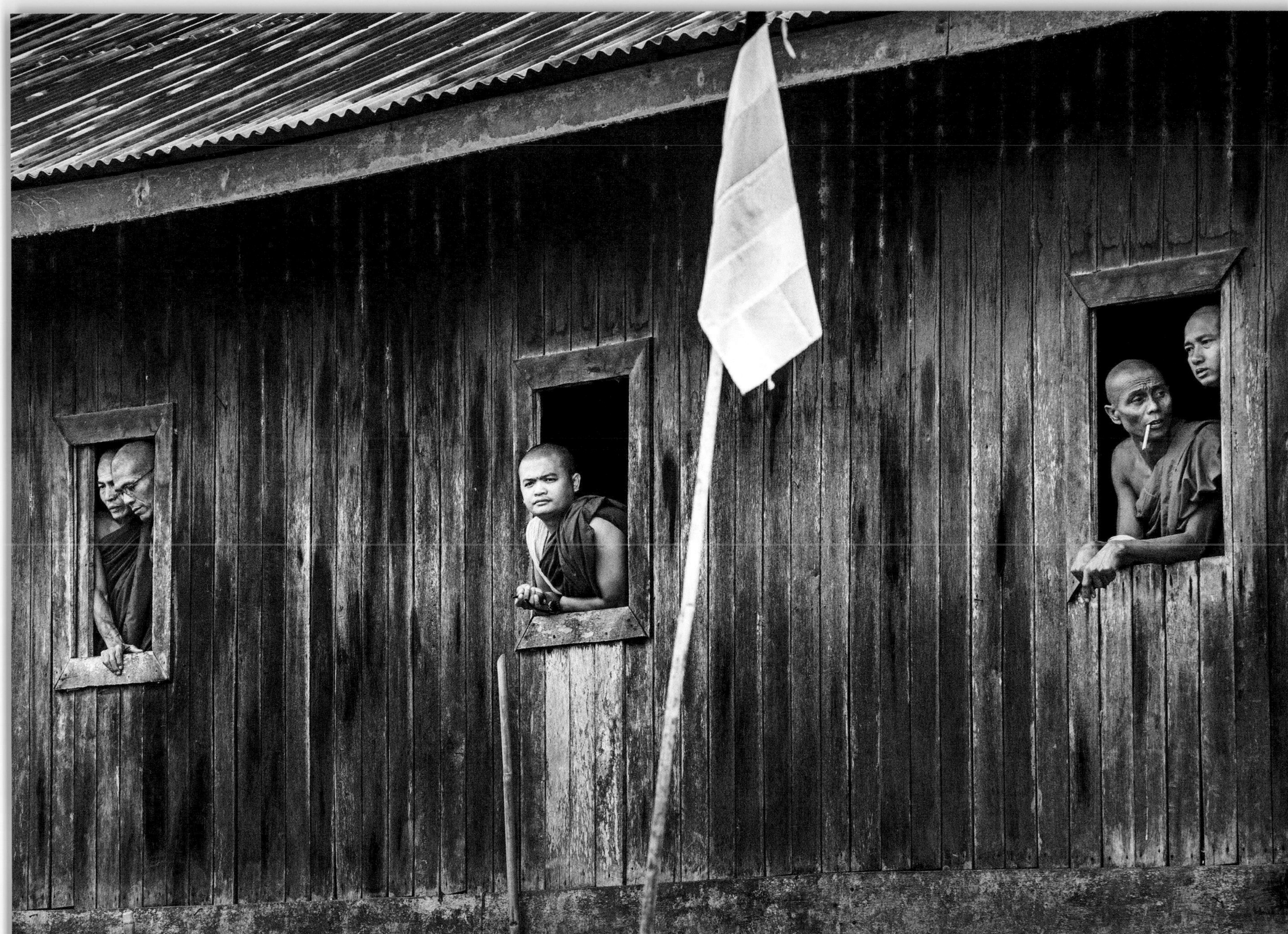

LON TON MONASTERY, INDAWGYI LAKE, KACHIN STATE, 2012

During the local pagoda festival these monks had a fine vantage point to look down at the festivities from their windows while avoiding the crowds.

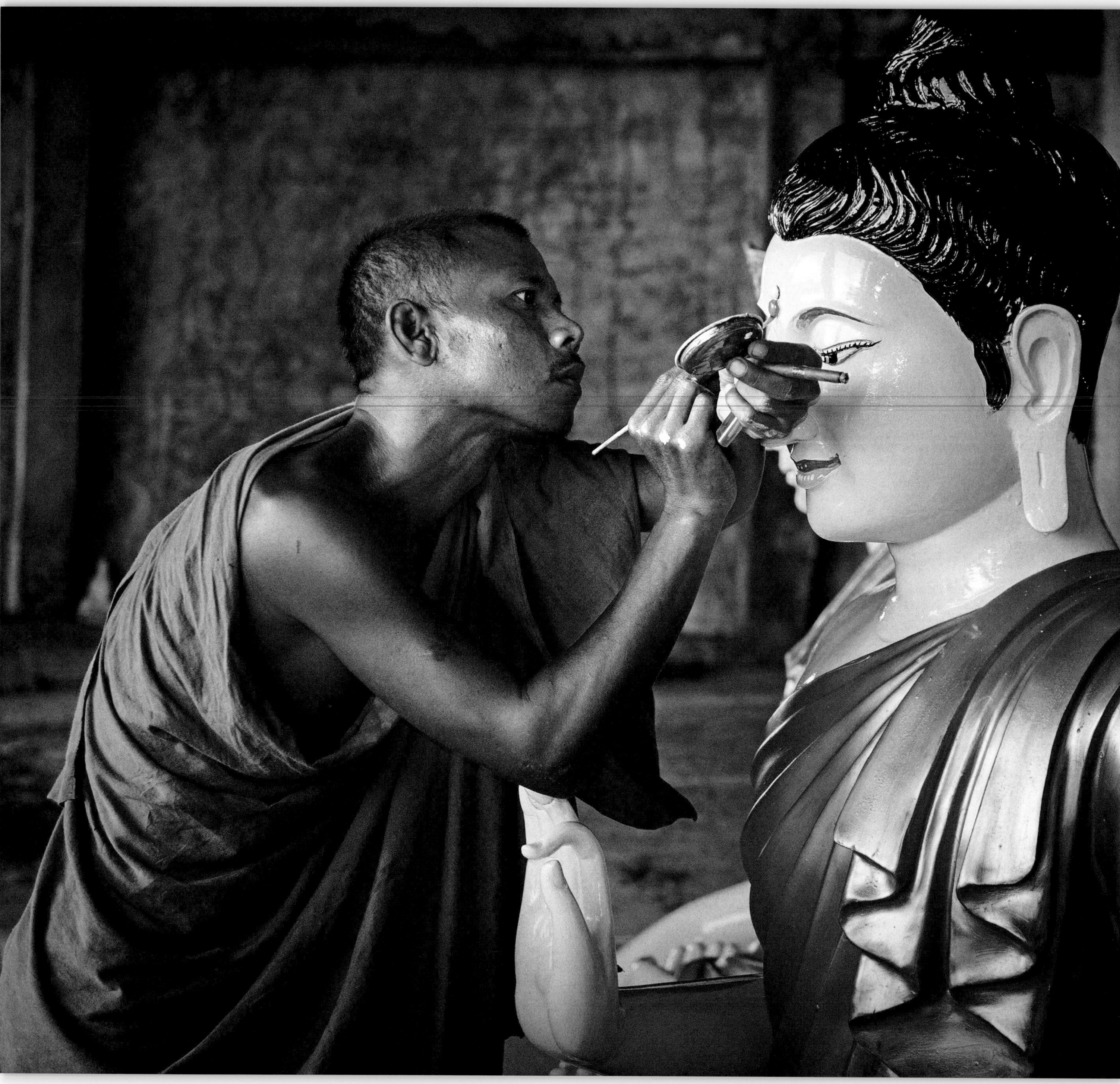

PAINTING THE BUDDHA'S FACE, MUDON, MON STATE, 2012

For a monk, being appointed to paint the face of a new Buddha statue is an honourable task and the face is often the final portion of the statue to be completed.

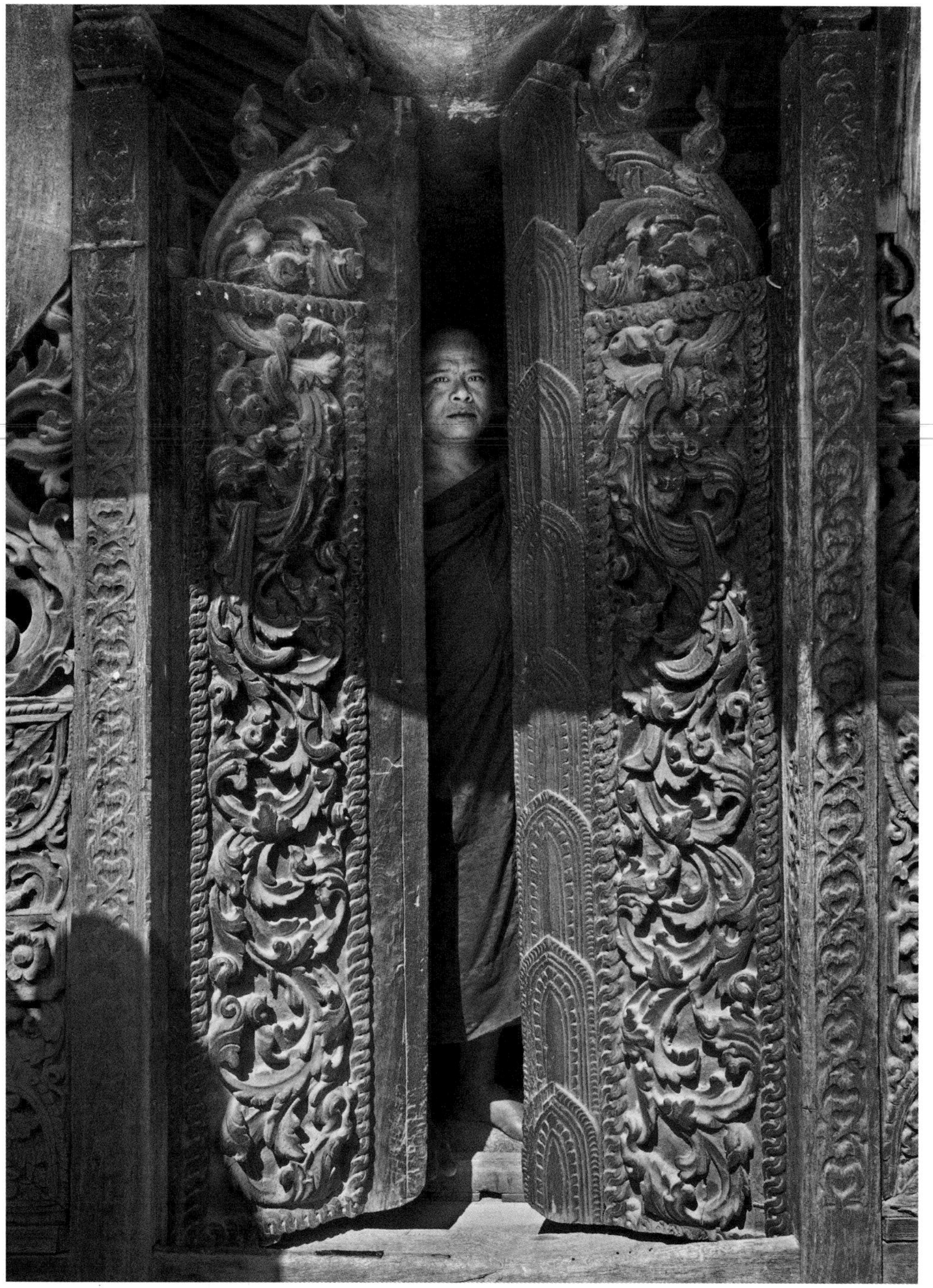

Abbot of the Tai Low Ko Wooden Monastery, Salay, Magway Region, 2012

Opposite: Evening recitals in the Shwe Kyin Monastery, Mandalay, 2015

Daily routines in a monastery follow a rigorous timetable.

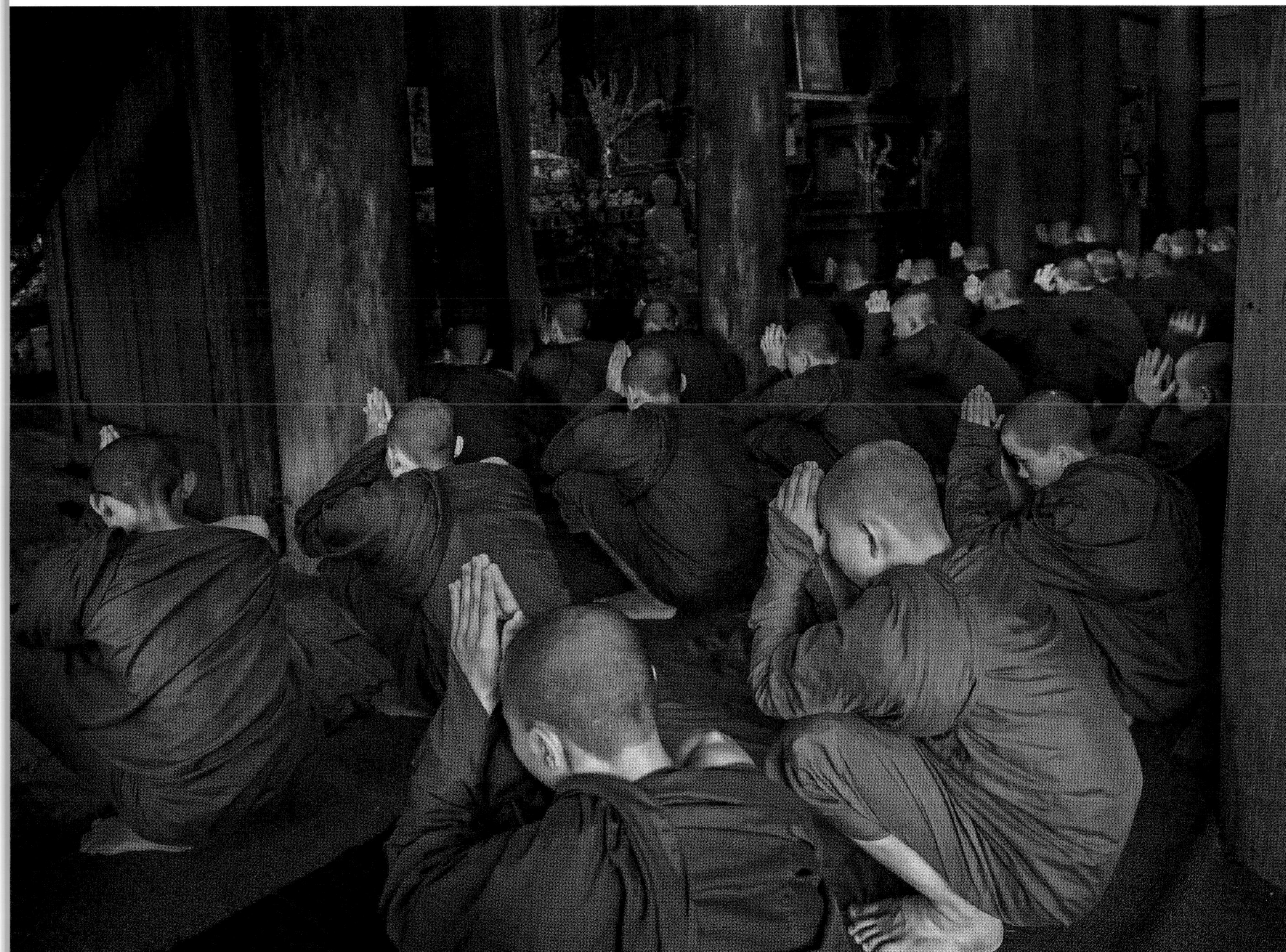

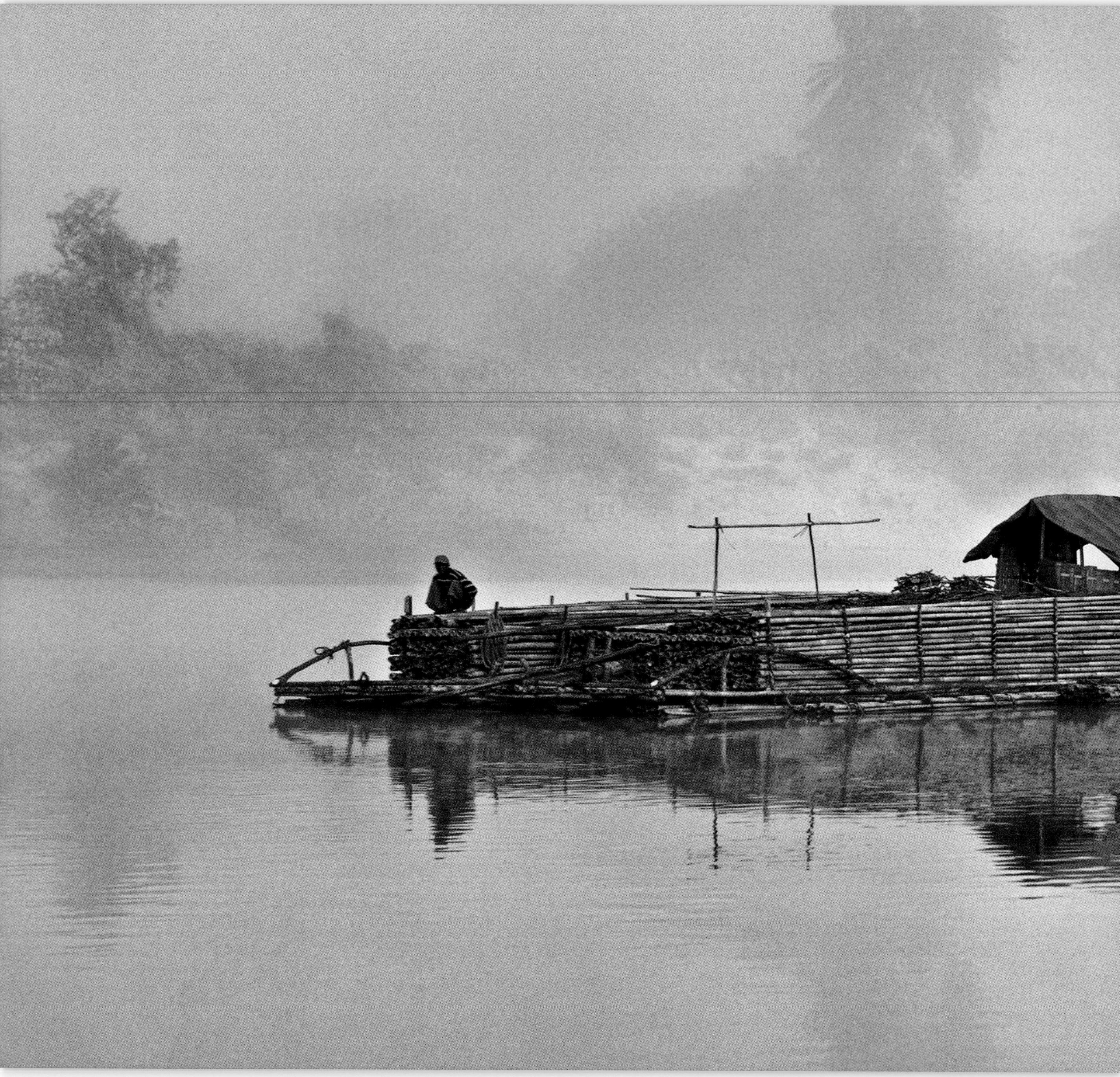

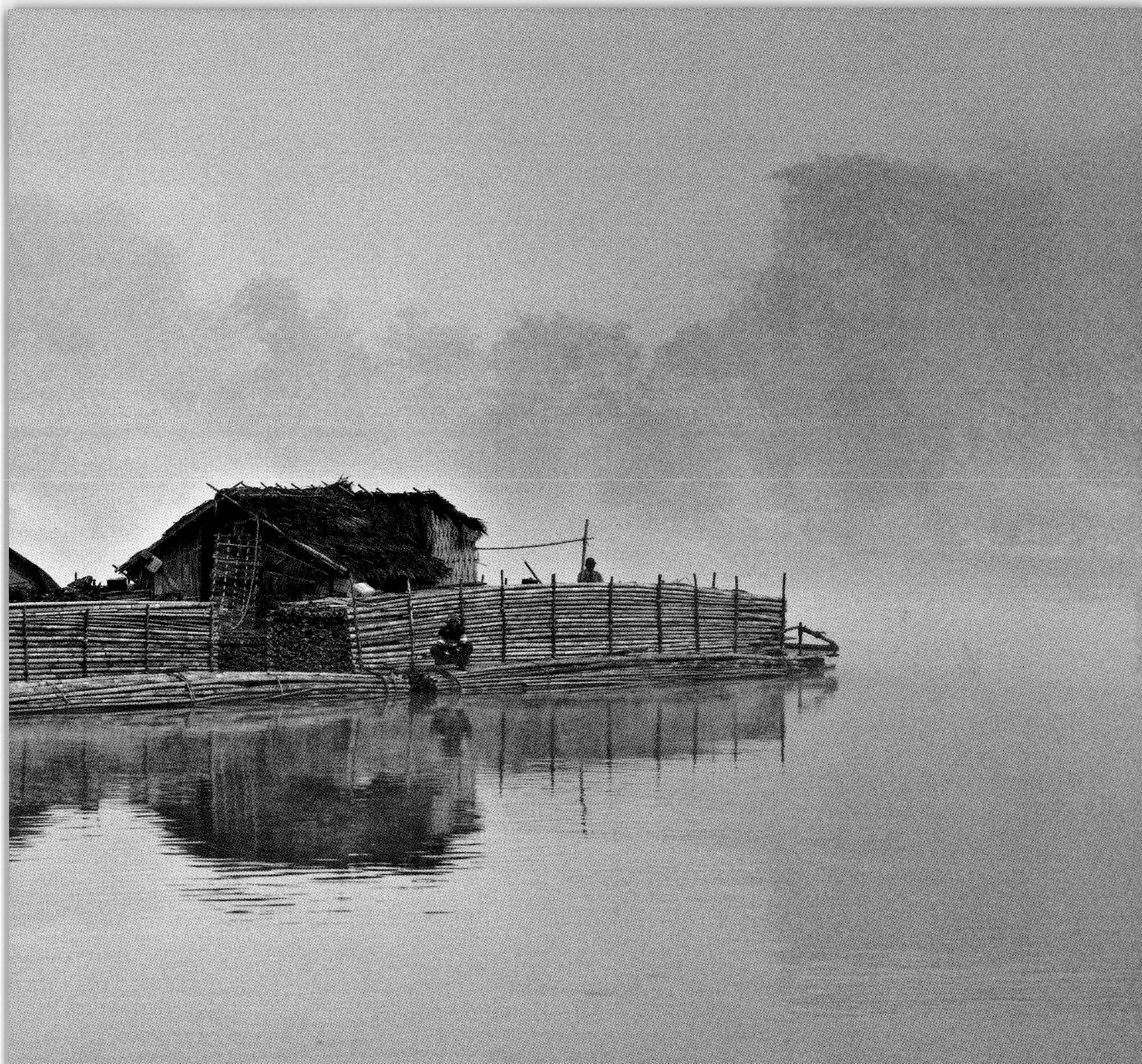

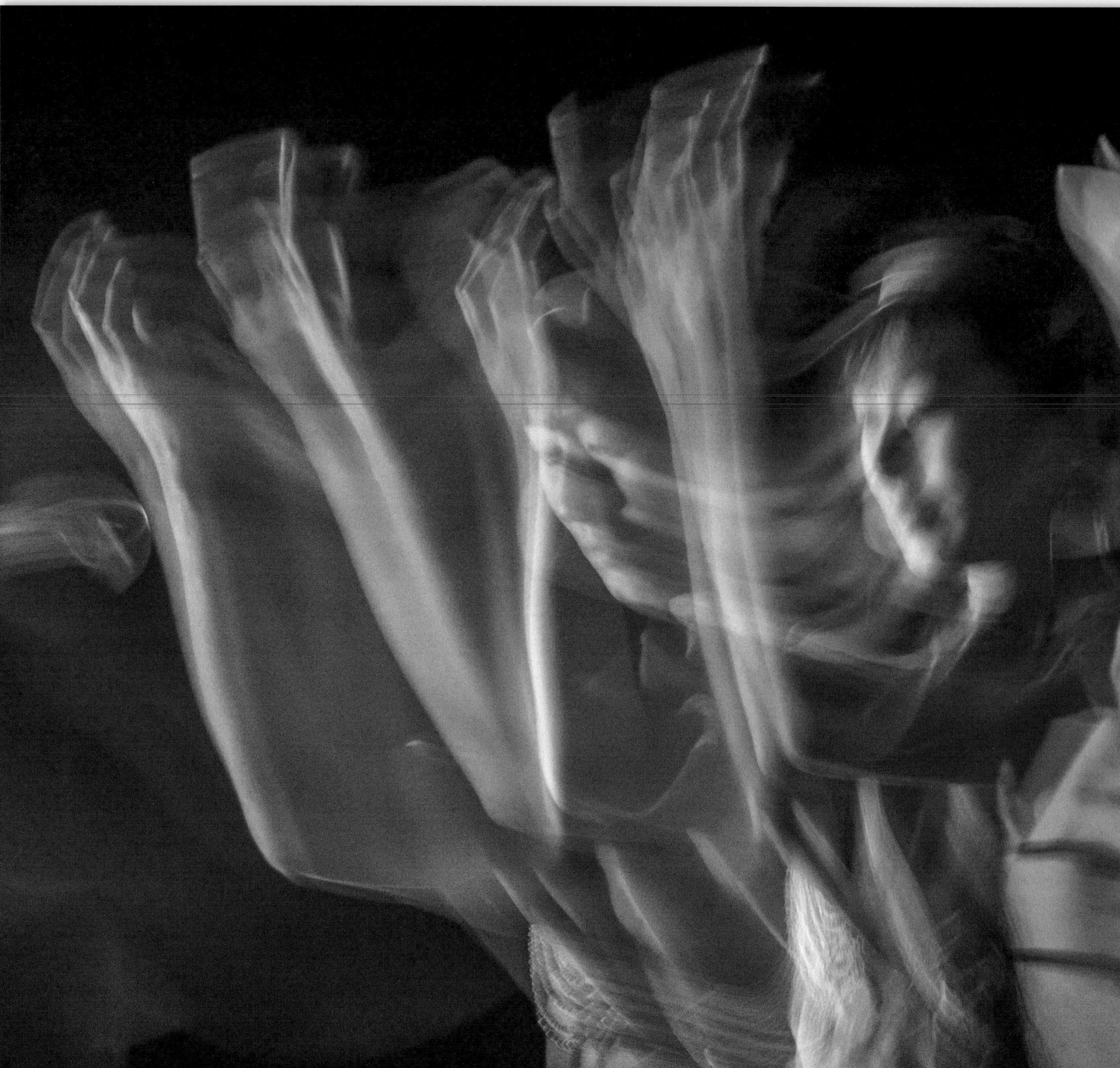

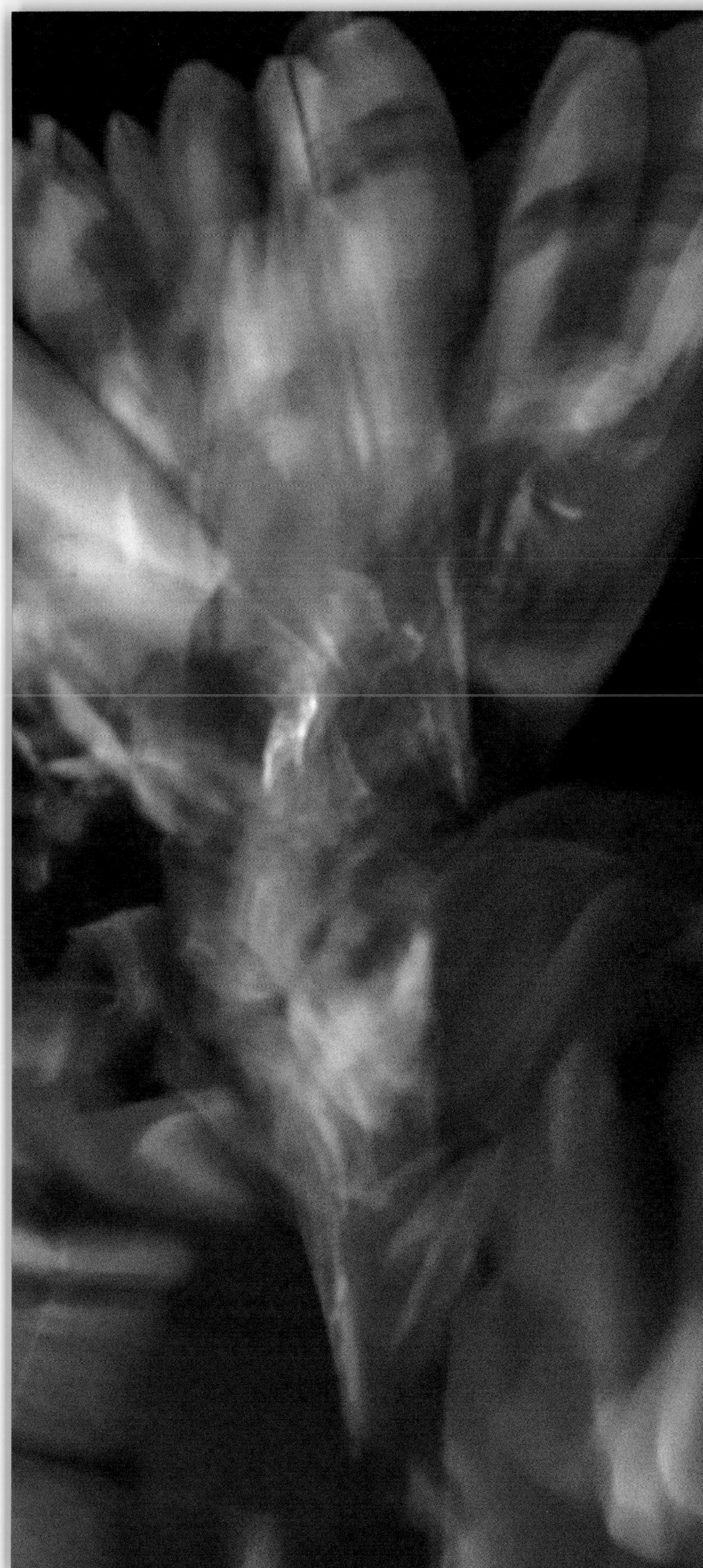

PREVIOUS PAGE: BAMBOO FLOAT ON THE CHINDWIN RIVER, SAGAING REGION, 2010

Rivers offer the easiest transportation routes in Myanmar. Whenever timber or bamboo needs to be transported, the material is often used to make a boat as well as any temporary housing needed for the journey – it can take a week or more to float downriver and the boatmen make themselves at home onboard.

WOMAN DANCING AT THE NAGA FESTIVAL, PA PHOU, SAGAING REGION, 2010

During the annual Naga festival in January, various Naga tribes demonstrate their dancing skills around a bonfire.

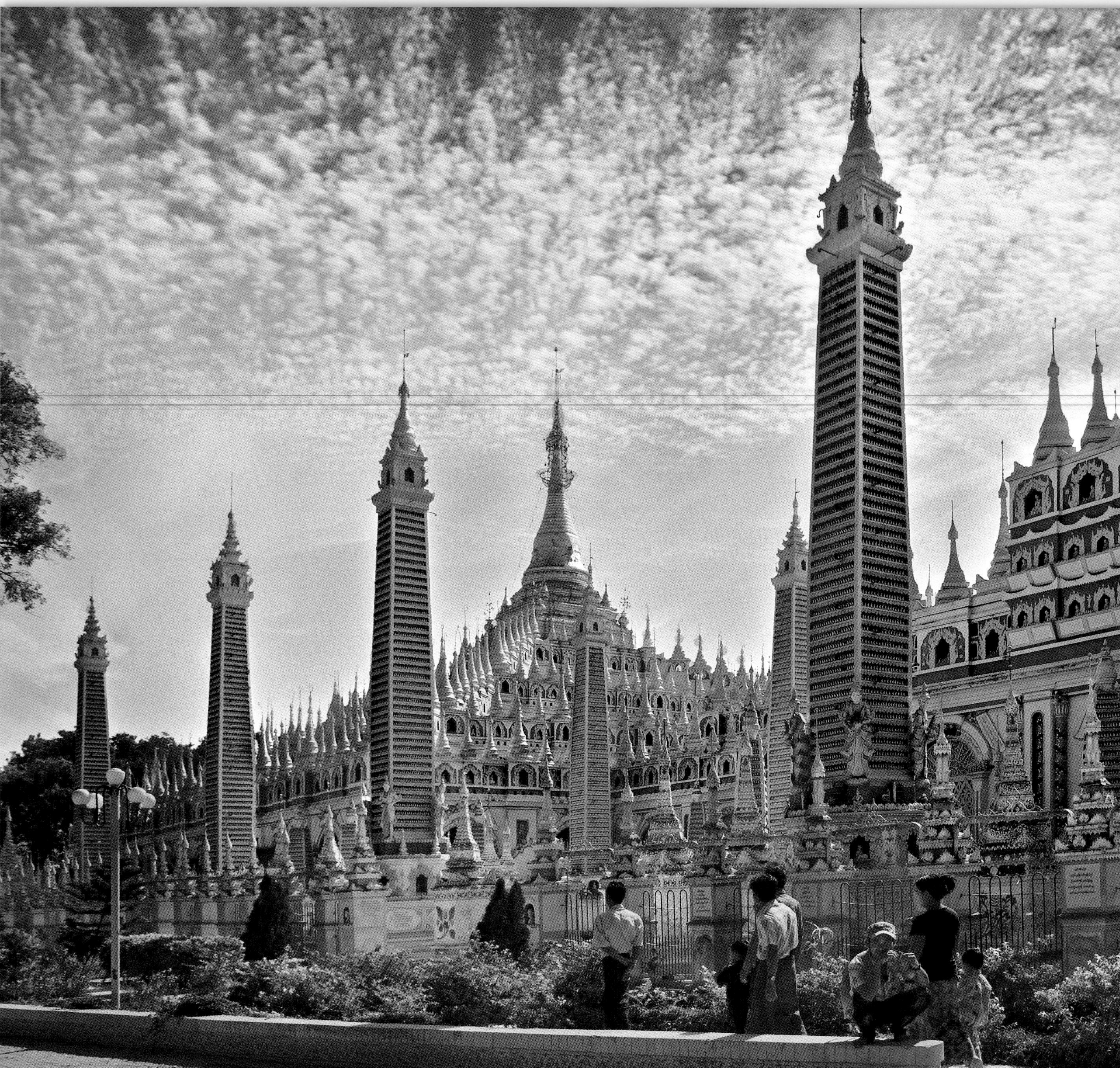

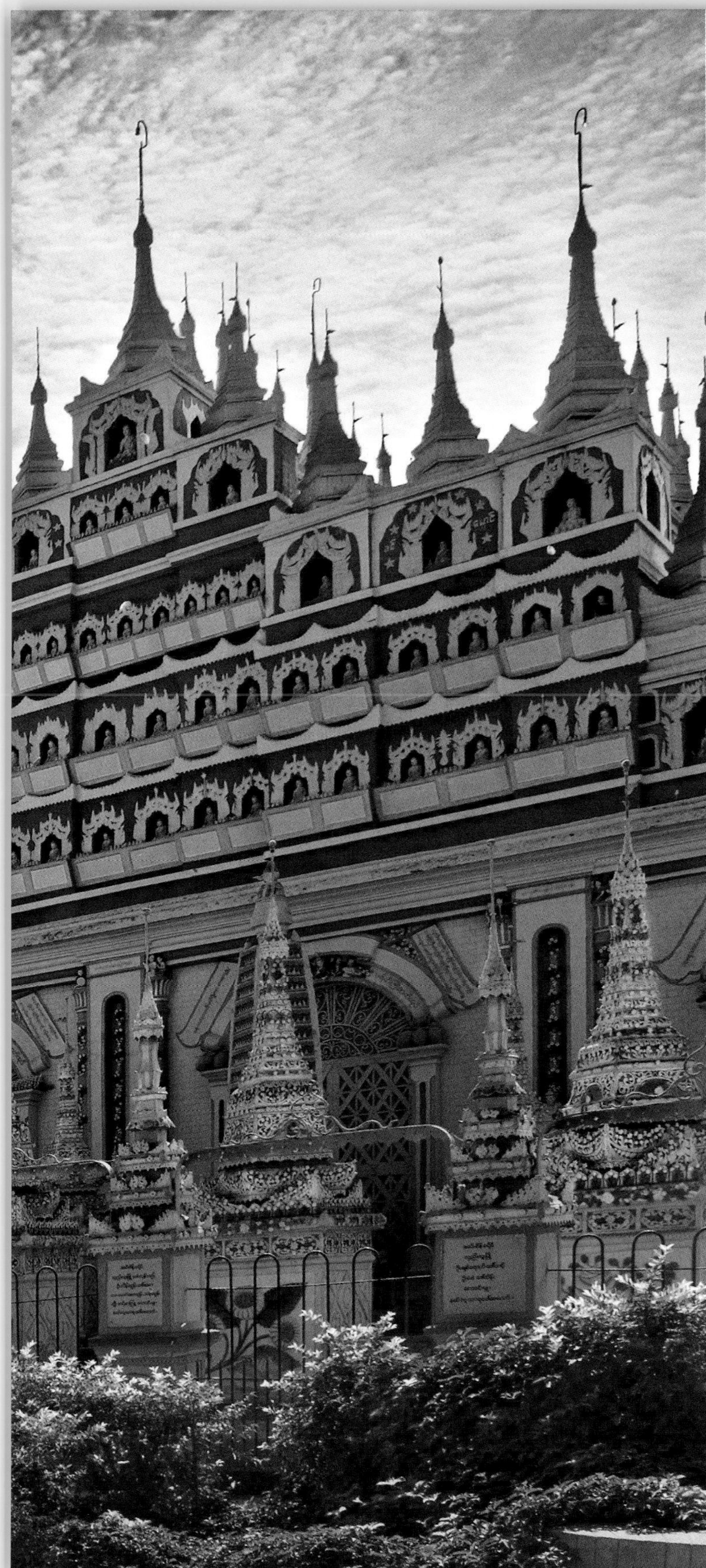

Thanboddhay Pagoda, Monywa, Sagaing Region, 2010

This pagoda is famous for having almost 600,000 small Buddha figures on its inner walls and outer façade.

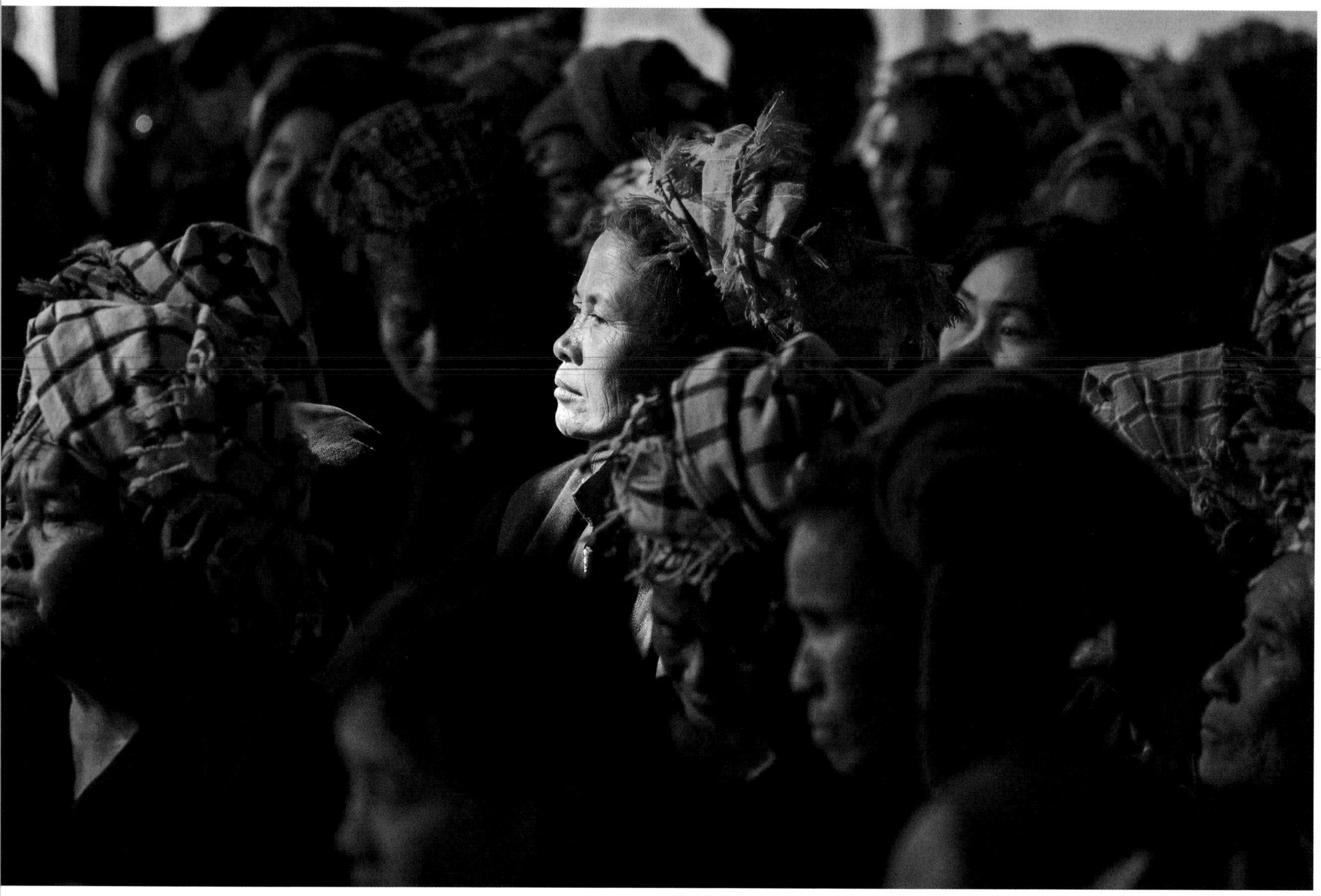

Pa-oh women, Inle Lake, Shan State, 2010

These women are members of the Pa-oh tribe. They gather annually at a different village each year to meet, pray, celebrate, and exchange news and gossip.

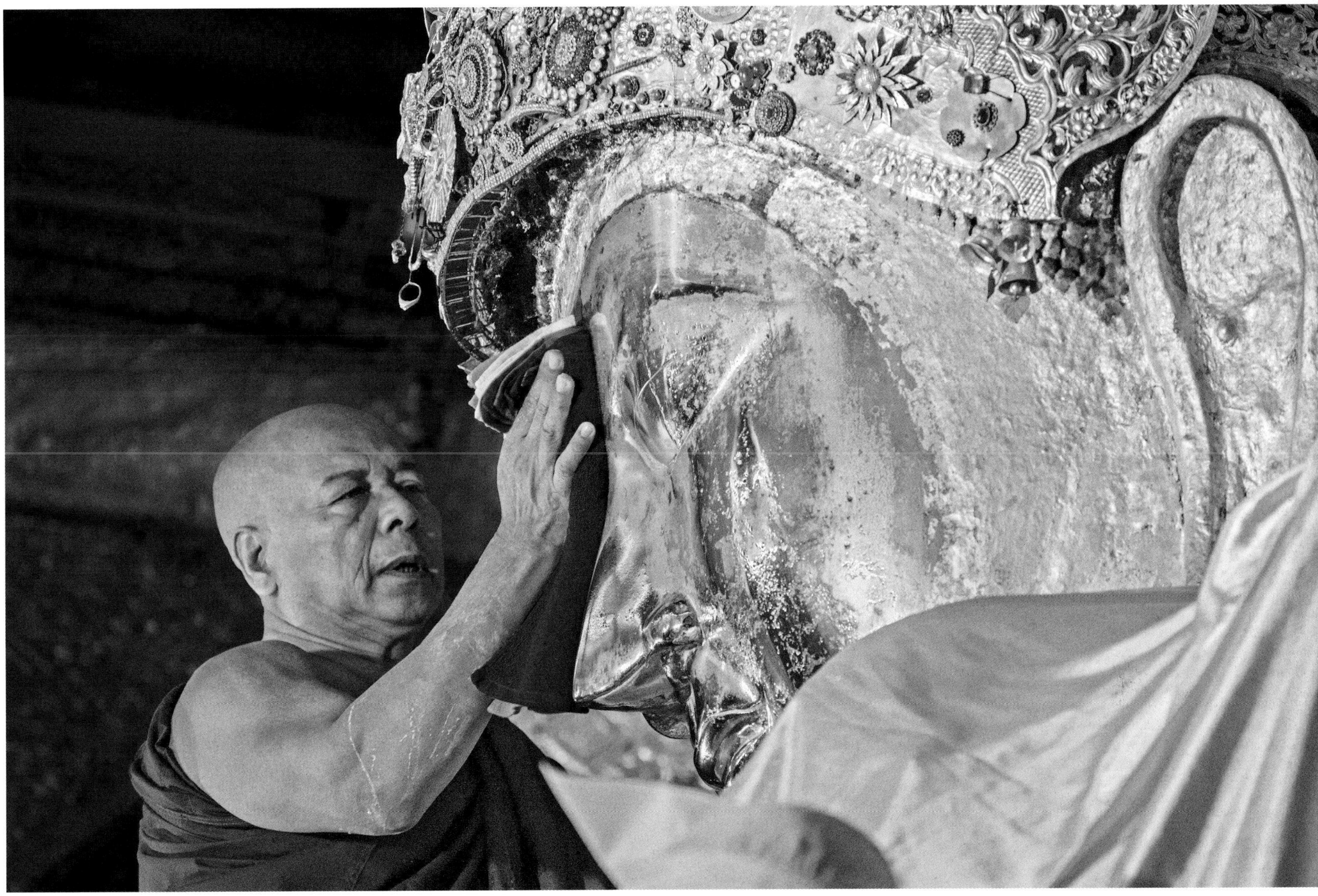

Face washing ceremony at the Mahamuni Pagoda,
Mandalay, 2013

Every morning at 4 a.m., a designated monk climbs up to the pagoda's revered Buddha statue to wash its golden face with a cloth, making sure it is polished and prepared for the day ahead.

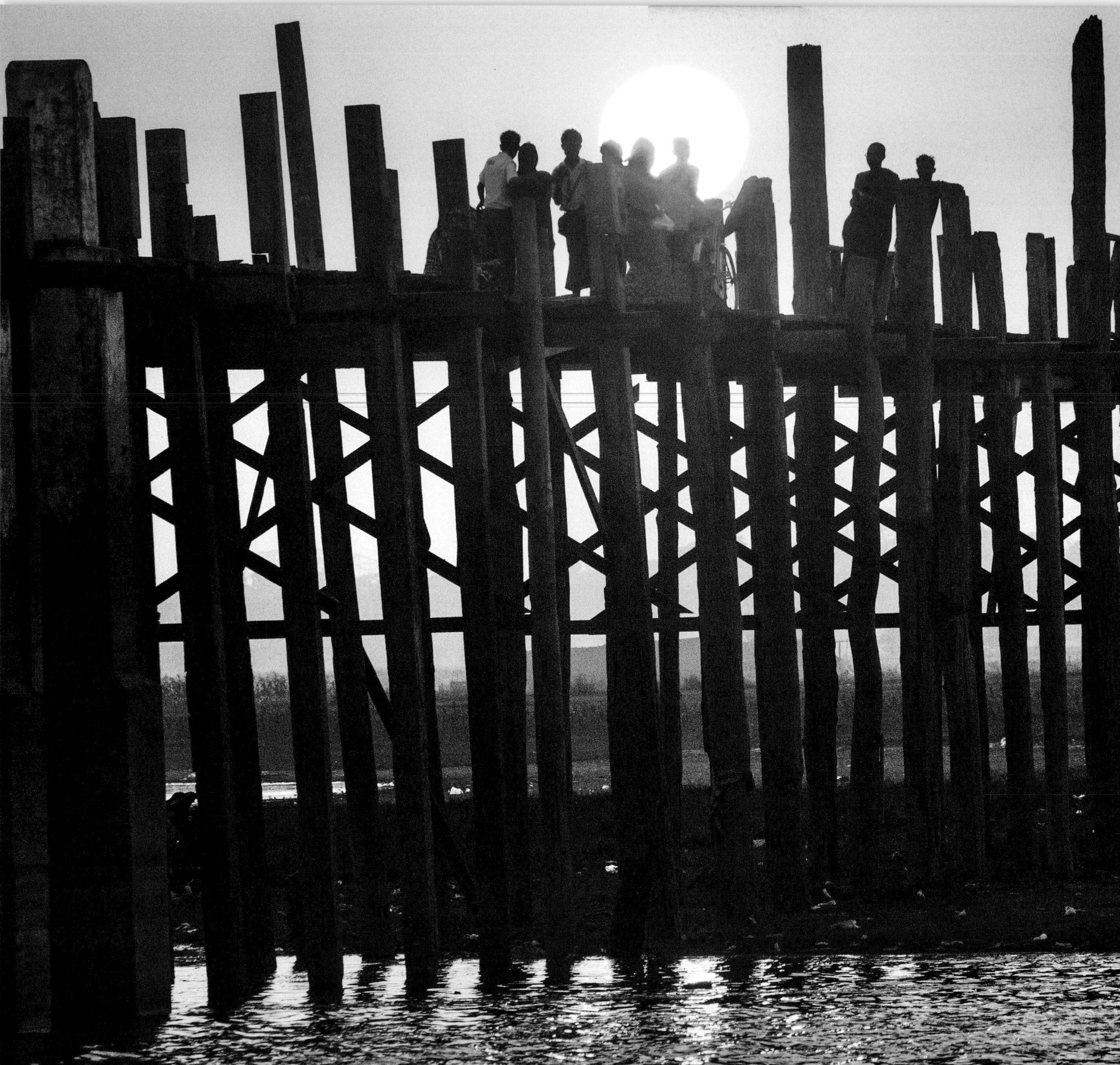

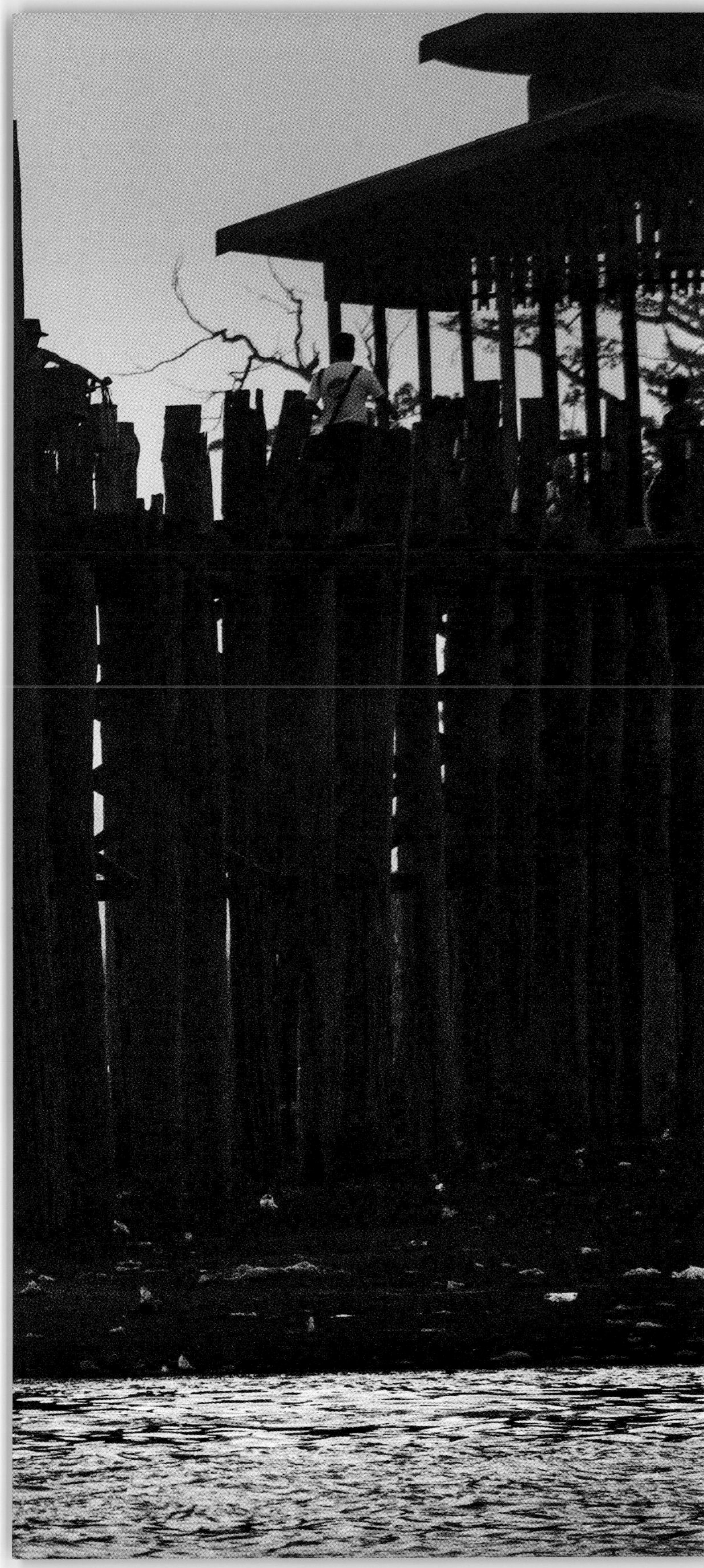

U Bein Bridge, Amarapura, Mandalay Region, 2011

Undoubtedly one of the most picturesque and photographed bridges in Myanmar, the U Bein Bridge was constructed from wood in 1850 to link two parts of a village separated by a lake. It still fulfils this purpose today.

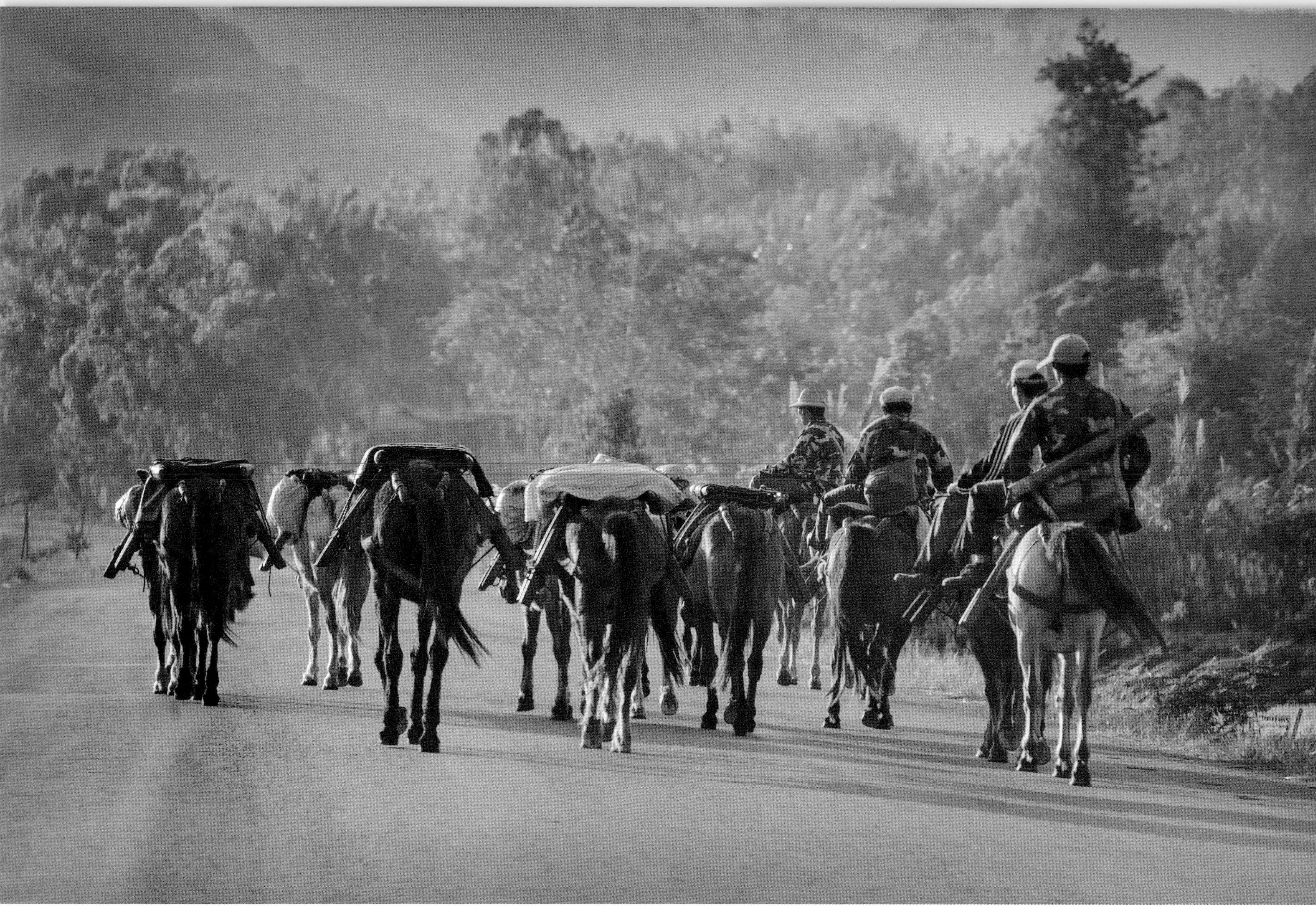

NOMAD TRADERS, KYAING TONG, SHAN STATE, 2011
Horses are still used to access remote areas for trade.

OPPOSITE: A MONK SEEN THROUGH A VILLAGE WINDOW, WON KANG VILLAGE, SHAN STATE, 2011

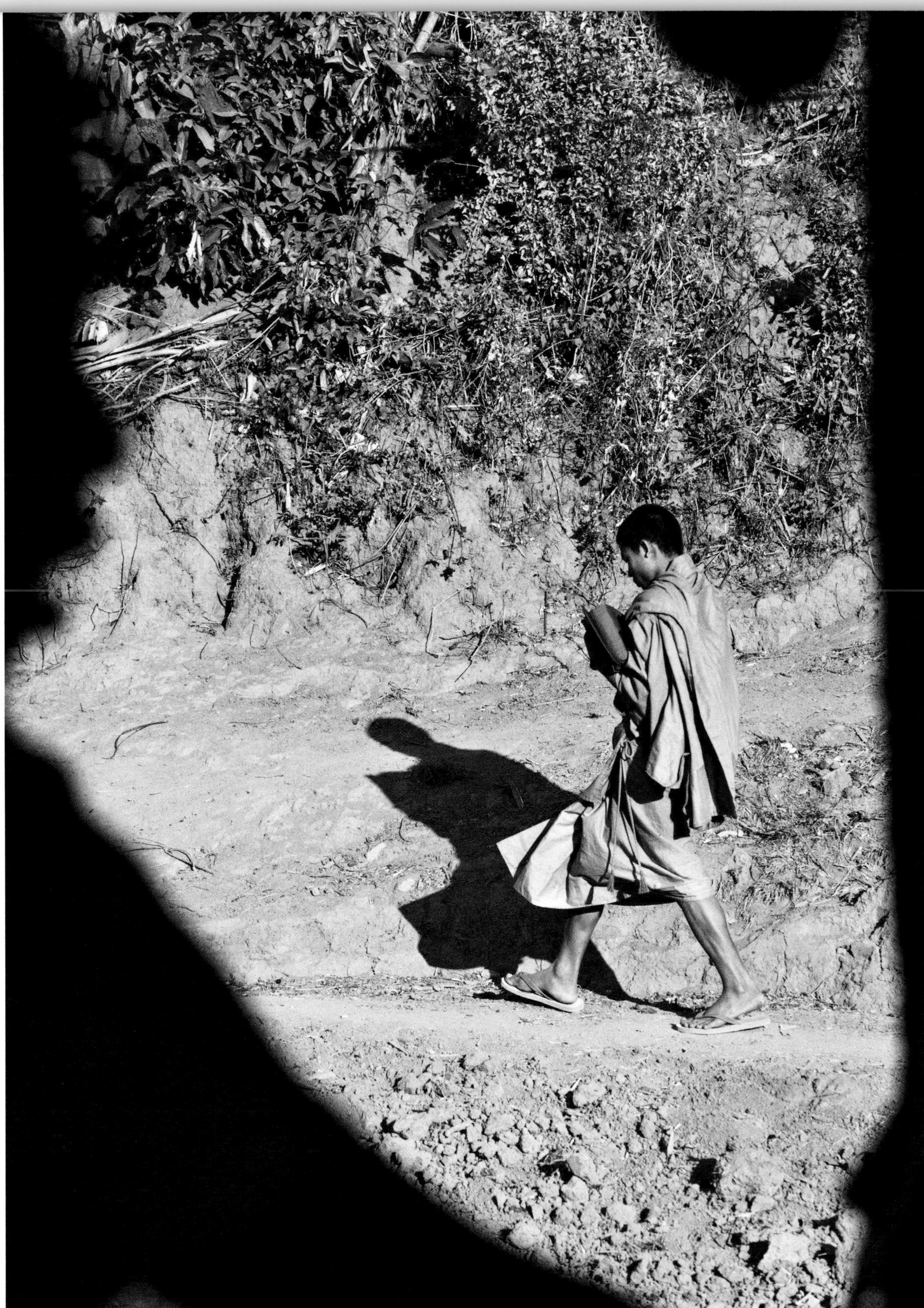

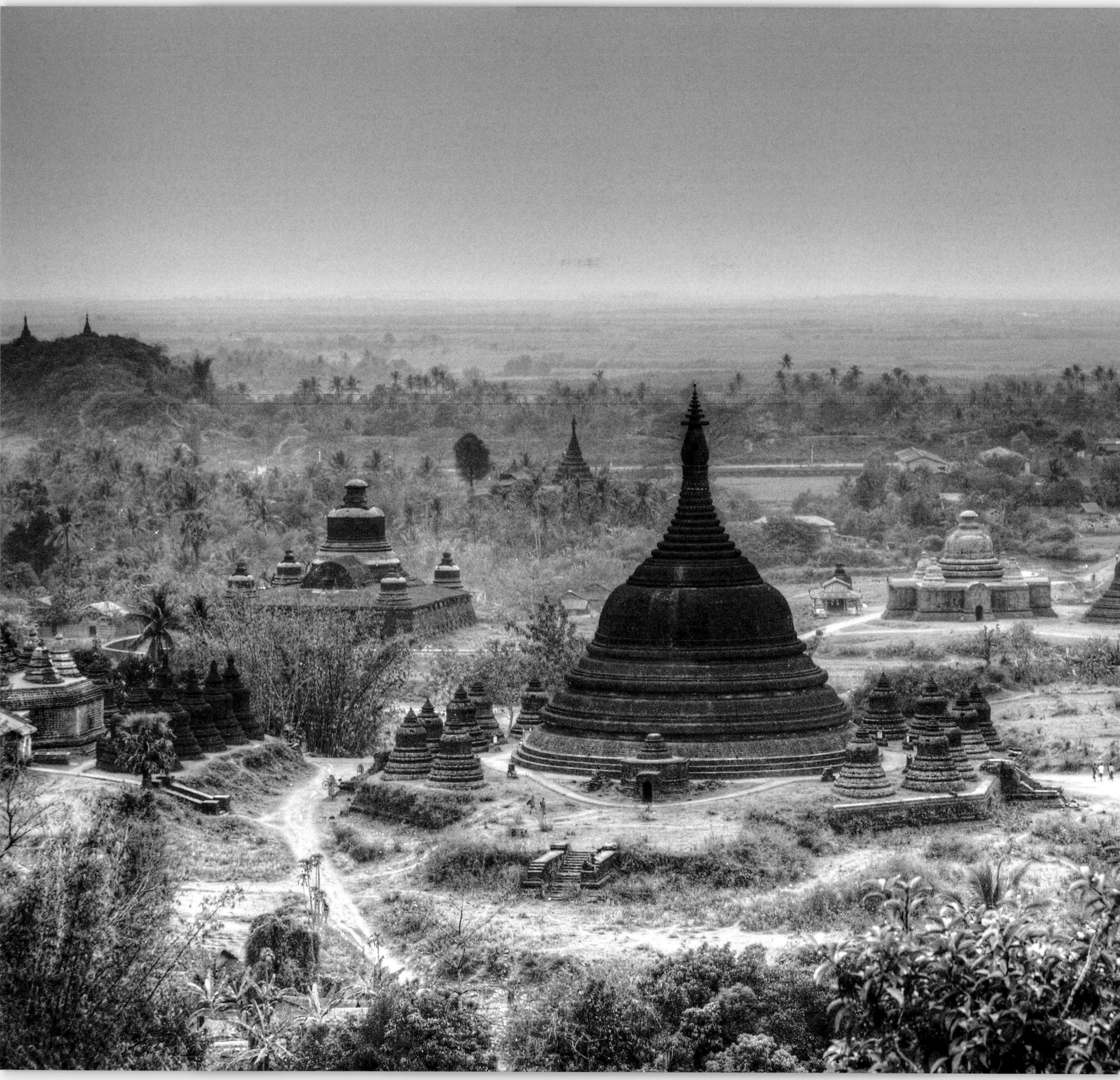

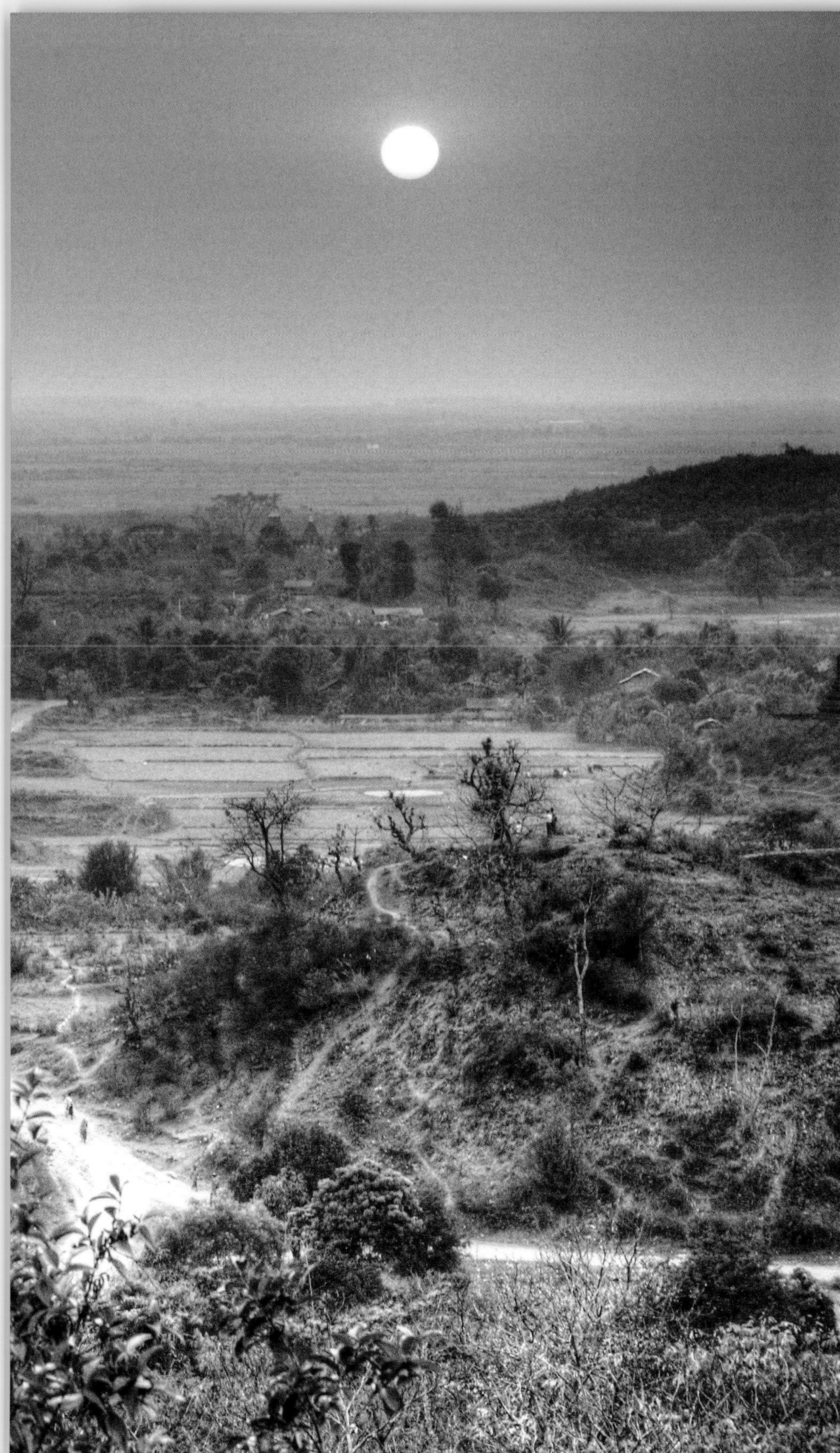

Sunset over the pagodas of Mrauk Oo, Chin State, 2011

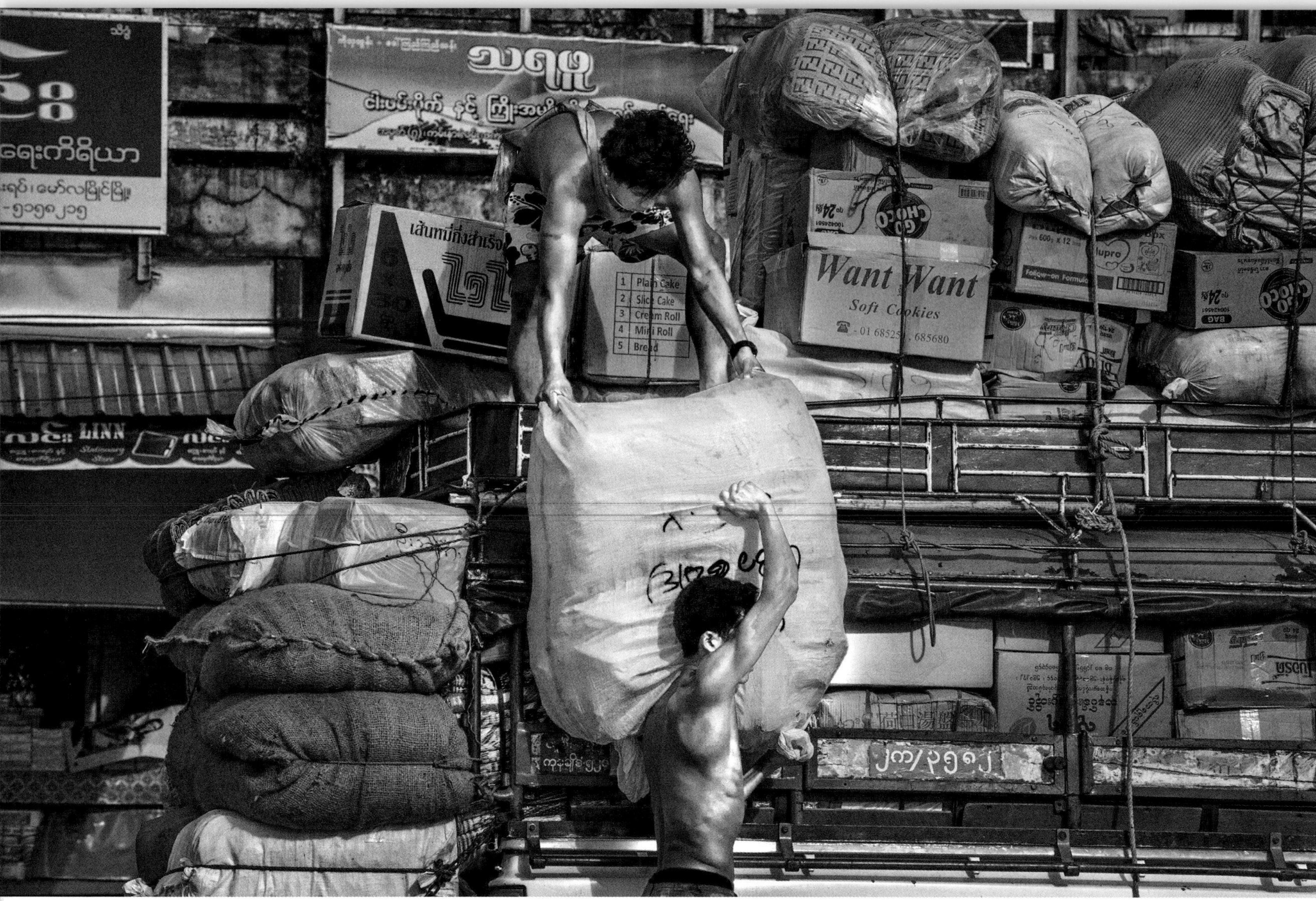

AT THE JETTY, MAWLAMYINE, MON STATE, 2011

Goods are unloaded at the jetty on the Thanlwin (Salween) River, which meets the sea close to the port of Mawlamyine. The river originates in the highlands of Tibet and then passes through China, Myanmar, and Thailand; in some parts forming the border between Myanmar and Thailand.

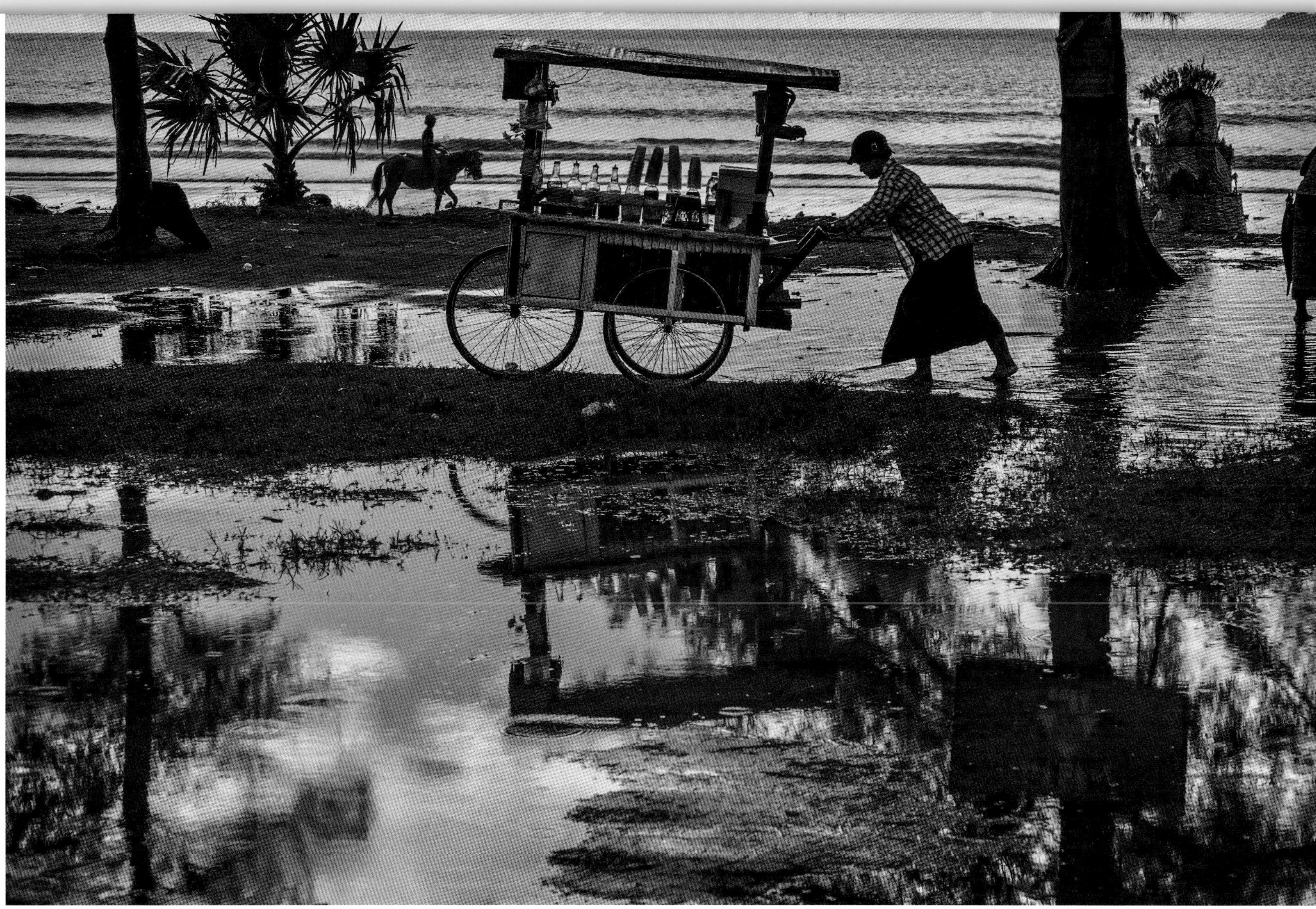

Beverage vendor at the beach, Setse Beach, Mon State, 2011

A stall-holder reemerges after a heavy rainfall ready to cater to tourists on Setse Beach.

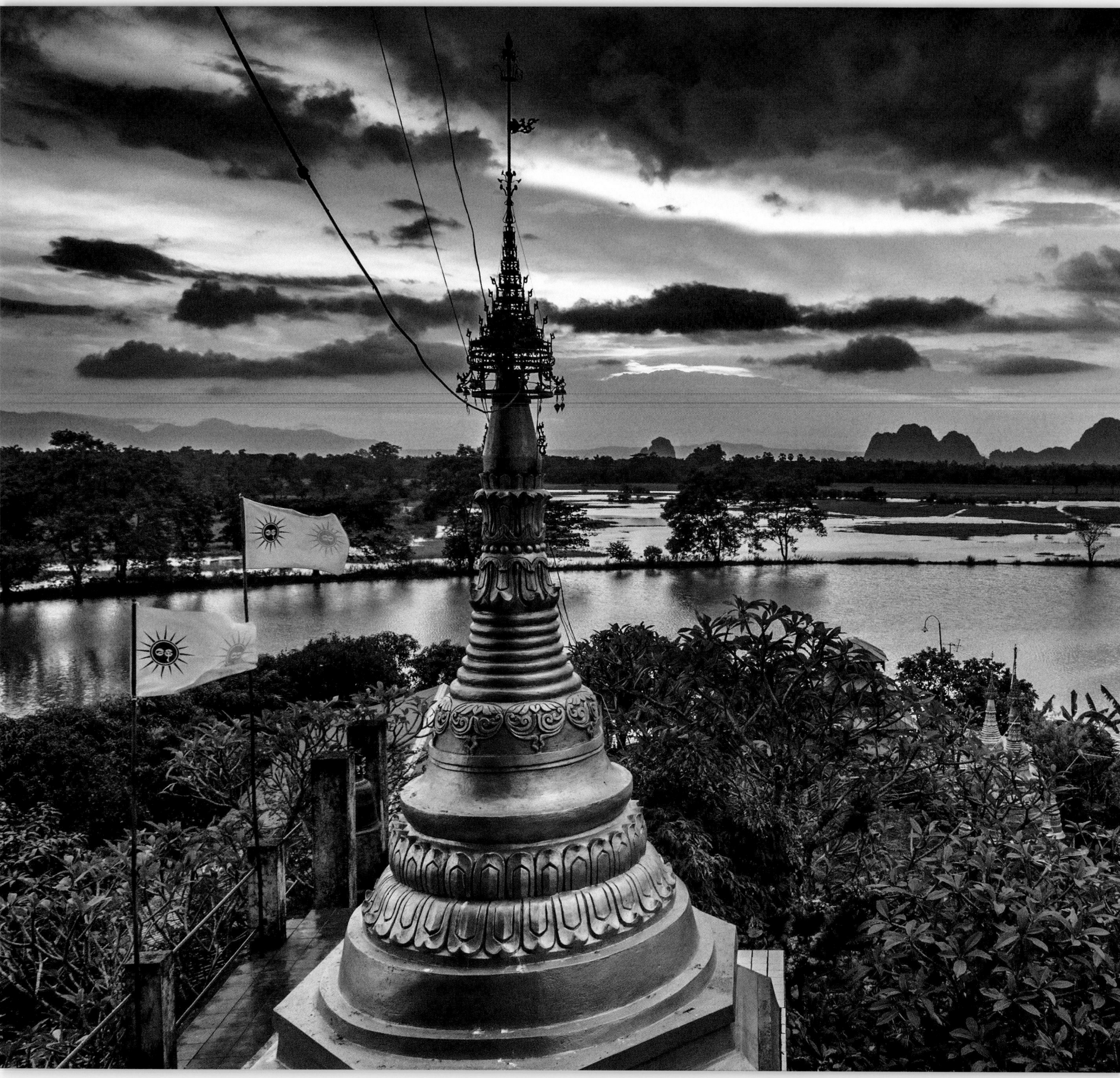

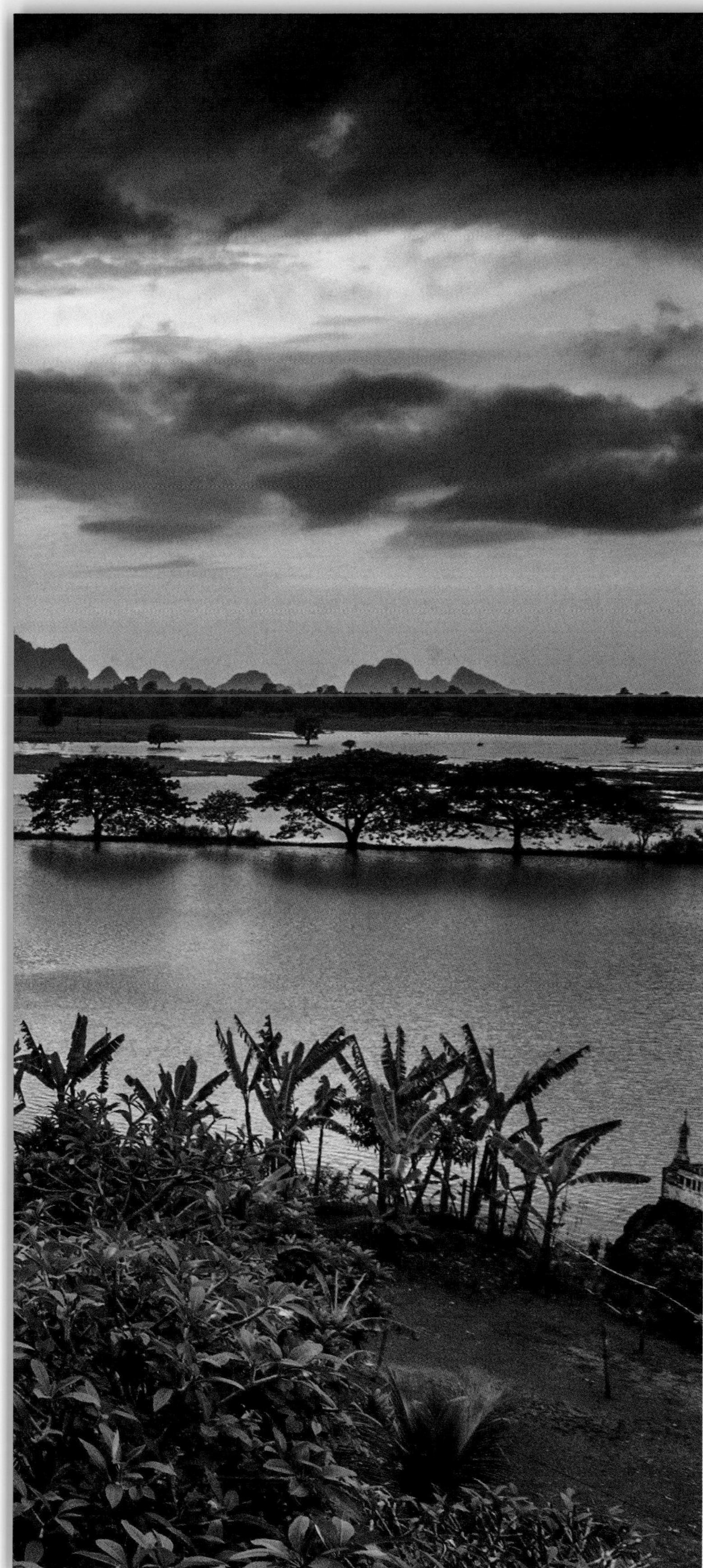

View from the Kyauk Kalat Pagoda, Hpa An, Kayin State, 2011

Pagodas often offer a stunning view of the surrounding countryside. In this photo, taken just after the rainy season, the land is lush and saturated with water.

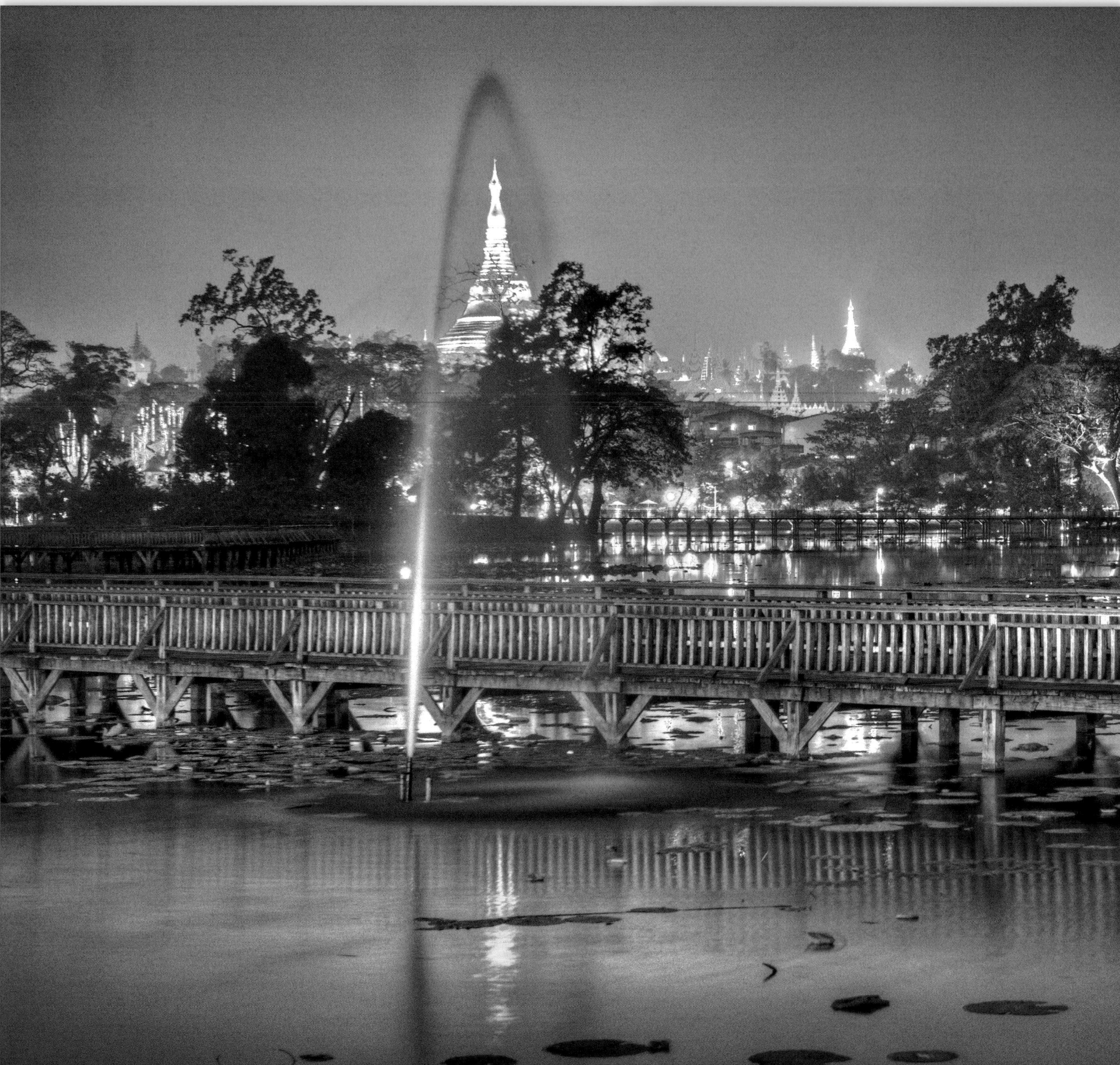

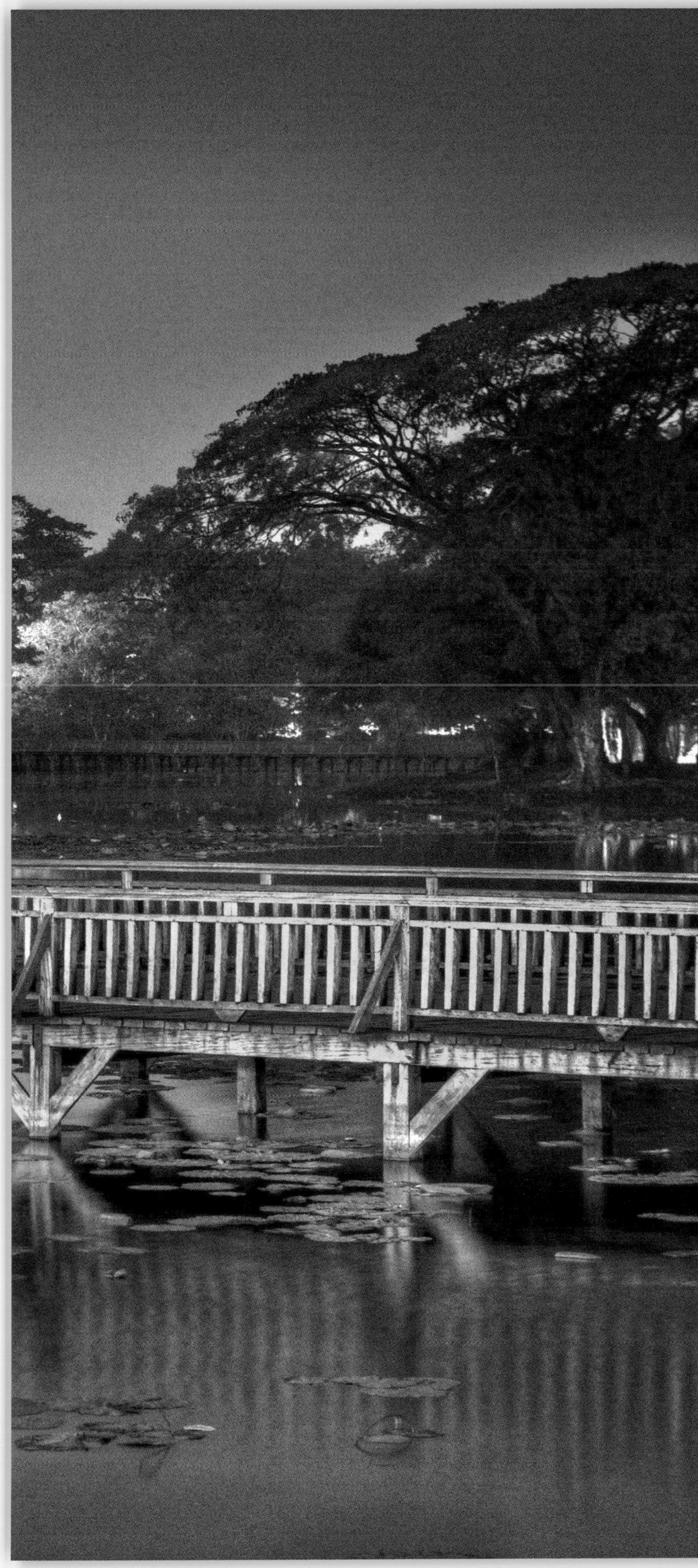

Night view of the Shwedagon Pagoda in the distance, taken from Kandawgyi Lake, Yangon, 2012

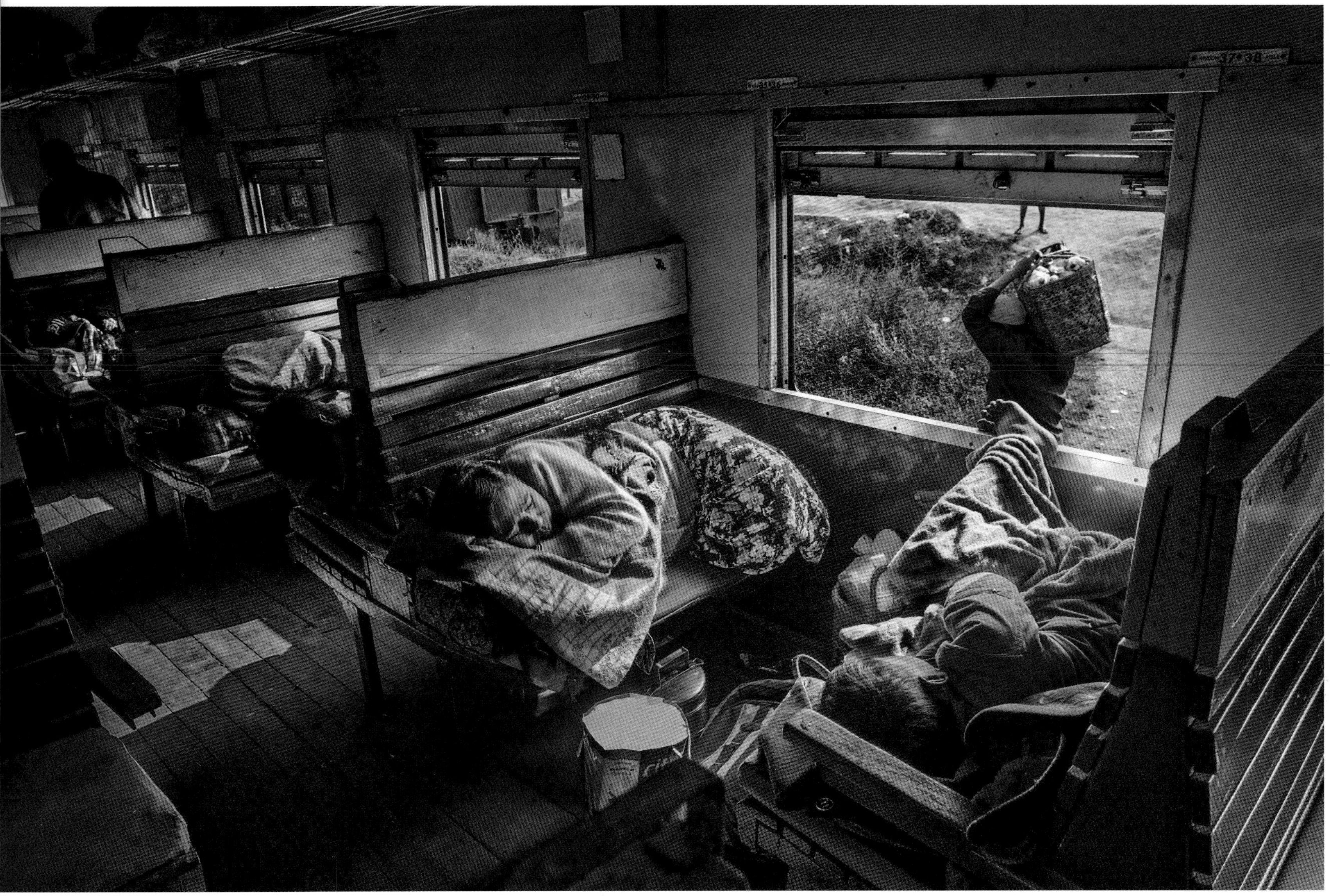

Train ride, Pyin Oo Lwin, Mandalay Region, 2012

Whenever the train between Pyin Oo Lwin (formerly the British hill station, May Myo) and Kyaukme comes to a halt, vendors converge around the train to sell snacks to passengers. As the train progresses along its route, the vendors are less successful as most passengers fall asleep despite, or perhaps because of, the jerking and rattling of the old carriages.

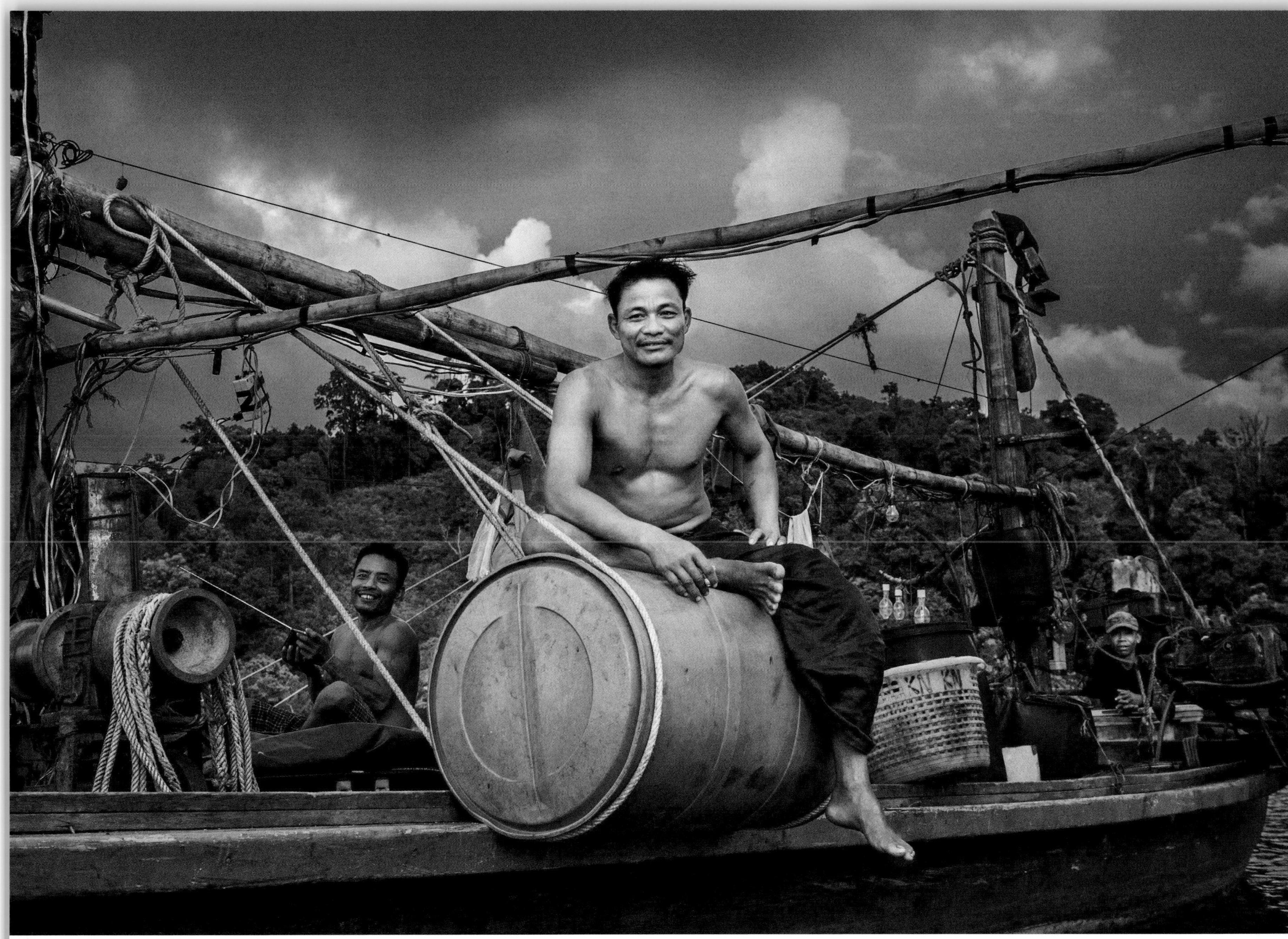

Fishing boat, Myeik Archipelago, Tanintharyi Region, 2012

Fishermen spend days out at sea on their boats before returning to shore to sell their catch. They are very busy, yet quick to offer a cup of tea if a visitor comes on board.

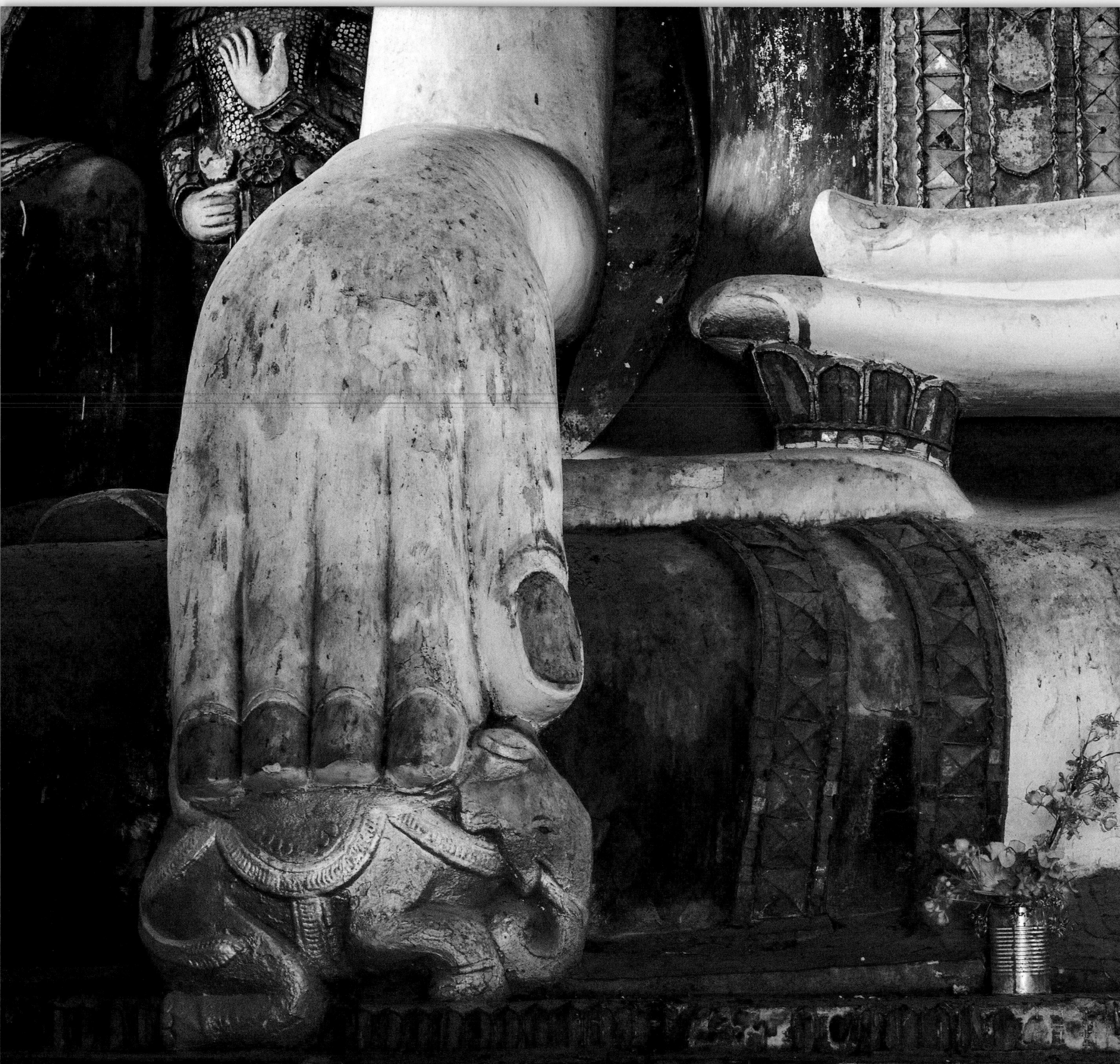

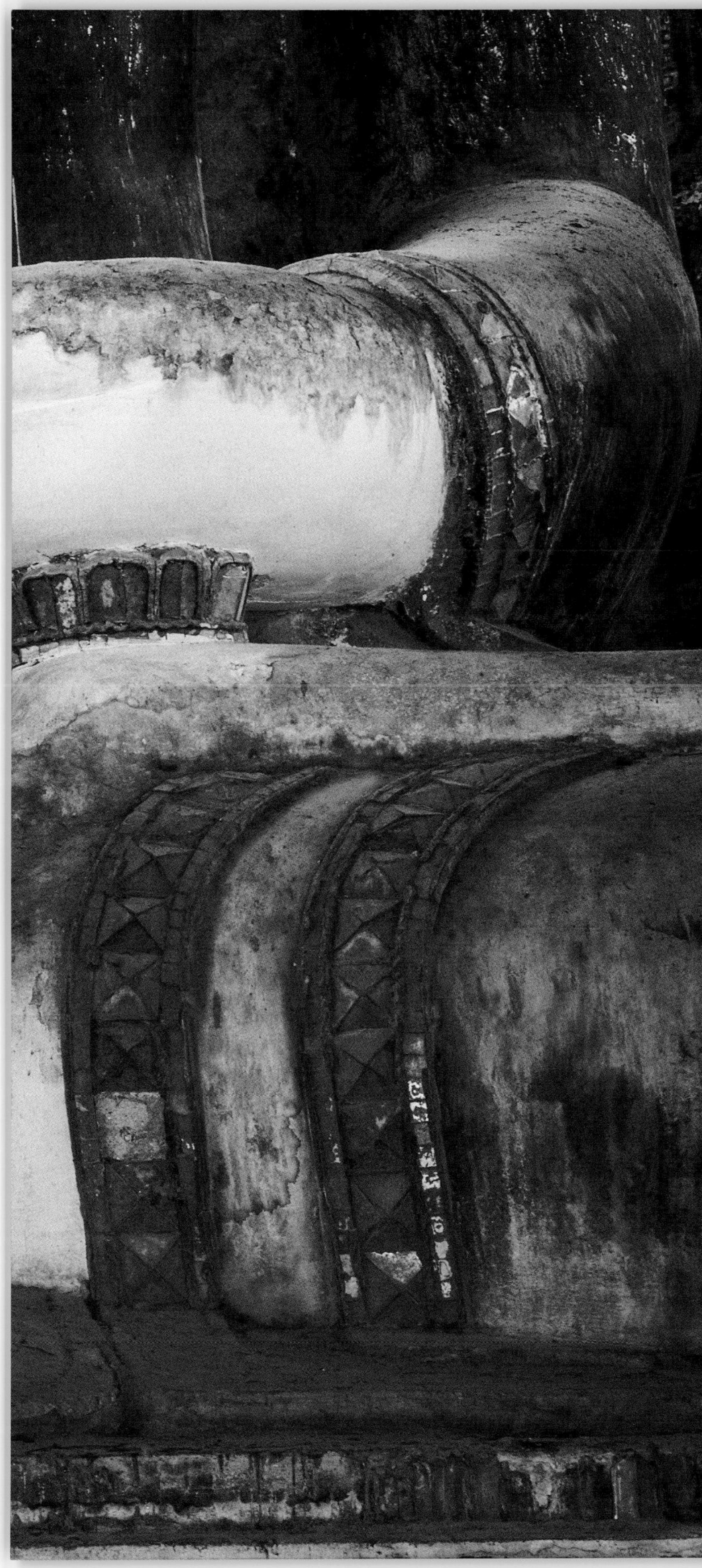

Thakaung Mwetaw Pagoda, Inle Lake, Shan State, 2012

It is rare to see an elephant beneath the main Buddha statue. In the Abhaya Mudra (which represents fearlessness and the granting of protection) the Buddha subdues a charging elephant that has been goaded on by a demon. Viewed with this in mind, this small sculpture may symbolize the submission of the elephant and a resulting liberation from fear.

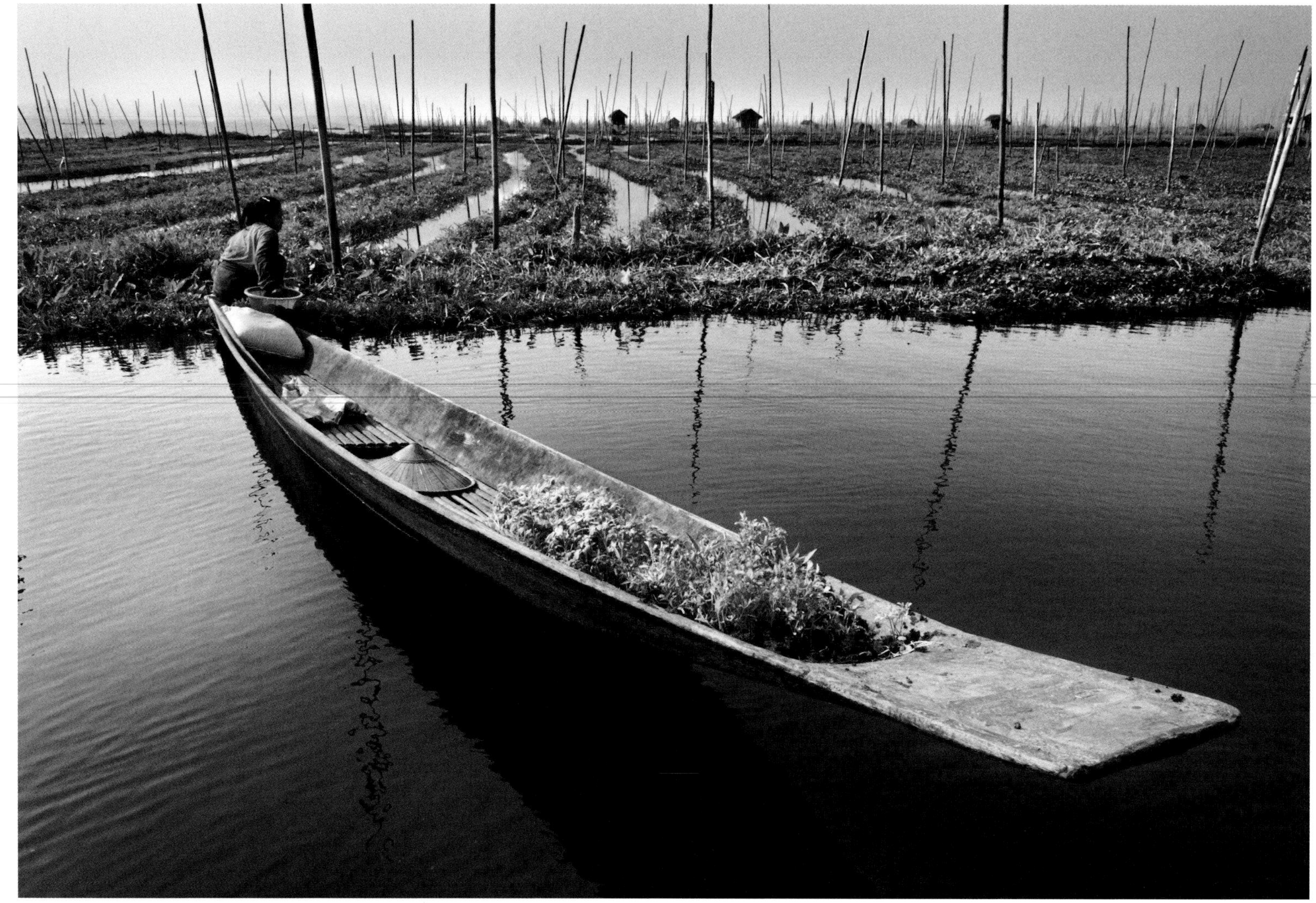

FLOATING GARDENS, INLE LAKE, SHAN STATE, 2012

These floating garden beds rise and fall along with seasonal changes in the water level. They are held in place by bamboo poles. The gardens are famous for producing the best tomatoes in the country.

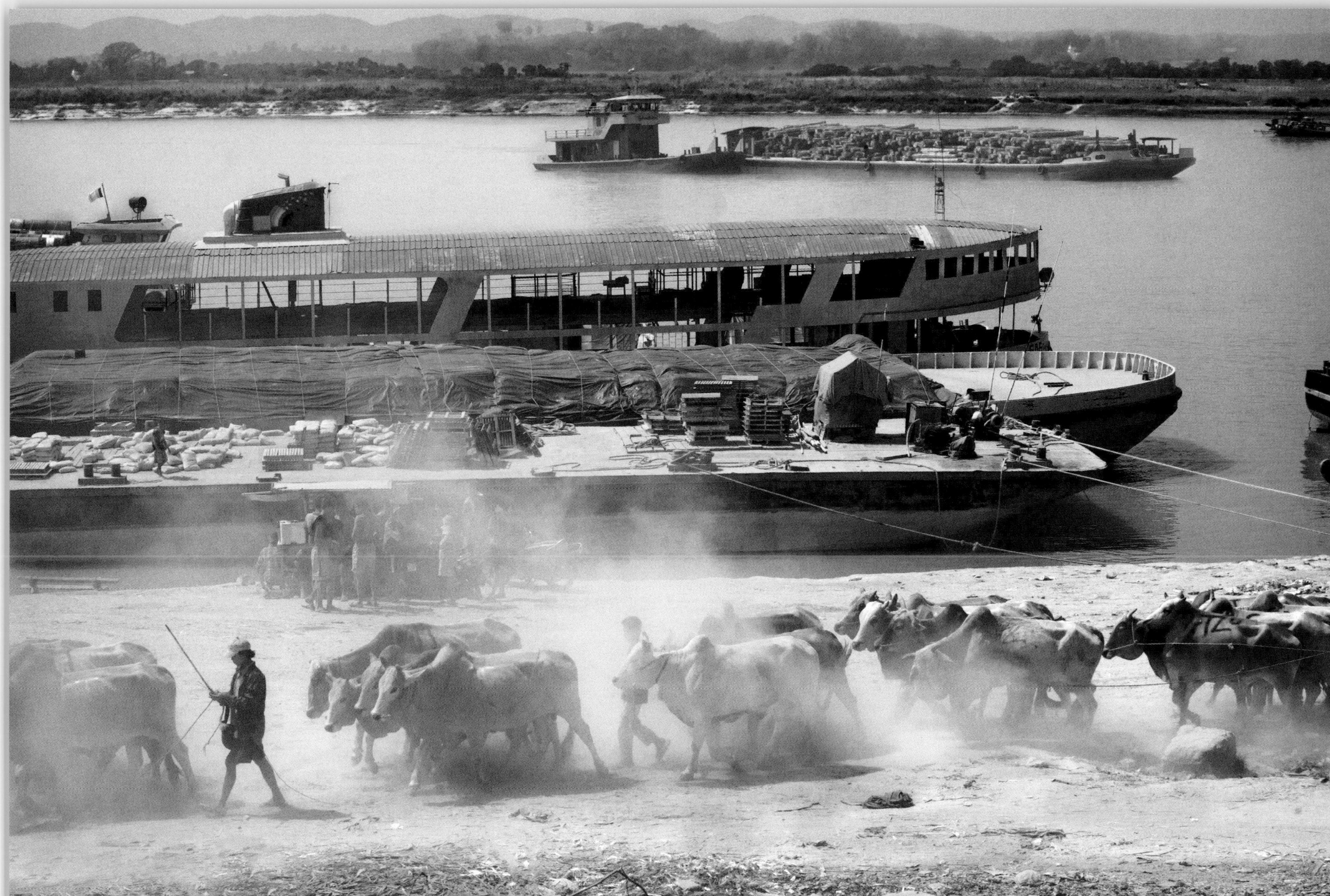

Oxen by the Ayeyarwady River, Mandalay, 2012

Oxen, rather than trucks, are still used to transport logs and other heavy goods to-and-from moored ships.

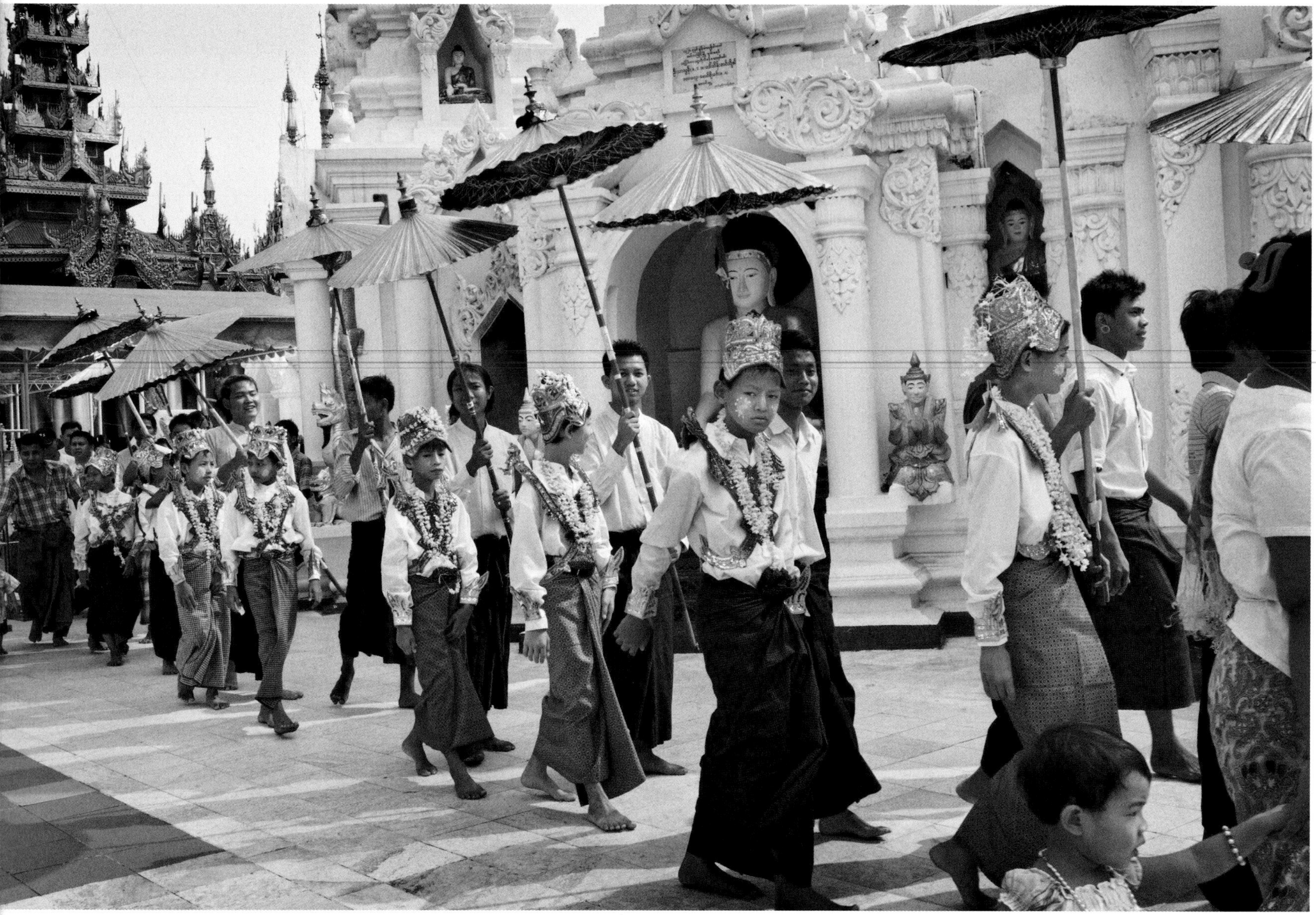

NOVITIATION CEREMONY AT THE SHWEDAGON PAGODA, YANGON, 2012

It must be a dream come true for a boy to celebrate his novitiation ceremony at Myanmar's most famous pagoda.

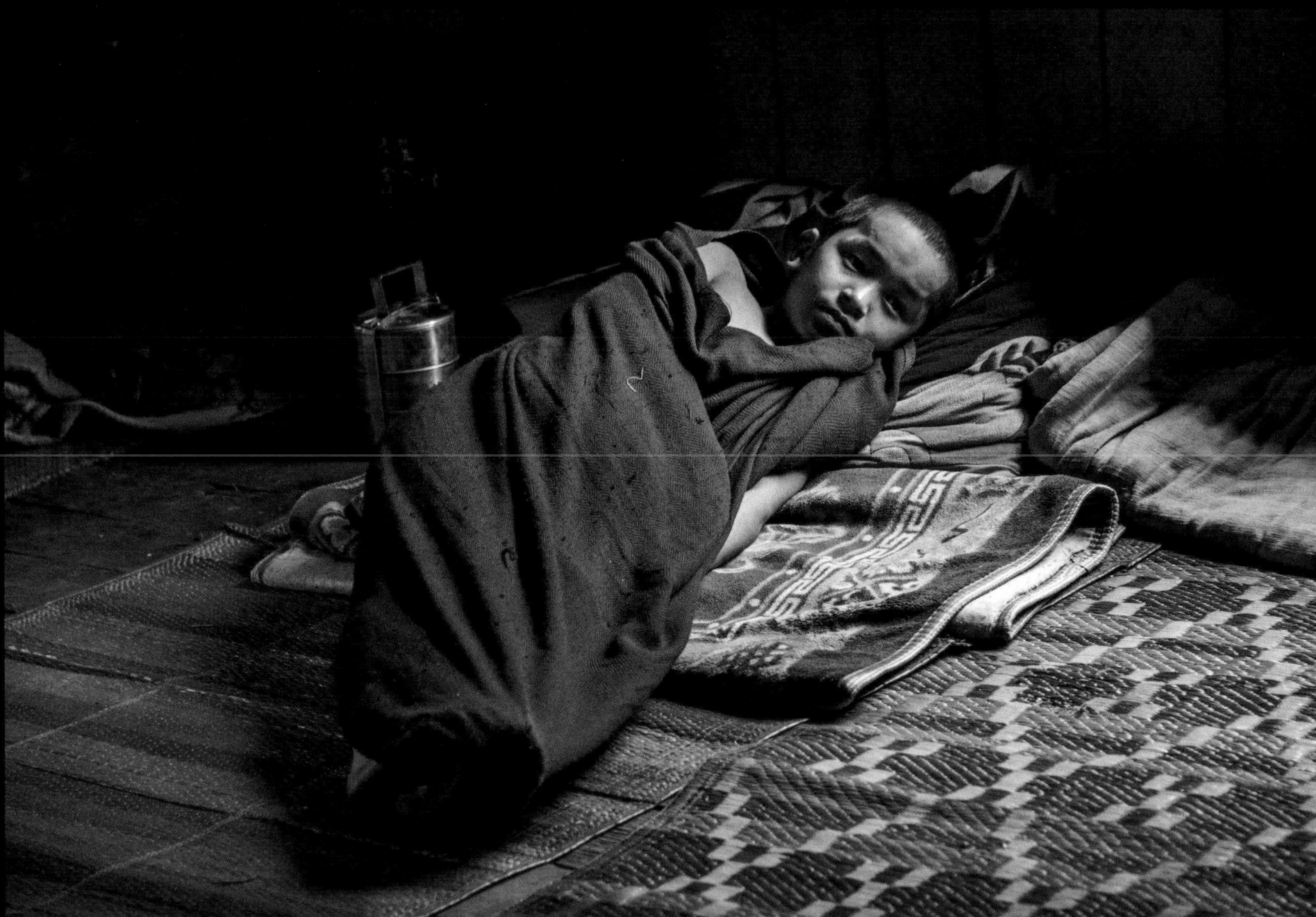

Novice at the Naung Yon Monastery, Hsipaw, Shan State, 2013

In a corner of the monastery, young novices have a place to rest and sleep.

Fish market, Sittwe, Rakhine State, 2011

At the Sittwe fish market, incoming boats are unloaded in the early morning mist. The mystical atmosphere ends abruptly as soon as you enter the adjacent fish market where the catch is immediately sold, either from vendor stalls or – if an especially big fish has been hauled in – at an impromptu auction.

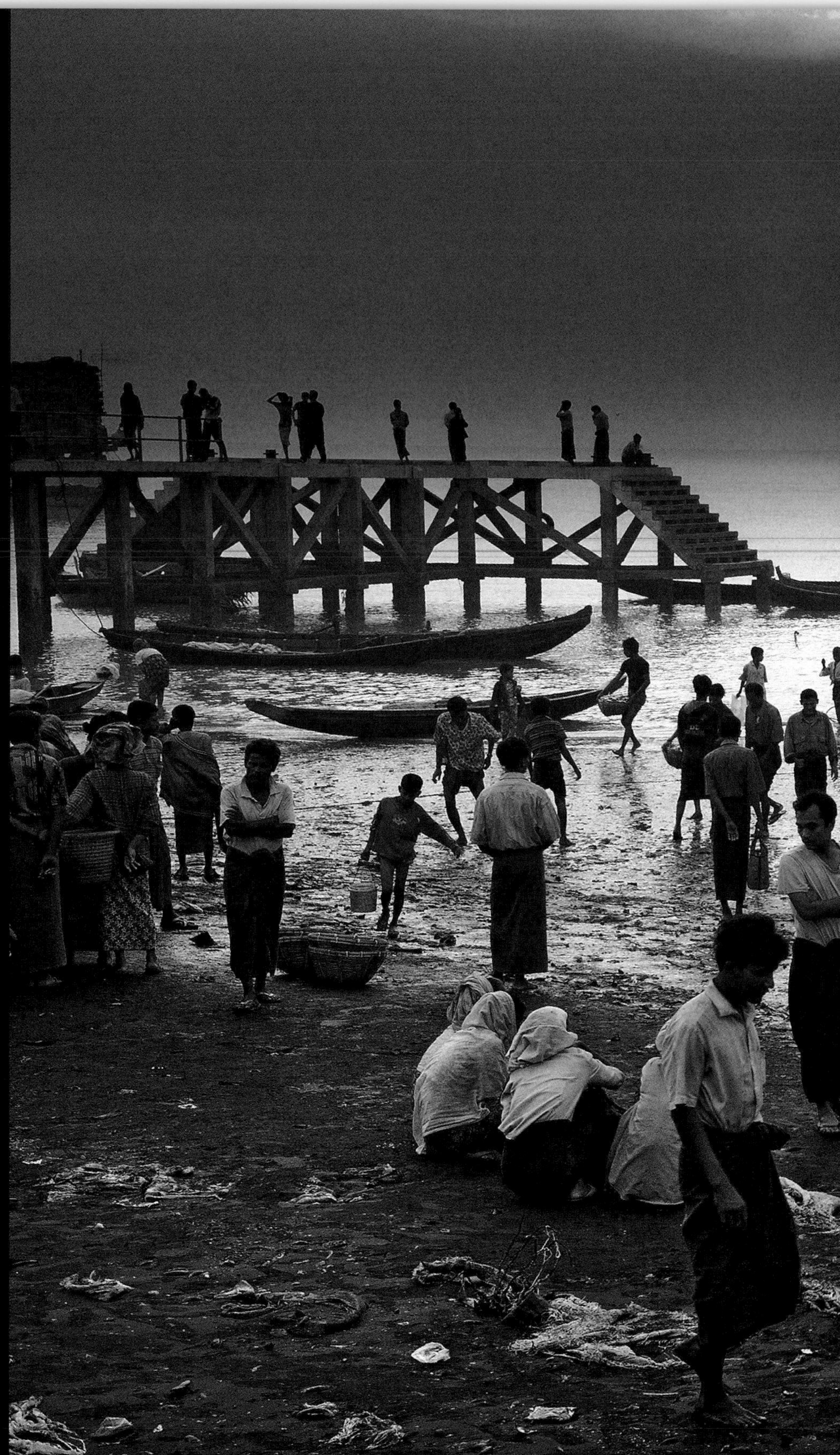

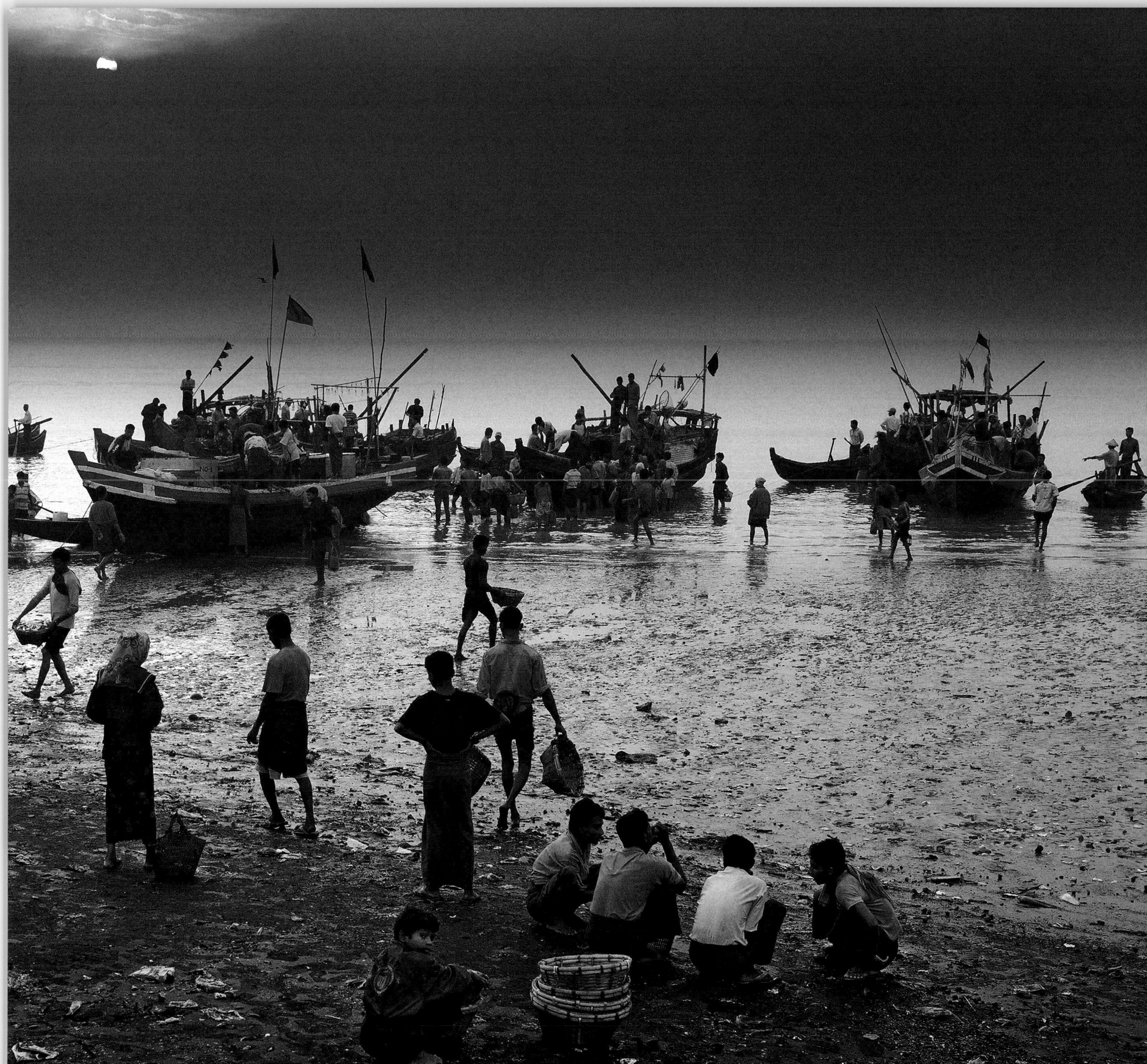

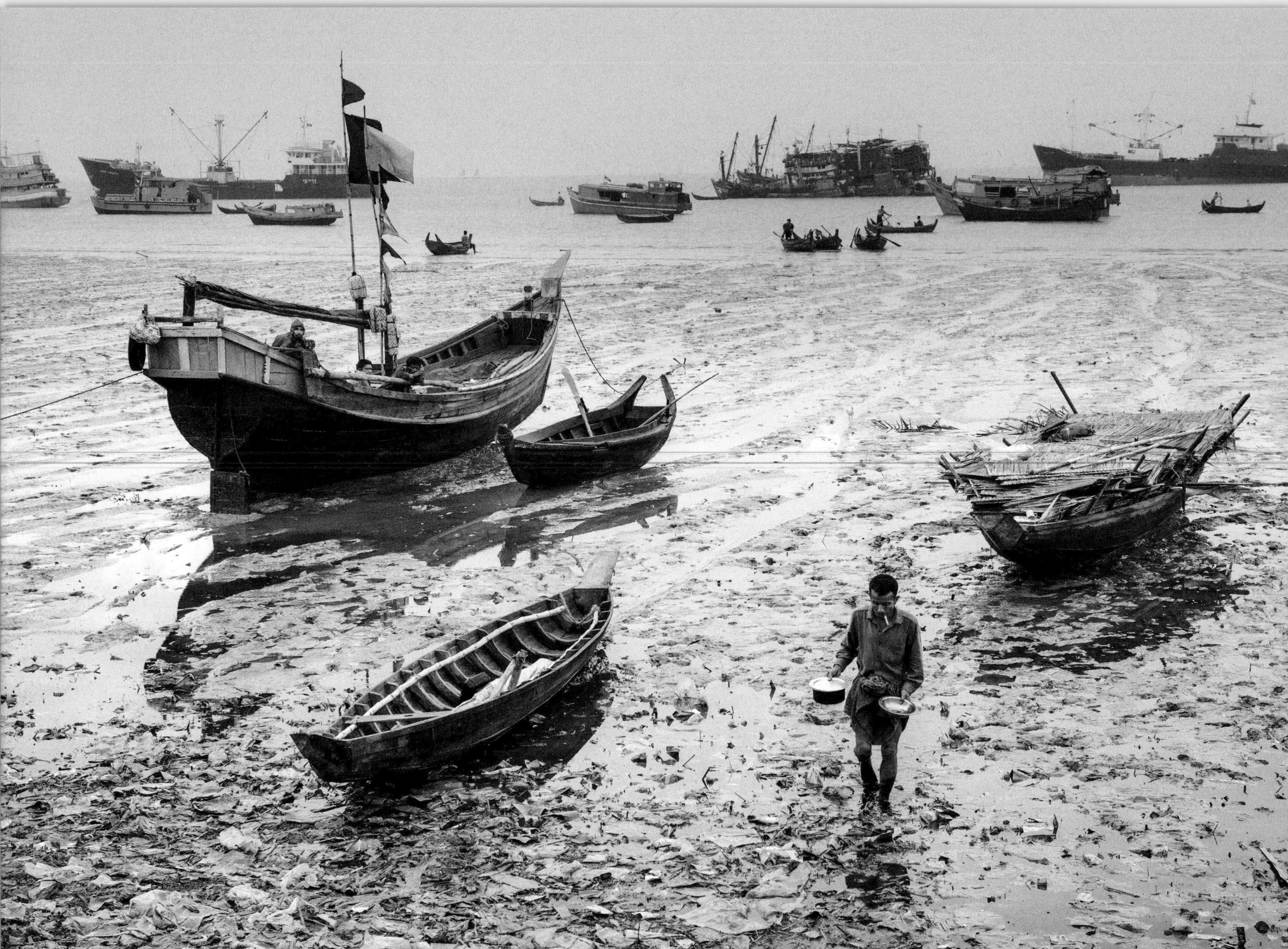

Early morning at the fishing harbor, Sittwe, Rakhine State, 2011

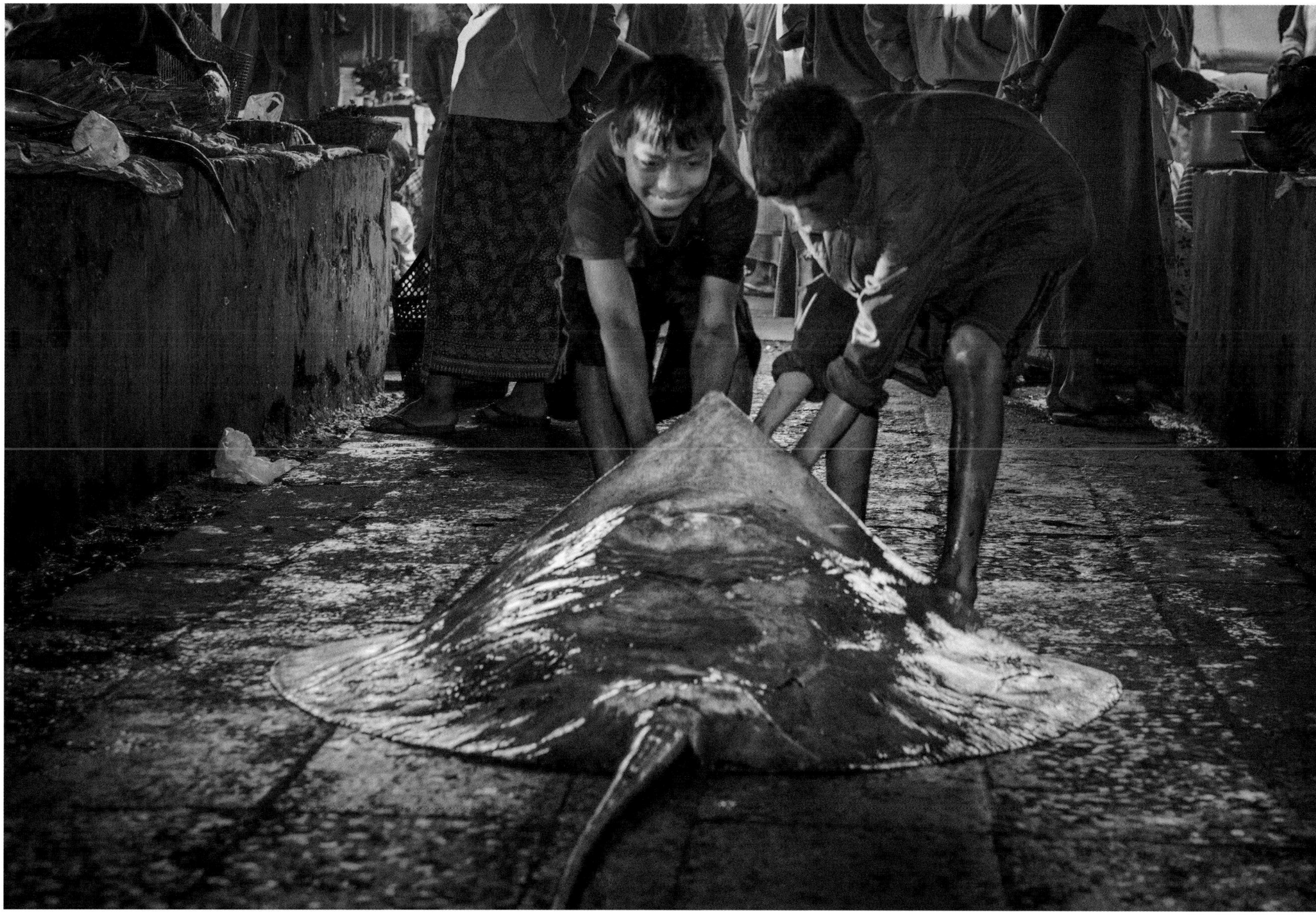

Boys dragging a ray at the fish market, Sittwe, Rakhine State, 2013

After an exceptionally large ray was unloaded from a boat, these two boys tried to transport it to the section of the fish market reserved for selling large catches. It proved too heavy and unwieldy to be carried so they had to drag it to its destination.

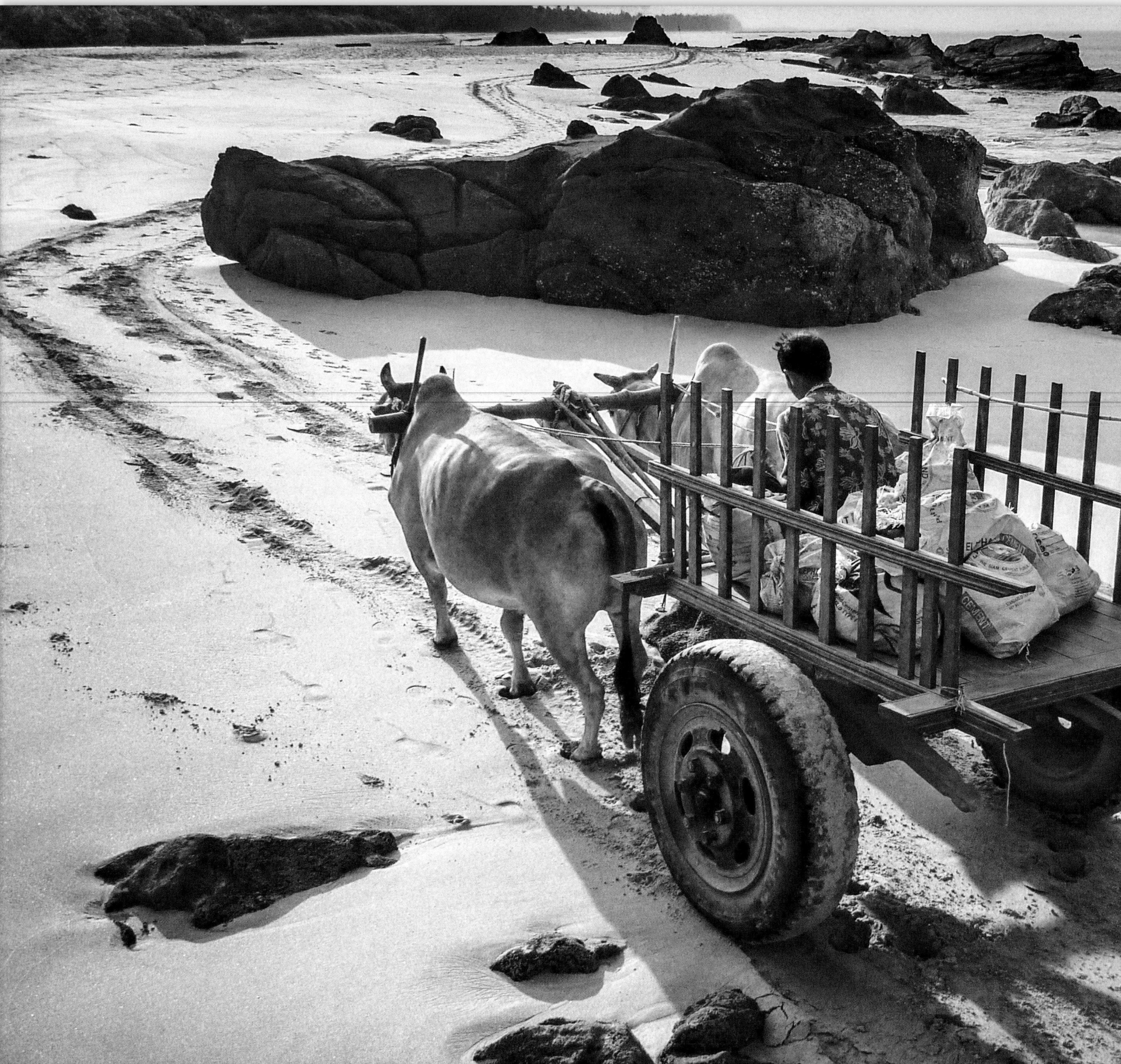

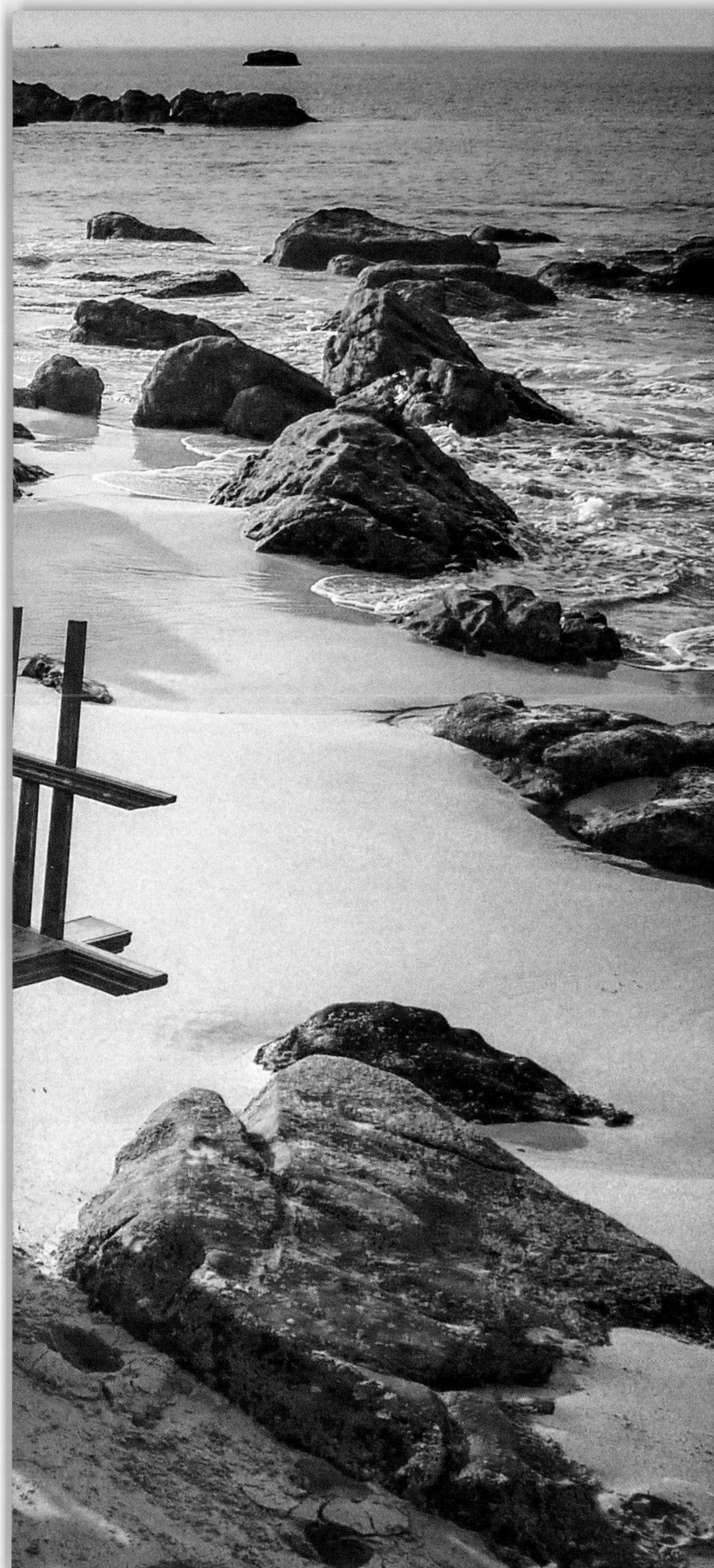

Ox cart on the beach, Thandwe, Rakhine State, 2014

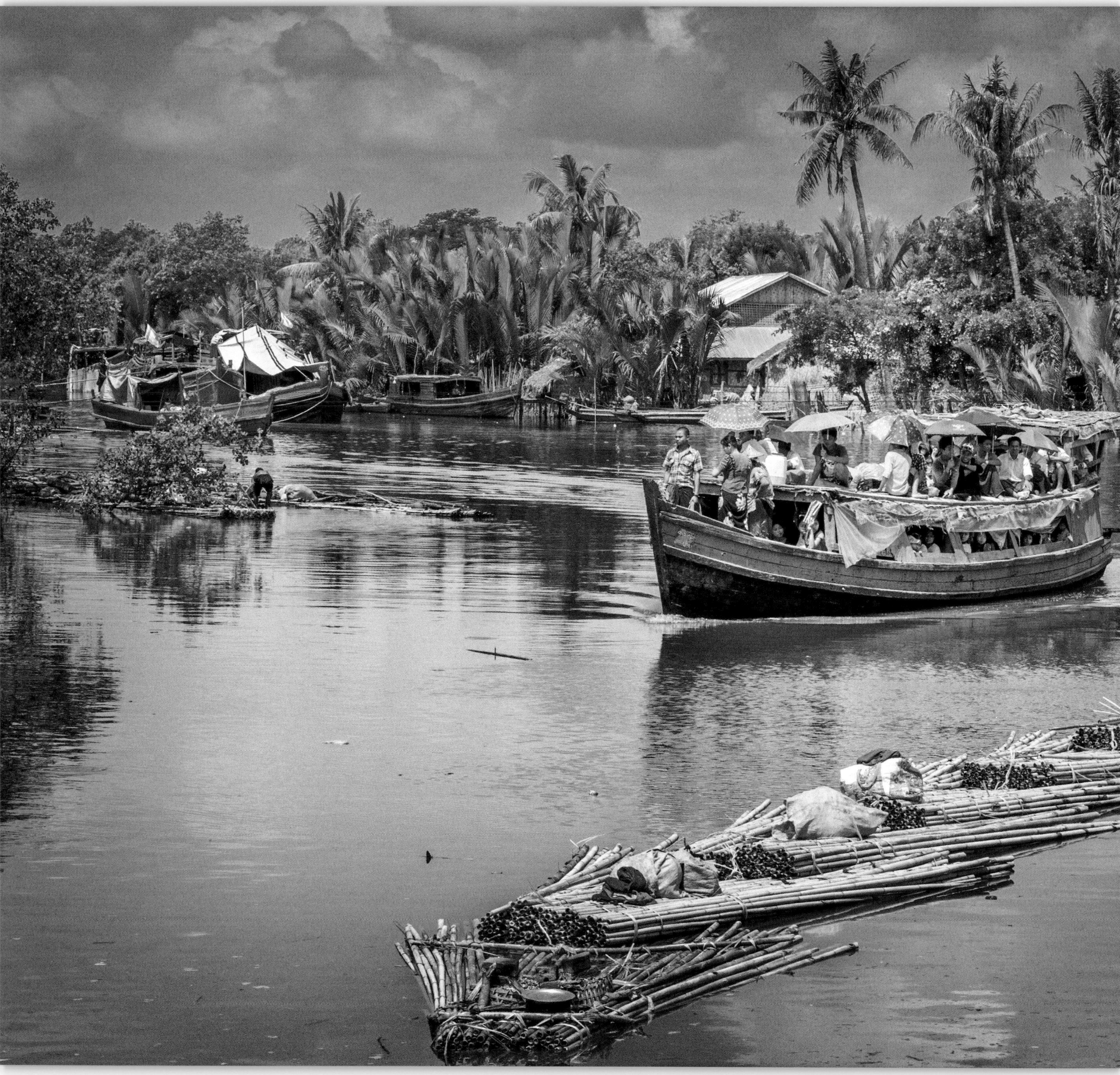

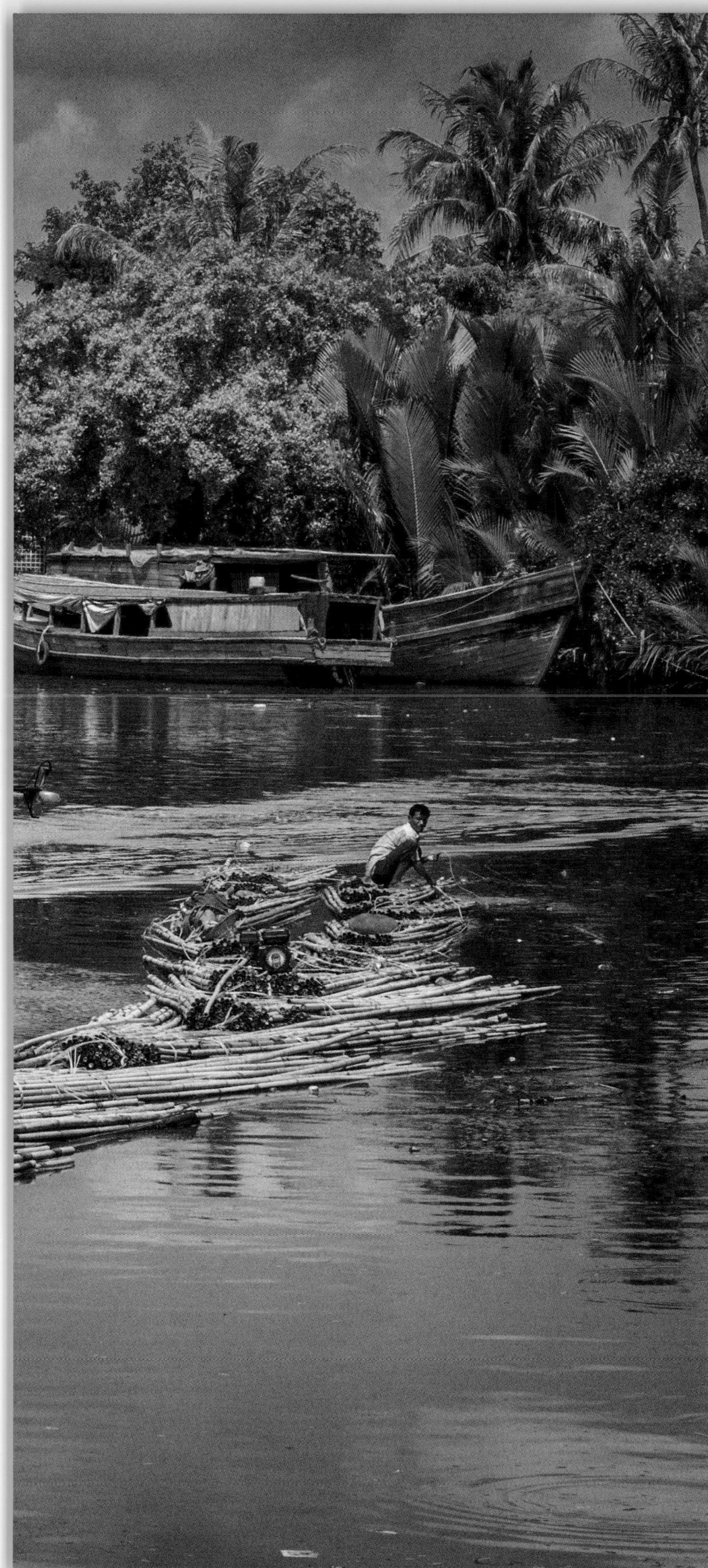

River scene with a passenger ferry and bamboo float, Mrauk Oo, Rakhine State, 2014

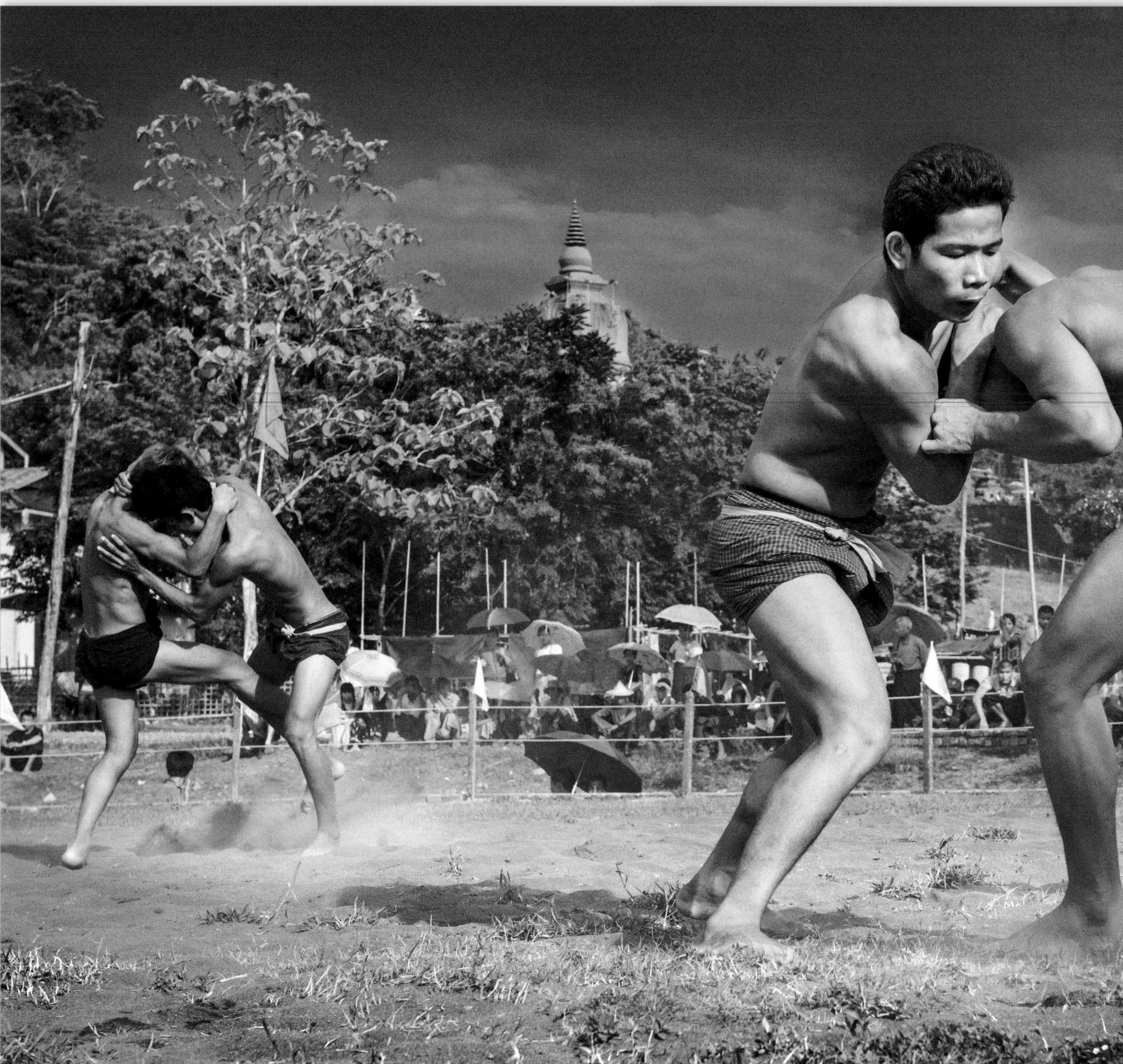

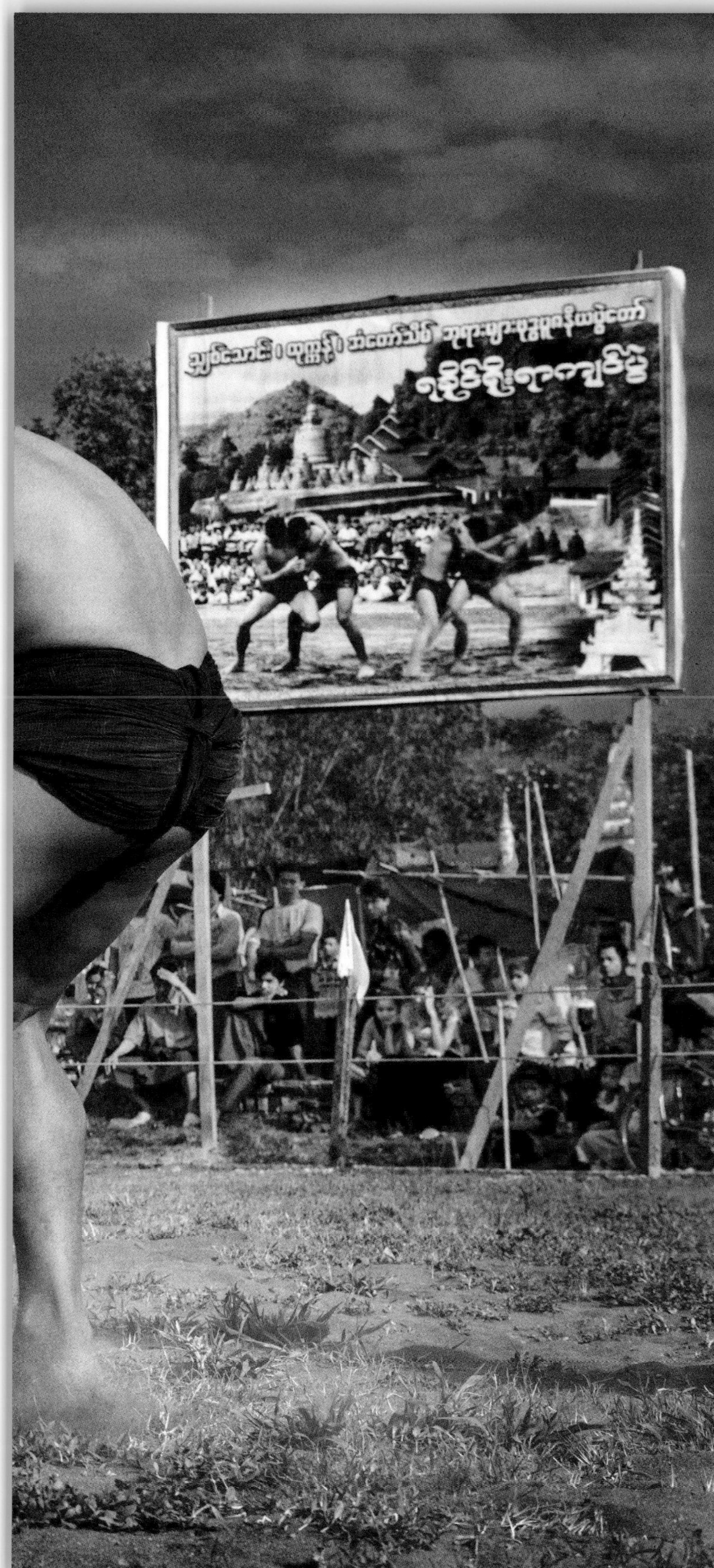

Wrestling competition, Mrauk Oo, Rakhine State, 2014

The annual Shittaung Pagoda Festival continues to keep alive traditions that are centuries old. Among the highlights are a boat race and this wrestling competition.

Overleaf: Bird's-eye view of the Manaw Festival, Myitkyina, Kachin State, 2015

The dances of the Kachin tribes follow a very strict choreography. The steps always match the rhythm of the music as a long row of dancers wind their way along lines painted on the festival ground. Only the dancers can interpret these intricate patterns and they know exactly where to go.

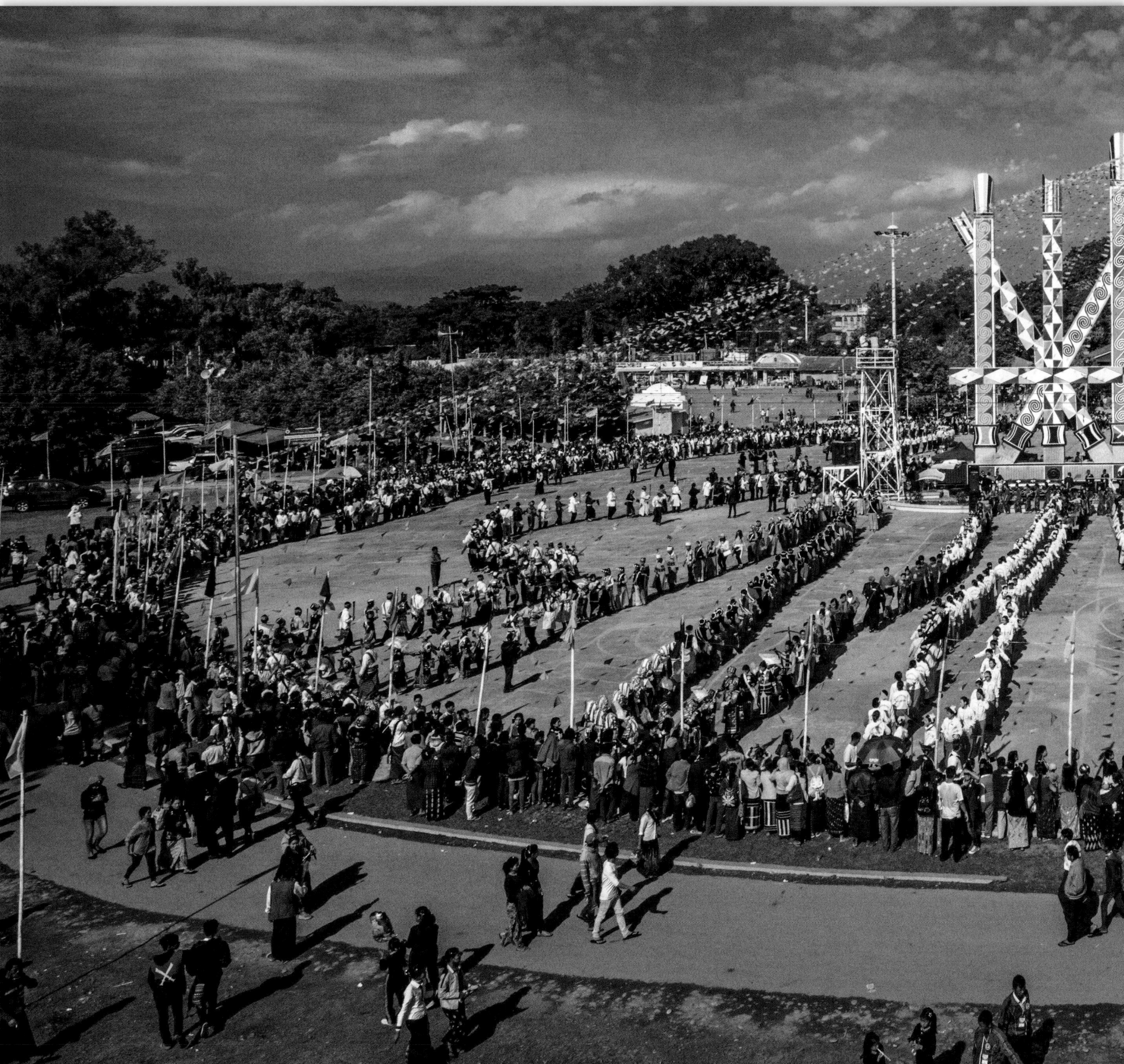

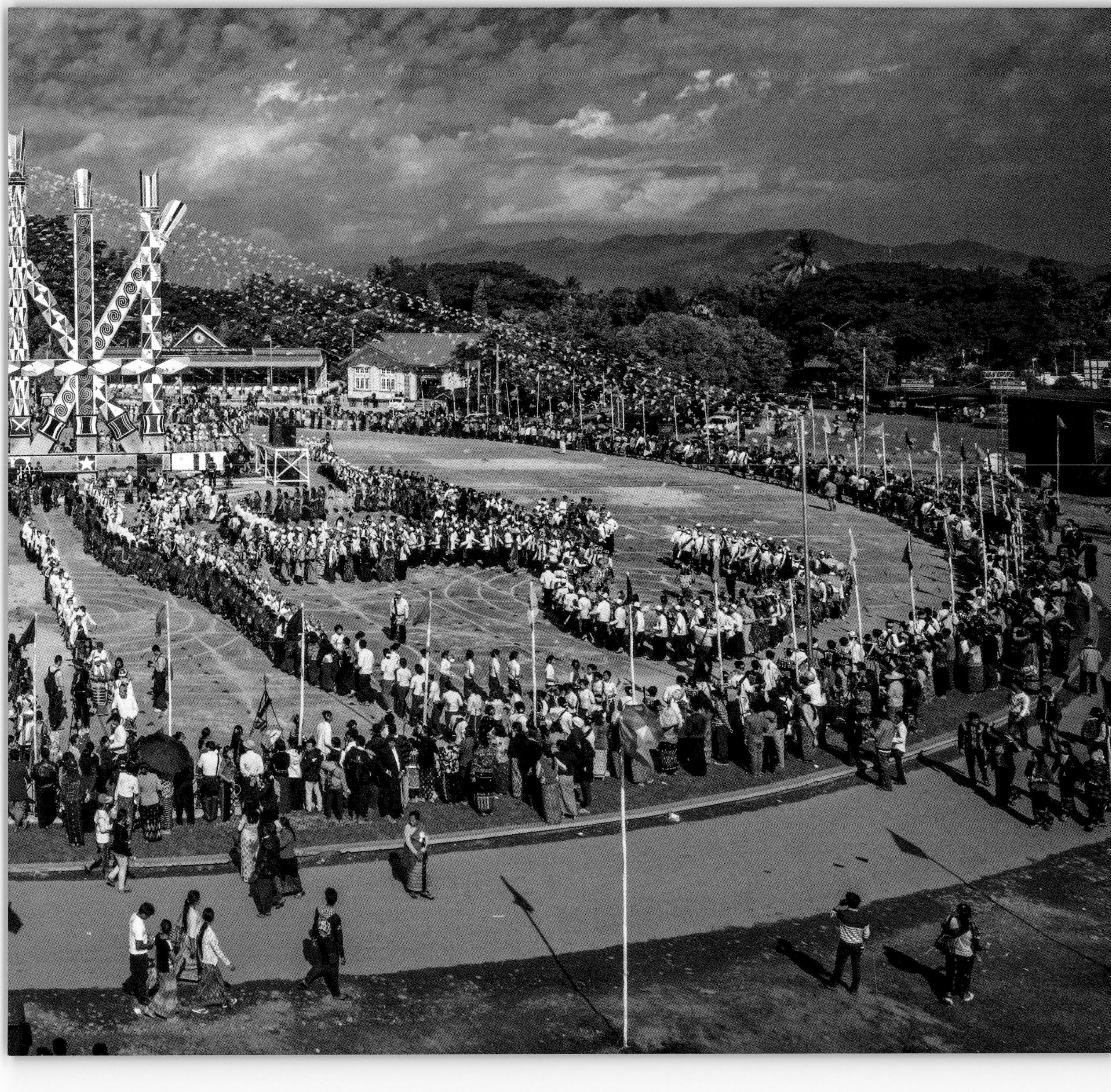

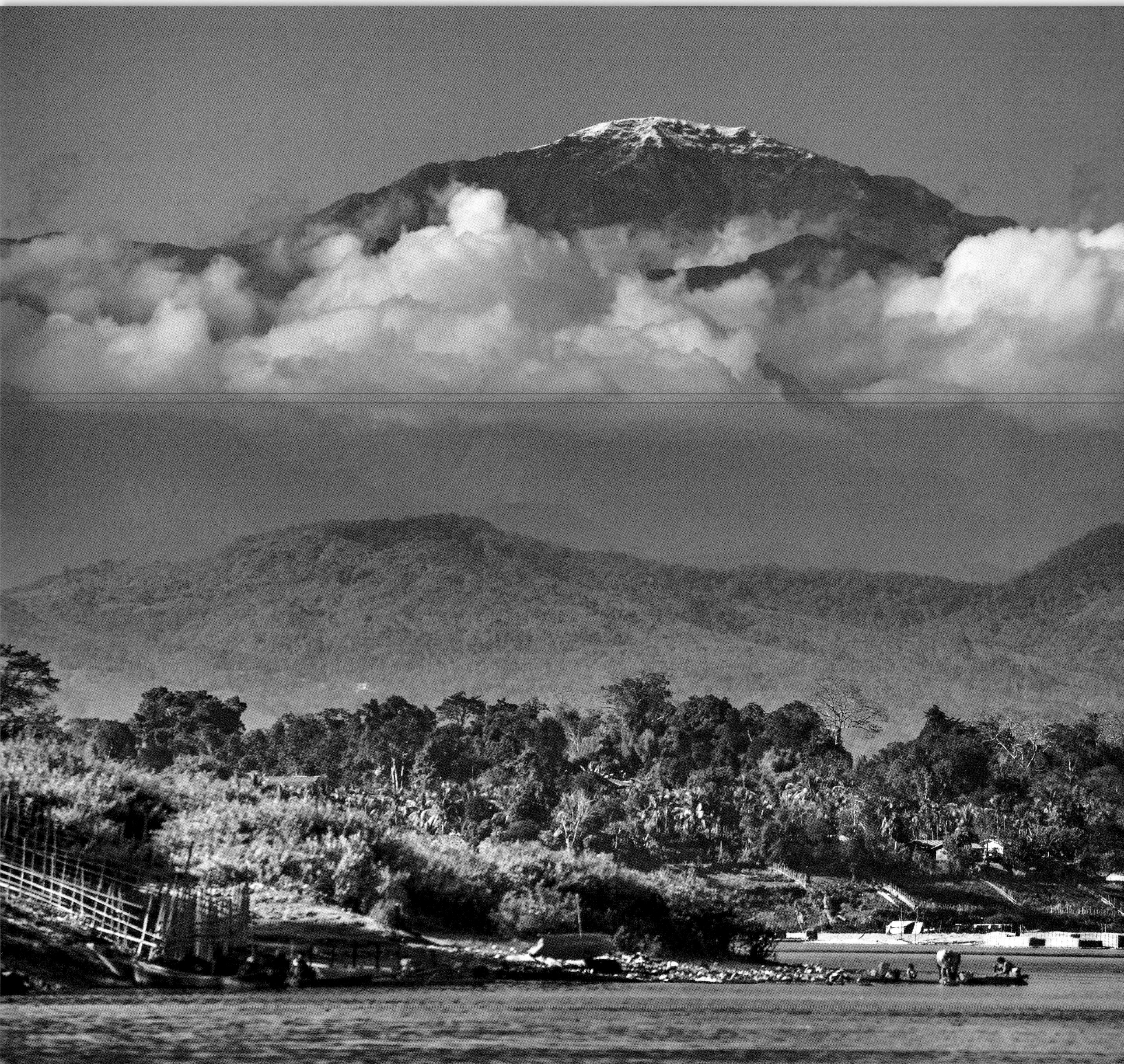

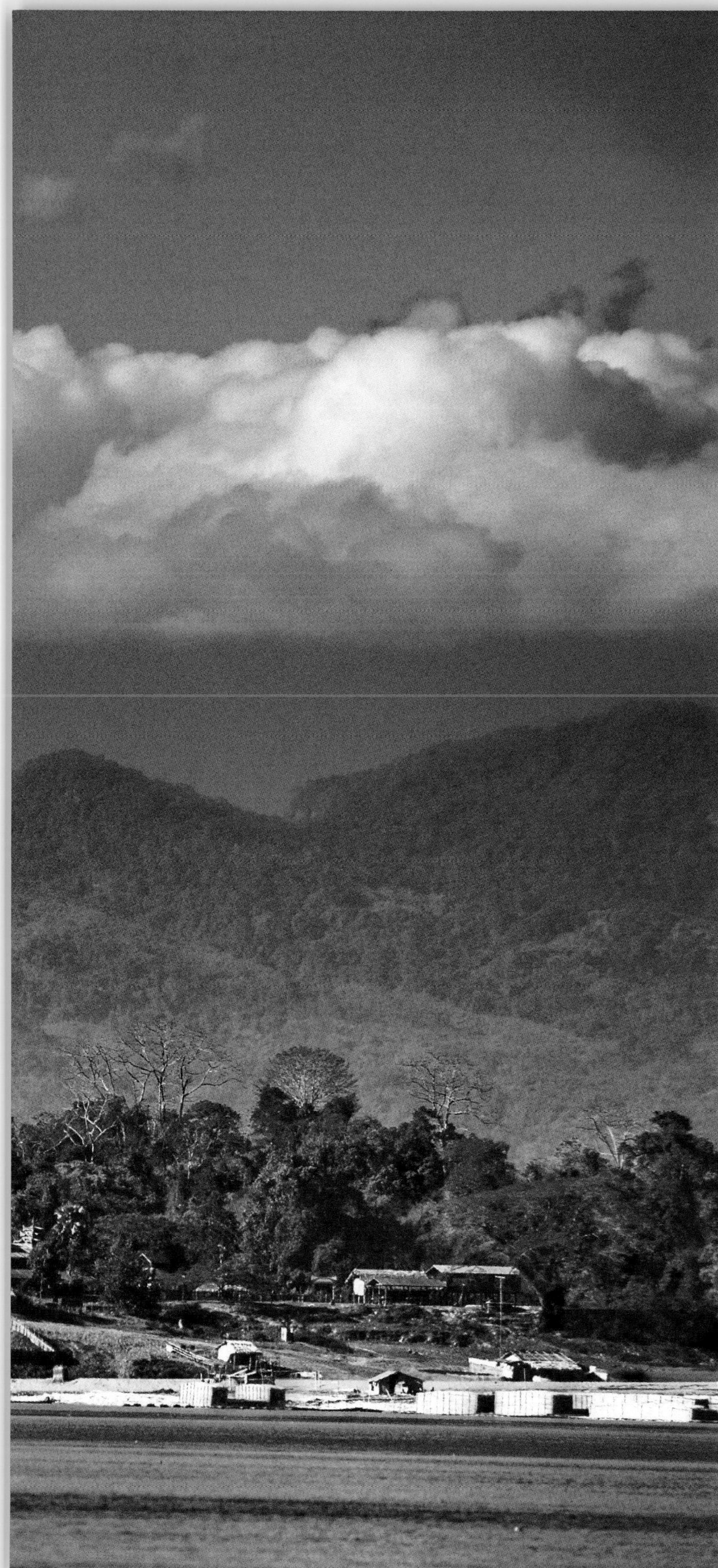

Where the Chindwin River meets the mountains, Thamanthi, Sagaing Region, 2015

The Chindwin is one of Myanmar's main rivers. It flows from the mountainous northwest region into the Ayeyarwady River further south.

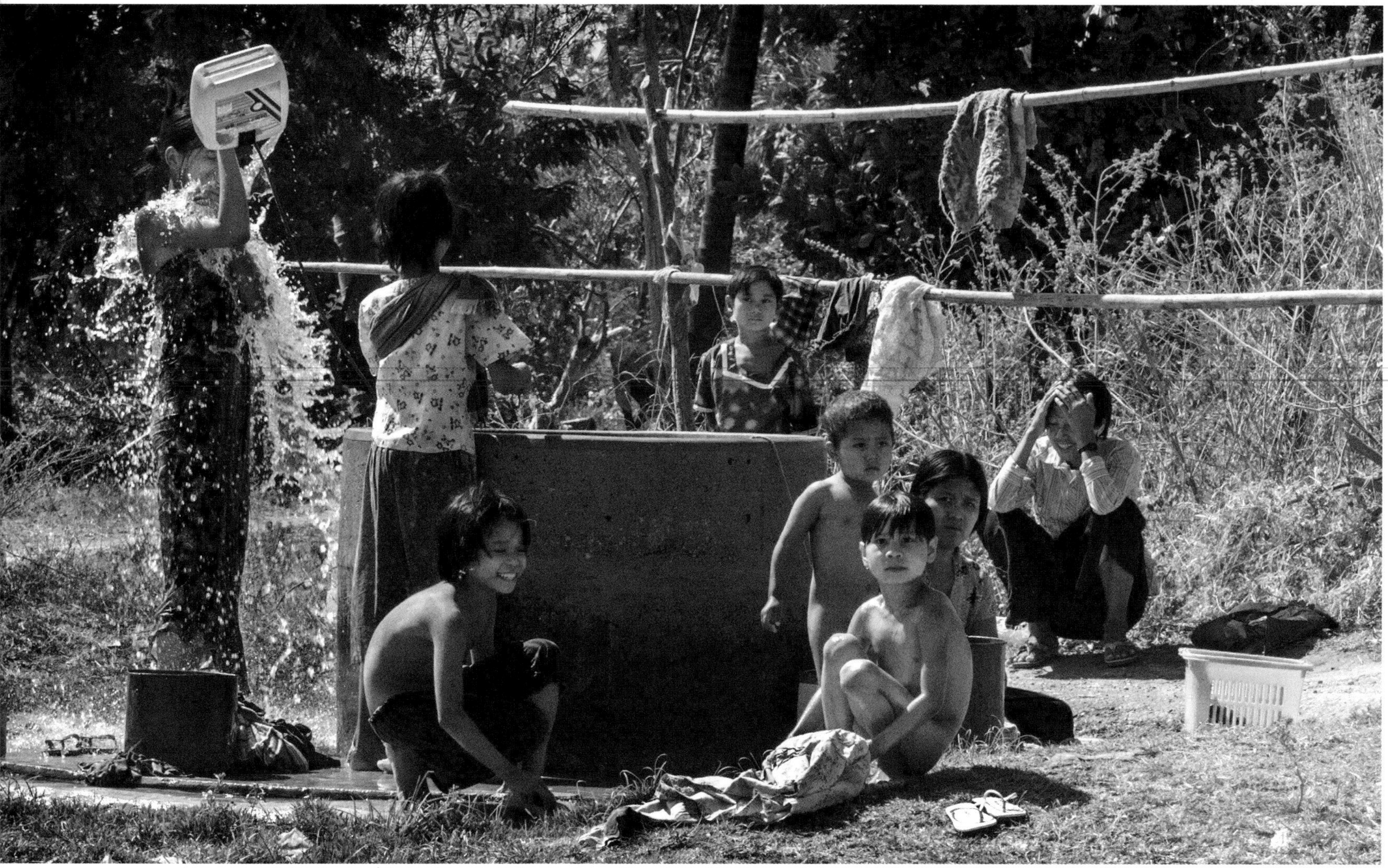

Village well, Kazunma village, Magway Region, 2011

When a village is located far from a river, the village well is a vital source of water and becomes a social hub where villagers chat while washing and bathing.

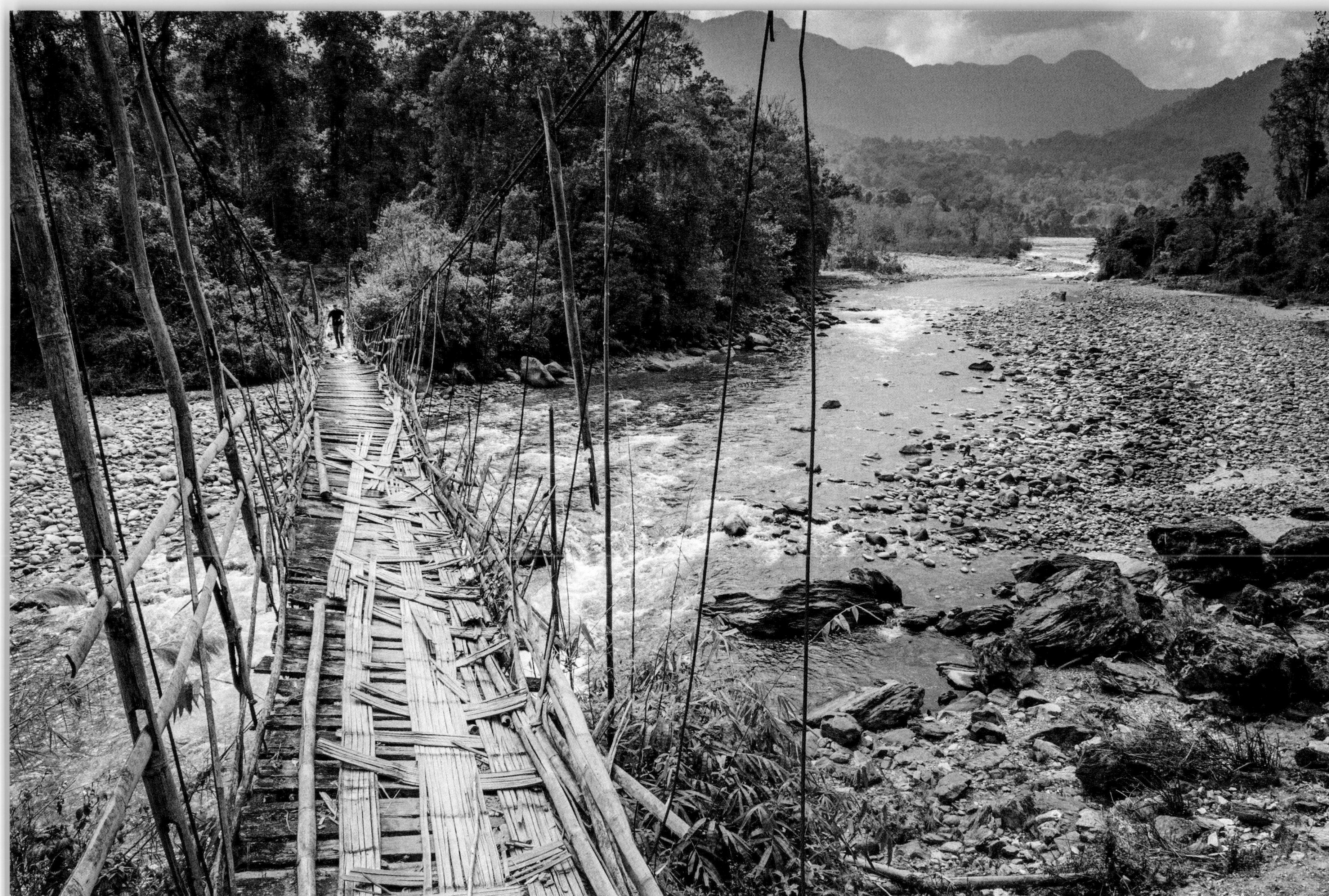

Foot bridge over a river, Awardon village, Kachin State, 2011

Roads end at Putao and the so-called "Icy Mountains", or the Himalayas, further north, are only accessible by trails and somewhat rickety bridges.

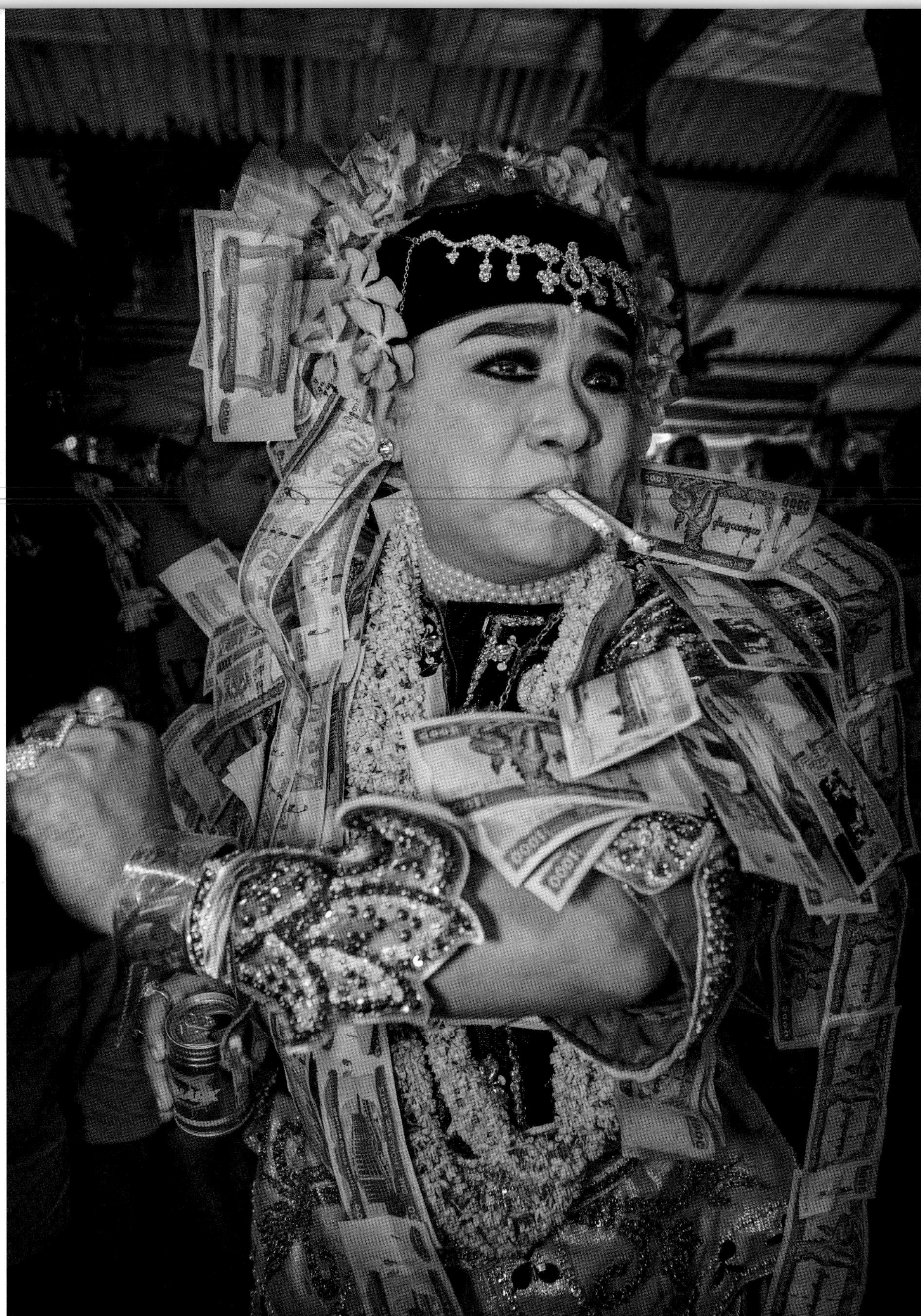

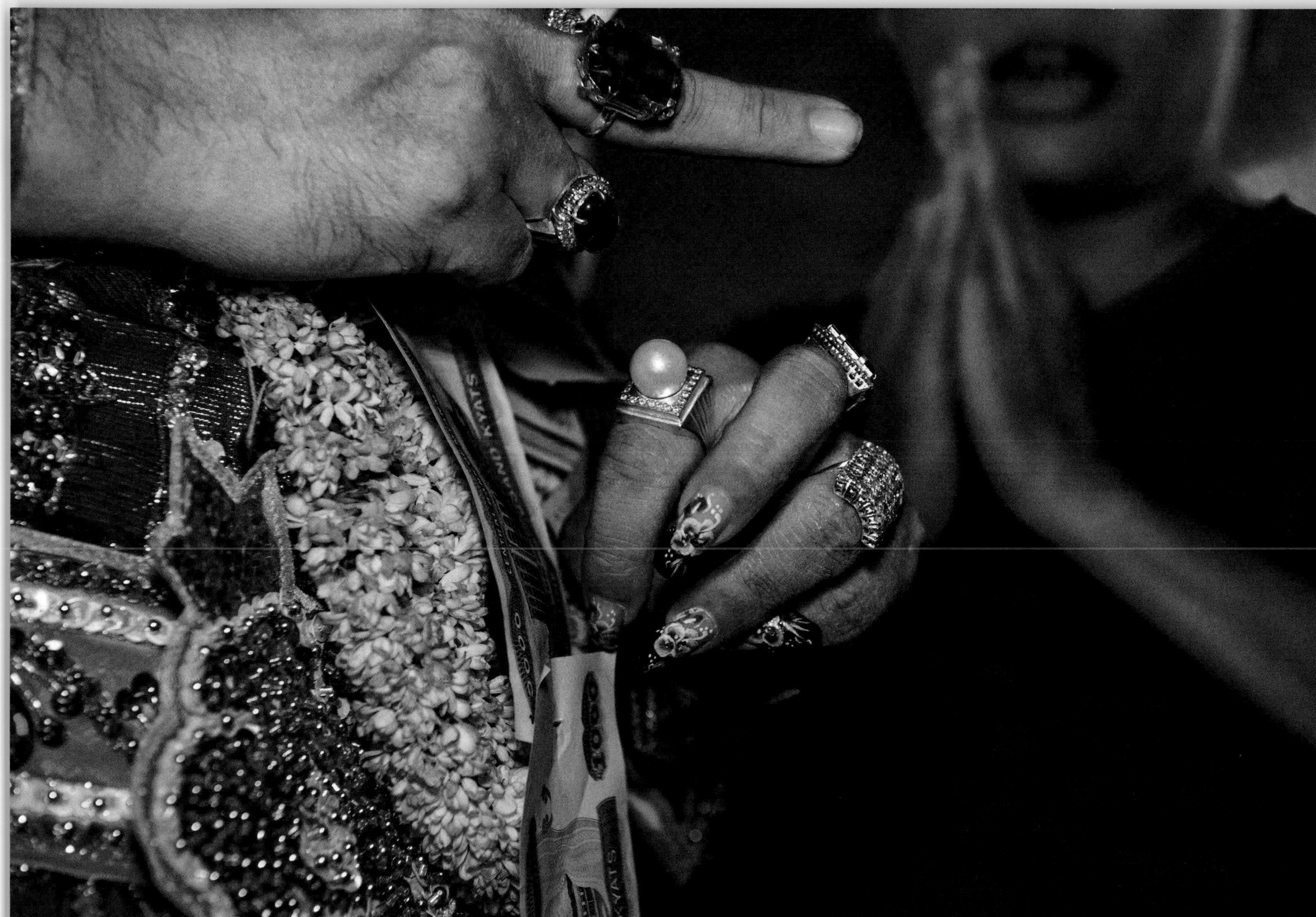

Above and opposite: Ceremonial dance by the *nat kadaw* Chiddae, Mingun, Sagaing Region, 2015

Chiddae is a well-known *nat kadaw*, a medium who connects to the *nat* spirits through a trance dance. During my many trips to Myanmar, I have come across several *nat pwe*, or spirit festivals to honour the *nat* and ask for their help with matters of love, wealth, or wellbeing. These lively animist festivals seem at odds with the country's predominant Buddhist beliefs and practices. How can Buddhist life, with its austerity and frugality, coexist with these primal and overabundant *nat* festivals? Somehow, the local culture has found a way to combine these two extremes and integrate superstition and spirit beliefs with Buddhism.

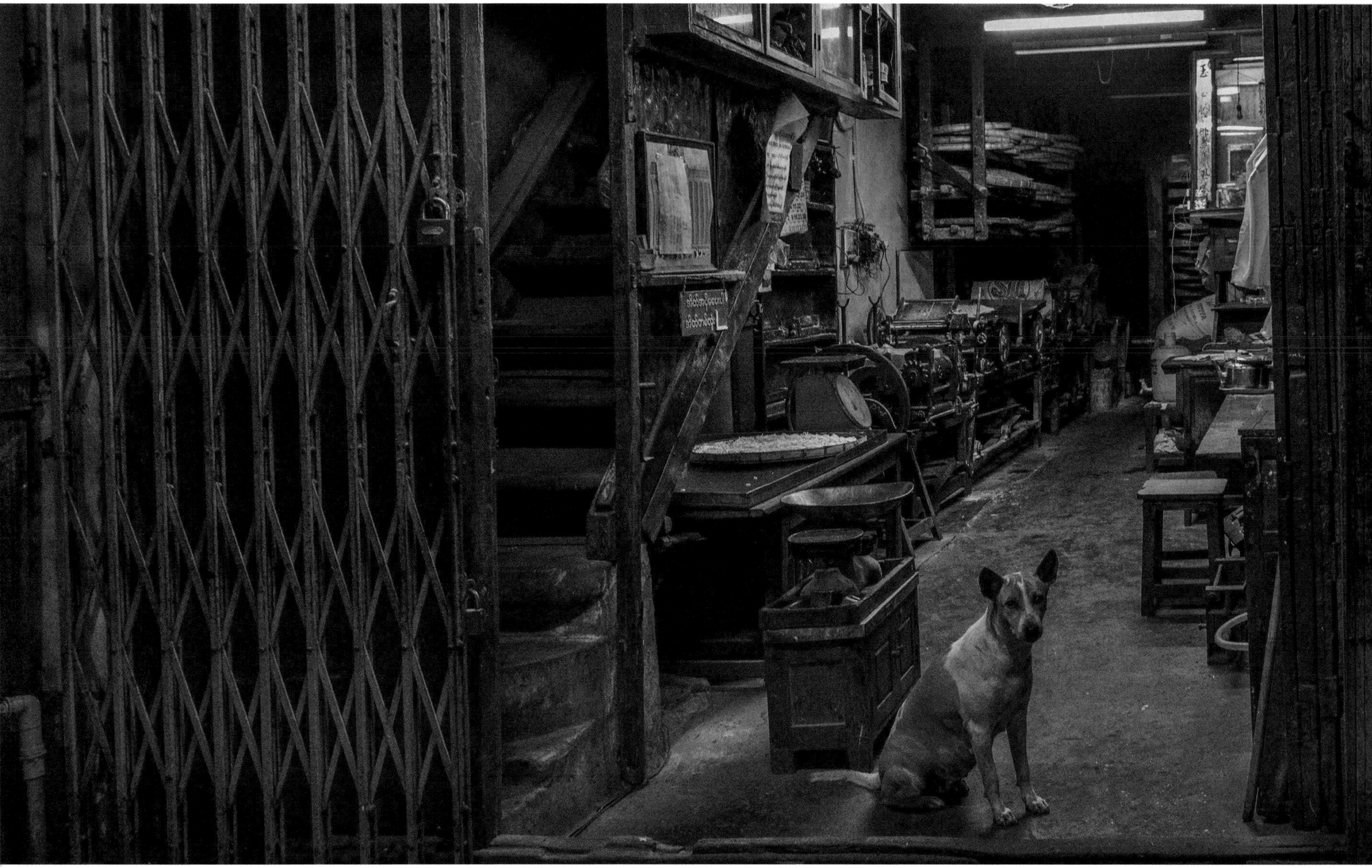

Dog in downtown shop-house, Yangon, 2016

In crowded downtown Yangon, there is often little or no separation between retail space, workshops, and living quarters. As a result, there are no boundaries between work life and family life. Similarly, the boundaries between inside and outside are not clear-cut and the shop-house interiors merge with the street outside as the gate that separates the two domains is kept mostly open.

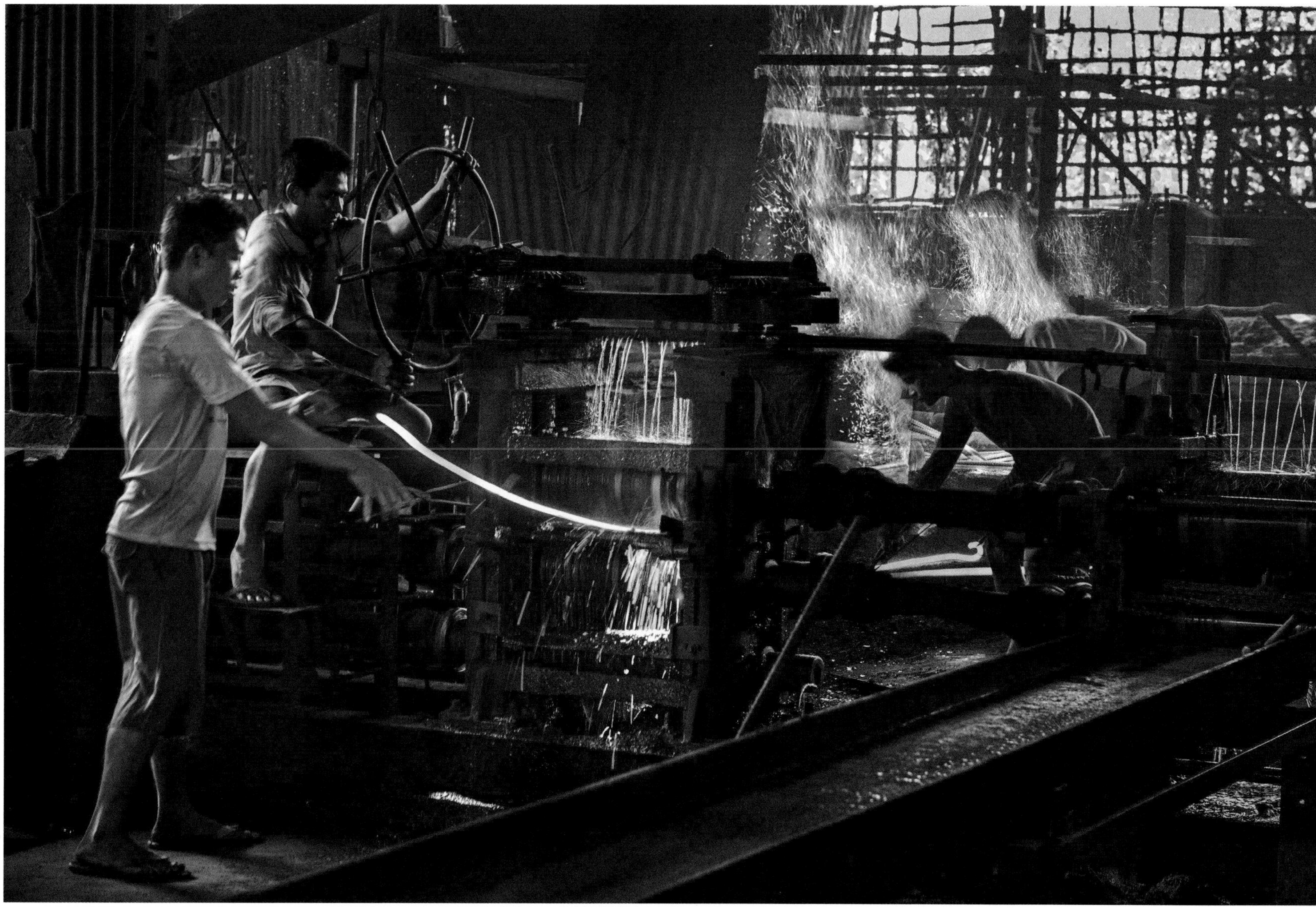

Recycling shop, Yangon, 2016

In an economy where many goods are in short supply or too expensive, recycling has become essential. As result, many products in Myanmar have more than one life. In this workshop, steel reinforcement rods are melted and reshaped into flat rods with the help of industrial rollers and manual labour.

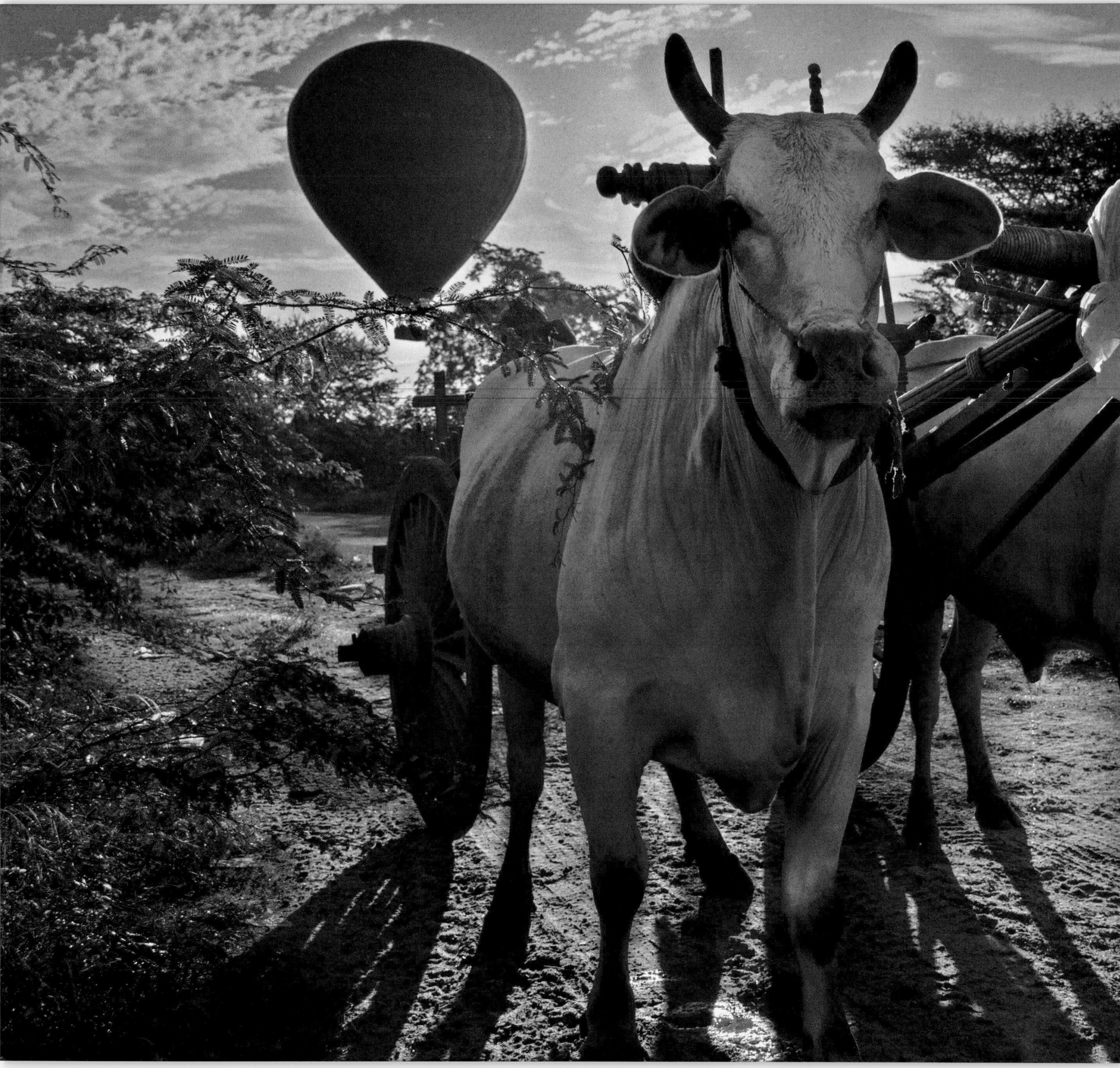

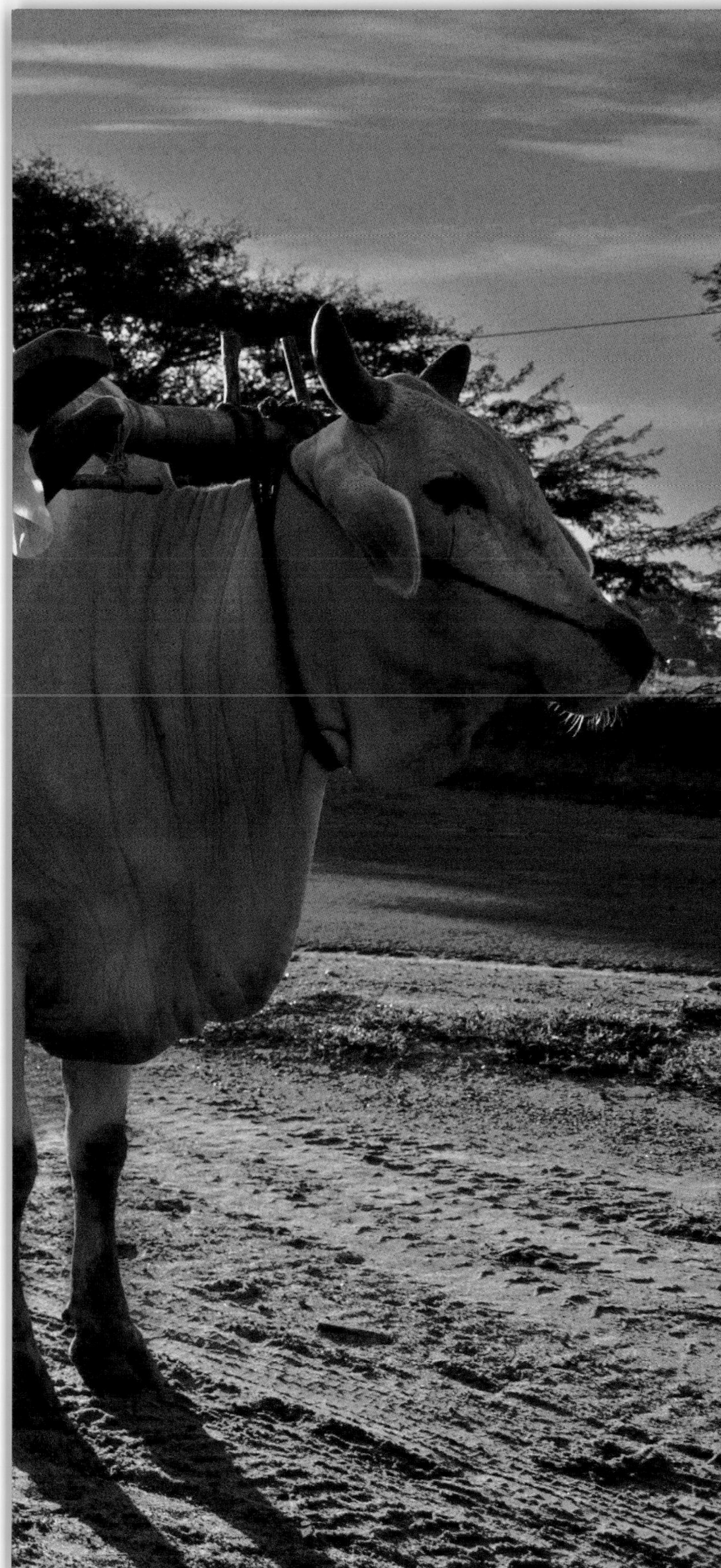

Ox cart with hot-air balloon, Bagan, Magway Region, 2015

An early morning hot-air balloon ride is a popular tourist attraction in Bagan, making balloons a ubiquitous sight on an early morning stroll.

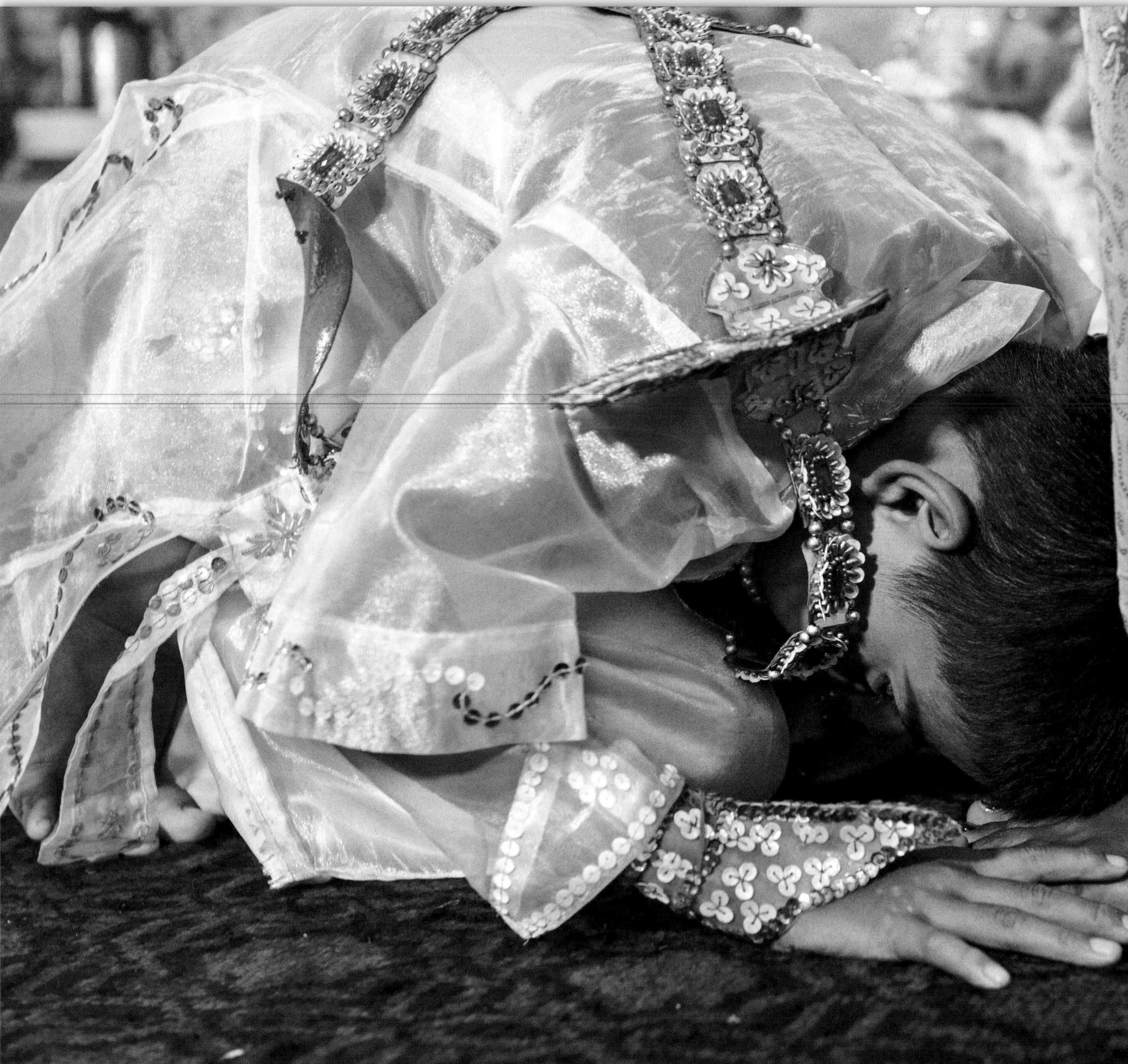

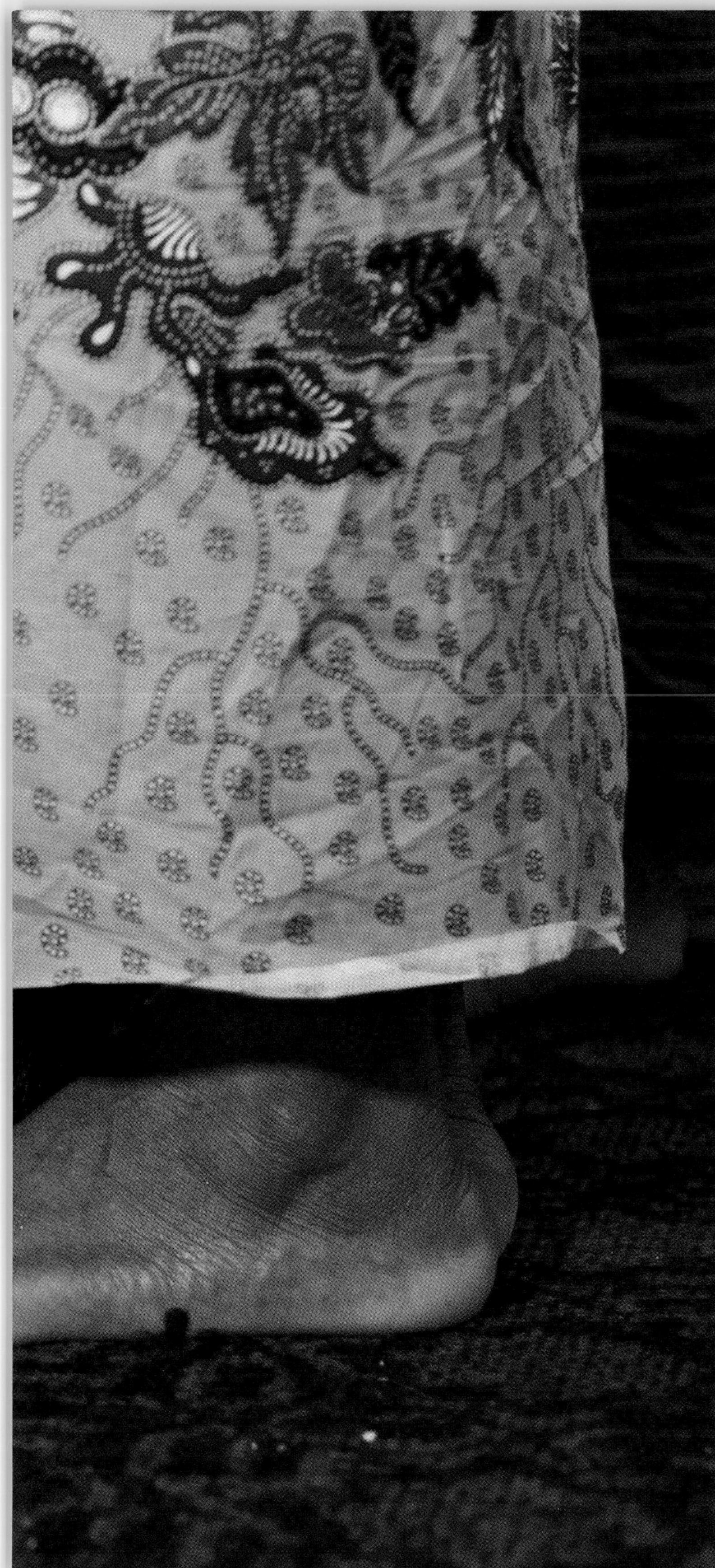

Young boy bowing at his mother's feet during his novitiation ceremony, Mandalay, 2015

As part of the novitiation ceremony, young boys bow at the feet of their parents in a gesture of gratitude for having been raised by them.

ACKNOWLEDGEMENTS

I visited Burma for the first time in 1981. Since 2010 (by which time it was officially called Myanmar), I have spent about two months a year there. I had the unique opportunity to explore the country as a documentary photographer including areas that are off the beaten track or sometimes out of reach for foreigners, all the while trying to find and catch moments and situations that wouldn't present themselves a second time. When I think of the range of people who have contributed in one way or another to this work, I feel humbled by the support, the trust, the knowledge, the enthusiasm, and the hospitality that has been extended to me over the years.

Many thanks to my dear Burmese friends who introduced me to the people and the culture, allowing me to make many more new friends along the way. I couldn't have completed this project without them. First and foremost, I would like to thank Kalayar Moe and her extended family for their friendship and Andrew Kan Htoo Aung who organized all my trips (www.amarabooking.com) and who never tired of my particular ideas and changes to the itinerary. Hninn Nwe Moe (Snow) and Khin La Pyae Win (La Pyae) worked miracles in facilitating organizational matters.

I thank my loving husband Jens who was able to join me on most of my trips. He has a great photographic eye of his own and understands the needs of a photographer. I feel blessed and grateful for his company, whether in Myanmar or elsewhere.

I also owe many thanks to my travel companions who have made each trip so special and shared many adventures with me, from hiking at the foot of the Himalayas, experiencing hard-to-reach festivals in the Sagaing mountains, and riding a motorbike through northern Shan State to cruising on an old cargo boat along the Chindwin River or in an old trawler on the Andaman Sea. I often tested the patience of my friends when I got up very early in the morning, pushed for certain destinations, and lingered too long with my camera when they wanted to move on. I apologize for any inconvenience I may have caused and thank you all for your love and patience.

I thank the friends, guides and drivers who helped me understand the wonders of Burmese life and culture through their explanations and translations. They also tirelessly researched access, permits, locations, and events to make sure I could get there and back without fail. In alphabetical order, they include: Aaron Hlamin, Latt Cha Mee, Ko Thein Naing, Htet Htet Aung, Thu Thu Aung, Nang Aung Kyi (Kyi Kyi), U Tin Ko Ko, Myo Lwin (Mr Bike), Swan Pyar Lynn (Thomas Lynn), Maung Maung Than, Aye Min Tun (Bryan), Nan Sam Moon, Nway Yu Zaw, Sai San Tint (Sai Sai), Ko Sitthu, and Win Zaw Oo (Ah Shae Gyi). There were many others along the way who are not mentioned here but who were equally supportive. Meeting all of you was a privilege; thank you for letting me enter your world.

Thanks go to Helen Frajman who helped me put together the selection of images and to Sophie Wingate and Julius Neiser for translating and editing.

Sincere appreciation and a special word of thanks go to my publisher Narisa Chakrabongse who enthusiastically took this book on board. Without Emma Larkin and Reutairat Nanta the final editing and design would not have gone so well and the book would not look as beautiful as it does now. *Catching the Light* is the result of teamwork rarely found. Thank you all.